THE RISE OF THE THERAPEUTIC STATE

THE CITY IN THE TWENTY-FIRST CENTURY BOOK SERIES

The Robert F. Wagner, Sr., Institute of Urban Public Policy
The Graduate School of The City University of New York

The City in the Twenty-First Century Book Series represents the volumes produced with support from the Robert F. Wagner, Sr., Institute of Urban Public Policy. The volumes are academic studies in the disciplines of the researchers and are intended to stimulate interaction between the research community and policymakers. Taken together, they provide a broad perspective of the issues facing the modern city. The general editor of The City in the Twenty-First Century series is Joseph S. Murphy, University Professor of Political Science and Chancellor of The City University of New York from 1982 to 1990. Asher Arian, Director of the Wagner Institute, is editor.

New York City is the exemplar of the emergent city of the twenty-first century. Its most striking characteristic is its uneven development and the sharp contrast it generates; growth is coupled with stagnation and decay. This has been called by some the "dual city," where—among other things—the affluence of the high-technology urban profession develops alongside poverty, homelessness, and a major influx of new migrants and cheap labor. In the dual city both class and ethnic cleavages become sharper.

The Robert F. Wagner, Sr., Institute of Urban Public Policy was established at The Graduate School and University Center of The City University of New York in 1987. Its goal is to bring the resources of the academic community to bear upon the understanding and solving of pressing urban and social problems in New York City and other urban centers. The Institute's agenda includes the exploration and analysis of the social, legislative, and political legacy associated with Senator Robert F. Wagner, Sr., a key architect of major components of the American welfare state.

THE RISE OF THE
THERAPEUTIC STATE

Andrew J. Polsky

PRINCETON UNIVERSITY PRESS   PRINCETON, NEW JERSEY

Library of Congress Cataloging-in-Publication Data

Polsky, Andrew Joseph.
The rise of the therapeutic state / Andrew J. Polsky.
p.   cm. — (The City in the twenty-first century book series)
Includes bibliographical references and index.
ISBN 0-691-07878-5(cl.)
ISBN 0-691-00084-0(pbk.)
1. Public welfare—United States—History.   2. Human services—
United States—History.   3. Social work with the socially
handicapped—United States—History.   I. Title.   II. Series.
HV91.P67   1991
361.973—dc20   91-9363

This book has been composed in Linotron Sabon

Princeton University Press books are printed on acid-free paper
and meet the guidelines for permanence and durability of the
Committee on Production Guidelines for Book Longevity of the
Council on Library Resources

Printed in the United States of America
First Princeton Paperback printing, 1993

10 9 8 7 6 5 4 3 2

To My Parents

Contents _____

Acknowledgments

THIS WORK began, longer ago than I like to think, as a doctoral dissertation under the auspices of the Politics Department at Princeton University. Although little of the dissertation remains intact, I still owe an enormous debt to my two advisors, Sheldon Wolin and Duane Lockard. They not only helped frame the argument but also affirmed my belief that the study of politics should be a critical enterprise organized around explicit value commitments. Several other scholars read the dissertation and made useful suggestions as I considered how best to revise it for publication. I would like to thank Jennifer Hochschild, Christopher Lasch, Ira Katznelson, Michael Katz, and Clarence Stone. During the past several years I have presented papers at conferences and forums that served as vehicles for clarifying key ideas. For their comments on these papers, I express my appreciation to Frances Fox Piven, Theda Skocpol, John Drew, George Curtis, John Forrester, Wendy Sarvasy, and Thomas Dalton. I also had the opportunity to explore my views of the juvenile court in *Studies in American Political Development*. The editors, Stephen Skowronek and Karen Orren, helped sharpen the focus of that essay, as did the anonymous reader they enlisted. The completed book manuscript was read by two anonymous readers for Princeton University Press to whom I am most grateful. It is also a pleasure to thank Barbara Nelson and Kathy Ferguson, both for their careful scrutiny of the manuscript and for their help in the past. Further credit is due Steven Rathgeb Smith and Nik Mistler for their responses to the material that appears in the last chapter. It goes without saying that none of the scholars and administrators with whom I have shared my writing agrees with everything I have written in these pages.

I am pleased to acknowledge several debts to those who have assisted in the research. The Hunter College Library was always helpful in obtaining obscure journal articles; Tom Jennings in particular went out of his way to make things easier for me. I also received welcome assistance from Josepha Cook and her associates in the Drew University interlibrary loan office. The generosity with which the Drew University library treated me, an outsider with no formal connection to the university, deserves special note. Also, in the course of my research I was most capably aided by Hunter College students Jenelline Connors, Lionel Francois, and Andrea Lewis. Peggy Wolff supplied valuable support in reproducing the manuscript and a welcome dose of humor in bleak moments.

Time may be the most precious commodity to any author. For providing a grant that gave me a semester free from teaching duties, I am happy to acknowledge the support of the Robert F. Wagner, Sr., Institute of Urban Public Policy. The Department of Political Science at Hunter College and then-Dean of the Social Sciences Walter Weiss took the administrative steps necessary to allow me to maximize the value of the Wagner Institute grant. A second semester without teaching responsibilities was made possible by additional grants from the Scholar Incentive Awards program of the City University of New York and the Professional Staff Congress/CUNY Faculty Research Award Program.

I am delighted to have the opportunity to note help of a less tangible sort, too. My colleagues in the Hunter College Political Science Department have helped create a congenial atmosphere under sometimes difficult circumstances. In addition, I have had any number of fruitful conversations with members of my department about subjects related to the manuscript.

Sandy Thatcher first expressed interest in the project for Princeton University Press, for which I will always be obliged. When Gail Ullman assumed responsibility for volumes on American politics, she continued to offer encouragement. I also appreciate her patience in the face of several unexpected delays during the writing and revisions.

It is customary in acknowledgments to recognize last those who really belong first. My family has always shown a great enthusiasm for this book. I am happy to dedicate it to my parents, with whom I first honed my argumentative skills. My wife's parents, Ralph and Mildred Morgenstern, have been steadfast in their support and generous with their time. During the 1988–1989 academic year, in which I wrote most of the manuscript, my daughter Sara was beginning her own academic career as a three-year-old in nursery school. I found her interruptions a (usually) welcome diversion from scholarly routine. Her brother Alexander arrived recently to add excitement as I finished the revisions. To my wife Beth Morgenstern I owe more than I can possibly say. Writing a book is not easy, but to live through someone else's writing is infinitely more difficult. She has weathered my storms and kept her faith. As long as she believed I had something to say, I believed it, too.

THE RISE OF THE THERAPEUTIC STATE

Introduction ————————————

The Problems of the Therapeutic State

To POLICYMAKERS, opinion leaders and pundits, and the concerned public, misery bespeaks marginality. The troubles that afflict an inner-city neighborhood today—poverty, substance abuse, delinquency, family violence and child neglect, homelessness, and more—seem to point up the distance between some citizens and the social mainstream. On the most obvious level, the mainstream revolves around participation in the modern post-industrial economy, which in turn requires advanced education and marketable job skills. Yet these people can find employment only in the low-wage service sector, which means insufficient income, poor benefits, and chronic insecurity. When the stresses of such a life find their way into the home, moreover, violence may erupt against spouses and children. Marginality thereby manifests itself in behavior patterns that the mainstream (rightly) defines as aberrant. In another vein, many young people in the neighborhood have dropped out of the legal economy entirely, idling away time or preferring the more lucrative opportunities that can be found in petty crime. Policy analysts and social critics worry that among the young the work ethic has collapsed. To put it another way, marginality also encompasses deviant norms and attitudes. Thus, people or groups are seen as marginal when they display one or more of the attributes—economic, behavioral, and attitudinal—that distinguish them from the social mainstream.

As part of its response to marginality, the modern welfare state incorporates programs and agencies that use an approach I term "therapeutic." It begins with the premise that some people are unable to adjust to the demands of everyday life or function according to the rules by which most of us operate. If they are to acquire the value structure that makes for self-sufficiency, healthy relationships, and positive self-esteem, they need expert help. Accordingly they become the clients of behavioral specialists, clinicians, and social workers—a group I refer to generically as social personnel. The therapeutic approach itself follows several distinct steps. First social personnel diagnose or assess the clients' situation and establish a friendly relationship with them. Then, through instruction, counseling, and supervision, clients are assisted in overcoming their personal deficiencies and learning to bear the pressures placed upon them.

Social personnel can maintain subsequent oversight to assure that clients have not slipped back into their former ways.

The therapeutic approach is not unique to public programs, but it takes on a different character when directed at marginal populations and pursued under authoritative state auspices. Any number of middle-class persons take advantage of counseling to cope with their anxieties, sometimes at public expense. Though the problems that bring middle-class clients to seek treatment may be serious, it is not seen as necessary to instill in them mainstream values to which they already subscribe. It should be added that they choose when to begin and end treatment. By contrast, public therapeutic intervention aimed at marginal citizens proceeds from the assumption that they cannot govern their own lives. The state therefore seeks to "normalize" them—an odd term, one that jars the ear, as well it should when we consider what the effort is all about. Lower-class clients do not seem to require merely a bit of support, like their middle-class counterparts, but instead wholesale personal and family reconstruction. Intervention sets out to foster new behaviors, instill another set of mores, and cultivate a different outlook toward self and family. By bringing about profound changes at the most intimate levels of human experience, the state aims to integrate marginal citizens into the social mainstream. Further, resistance on their part will not be tolerated. The state has the legal tools to impose client status upon marginal citizens and the coercive instruments to compel them to remain in that exposed position.

In the institutions of the American welfare state, the therapeutic approach finds many outlets.[1] Some social welfare programs, it is true, provide only material support. But others do not stop at concrete assistance and seek in addition to give recipients better psychological tools and stronger emotional resources so they can overcome what is perceived as an attitude of dependency. Similarly, though many courts are content to render a verdict on antisocial acts, certain judicial institutions profess a desire to help violators develop more acceptable behavioral standards. A complete listing of public "human services"—agencies that use the therapeutic approach[2]—would include juvenile courts, child welfare departments, vocational rehabilitation and training centers, shelters for the homeless, community mental health programs, public assistance departments, chemical dependency treatment clinics, shelters for battered women, and Veterans' Administration services. Often the state offers therapeutic treatment through private nonprofit organizations by purchasing their services. Because public funds are at stake and policy objectives are set forth by elected policymakers, contract services should be viewed as a component of the public therapeutic sector. All told, the number of persons brought under the domain of the human service apparatus ranges into the millions.[3]

In concept and in potential scope, then, the therapeutic sector looms as a menacing Leviathan. Yet in practice it amounts to something a good deal less imposing. To begin with, public human services occupy a clearly subordinate position in the larger scheme of social policy. The expenditures for adjustment services are dwarfed by the massive outlays for entitlement programs like Medicare or social security. Even within agencies that pursue the therapeutic approach, a relatively small percentage of the budget may be spent on casework. Therapeutic practitioners complain incessantly of insufficient resources.

The therapeutic approach claims only a secondary role in much policy debate, too. While analysts across the political spectrum endorse normalizing intervention as one antidote to marginality, they treat human services largely as an afterthought. Liberals and conservatives alike mention the need to address the behavioral and motivational weaknesses of the poor, but little is said about therapeutic casework. Instead, the debate centers on the merits of various cash transfer programs or provisions that require welfare recipients to work.[4] We may take this as evidence that the therapeutic idea has become an accepted feature of social policy, yet at the same time one to which key policy actors today attach limited significance.

An examination of what happens within therapeutic or "social" agencies further confirms that the therapeutic sector rarely measures up to its grand design. As the most cursory inspection will disclose, the record compiled by the human services is dismal, filled with episodes of bungled treatment and clients who do not respond to the overtures of caseworkers. This wretched performance cannot be blamed on inadequate agency budgets. Instead we must look to client actions and the flaws in the therapeutic method. Clients do not passively cooperate with the agency, but rather try to manipulate intervention to achieve their own purposes. Sometimes this moves them to appear to accept a caseworker's suggestions while they go on leading their lives as before. In other instances, they draw the agency into family power struggles; social personnel, by taking sides, sacrifice the essential friendly relations they are supposed to maintain with all family members. Agencies should be able to see through such client tactics. But as the mishandling of cases by agencies responsible for juvenile probation or child abuse prevention attests, social personnel cannot reliably predict or modify behavior, even when therapeutic resources are intensively applied.

Finally, where the human services are supposed to form an orderly system, the therapeutic apparatus is disjointed and poorly coordinated. The constitutive elements lack a shared identity or sense of mission even though they are connected by an intricate web of working relationships. No common dialogue binds together social agencies making use of the therapeutic approach. Juvenile justice, for example, forms a discrete policy field, and those who participate in the ongoing debates about court-sponsored treatment rarely communicate with those outside their own narrow circle. Attempts to impose a rational structure on the whole apparatus from above have only contributed to the bureaucratization of each agency. It is no wonder, then, that the therapeutic state remains an elusive object of analysis.[5] More to the point, fragmentation and divided effort let marginal populations elude normalizing intervention. Many potential clients slip between and around social agencies.

When we consider all the limitations of the therapeutic sector, it may appear that we have scant reason to inquire further into its activities. But there is another side to this story that we must recognize. The therapeutic sector matters far more to the marginal populations caught in its web. A given low-income community will feature a variety of social agencies. There is a high probability that individuals or families will come into contact with one of these. Often it can be brushed aside; as I have said, caseworkers are easily manipulated. Yet when files are opened, some clients face the very real prospect that they will be drawn into an extended series of interventions stretching over months or even years. Typically the encounters will be sporadic and inconsistent, with intervals in which no contact occurs until some new episode triggers the interest of another agency. At that point the entire dossier may be reactivated, the record of past transgressions and inadequacies brought to life again. Demands are made that clients mend their ways and conform to the agency's behavioral expectation. In certain cases agency edicts are backed by the threat that a family will be broken up or a client placed in a secure treatment facility.

Any evaluation of the importance of the therapeutic state must also take account of its continued expansion. In the past twenty years the human services have suffered a succession of blows—fierce client opposition and a vigorous movement among attorneys to restore clients' formal-legal rights, public criticism and hostility from lawmakers as the failure of normalizing intervention became evident, and the sharp retrenchment brought on by the spending reductions of the Reagan administration. Yet, despite this inhospitable political climate, important components of the therapeutic apparatus have actually expanded. We continue to turn to social agencies to deal with old problems that they previously failed to resolve and with new ones that capture our attention. Growth is evident in, to take two leading examples, the juvenile justice and child welfare fields. It follows that the sort of interventions that recall an invasive Leviathan are likely to become more common.

Thus, while the therapeutic state cannot be regarded as a behemoth set loose to prey upon all marginal populations, it is sufficiently potent to call for critical scrutiny. Normalizing intervention confronts policymakers and the public at-large with vexing moral choices. We—officials and citizens alike—look to public human services to deal with forms of distress that arouse our compassion by altering forms of behavior that unnerve us. Inaction in the face of, say, family violence is unacceptable, and we are at a loss for other policies to address the situation. We therefore invite public authority to probe the inner recesses of people's lives. But we also appreciate that a society can limit the power of the state only by insisting that it respect the sovereignty of the individual mind and personality. Moreover, in a democratic community, there must be settings beyond the reach of public authority in which citizens can express themselves and discover their shared concerns. Privacy and autonomy, however, are routinely violated by social personnel. Though their actions might be justified in the case of obvious mental incompetence, we compromise fundamental values when we extend state-sponsored intervention to the vast number of clients caught up today in the therapeutic apparatus.

The contradictory nature of the therapeutic state—a sprawling, disjointed network that often misses its mark yet in other instances inflicts great mischief upon its clients—raises three fundamental issues. First, although we recognize a common approach across a range of agencies, the entire state sector so lacks coherence that it is difficult to locate it as a subject for analysis. Were its components ever bound together, as their shared method suggests? If so, what has driven them apart? Second, on a normative level, intervention poses what might be termed the question of citizenship. We embrace an exercise of power by the state that is at odds with our belief that some aspects of a citizen's life should lie beyond its reach. How have we come to accept, nay, to insist upon, this surrender of democratic independence in favor of a standard of behavior? Third, in view of the fact that policy failure in the human services has produced more agencies and programs, we must address the political question of organizational tenacity. Where public agencies enjoy the support of powerful constituency groups, survival perhaps requires no elaborate analysis. But social agencies, staffed by low-status professionals and serving those with the least political voice, would appear to have few friends who count. How is it that the therapeutic apparatus has established itself so firmly that, despite substantial opposition, it can continue to expand even when its ineptitude is starkly evident?

History, Discourse, and Politics

As my formulation of these questions suggests, I believe the core issues presented by the therapeutic state can be resolved only through an account of its development. We can most easily sketch the full dimensions of the therapeutic sector if we start with its foundation. In the course of a historical inquiry, too, we can explore why the sector as a whole seems to have slipped out of sight. Besides sharpening our analytical focus, a historical study permits us to best illuminate the urgent problems of principle and politics that the therapeutic state raises. Today policy elites are so much under the sway of the doctrine of the human services that they find it difficult to reconsider their commitment to the mode of intervention it represents. To recover the problem of the marginal citizen as a subject for discussion, we need to appreciate the intellectual forces that have driven it from our awareness. By the same token, as therapeutic practitioners march ahead despite their thin record of accomplishment, their political resilience seems inexplicable. To grasp the mystery of how they have made their approach the basis for so many initiatives and institutions, we must step back from the present, to unearth earlier political strategies and long-buried compromises.

Such a historical study must be faithful to the complexity of the therapeutic state itself. Social agencies embody, in their broad diversity, different notions about marginal populations, the nature of therapeutic power, and techniques of intervention. We need to attend to the shifting intellectual currents that have yielded so heterogeneous a set of organizations. At the same time, the varying commitments of public agencies to therapeutic methods and the uneven influence that social personnel exercise upon their institutions make it clear that their discourse has not dominated the entire evolution of social policy. Though ideas have left their mark, the configuration of the human service apparatus is a political outcome. Thus we must follow closely the strategies that proponents of therapeutic intervention—therapeutic activists—have devised to secure political support and neutralize opposition, and the role played by any policy competitors. We have need of an approach to political development that lets us give due weight to the intellectual and the political alike and helps us comprehend the interaction between them. Furthermore, clients have sometimes disturbed the therapeutic design by bending interventions to suit their own purposes. The mode of inquiry we use must recognize how clients as active agents shape the therapeutic sector.

For tracing the impact of ideas upon the way in which the state has dealt with marginal populations, the work of Foucault is particularly suggestive. His argument, in condensed and simplified form, goes something like this: The effort to normalize marginal groups took shape in the nineteenth century when it became evident that blunt repression could not prepare them for productive tasks in the emerging capitalist economy. Through fields such as public health, a rising corps of social experts began to accumulate knowledge about marginality and to contemplate new techniques through which it would be possible to refashion the poor and the deviant into positive social assets—initiating, that is, a discourse on intervention. Putting their insights to the test in a host of local experiments, the first social practitioners invented a different form of power, one that penetrated to the most minute level of everyday life to evoke higher desires and appropriate economic attitudes. Later, when the value of this constructive power to dominant groups became clear, it was absorbed into the state. This process began, again, through local applications, where the apparent conflict between normalizing discourse and the liberal doctrine of individual rights went unnoticed. The technology of normalization has since attained a secure place within the state, sustained by the ongoing accumulation of bodies of knowledge and an elaborate mechanism of surveillance.[6]

Foucault recognizes that we need to investigate more closely how normalizing activity made the leap from disjointed, small-scale practice to an elaborate enterprise conducted under the auspices of the state. In part he is hampered, I suspect, by a reluctance to "subjectivize" history, to identify the specific actors who translate ideas into concrete programs and public policies. But building upon his remarks about the role of early social experts, we can hypothesize that the pioneers in normalizing intervention constituted a "discursive movement." Foucault indicates that they shared a conception of marginality, an enthusiasm for their methodological innovations, and a desire to expand their modest efforts into a more global project of social reconstruction. Certainly this should have sufficed to yield a common identity among the first practitioners of the normalizing approach, however they might have differed over points of emphasis. By positing a discursive movement that sought to realize the potential of the new approach, we fill the political void in Foucault's scenario. We would expect to find the proponents of the normalizing method leading the drive to link their new technology to the state.

Drawing upon Foucault's insights into the relationship between discursive strategies and the positive exercise of power, Donzelot presents a much more detailed account of the attempts to integrate marginal populations into the social mainstream. He argues that modern family life has been shaped by several distinct lines of discursive activity. For the middle-class household, medical experts in the nineteenth century and psychoanalysis in our own era have been decisive influences, each in turn suggesting certain norms that family members have willingly sought to uphold. But among the working class, especially its fringe elements, efforts by philanthropy during the nineteenth century to encourage standards of labor discipline and savings faltered, confounded by resistance from clients and their artful manipulation of intervention to realize their own aims. Philanthropic organizations then sought to enlist the cooperation of the state. Early in the present century these efforts resulted in the appearance of what Donzelot calls "the social," a hybrid public-private sphere organized around therapeutic intervention and the surveillance of marginal clients. Social personnel sought through mandatory tutelage—educative casework backed by sanctions—to impose upon working-class families bourgeois norms for family relations and personal adjustment. Yet that is not the whole story. For if the broad outline of the therapeutic sector was established decades ago, the human services today differ significantly from the first experiments. Donzelot observes that new techniques have caught on among practitioners and that the middle-class norms they promote have continued to change.[7]

Missing from this rich analysis, alas, is an appreciation of the political realm. Donzelot understands that the state, through its coercive resources and surveillance mechanisms, adds something to the therapeutic project. But the state cannot simply be manipulated, put to use to advance discursive schemes. It has its own history and therefore its established biases. For example, where therapeutic intervention is supposed to rest upon the expertise of social technicians, the American state traditionally has been most respectful of local sentiments, however backward or unenlightened. It seems more likely that such a state would conduct public tutelage in a manner not approved by therapeutic practitioners. In much the same way, although Donzelot pays heed to conflicts within public social agencies, disputes over public policy may be much broader, conditioning the entire context in which agencies operate. We need to go a good deal further in our exploration of the competition that philanthropic practitioners faced when they set out to secure the backing of the state and the political forces that have subsequently constrained social personnel.

Accordingly, while we might begin with the insights of Foucault and Donzelot, our historical investigation of the human services must also probe "state building" as a political activity. The phenomenon of state building—creating new forms of state organization—has been the focus of much recent scholarship. These studies make clear that functional social needs or demands from various classes and interest groups do not suffice to produce new governing structures. For such external pressures to make themselves felt, they require champions within the existing political system, political entrepreneurs eager to support innovation for their own (often political) reasons. They in turn must do battle against established political forces and institutions that seek to resist, contain, or subvert change. The new state apparatus emerges from the friction between entrepreneurs and conservative power centers.[8] Extending this kind of argument to the attempt to connect normalizing techniques to public authority, we would look for the same pattern of policy advocacy and resistance. We must be alert to the possibility that political entrepreneurs and the reigning political order have skewed the therapeutic sector to their own purposes. At the same time, if therapeutic activists have learned to negotiate their way through this political maze, later human service reforms may reflect their increased political acumen.

The approach I adopt, then, combines discursive and political analyses. Through an examination of the public statements of therapeutic activists, I seek to make clear the design behind their enterprise, to lay open for critical discussion the kind of power it incorporates, and to bring into sharp relief the ideal of public tutelage and the unifying vision behind the therapeutic state. We can then consider the place of personal autonomy and democratic citizenship in the discursive strategy for integrating marginal populations into the social mainstream. Moreover, since we need to go beyond idealized models to consider discursive practice, as Donzelot and several others have recently emphasized,[9] I explore the effects on clients and their own role in shaping normalizing intervention. I also focus on the political struggles surrounding the therapeutic state. By treating therapeutic activists as political entrepreneurs in their own right and reviewing their tactics, I endeavor to account for the initial triumph that saw their doctrine incorporated by various state agencies. I continue to pursue a political inquiry, investigating the strategies subsequently favored by social personnel, in an effort to uncover the driving force behind the later expansion of public human services. On the other side, through a full reckoning of the political obstacles that therapeutic activists have faced, I intend to show why many social agencies suffer from a split personality and why the therapeutic sector as a whole lacks coherence.

The Hazards of Imperfect Victories

In my account of the rise of the therapeutic state, I recognize the pivotal importance of normalizing discourse and the movement constituted by its proponents. The discourse itself was an outgrowth of philanthropic activity in the nineteenth century, when techniques of intervention were first tested. During the Progressive period, beginning about 1890, social personnel refined their methods for reshaping the working-class family, and came to believe that they had invented a tool of extraordinary constructive possibilities. They proceeded with great enthusiasm and considerable political skill to secure official backing. Judicial institutions and social agencies in fields like public assistance incorporated casework goals and called upon the services of therapeutic practitioners. Over the following decades therapeutic activists have continued to be inspired by their faith in the utility of the therapeutic approach for helping the client in distress to abide by social standards or function at a higher level of personal competence. This credo has prompted social personnel to press for an expansion in the scope of public tutelage, to seek more resources and a greater public investment in training skilled caseworkers, and to agitate for a major role for themselves whenever some new manifestation of marginality has come to our notice.

Still, though therapeutic doctrine has been the catalyst in the development of the human services, I maintain that the new state sector has been significantly affected by other discourses. The most significant draw upon the commitment, deeply embedded in our liberal/Protestant culture, to individual moral responsibility. In the economic realm, the notion that each family head bears the burden to support self and dependents has shaped the free-market discourse of political economy since the beginning of the industrial era in the nineteenth century. Individuals are presumed to be accountable for their own fate. When they fall prey to poverty, therefore, they are to blame for their plight. Under such economic moralism, their suffering is earned, the proper reward for the evils of indolence and dissipation. Though not wholly incompatible with the therapeutic approach—which might be used, after all, to instill in the poor a desire to be self-sufficient—political economy differs sharply in emphasis, for it stresses the need to condemn persons who do not look after and control themselves. Similarly, in the field of law, popular opinion has often favored a moralistic jurisprudence that pronounces harsh judgment upon offenders. Social personnel insist instead on the need to understand violators and to rehabilitate them rather than to inflict punishment. I further show that, thanks to our understanding of democracy and our political arrangements, the popular faith in individual responsibility has had a major impact upon social policy. Public officials have long subscribed to an ideology of localism, according to which they have an obligation to express the popular values of the community they serve. As if that were not enough, state structures, notably decentralized courts and small legislative districts, are perfectly suited to allow grassroots individualism to make itself felt.

Therapeutic activists have been challenged at times, too, by less universal discursive forces. Where social policy borders on the legal system, in an institution like the juvenile court, opposition to social personnel has arisen over the past several decades from formal-rights advocates. They represent a strain in legal discourse that demands meticulous adherence to due process. Though distinct from and perhaps incompatible with legal-moralism, this proceduralism also stands sharply at odds with a therapeutic jurisprudence that sees courtroom formalities as an obstacle to proper diagnosis of an offender's condition. On a different level, therapeutic activists have been confronted sporadically by those who believe marginality can best be overcome through political action. According to this discourse of democratic participation, social membership is achieved not through normalizing intervention but through the collective efforts of autonomous citizens to fashion their own communities.

With still other discourses the therapeutic enterprise has enjoyed a more ambiguous relationship. Social personnel have had to answer to policy actors who reflect the discourse of rational management or modern disciplines like economics. Early on, during the Progressive era, the relationship was congenial, with therapeutic practitioners eager to borrow from other schools of thought. Since the 1960s, however, there has been a sharp struggle for dominance within the policy process and for control over social agencies themselves. A similar pattern can be found in the interaction between the therapeutic approach and feminism. At the turn of the century feminist doctrine contributed to the formulation of the therapeutic method and encouraged the development of the first normalizing agencies. But over the past two decades, feminist thought has reversed direction, questioning the biases of the helping professions and inspiring the creation of alternative support networks.

Only under rare circumstances have therapeutic activists established their practical ascendancy over these competing discursive interests. On occasion social personnel have seized upon a favorable opening, created by some policy crisis, to bring about significant expansion in the therapeutic sector. They rode the wave of Progressive reform to their first successes, insinuated themselves into key policymaking positions during the New Deal to bring federal resources into the human services, and capitalized upon popular concerns about juvenile delinquency and the rise in the welfare rolls during the 1950s and 1960s. But I demonstrate that whenever other discursive forces have aroused themselves, therapeutic activists have been soundly trounced. They have been hounded from the positions of influence they attained during the bursts of program innovation and growth. And once their foes have assumed control over policy or within social agencies, they have successfully resisted efforts by social personnel to dislodge them.

These defeats have owed much to the political weaknesses of therapeutic activists as a discursive movement. Social personnel represent something of an object lesson in how not to organize for political influence. In a political system that invites local opinion to make itself felt, they tend to be cosmopolitans, ill at ease in the parochial, common-sense world of community politics.[10] They also have few natural allies. During the Progressive era, as I mentioned, they drew significant support from various social reform movements. But with the collapse of the reform project in the wake of the First World War, the therapeutic enterprise was left dependent upon its own handful of proponents. They have found it difficult to repeat the initial connection to any broader coalition, though they have had sporadic successes that I discuss. Also, where administrators of entitlement programs can readily enlist constituents in the political arena, for social personnel this backing has been problematic. The poor and delinquent are unenthusiastic about the therapeutic project; even if they were prepared to endorse it, they form perhaps the least influential base of support one might muster. By comparison, to cite but one example, juvenile court judges who choose to punish delinquent acts rather than counsel the young offender can count on strong backing from local elites and the public in general.

Social personnel have also been undermined, I hold, by the failure of normalizing intervention itself. Having gained initial success by promising low-cost solutions to pressing social problems, they could not deliver on their word. Foucault claims that the exercise of power leads to the further development of knowledge, which in turn makes power more effective. It would be more accurate to say, however, that clinicians and social work educators have embarked upon a relentless quest for knowledge, hoping all along that some new discipline would allow them to demonstrate the superiority of the therapeutic approach. But despite innumerable pilot projects and experiments, therapeutic practitioners have yet to show they can bring about the normalization of marginal clients on a consistent basis. For this failure clients have been largely responsible. They have feigned cooperation and invented appearances to please caseworkers, responded with sullen passivity, or tried to initiate intervention to alter the terms of intrafamily conflict. Though clients rarely have achieved what they wanted, their willfulness sufficed to defeat the therapeutic agenda. As a consequence, discursive competitors have found it easy to ignore therapeutic doctrine or to use the disappointing record of intervention to discredit social personnel.

All the same, notwithstanding the forces arrayed against them and their own liabilities, therapeutic activists have preserved many of the footholds they have secured and gone on to conquer new ground. Extensive use has been made of policy instruments, like centralized bureaucracy, that are less vulnerable to popular counter-discourses; through schools of social work, the supply of trained therapeutic practitioners has been enlarged; and where social personnel have lost their influence upon an institution, alternative agency structures have been created in which therapeutic methods might be systematically applied. I contend that such strategies have entailed a substantial cost to the therapeutic enterprise. Therapeutic activists lost their identity as a movement and their common sense of mission as they divided along bureaucratic fault lines into narrow policy clusters. This has contributed to the loss of coherence in the therapeutic sector. So, too, has the multiplication of agencies, brought on by the desire to create practice settings not contaminated by other discursive tendencies. Nevertheless, whatever the losses, they have seemed worth it to social personnel. The therapeutic state has been sustained.

Along the way, moreover, therapeutic tenets have become a part of our broader public discourse on marginality. The normalizing approach now shapes our reflexive response when we are confronted with new manifestations of human misery. I suggest we have not abandoned our belief in individual responsibility. But while some commentators continue to voice moral condemnation of the poor in the traditional form, it is more fashionable to describe their problems in terms drawn from the diagnostic language employed by clinicians and caseworkers. And even those analysts who utter harsh judgments of such marginal archetypes as the unmarried teenage mother on welfare recommend that the policy response include, along with mandatory employment, therapeutic counseling and instruction.

Social personnel have not often stopped to reflect critically upon the assumptions and categories they have bequeathed us. In their eagerness to put normalizing technology to the test, Progressive therapeutic activists did not pause to consider the harm they might do to clients or how the therapeutic enterprise might weaken the conditions for democratic citizenship. They saw only that power might be used in a positive fashion, not to repress but to instill bourgeois norms toward self and family. Meanwhile, in their unbounded confidence in the efficacy of the new tools of intervention, therapeutic activists betrayed a dangerous conceit of the scientific spirit, a blind certainty that marginality could be excised through the application of correct behavioral knowledge. We must note, too, that the activists were mostly women, and the new power seemed less menacing for its feminized quality—it was benign, softened, nurturing. This image of power remained firmly held even when the coercive resources of the state were added to the therapeutic mix. Later, especially during the Great Depression and during the 1960s, social personnel have come under sharp attack from outside and from defectors within their own ranks. Yet most practitioners have continued to assert that intervention was in the interest of clients and society. Indeed, those who say otherwise are treated as blasphemers.

We cannot permit ourselves to fall prey to the therapeutic mindset. As I recount the rise of the human services, I stress that the fascination with normalizing technique and its associated implements of power has had disastrous consequences. To begin with, because social personnel have seen only the positive side of therapeutic power, they have tolerated the abuses too often inflicted upon marginal populations under public tutelage. When intervention techniques have proved wanting, the conviction among therapeutic practitioners that science can still yield the solution has left clients acutely vulnerable. New methods must be tested. And so clients have become human "laboratory rats," subjected to each fad treatment in personality reconstruction or behavioral modification. Social personnel have also acquiesced in the use of coercion by the state to regulate the most private dimensions of clients' lives. As critics have charged, those drawn into the public tutelary apparatus have faced demands that they change how they rear their children, adopt different spending habits, find a new residence, maintain sexual abstinence, and more; refusal to comply can mean the breakup of a family or incarceration. Mercifully, most marginal citizens have been spared the worst. Due to the check imposed upon the expansion of the human services by other discursive forces, I note, therapeutic resources have simply been too limited to encompass all potential clients.

Second, under the impress of therapeutic discourse, policymakers and the larger public have learned to devalue personal autonomy. Social personnel steadfastly deny that this was their intention. They insist that unless someone's well-being is at risk, nothing should be imposed upon clients against their will. Even where it is necessary to protect clients from themselves, the line continues, intervention seeks only to restore them to a higher level of independent functioning. But disciplines like psychoanalysis have been embraced because they seem better able to get beneath the defenses that clients erect. In addition, thanks to an elaborate mechanism of referral, some clients find themselves placed under permanent surveillance. Cases are continued indefinitely; if any backsliding is detected, intervention resumes. By proceeding in a way that demonstrates that autonomy counts for little, therapeutic practitioners have helped convince others of the same. The notion that citizens must have some space in which to define their concerns in their own language has been subordinated to the premise, drawn from therapeutic discourse, that intervention will leave clients better able in the end to stand on their own two feet.

Finally, convinced that normalizing intervention alone was the best means to link marginal populations to the social mainstream, social personnel have done much to foreclose certain alternative approaches. I examine how interest peaked during the Progressive era and again during the 1960s in the discourse of citizen participation. First the settlement workers and later the community action proponents asserted that marginal groups, through their own collective efforts, could solve problems, forge their own sense of communal identity and membership, and thereby link themselves to the larger society. What was required was not counseling and instruction by caseworkers but opportunities for the direct exercise of power. But when presented with the chance to support political activism among their clients, social personnel made clear that they preferred instead to treat marginal groups as objects upon whom power might be applied. They dismissed client organizing or sought to co-opt client militancy. Having helped to shut off the political path to social membership, therapeutic activists hardly speak of it, and policy elites have followed their lead.

Overview

I pursue these analytical and normative themes through a roughly chronological survey of the development of the therapeutic state. In part 1 I examine the precursors to therapeutic discourse and the discourse itself. The Progressive notion that marginal populations could be normalized through casework intervention, especially with the support of the state, derived from the efforts of philanthropy during the nineteenth century. Accordingly, I begin in the first chapter with an analysis of philanthropy in the earlier period. Philanthropic activists were determined to heal the fissures that seemed about to split American society along class lines. In this desire they were inspired by a vision of community that stressed the obligation of elites to seek the moral uplift of the less fortunate. Philanthropic activists expressed their commitment through vigorous work to promote modernization of the slums, protect children from city streets and blighted homes, administer private relief, and reform institutions in which children and the poor were confined. Through these distinct lines of activity, casework methods began to emerge; moreover, we can discern a definite conception of how the state might contribute to the integration of marginal groups. The practical and theoretical accomplishments of nineteenth-century philanthropy established a discursive pattern that its successors, worried over the same social problems, were predisposed to follow.

This is not to say, however, that Progressive social personnel merely took up method and doctrine as these were left to them. As I explain in chapter 2, the Progressive generation became true therapeutic activists: they refined the approach toward the working-class family, grasped the vast constructive potential of normalizing intervention, and set out to make their credo the basis for a new public sector. Under the impact of economic crisis in the early 1890s, effective steps for closing the gaps between classes seemed more urgent. Reform movements showed new vigor, especially through the efforts of middle-class women seeking a public role beyond their own households, and philanthropic activists joined this ferment to urge expanded social provision for the working-class family. But convinced that marginality had to be overcome through direct intervention in the family itself, charity workers and residents of the new settlement houses resumed the quest for better techniques to repair damaged lives. From this came an elaborate casework ideal and what we recognize immediately as the therapeutic discourse of the modern human services. We find here an explicit awareness that intervention entailed the application of power to remold clients' volitions, aspirations, and sense of personal identity. Little of this could be accomplished by philanthropy alone, to be sure, as its resources were insufficient. So proponents of the new casework approach urged an alliance with the state, and pronounced themselves ready to serve the new public human service agencies they hoped to create.

I describe in part 2 the early success gained by therapeutic activists in creating an apparatus of public tutelage, the problems they encountered, and their triumph over the community-mobilization approach to the problem of marginality. Philanthropic casework technology, I show in the third chapter, became the basis upon which social personnel constructed an even more intricate model of public tutelage. They presumed therapeutic means and public authority could reinforce each other, so that intervention might gain greater scope, consistency, and impact. In the new juvenile court, diagnostic and rehabilitative methods were combined with formidable coercive powers. Proponents of the institution formulated an idealized view of its operation that suggested that young offenders would be diagnosed rather than condemned and then treated according to their individual needs rather than punished for what they had done. Similarly, in the mothers'-aid programs that provided public assistance for widows with young children, normalizing intervention was seen as an essential adjunct to material support. Where poverty had allowed wasteful habits to take hold, caseworkers were expected to fashion treatment plans for recipients, develop an intimate relationship with them, keep them under close surveillance, and even threaten sanctions if they did not do as expected. The added support provided by the state, it seemed clear, would greatly enhance the impact of the constructive power implicit in the therapeutic enterprise.

Although therapeutic activists made significant strides by 1920 in creating a human service apparatus, they also encountered unanticipated obstacles. Juvenile courts and mothers'-aid programs spread rapidly before and during the First World War, and other experiments in public tutelage followed. But as I argue in chapter 4, this swift advance brought social personnel into conflict with policy actors representing different discursive traditions. Because juvenile court judges, elected officials, and overseers of the poor saw themselves as representatives of community opinion, the agencies they ran reflected local popular sentiment. Clients were usually dealt with according to precepts derived from the venerable ideology of individual responsibility, much to the dismay of advocates of the therapeutic approach. As they saw it, the fault lay primarily with a political system that catered to lay prejudice and with administrative mechanisms too open to democratic influence. Yet some of the blame, social personnel also conceded, rested upon the therapeutic movement itself, for it had not demonstrated that its methods were clearly superior in helping clients adjust to social expectations.

I examine in the following chapter the strategies that supporters of the therapeutic agenda developed after the First World War to shield their instruments from corruption by other political currents. Since it seemed vital to lessen lay interference, social personnel urged reforms, notably centralization and a bureaucratic form of organization, that would allow them to impose their authority over local agencies. Also, where political circumstances had forced therapeutic activists into improvised service arrangements, the division of tasks could be rearranged. Local cooperation was to be assured by installing more agents of the therapeutic method in the field, where they could instruct judges and mothers'-aid officials on what casework entailed. The latter would be likely to respond, of course, only if intervention techniques were improved. This seemed to require a better science of human personality, one that might overcome the resistance to change clients had demonstrated. After much searching for a suitable behavioral discipline by clinicians and casework educators, they began to fasten onto Freudian psychoanalysis in the late 1920s as the proper scientific instrument. These strategies were at best partial successes, but they sufficed to permit the survival of the therapeutic sector after the collapse of Progressivism.

During the founding period of public tutelage, social personnel withstood a separate discursive challenge from those who believed social membership might be achieved through collective action. I indicate in chapter 6 that settlement house residents not only contributed to the elaboration of therapeutic methods but took a keen interest in the capacity of working people, however impoverished, to sustain their own group initiatives. If these efforts were encouraged through a decentralization of political power and administrative responsibility, it seemed possible to foster neighborhood cohesion and a strong sense of belonging, and with this an identification with the larger community. For a brief time just before the war there was a flurry of activity to promote community organization. But this waned amidst an intellectual ethos that was increasingly oriented toward technocratic rather than political approaches to social problems. Even the first enthusiasts of community organization gradually lost their taste for grassroots political action. With their retreat the position of therapeutic practitioners in policy circles became more secure.

The therapeutic apparatus has expanded dramatically over time, though its backers have often been checked in their most grandiose ambitions. I discuss in part 3 the broadening of the human services since the Great Depression and the continuing conflicts in which social personnel have been embroiled. Perhaps the most important gain recorded by therapeutic activists was their success in enlisting the support of the federal government. They accomplished this, I indicate in chapter 7, by capitalizing upon political opportunities and by continuing to pursue the strategies they had earlier introduced to foil their adversaries. When the Depression itself pointed up the inadequacies of existing forms of social provision for the needy, key political leaders suddenly showed great eagerness to consider new programs. Social personnel again demonstrated shrewd entrepreneurial skills, first carving out a niche for themselves in the emergency relief mechanism of the early New Deal and then building support among the architects of the Social Security Act for federal subsidies for existing human services. From the late 1930s through the 1960s, caseworkers within the federal bureaucracy sought to use the resources of the national state to advance the idea of normalizing intervention in public assistance and child welfare. They had sufficient control over policy discussion to assure that, when public concern over delinquency and welfare rose during the 1950s and early 1960s, their voice would be the one heard most clearly by policymakers at the national level.

Notwithstanding their ability to attain ever greater federal support, however, social personnel struggled vainly to gain command in the field. I explore in chapter 8 how they were routed from public social agencies during the 1960s, a defeat that also permitted their discursive competitors to dislodge them from their favored position in the higher reaches of social policymaking. In the juvenile justice system, therapeutic practitioners found themselves pushed aside by legal moralists and proceduralists. Meanwhile, vigorous if short-lived community action and welfare rights movements disrupted local social agencies and challenged the appropriateness of therapeutic methods as tools to combat poverty. Finally, having sold policymakers on the value of normalizing services to contain the surge in public assistance costs, social personnel were embarrassed when welfare caseloads began to increase at an even more rapid rate. By the close of the decade, Congress wanted nothing further to do with caseworkers, and within social agencies a new breed of managers arrived to put into practice cost containment methods derived from the business world.

Yet the therapeutic enterprise endured these setbacks, and the human services at present are larger than they were in the 1960s. As I observe in the last chapter, the therapeutic sector has weathered its crises in large measure because social personnel have accommodated themselves to political realities. They have promoted the creation of still more agencies and sub-units in fields like juvenile justice and public welfare, and then have acquiesced in the subordination of these to other institutions dominated by competing policy actors. In another adroit move, when the middle class began to take advantage of social services, therapeutic activists welcomed the opportunity to minister to a new constituency, even though fewer resources would be available to serve the poor. Social agencies have also learned to mobilize their better-off clientele to protect their budgets from retrenchment-minded politicians. Meanwhile, as new problems of marginality have come to public notice, social personnel have stepped into the breach to offer their services. The recent strategies have preserved the therapeutic state, but again at a steep price, for the human services have become ever more politicized and bureaucratized. Even so, therapeutic activists have recovered their confidence, and their faith in the constructive possibilities of casework remains deeply held. Clients, on the other hand, are more vulnerable to the excesses of intervention.

I believe it is vital to restore to a central place in our discussion the question of whether a democratic society ought to engage in normalizing intervention. Unfortunately, as I note in the conclusion, the question is complicated by the therapeutic sector that confronts us now. We can condemn it for its repeated failures and certainly imagine another way to approach marginality that does not rest upon casework mechanisms or violate citizen autonomy. But as a practical matter, we cannot sidestep the past. The efforts of therapeutic activists have left us with a formidable obstacle to change. We must reckon with agencies that will not graciously step aside and a policy process in which they retain enormous advantages. Much as we would like to translate our noble sentiments into deeds, we find ourselves with little room in which to maneuver.

Part One

THE SOCIAL QUESTION

One

Moral Economy and Philanthropy

THE PROBLEM of marginality as it came to be seen in bourgeois circles during the nineteenth century reveals less about the poor than it does about the community notables, social reformers, and charity operatives who dealt with them. It has long been recognized that theirs was an era of profound social change, brought about by the rise of industrial capitalism and the associated rapid urbanization. In speaking of the dislocations and suffering associated with capitalist development, these social observers used a language that reflected a sensibility alien to the new era that was unfolding. They worried not just about poverty but about the loss of contact between elites and the lower ranks of society. As the ministers and other bourgeois commentators recalled things, in the preindustrial community the more prosperous citizens had exercised stewardship over the behavior and values of others, especially those least able to look after themselves. But urban elites had lost their sense of mission, and so the bonds across class lines broke down. Marginal groups themselves could hardly be expected to abide by established moral codes. In the emerging slums, working-class families demonstrated their lack of moral bearings through displays of reprehensible and self-destructive behavior. Worse yet, among the working population, wealth no longer was seen as a just reward for discipline and upright character. Class antagonisms became more pronounced. Community notables feared a crisis, an eruption of social disorder, unless some new means could be found to lower class hostility.

Just as the vision of a preindustrial community framed the analysis of marginality, so, too, did it point to a plan of action. The conviction that elites had once accepted responsibility for the conduct of their social inferiors made clear what had to be done. Urban and industrial conditions did the most damage in the working-class family. Enter the philanthropists in their many guises. Having identified the family as the point of contagion, they struggled to erect barriers around it and make it the vehicle for the regeneration of morals. Ultimately this required a direct challenge to the family's autonomy. Through such philanthropic activities as child protection and private relief, marginal populations during the latter half of the nineteenth century were exposed to increasingly invasive moralizing intervention. As philanthropic activists elaborated various methods for erecting moral props beneath the working-class family, moreover, they came to recognize that they were pursuing different means toward the same end. A diversity of practical experiments, most very local in scope, yielded a discursive movement with a shared sense of mission.

This movement matured quickly. In their attempt to define the shape of social policy, philanthropic activists met with considerable resistance. They mastered it in a number of instances by forging tactical alliances with more influential interest groups. Philanthropic ventures continued to multiply, suggesting the many ways in which the working-class family might be approached. Furthermore, as philanthropy accumulated experience in dealing with marginal populations, it began to stabilize its organization of labor and specify its preferred techniques. It also moved, less overtly, to define a new role for the state, one that would place public authority squarely at the center of the moralizing project. Both the philanthropic apparatus and the discourse of intervention that took shape around it would cast a long shadow, inviting further investment while inhibiting any attempt to think afresh about marginality.

Moral Economy and the Dangerous Classes

For an influential segment of the middle class, the darker side of American economic expansion and the rise of great cities stood out only too clearly. The professionals and reformers who circulated through the swelling urban slums worried that American cities were reduced to centers of human degradation. To many evangelical ministers and charity activists, such poverty originated in common infirmities of the human character that city life unfortunately magnified. Others held that unique urban economic and social circumstances induced new forms of misery.[1] Some victims, concluded the antebellum Boston charity worker Joseph Tuckerman, suffered not for their own laziness but because the urban economy went through periods of insufficient demand for labor. Marginal families in the city, moreover, were forced to live in overcrowded housing, without proper sanitation or any privacy.[2] Middle-class observers agreed that urban conditions often meant moral decay for those in the slums. Family breadwinners lost the will to support themselves and degenerated into pauperism. And the deterioration reproduced itself, because the families of the poor functioned as a source of moral infection. Through their own homes, children were initiated into a poverty lifecycle—they were neglected or exploited by drunken parents and later as youths were left free to roam the streets, until they finally matured into a shiftless adulthood and began to pass the same habits on to the next generation.[3]

The particular terms that community notables used to describe marginality reflected in part the harsher view of poverty that historians identify in bourgeois public opinion after 1820. Poverty during the colonial and postcolonial eras had appeared natural and inevitable, at least in certain cases. When these worthy persons fell into distress, elites welcomed the opportunity to demonstrate their sense of charity and mercy. There was a communal responsibility to lend aid, as expressed in the elaborate structure of poor laws dating back to the early colonial settlements. The poor law apparatus recognized that not all poor persons were equally deserving, of course, and some received harsh treatment, but the system itself did not presume that misfortune was a moral affront. With the rise of aggressive commerce and the factory system, however, values associated with a market-oriented political economy came to the fore. Individuals were held strictly responsible for supporting themselves through hard work. When many could not do so, their failure became proof of bad character.[4]

Yet the nineteenth-century reflections on poverty by ministers, reformers, and charity workers suggest strongly their own misgivings about the new economic order. Where that order stood for the relentless pursuit of wealth, they still subscribed to an older ideal of a moral economy in which strong mutual bonds tied together different social ranks. Many urban professionals hailed from small towns, especially the storied villages of New England, and their past was shaped into a collective memory about how life was ordered in a preindustrial community.[5] According to the moral economy conception, town leaders had had a vital duty to keep watch over their less fortunate brethren, to hold up for them examples of right conduct. The exercise of moral guidance by elites, it was held, did much to foster both better behavior among the poor and loyalty to the community as a whole among all groups.[6]

Viewed from this moral economy perspective, urban elites were violating a public trust, choosing self-aggrandizement over the exercise of their responsibility toward the lower classes. A culture of consumption and promiscuous spending had taken hold in the metropolis. The barons of commerce and industry built elaborate homes to display their success, while the ordinary bourgeoisie did their best to ape the practice.[7] Yet literally in the shadow of these abodes, the poor lived in squalor, unnoticed. Class isolation became more extreme after mid-century, when a general movement began among the more prosperous citydwellers to regroup into their own neighborhoods. "It is the great evil of our city life," noted one philanthropic activist at the time, "that our classes become so separated." Spatial divisions erased any lingering trace of civic obligation among the well-to-do to attend to the fate of the poor.[8]

The consequences of the collapse of preindustrial solidarities deeply disturbed those who studied firsthand the condition of marginal populations. Where base instincts and destructive appetites were restrained in the small town by the scrutiny of neighbors, no one in the industrial city took notice.[9] Workers felt free to indulge their impulses, dissipate their wages and savings, and then accept the handouts that undermined their will to support themselves. Because parents in the working-class household had not been taught the correct bourgeois view that children were precious assets to be shielded from premature contact with the adult world, their youngsters were sent out to beg or work in factories. Immigrants seemed especially prone to moral decline, for, given their typically peasant background, they had been exposed least to decent behavioral norms.[10] Furthermore, now that marginal groups were left to themselves, they nursed a deepening resentment of those who lived in luxury. It was claimed that personal stewardship by the rich had legitimized hierarchy, for the poor were convinced by example that status reflected earned reward and that they occupied the rank they deserved. But in the absence of such contact, they saw nothing rightful about their position. The unequal division of property became an invitation to seize what otherwise was beyond reach.[11]

It did not escape notice that marginal populations had begun to turn to collective action. Politicians understood that the urban masses could be mobilized by a grassroots party organization that offered them recognition, ready access to public outdoor relief, and the spoils of office. To the genteel professionals, this smacked of the lowest kind of rabble-rousing and manipulation. They claimed, too, that unscrupulous ward leaders hired gangs of street youths to physically intimidate honest voters.[12] More alarming by far were the signs that working people were becoming conscious of themselves as a class. As the factory system made skilled labor obsolete, mechanics and tradesmen expressed a deep rage over the destruction of their way of life. They, too, drew upon a shared memory of the preindustrial past, but it was a very different sort of moral economy that they recalled. Before the factory had arrived, they believed, labor had been appreciated as an activity of worth in its own right rather than merely a means of survival. More than that, they had asserted their membership in the community through a degree of participation in collective decision making that had disappeared in the industrial city. They fought to keep alive their own ideal of a community in which skilled labor was respected, property was widely distributed, and ordinary people preserved a measure of democratic control over their own fate. Toward these ends craft unions and workingmen's parties were formed during the antebellum era. Later, unskilled industrial workers also struggled to organize themselves, though the surplus of labor pouring into the cities made them easily replaceable. At first labor agitation was episodic, undermined by business panics and episodes of high unemployment, but by the 1880s the turmoil seemed a constant by-product of the industrial order. And working people seemed increasingly receptive to socialist doctrine and other radical schemes for redistributing wealth.[13]

As the stirrings of the working class became more vigorous, bourgeois reformers in the larger cities began to fear that the destruction of the moral economy had brought America face-to-face with class warfare and an attack upon the sacred foundations of the liberal social order. Fringe elements in the working class, in the words of the important philanthropist Charles Loring Brace, might explode at any moment to "leave the city in ashes and blood."[14] Marginality under industrial capitalism convinced community notables that they were confronted by "the social question": in the wake of the erosion of older forms of authority, how was class conflict to be averted? We are not used to thinking of this as an American problem, for we prefer to regard our class system as more flexible—part of what is sometimes called American exceptionalism. But to these observers, the American city looked very much like its European counterpart, seething with proletarian unrest. Whether or not they had an accurate grasp of the situation, they would act according to their perception. It seemed urgent to find some way under the new urban-industrial system to restore class harmony.

Philanthropy Ascendant

As the social question began to prey upon the bourgeois mind in the decades before the Civil War, reformers groped for an antidote to the deterioration they had noted in the working class. They were drawn quite naturally to surrogate measures that might restore elite guidance over marginal groups according to the pattern of the older moral economy. These early ventures, including religious proselytizing and Sunday schools, stressed the moral uplift of the fallen and wayward. Since even supporters quickly dismissed the campaigns as superficial and they had little subsequent influence, I will not recapitulate their history here.[15] Before passing beyond the early nineteenth century, however, I must note two forms of antebellum practice that endured to shape later philanthropic developments. First, the mounting demand for outdoor public and private relief in several cities by the 1820s prompted reformers and charity activists to redefine private relief. They experimented with a system of elite visiting to the poor, pronounced this superior to material

assistance, and codified the methods.[16] Moralizing casework, a technique
I discuss below, then served as the basis for many later private relief ventures. Second, during the Jacksonian era, many asylums and other carceral institutions were established to segregate children, paupers, and
other degraded groups from the larger community so they might be rehabilitated. Reformatory confinement continued to be a vital field for
philanthropic activity, though this largely reduced itself to reform of the
very institutions earlier generations of reformers had created. Through
the work of Foucault and Rothman in particular, asylums have been
given much attention in the history of philanthropy, but we must be wary
lest their role be exaggerated.[17] When middle-class activists sought an
answer to the social question, they recognized the need to restore class
harmony in the modern industrial city itself, where the moral economy
had been torn asunder, rather than in places of confinement.

Our gaze is properly directed, then, at the tactical steps that bourgeois
activists took during the second half of the nineteenth century to counter
the core problem they believed lay behind the social question—the decay
of the working-class family. Organizational and public resources not previously imagined were brought to bear upon the family unit. On one side,
because it was agreed that decent homes were undermined by their slum
surroundings, some of these resources were used to modify the family
environment. But moral economy analysis indicated the family itself now
compromised decent values. It would perpetuate bad habits and ugly behavior among marginal populations, bourgeois activists maintained, unless other new tools were used to excise its degenerate tendencies and
revive it as a repository of higher standards. Accordingly, by comparison
with what had come before, intervention was designed to be far more
invasive, to penetrate superficial conformity and reach the level of emotions and desires. The degraded poor were to be taught to embrace bourgeois norms of sanitary housekeeping, enlightened child nurture, self-
sufficiency in the wage labor market, and thrift.

Dangerous urban conditions prompted a series of philanthropic efforts
that might be grouped together under the heading "social modernization." According to the famous urban landscape designer Frederick Law
Olmsted, property owners built structures as they saw fit, without regard
to the quality of life in a neighborhood, the health of the residents, or the
impact upon class tensions. The result was an environment that, as moral
economy discourse had frankly acknowledged, despoiled and corrupted
the working class. Only certain social remedies would make possible its
recovery. Proponents of environmental correctives intended to apply recent scientific advances to the industrial city, thereby neutralizing the external threat to physical health and spiritual integrity.[18] Translated into a
concrete agenda, social modernization entailed both the planned use of

social space and measures focused more narrowly upon the quality of working-class housing.

Community planning, designed to counter the effects of profit-oriented land-use decisions, rested primarily upon public health reforms and urban parks. Sanitation improvements were advocated after 1850 for working-class districts as a way to reduce illness and dependency; the necessary technology had been introduced in the early nineteenth century in middle-class neighborhoods.[19] At roughly the same time, Olmsted and his allies began to urge park construction in the proximity of the slums. Large parks were justified as a means to relieve the drudgery of factory labor, give the working-class family a quiet retreat in which to renew its emotional ties, and promote mingling among social classes.[20] Beyond containing the damage caused by industrial life, philanthropists hoped, planning would enhance the human resources upon which the factory system relied and restore the social bonds that had knit together a moral economy.

The moral tone of working-class life could also be improved if the home itself were reconfigured physically so that it more closely resembled its middle-class counterpart. Public health proponents followed up their campaigns for better urban sanitation with calls for the introduction of running water to individual tenement buildings. The remedial logic was explicitly noted: "By facilitating the means of frequent bathing in families—particularly the poor and laboring classes—the effect would soon be apparent, by removing a prominent cause of disease, and contribute to the moral, as well as physical improvement of the lower classes."[21] Other philanthropists, linking overcrowding to disease and loose sexual morals, urged that the tenement be redesigned so that it would be made suitable for decent family relations. In particular, working-class girls needed greater privacy so their virtue might be safeguarded. Beginning as early as the 1850s philanthropic groups like the New York Association for Improving the Condition of the Poor sponsored social housing in the slums. The model tenement units were intended to show that if living arrangements no longer encouraged bad habits, the working poor would be able to triumph over their character defects.[22]

However, with little support from the middle and upper classes and modest resources available for what promised to be costly physical investments, social modernization efforts yielded very limited benefits. Sanitary improvements and parks enjoyed a brief vogue before taxpayers began to complain about the cost.[23] For philanthropy, the opposition taught an important lesson: even if they would benefit from harmonious class relations, propertied interests were reluctant to subsidize public improvements. Social housing, on the other hand, was a voluntary initiative that implied no public commitment. Alas, the few small projects undertaken by philanthropic groups did not begin to offset the decay in the housing stock or the construction of new dwellings that repeated the evils philanthropists had discovered in the slums and tenements.

A second line of philanthropic activity took as its objective child protection or, as it was known, "child saving." Child protection originated in the conviction among bourgeois observers that working-class children deserved special attention, for they were at once the most vulnerable of marginal populations and the medium by which the ranks of certain antisocial elements would be replenished. To some child-protection advocates like Charles Loring Brace, children were mistreated and exploited by their parents, and the family bond thus seemed to be an obstacle that should be broken. Urban street life also was a focus of alarm, for young people were exposed to destructive influences. Tainted by their homes and streets, children became hardened and mean, eventually being drawn into a shiftless underclass that survived through crime and pauperism.[24]

This analysis gave rise to vigorous efforts by voluntary organizations to shield children from the varied hazards of working-class life. The New York Children's Aid Society, established during the 1850s under Brace's leadership, sought to remove children from the homes of the casual laboring element by placing them out in rural communities or by enrolling them in industrial training schools where they might learn both useful skills and the discipline of the workplace. The problem of youngsters already abandoned to the streets likewise demanded a forceful response, so Children's Aid tried to entice these children into its placement or training programs. Over the next several decades the Children's Aid model was copied in a number of cities.[25] These organizations shared the child protection field with societies for the prevention of cruelty to children (SPCCs), formed in the 1870s in response to mounting middle-class concerns with child abuse. Some SPCCs thought it best to strengthen the home and preferred to earn the cooperation of the family. But an abiding disdain for working-class parents seems to have predominated in SPCC work, and the Societies favored coercive measures to rescue children. They used their political influence at the state level to secure laws against juvenile vagrancy and street begging and win passage of statutes that permitted the SPCCs to gain legal responsibility over children when it could be shown that they had been exploited by their parents. To make sure that the legislation would be used, the agents for the Societies established good working relations with local judges and police.[26]

A certain timidity at first marked the practice of child protection groups in their dealings with the working-class family, but they soon became quite bold. Placing-out by the Children's Aid Society threatened to set it in open conflict with a child's parents. Such parental objections outraged Brace, who regarded the adults as an irremediable source of corruption. Still, for all his shrill rhetoric, his organization was not eager to interpose itself between parent and child. Youngsters were recruited for transport to the country only when their ties to the home had been clearly severed. Many SPCCS, by contrast, did not shy from confrontation; they were willing, even eager, to prosecute parents as a means to refashion family norms. In fact, the New York chapter in 1881 gained the power to make arrests, while other SPCCS routinely called upon the police. Statutes permitted the Societies to be appointed as guardian in neglect cases and to be given immediate custody of very young children. Courts looked to SPCC agents for recommendations and usually followed their advice, which often was to separate a child from his or her family. It was no wonder, then, that the poor called the SPCC "the Cruelty" and dreaded the appearance of its representative on their doorstep.[27]

Through a third major line of activity, philanthropic relief, bourgeois voluntary organizations attempted to correct what they saw as the indifferent attitude of working-class adults toward wage labor and thrift. Relief represented one of the earliest philanthropic enterprises, but in the 1860s and 1870s it took on a vastly enlarged ideological significance. The change was set in motion as philanthropic relief leaders became alarmed by a surge in public relief expenditures. High unemployment after the Civil War and during the industrial depression of the 1870s seem to have produced the political conditions that Piven and Cloward have identified as catalysts for an explosion in public relief. Not only were social disturbances common, but urban political machines saw the distribution of relief as a tool for securing working-class support.[28] Always hostile toward "outdoor" public relief because it seemed too attractive an alternative to the poorhouse, charity activists denounced machine-administered alms with particular bitterness. When relief was politicized, it was charged, the working-class family lost sight of the connection between its own flaws and its misery. Economic moralism was very much a part of the conception of a moral economy to which private relief leaders remained devoted. They worried, too, that the easy availability of relief would remove the spur of necessity and so compromise the integrity of the system of wage labor.[29] If relief were left in their own more competent hands, it would be administered with greater discrimination so that dependency would not become a way of life among the able-bodied.

Charity activists in key eastern cities formed an alliance with middle-class reform politicians to contain the public relief menace. By the late 1870s all public home relief in Brooklyn and New York City was eliminated, and reform coalitions temporarily dislodged the party organizations from city office. Over the next few years philanthropists in several other Eastern cities shut down public aid departments.[30] What had seemed a major challenge to labor discipline—public subsidy of the work-

ing class—thus disappeared by means of a deliberate strategy to depoliticize and privatize relief.[31] If the victories over public aid were confined to
one region of the country, here at least a message had been sent to the
casual laboring class. State resources could be withheld to place the poor
once again in a condition of economic insecurity and remind them that
they could not use their political strength to escape their natural obligation to toil.

Having reined in the misguided public relief operation, private relief
leaders faced the task of fulfilling their promise that they could better
cope with the needs of all those legitimately in distress. They met the
challenge, if only to their own satisfaction, through better coordination
and an expanded program of home visiting among the poor. In the opinion of charity leaders, many cities were "overcharitied," with aid too
readily available from the many private agencies, none of which took the
trouble to attend to the moral needs of their beneficiaries. Charity organization societies (COSs) were formed in the 1870s and 1880s, then, to
establish greater central direction over the fragmented private relief apparatus. In turn it would be possible to reduce fraud among recipients and
promote the character reform that charity activists believed so essential in
overcoming pauperism. The COS employed professional investigators
(usually men) to uncover imposture, compiled dossiers on each applicant,
and established an information exchange to discourage duplicate claims.
Genteel women volunteers, "friendly visitors," were then sent into the
homes of relief applicants to re-create the elite stewardship of the preindustrial community.[32]

Proponents of the COS touted its methods of investigation and personal
contact as the best instruments for rehabilitating marginal families and
binding the social wounds inflicted by industrialization. The initial inquiry sought not merely to distinguish genuine distress from deception,
but also, in the authentic cases, to reveal the character flaws that lay beneath poverty. Once these were identified, the friendly visitor attempted
to make the family acknowledge its deficiencies. Material aid was discouraged, the COS arranging for other agencies to provide it only where
absolutely necessary. Instead the visitor was supposed to instill in her
charges the determination to bear up to their responsibilities through
their own efforts. Her counseling rested upon optimistic premises: to the
COS, unlike the prosecution-minded SPCCs, impoverished adults were candidates for redemption. Through the person of the friendly visitor, as
Donzelot says, philanthropic relief tried to project itself deeply into the
working-class family, so as to moralize it from within. The male breadwinner would be taught the importance of self-support and savings, while
the woman would be guided to turn her home into a refuge for him and
her children. Despite its humble station, the family would then resemble
the contemporary bourgeois model of a well-ordered household. In the

process understanding between classes was to be promoted and the extremes of society were to be brought together.[33]

Much of the burden for this domestic transformation rested with the woman in the marginal family. To the friendly visitor, seeking a point of entry into the family circle, the mother seemed easiest to reach, for while there was a vast cultural difference between them their common gender served as a bond. The mother therefore found herself the target of many suggestions—she must save money, make her home an inviting refuge for her mate so he would not seek the comforts of the tavern, keep alcohol out of the house, give male and female children separate beds, and so forth. Her husband did not escape attention, of course, because his sobriety and his enthusiasm for work had to be stimulated. Yet here, too, she had a role, putting further pressure upon him, possibly by threatening to remove her children. At the same time, she dared not drive him away, because the COS also regarded desertion as a social menace of the first order. If he fled and she could not support herself, she would have no recourse but to surrender her children.[34]

We can now properly consider the final important line of philanthropic activity, institutional reform. At the outset of this discussion I noted that since the Jacksonian period much philanthropic effort had been invested in this field. However, despite a proliferation of specialized institutions, there was still deep dissatisfaction with the techniques of confinement. In a renewed effort that began during the Civil War, reformers attempted to improve the rehabilitative performance of institutions. New correctional theories led philanthropic activists to recommend innovations including adult and juvenile probation and the substitution of cottage-sized facilities for large congregate institutions.[35] Asylum reformers also recognized that the failure of reformatory institutions lay partly with their administration. Facilities like workhouses and juvenile homes were enmeshed in a political web woven by state and county politicians who sought to reduce subsidies, asylum superintendents who tried to hold down costs and satisfy competing local demands for discipline and laxity, casual laborers who sought seasonal refuge, and local businessmen who viewed the institution as a customer first and foremost. Beginning in Massachusetts, philanthropic leaders tried to counter this excessive political interference by promoting state boards under their own direction with broad powers to supervise public, publicly-subsidized, and private institutions.[36] The campaign to establish state oversight reflected, as did the COSs, a willingness to embrace the administrative method of centralized control. But in this case philanthropy sought explicit public sanction, in the form of state legislation and/or gubernatorial appointment.

Although institutional reform was inspired by an autonomous strain of philanthropic discourse, we need to appreciate the relationship between remedial confinement and other philanthropic enterprises. The great attention devoted to institutions that segregated marginal populations reflected an implicit awareness that not all members of such groups could be moralized in their given surroundings. Quite the contrary, the philanthropic enterprises that reached into working-class communities—child protection and private relief—required carceral options to back up their operations. It was understood that the severe moral or physical decay of certain individuals made it too risky to leave them in a position where they might continue to contaminate their families, peers, and communities. For example, cos leaders urged that women who gave birth to more than one child out of wedlock be sent to a reformatory asylum so that their promiscuity would not spread as a plague through the slums. These mothers were to be separated from their children, too, so the young would not be infected with the same moral weakness.[37]

Thus far I have spoken of the different forms of philanthropic endeavor as discrete entities, but we should appreciate the coherence of the philanthropic enterprise as a whole. It is true that enthusiasts of each field sometimes saw themselves in competition with the others. Yet a common outlook—fear of class conflict coupled with a conviction that some artificial means had to be invented for restoring moral-economy social relationships—bound most philanthropic activists together. They understood that the stewardship they wished to exercise depended upon coercive instruments that would allow them to overcome the autonomy and passive resistance of marginal groups. Thus child protection groups turned to the courts, asylum advocates proposed confinement, and charity leaders manipulated outdoor relief policy. Furthermore, though bourgeois activists might devote themselves to but one branch of philanthropic work, they grasped that interventions were mutually supporting; no single approach could excise the demoralization of the working-class family where that demoralization had many sources and found many expressions. The strategic unity of the several forms of philanthropic practice requires that we treat them henceforth as a collective subject, philanthropy.

The Philanthropic Apparatus and State Power

Philanthropic practice, we must acknowledge, fell far short of the aspirations of proponents for moralizing the industrial working class. For the purpose of a full historical account, it would be necessary to point out that philanthropy nowhere established the hegemony of its approach. Public relief did not disappear from most cities, so politicians went on appealing to impoverished workers by offering cash aid and in-kind benefits; institutions defied every effort at oversight and made a mockery of new correctional theories; and sectarian agencies fought Protestant-dominated child protection efforts. Working-class families tried to use agencies, especially the SPCCs, to settle internal quarrels or squabbles with their neighbors. Philanthropic leaders spent much of the time at their conferences condemning political interference, client obduracy, and public indifference.[38] Even on a theoretical level, the philanthropic approach to poverty was sharply contested. For example, from the perspective of an extreme Social Darwinism, poverty represented evolutionary selection at work, and it was a crime against nature to interfere with the process out of some misguided compassion for the victims. Any number of intellectuals and business leaders subscribed to this position and maintained that the proper social policy was to do nothing.[39]

Appreciating that their endeavors had been checked at many points, philanthropic activists set out to do better. A discursive movement is not easily deterred by a nonconforming reality. Having created for themselves an elaborate framework for interpreting the world, the participants filter experience through this mental construct, fitting even the most unpleasant facts comfortably into place. Rather than raise doubt about the movement's premises, failure is attributed instead to temporary difficulties that merely indicate what proponents must do next to advance their cause. The political machines that philanthropists saw corrupting the working class might have led them to conclude that mass democracy would never tolerate the elite oversight they had in mind; likewise, elite and taxpayer opposition to social modernization might have convinced them to give up this line of their work entirely. But in both cases, philanthropic activists told themselves that they simply had not amassed sufficient backing, and so they determined to add to their political support.

They did this by finding allies in various quarters. The campaign against public outdoor relief brought together relief activists and upper-crust urban reform elements. For example, well-to-do men in Philadelphia, active backers of political reform, supported the local COS as it successfully fought to abolish outdoor assistance—it seems they preferred to send their wives into the slums rather than pay taxes to subsidize relief.[40] By contrast, when faced with business or other elite opposition, philanthropic types joined in coalitions that crossed class lines. Some child protection leaders became early advocates of child-labor and compulsory-schooling laws promoted by trade unionists. Of course, the most natural base of support was the middle class itself, then growing in size and political influence. This constituency would find its hallowed ideological traditions, particularly the doctrine of individual responsibility, honored by philanthropy. In addition, the movement could accommodate contemporary bourgeois intellectual currents. Social Darwinists who thought the mischief of heredity open to human correction would be able to support any line of philanthropic effort.[41] Philanthropic activists made good use of the many periodicals aimed at the literate middle class to preach the merits of their response to the social question.

Due in no small measure to the friends it had made, philanthropy in the late nineteenth century could point to a wide array of local initiatives mounted under its auspices. These might be taken as the first tangible outline of a comprehensive program for moralizing marginal populations. Social modernization, child protection, and philanthropic relief suggested many answers to the question of what to do with the unfit working-class family. Its renovation might be accomplished through sanitary improvements, access to public parks and social housing, removal or training of its children, prudent distribution of relief (preferably in-kind rather than cash), and genteel advice. For truly extreme cases, new specialized institutions promised to replace mere confinement with enlightened care. It would be possible to build upon this practical foundation, to elaborate further each of the lines of activity.

The field experiments suggested lessons about what made for effective moralizing, so philanthropy began to refine the organization and technique of social intervention. In the process the movement committed itself more firmly to the course upon which it had already embarked. The different branches of philanthropy were seen to have found their proper niches, and were so recognized in the division of section meetings at philanthropic conferences. Accordingly, each branch took on a life of its own, ordering the discursive conception of appropriate practice. For example, when confronted with children in any sort of distress, philanthropic activists turned for inspiration to the well-elaborated enterprise of child protection, with its stress on judicial support and its deep mistrust of working-class parents. Within the particular lines of philanthropic activity, similarly, the approaches and techniques already in use were regarded as the correct tools for reaching the marginal family. We may take as a case in point the praise heaped upon the early casework methods developed through friendly visiting. Although by most accounts the well-intended visitors often failed in their task, philanthropic activists were still confident that a sound personal relationship would permit bourgeois outsiders to bring moral uplift to an impoverished family.

As part of this ongoing clarification of how it proposed to approach marginality, philanthropy built upon its first interactions with government to suggest a new model for the relationship between the state and civil society. This theoretical achievement has been overlooked in most historical accounts of the early philanthropic movement. We can readily understand the omission. Through most of the nineteenth century Americans did not speak of the state, for state power was so diffuse as to be all but invisible. They had forgotten the experience of the colonial era and the early national period, when public authority was used more vigorously in enterprises as diverse as economic development and public welfare.[42] Philanthropists therefore did not identify the state as a recognizable abstraction but buried it, talking about public power indirectly and in the most deceptively mundane terms. Just as important, since philanthropic discourse appeared to accept as a given the classical limitations upon the role of the state in liberal society, the movement itself did not appreciate that it held a distinctive political view. I contend, however, that philanthropy, keenly aware of the need to harness legal authority and administrative resources to its moralizing project, expressed a consistent view of the state that would require nothing less than a reconfiguration of political power.

Given that philanthropy's ideal of the state was embedded in the various lines of philanthropic activity, we can only reconstruct it by reviewing how each field contemplated the use of public power. To begin again with social modernization, it should be observed that many measures to remake the urban environment depended upon the exercise of eminent domain. They required, then, the expansion of state power at a most sensitive point—where it encroached upon the property rights of dominant social groups. In addition, sanitation improvements and parks implied some redistribution of wealth, for local governments financed these measures through higher taxes on property owners. When social modernization campaigns stalled, proponents had to recognize that for the time being they lacked the political weight to alter the state/society relationship on property questions. Their tactical retreat made it appear that they accepted prevailing notions of limited government. But the matter is not so simple, for philanthropy had asserted a principle: property rights ought to be restricted where their free exercise brought on the human moral decay witnessed in working-class households.

Let us consider next child protection, where the theoretical commitment to state power was more closely matched by the practical results. In early American history courts demonstrated a great reluctance to interfere with internal family governance, respecting patriarchal authority unless a father's control over his household had completely collapsed.[43] Child-saving agencies at first called upon the judiciary to continue its traditional role. The Children's Aid Society and the SPCCs, determined to separate children from their parents in cases of flagrant neglect or exploitation, sought to enlist judicial authority against nonfunctioning family units. Over time, however, it seemed essential to use the courts against less extreme forms of mistreatment—indeed, in response to forms of behavior seen as quite normal in impoverished working-class communities. Under the new antibegging and compulsory school attendance statutes,

SPCCs asked judges to compel parents to fulfill what the societies took to be their basic obligations to provide shelter and care. Child-protection agents then acted as an arm of the courts to make certain their directives were followed. By responding to the prodding by SPCCs for earlier action and delegating enforcement powers to their agents, the judiciary allowed itself to be invested with a new responsibility to enforce bourgeois child-raising norms within the working-class household. This represented a significant extension of state power.[44] That it drew no notice can be explained by the fact that, in contemporary bourgeois opinion, courts were regarded as neutral legal organs rather than as part of a political state. Inflated judicial power would be seen only by those marginal families caught directly in its path.

In the third field of philanthropic effort, relief work, the call for a retreat from public action contributed more obliquely to the articulation of state power. Power can be seen to expand, of course, when the state enters upon some task. Yet when government ceases to provide some service or benefit, this act of withdrawal may likewise enhance its capacity to shape behavior—most particularly, the behavior of those who have just been denied access to the public largesse. So it is with public aid and the poor. They are forcefully reminded, when the state reduces or eliminates assistance, of the variability of official kindliness and impressed with their acute vulnerability.[45] In the 1870s philanthropy waged (and in some places won) a struggle to "depoliticize" relief, demanding that control of relief funds be transferred to private hands. The message—that the state might now take back what it had given—could hardly have been lost upon dependent groups even in the cities where philanthropy did not succeed in its quest to eliminate public relief. Unlike some of the other philanthropic contributions to the refashioning of public authority, this one was the subject of much discussion. To charity leaders and political reformers, the state had moved at a critical moment to reaffirm its limited mandate under the liberal social constitution.

Institutional reform, the final component of the philanthropic enterprise, advanced another kind of change in the shape of state power. This involved a shift in the locus at which power would be exercised. Asylum advocates had always been mistrustful of local politics. Unfortunately, since the upkeep of an institution was a community or county responsibility and since confinement might have to be ordered by the town judge, they had been dependent upon local officialdom. When philanthropy in the late nineteenth century launched its drive to establish state supervision over institutions, it put its weight behind the centralization of state activities. Philanthropic leaders who agitated for state boards believed that at this higher level of public organization, where philanthropic ideas did not have to compete with local sentiment and prejudice, the commitment to moralizing confinement would be pursued more consistently. The central state apparatus came to be viewed as the only public structure that might embody the public interest in the philanthropic agenda.

We can now grasp the unifying themes in philanthropy's attempts to make over state power. Preservation of the working-class family, especially its moral integrity in bourgeois terms, became the standard by which to judge the appropriateness of public intervention. The state emerged with a new combination of duties and limits. Where the threat to the family could only be neutralized by authoritative action, philanthropy sought state support, even at the risk of conflict with agency clients or those required to bear the financial cost. Child protection, sanitary improvements, and urban parks all depended upon the exercise of legal prerogatives available through the state alone. By contrast, where public programs were seen to imperil the family, undermining its discipline to work and save, philanthropy fought to circumscribe public responsibility. Hence direct public subsidies to the poor in their own homes were to be shunned. State authority, expressed here in the refusal to continue an action, would be brought to bear to warn the working-class family that public resources were not to be taken for granted. At any point this remodeled state might violate local popular views of the role of government. When such a conflict became evident, the moralizing activity in question would be placed under a more central state organization, and so would be insulated from lay opinion. Philanthropy had taken the first step with its advocacy of state supervision of institutions.

In practice and in theory, then, philanthropy established new terms through which the problem of marginal populations could be systematically addressed. Philanthropic discourse designated the targets for intervention, defined the fields of practice, suggested the techniques that should be pursued, and hinted at an enlarged role for the state in moralizing the working-class family. If certain issues appeared settled, the enterprise was still in its formative stage, and there remained considerable room for further practice and inquiry. Those eager to make their contribution to resolving the social question therefore flocked to the banner of the philanthropic movement. But the lines of activity and the discursive categories and assumptions would also act as constraints upon subsequent innovation and intellectual exploration. Although the next generation of activists might wish to rebel against the discursive framework, such a legacy simply could not be avoided.

Two

The Discourse of the Human Services

THAT THE PAST would weigh heavily on philanthropy becomes clear when we examine the rebellion against established philanthropic doctrine that began among settlement house residents, charity workers, and other middle-class activists in the 1890s. They insisted upon their distance from their philanthropic predecessors. Yet the Progressive-era attempt to repudiate the inherited framework could not overcome fundamental continuities in the philanthropic movement. Its old preoccupation with social upheaval among the working-class endured, in different language, into the twentieth century. As Progressive social personnel sought solutions to the social question, moreover, they could not escape the practical side of their discursive heritage. The working-class family, regarded still as unable to cope with modern conditions, continued to be the target of philanthropic intervention. Rather than shed completely what had come before, Progressive philanthropy devised a model that would raise this intervention to a new pitch of intensity.

Critical scrutiny of philanthropic assumptions was stimulated by new intellectual currents, an influx of activists with different ideals, and the economic collapse of the mid-1890s. In the universities social scientists spoke of the "interdependence" of social forces and social classes. Such a perspective suggested that marginal populations might be the innocent victims of circumstances they could not control, rather than of their own weak character. As college-educated volunteers circulated in the slums and witnessed firsthand the high unemployment brought on by the depression of 1893, they repudiated the verdict on the moral defects of the poor that philanthropy had pronounced. Many of the new activists were women who, sensing their own uncertain position in American life, empathized with others on the fringe of the social mainstream. They were also most eager to make a place for themselves by doing more for the forgotten half of society. Pressed by this younger generation of activists, philanthropy embraced a broader conception of social rights under which persons placed in distress by social conditions could make a claim on the community for help.

For all the talk of securing justice for the poor, it was still necessary to formulate a concrete program. Interdependence, I will suggest, is a vacuous concept, which leaves entirely open the kind of service owed to those in distress. And the notion that people are entitled to a living standard might be taken to encompass many things. If new ideas are not sufficiently specific to guide action, it can only be grounded in older forms of practice. Here philanthropy, as the dominant discursive approach, occupied a commanding position. Methods of intervention had been carefully elaborated, a division of labor had been established, and philanthropic groups were already well connected to other social movements and to state structures. The old avenues invited further investment. Although Progressive social personnel fashioned their own discourse—what we recognize today as the discourse of the human services—the mark of philanthropy is unmistakable. The family unit was regarded by charity visitors, settlement residents, and others as the focal point for intervention. For the family to survive it would have to be adjusted—as Donzelot puts it, not moralized but normalized.

On the other hand, it would be a serious mistake to represent the Progressive accomplishment as nothing more than a change in terminology. Philanthropic leaders set out to refine the methods of the friendly visitor into a precise casework technology that could bring about profound changes in habits, attitudes, and behaviors. Nineteenth-century philanthropy, always conscious of sin and the weaknesses of its targets, had admitted definite limits to what genteel influence could accomplish. A boundless faith in science relieved Progressive social personnel of any such modesty. Enthralled by the tools they had devised, moreover, they did not pause to consider the risks their enterprise might pose to the personal autonomy of their clients. Instead they leaped to make a connection between their casework program and the Progressive living standard doctrine, so that normalizing marginal populations became a community obligation. It followed that the state would have to be drawn wholesale into the enterprise. Where their predecessors had obliquely raised the possibility that public authority ought to be used to restore the working-class family, Progressive philanthropic activists openly determined to make it their instrument.

New Inspirations

Much as philanthropy had originally been shaped by the larger drift of middle-class thought during the nineteenth century, the turmoil within Progressive philanthropic circles reflected the changing tide of bourgeois opinion at the end of the nineteenth century. We can identify two larger intellectual forces that helped to modify how the middle class viewed American society and the problems of poverty and class tension. The first of these forces was social science, at the time just assuming the disciplinary configuration we recognize today. University intellectuals rejected the moral-economy framework as archaic and unscientific. Industry and commerce on an unprecedented scale had remade social life, and little wisdom could be gleaned by clinging to a vision of a form of community that had vanished. It was necessary instead to take an empirical approach to social subjects, to accumulate data without viewing the results through a distorting normative lens.[1]

When sociologists and political economists put their method to the test, they found a society that was highly complex, with intricate relationships among its component elements and indirect and often obscure lines of social causation. Such a society could best be compared to the living organisms studied by biologists. For, like the organism, society was interdependent, its multifold cells necessarily influencing each other, the disturbances in any one limb spreading outward in ever-widening circles to upset the entire social body. The social scientists accordingly did not dwell upon individual responsibility, but sought to illuminate the full depth of interdependence and its unseen consequences.

Despite the pretense of objectivity, the new social science embraced definite value choices. It still suggested, as had moral-economy discourse, the rejection of narrow economic thinking and the need for class reciprocity and gradual social change. In an organism each cell or part depends upon every other one. So also in modern society: each element, no matter how powerful it appeared, could not survive without the cooperation of all others, could not prosper at their expense. Rapacious behavior, the vulgar product of a market-dominated society, was condemned as before for tearing apart the social fabric.[2] At the same time, if one explained "interdependence" by means of soothing organic metaphors, it was possible to deny again the intractability of class conflict. Tensions between classes were more properly seen as the product of misguided thinking.[3] The damage done to the social organism by greed, irresponsibility, and class hostility had to be repaired, of course, but like any living thing the social body could not be rebuilt from scratch. Social science stressed that the task was a delicate one that required evolutionary correction, not abrupt radical reform.[4]

Progressive philanthropy embraced the premises of university social science. Working-class families and neighborhoods would be studied without the presupposition that misery meant depravity; instead, social facts would suggest their own inevitable interpretations. The settlement houses have been celebrated as the quintessential vehicle of the new empiricism. Their residents immersed themselves in slum life, seeking to view it from the level of marginal groups themselves.[5] And in the meliorist spirit of social science, the settlements insisted the study of urban conditions was no end in itself; the settlement, as Jane Addams maintained, expressed the desire to apply knowledge effectively in human affairs. Social science could modify its own subject, could eliminate the social pathologies that left people in poverty and despair.[6]

Feminism constituted a second intellectual movement reshaping the middle-class mind at the close of the nineteenth century. Bourgeois women in increasing numbers sought to escape the confines of domesticity by defining for themselves a public role. Since the notion that women belonged in a separate sphere still held strong, their choices remained limited. Conventional party politics, for example, was an exclusively male preserve. But if women could find outlets that seemed to call upon their particular concerns, especially with home and family, they might establish themselves in the public world. They would also be in a position to make use of the moral capital they claimed by virtue of their acknowledged devotion to the values of a healthy family life.[7]

Philanthropy was one such outlet, and women flooded its ranks in the 1890s, often moving directly from the universities into settlement or charity work. In part, perhaps, they were only following an established pattern, for women had already made themselves an integral part of such ventures as charity visiting. But that had been a part-time pursuit, carried on within an organization dominated by men.[8] Progressive women wanted to put their own stamp on philanthropy. Here was a form of activity that was at once a natural elaboration upon the traditional domestic sphere and an escape from the suffocating restraints of the purely private life of the middle-class homemaker. Philanthropy offered an opportunity to translate values associated with women—concern for children, caring for those in distress—into a laudable public role. Women volunteers seized the chance, assuming a far more prominent position in many philanthropic efforts than had their predecessors.[9]

To their work in the settlement houses and the COSs, Progressive women activists brought a special sensitivity. They recognized that, whatever a woman's particular talents, she had been trapped until now in the household, condemned by cultural norms to the periphery of the social world. With this imposed subordination a fresh memory, they felt special sympathy for others who could not control their own destiny. The social science that young middle-class women absorbed in the universities spoke of the poor as victims of "impersonal social forces." For those who had just transcended their own marginal status, it was plain that the poor should not be condemned for theirs. Better to extend to them, too, the prospect of a release from their marginality and the means to enter the social mainstream. When coupled with the eagerness of women volunteers to stake out for themselves a larger place in American life, their determination to liberate the poor from the circumstances that bred misery became a potent source of imperial energy for philanthropy.[10]

Marginality and the Social Living Standard

The surge in unemployment in 1893 spurred a reappraisal of philan-thropic social analysis that was shaped in turn by the new intellectual currents I have just outlined. Settlement house residents, who began to establish themselves in the slums at just this moment, refused to accept the simple notion that cyclical unemployment reflected personal moral weakness. Trying to view their neighbors without condemnation, the set-tlement workers found that the mass of unemployed workers were of sound character.[11] It has been argued that this modern outlook distin-guished the settlement houses from mainstream philanthropy. But that is merely how settlement leaders liked to applaud themselves.[12] In fact, the unemployment crisis led charity organization field staff to come to the same conclusion. Friendly visitors realized that most of those seeking emergency relief had managed before the crisis to support their families. Their presence now at the COS office cast doubt upon private relief's core assumptions about character, individual responsibility, and misery. So-cial conditions, it was conceded, did not necessarily destroy character even though they had reduced people to poverty.[13]

Among philanthropic ranks a new understanding of social marginality took hold that represented a partial break with the past. To begin with, Progressive philanthropy made the category of marginality far more in-clusive. Social research by settlement residents showed that the vast ma-jority of working-class families lived in meager circumstances, often on the verge of dependency.[14] Social science thus led philanthropy to see that the problem of poverty was of greater magnitude than even the most alarmist moral-economy analysis had suggested, lending new urgency to the philanthropic enterprise as a whole. As the problem of marginality grew in scale, moreover, its causes became more remote. The logic of interdependence demanded that the study of marginality be pushed back from the victims to the dominant social forces. For the most part general-ized poverty could not be traced to indolence or other character short-comings. Instead, the focus of analysis shifted to the instabilities of the industrial economy. Workers suffered from the exploitation of their labor and an "inefficient" business cycle that discarded productive labor ac-cording to the whims of the market, while their income was insufficient to provide their families with any insurance against catastrophe. The indus-trial environment, concluded leading reformer Lee K. Frankel, made it "a physical impossibility to eke out a decent living and to maintain a decent standard of existence."[15]

Field research also yielded a different assessment of the working-class family. Simple dismissal of the marginal household as a breeding ground for degraded values gave way to a more nuanced understanding—the family was resourceful yet seriously endangered. Again it was the settlement house residents who best appreciated the resilience of family life and the steadfastness of family affections.[16] Nevertheless, amidst a bewildering urban environment, the family was, to use the new objective rhetoric, "maladjusted"—it coped poorly with the conditions in which it found itself, everything from overcrowded housing to low wages.[17] In the contest between strong families and a brutal industrial order, the former were overmatched.

With attention fixed on the broader causes of marginality, the condition of social casualties raised for Progressive philanthropy a question of justice rather than charity. Philanthropic discourse began to grapple with the idea of a social living standard as a communal obligation. The standard seemed to include, at a minimum, decent housing, sufficient food, basic medical care, some access to recreational and cultural programs, an elementary school education, vocational training, and safe working conditions.[18] That society denied many of its members the bare minimum they needed for an adequate standard of living was seen as an affront to their human dignity.[19] More than that, philanthropy treated the social living standard as a precondition for democratic citizenship. "Democracy," asserted Mary Kingsbury Simkhovitch, a settlement leader, "implies that poverty is not to be tolerated, every individual must have his chance to become a real person and add his strength to the life of the whole." By denying marginal groups the chance to contribute to the larger community, society violated their fundamental democratic rights.[20] Simkhovitch and her peers thus echoed the old moral-economy faith that noneconomic values ought to be respected, but a rhetoric of citizenship replaced that of class stewardship.

Having raised an adequate living standard to the status of a right, philanthropy had to acknowledge that marginal groups could make a valid claim upon the community. Mainstream charity leaders like Edward T. Devine suggested that society incurred a twofold obligation toward its members: first, to place each in a position where self support became possible and, second, to rectify damaging industrial and urban conditions that lay beyond individual control.[21] Until both commitments were fulfilled, many working-class families would be unable to sustain the living standard through their own effort. Therefore the responsibility rested on the community to meet their vital material needs and so renew their sense of self-worth.[22]

At this point the new analysis of poverty circled back to reach a familiar conclusion. Although Progressive philanthropy rejected the earlier moralizing posture, the social question was not forgotten but merely rephrased. It was posed now in a way that made it consistent with the prevailing social scientific outlook. Because of interdependence, social forces brought great pain upon unsuspecting and defenseless victims. The result was a laboring population prone to unrest, hostile to the urban-capitalist system that both dominated it and depended upon it. No observer could fail to see the connection between misery on one side and labor strife and socialist agitation on the other. Hence the question: how could the elements of an interdependent society be brought into harmony? How, that is, could class antagonisms be contained?[23] Bourgeois activists a half century earlier had concluded that they faced a very similar challenge.

Social science, alas, did not point clearly to a solution. Moral-economy discourse had drawn upon a definite model of social relations to provide a basis for bourgeois activism; genteel stewardship and family moralization followed naturally from the analytical premises. By contrast, interdependence expressed a vague wish that social forces, especially labor and capital, learn to appreciate that they needed each other. How such a result was to be achieved remained completely obscure. Only the notion that the community had a responsibility to provide a minimum standard of living offered any help to those seeking practical direction. If the community acknowledged its obligation, it appeared, the discordant parts of the social organism could be drawn together again. Yet, significantly, the social living standard was itself an unbounded concept. We have observed that philanthropy aimed not just to assure physical survival, but to provide for a higher level of existence needed to create democratic citizens. The full dimensions of that standard were yet to be defined.

Technology of Adjustment

Where grand ideology provides an inadequate plan for action, an established discursive movement still has sources upon which it can draw for strategic guidance. Past practices embody a design for exercising power. Though some may be discredited, it would be extraordinary if the movement had lost all capacity to adapt to new demands. Philanthropy in the Progressive Era remained vital and open, willing to learn from its mistakes and shortcomings. The various lines of activity offered different paths via which an answer to the social question could be found. If social science urged an awareness of interdependence, philanthropy would continue in its efforts to realize a bond between classes. If the task was to secure a decent standard of living for marginal populations, philanthropy, as the enlightened vehicle of the community, would build upon its many agencies to make good the community's obligation. A strategy thus emerged through the elaboration of previous philanthropic endeavors.

First, to reshape the destructive slum environment, philanthropy expanded upon its earlier efforts in social modernization and child protection. The former was revived with particular enthusiasm. Philanthropic activists, with the settlement house residents in the lead, pressed for legislation to control both social space and private housing standards.[24] We have seen that earlier social modernization efforts faltered in the face of elite indifference or opposition. However, Progressive philanthropy cultivated important allies at the local level, including organized labor and certain urban reformers. Besides urging such environmental correctives as strict building codes and improved public health regulations, the social reform coalitions sought to bring basic material benefits to working-class families. The subsidized public utilities, low-cost public housing, and municipal pure milk stations and medical dispensaries that were introduced in a few cities stood as proud examples of what philanthropy imagined when it spoke of a community commitment to a material social living standard. In conjunction with other middle-class reformers, some erstwhile settlement residents began to form a public administration movement to proselytize for the extension of public social provision.[25] (About this important movement I shall have more to say in chapters 5 and 6.) Child-protection groups also stepped up their campaigns for broadly targeted legislation and social policy. In conjunction with organized labor, they demanded child-labor laws; on their own they fought for public playgrounds to create a secure space for children off the streets.[26]

Philanthropy, however, regarded social modernization and social provision as insufficient. These measures were fine so far as they went, but they operated at too general a level to serve as a remedy for specific manifestations of maladjustment. Statutes, codes, and programs to make basic benefits available to everyone would not reverse the pathologies that infected a given family unit—its demoralization, its low values, its inability to cope with the demands placed upon it. Hence the second item on Progressive philanthropy's agenda: direct intervention in the family, to repair its internal workings and give it the capacity to sustain its burdens. The working-class family, long regarded as unfit, was now deemed incompetent and therefore still in need of close philanthropic attention.[27]

We cannot help but be struck by this enduring fascination with the presumed debilitating effects of misery on working-class families. It may have derived in part from the feminist concern with the integrity of the home. Middle-class women activists still regarded their own domestic arrangements as the standard for a secure and nurturing home, and felt keenly the need to preserve or restore that standard in working-class households. To an even greater degree, the commitment to remedial intervention to secure family adjustment reflected continuity at the operational level of discursive practice. Charity work and most settlement house activities still focused upon individual family units.[28]

Philanthropic field staff used their experience with families to refine the casework techniques inherited from private relief into a more rigorous approach to family rehabilitation. The condition of the working-class family was viewed as "diseased," requiring treatment for its specific symptoms much in the way that modern medicine approached illness. We see the influence of the medical pattern not only in charity practice, where we might expect to find it given the longstanding emphasis on domestic pathology, but also in the settlement house programs. Robert A. Woods, along with Addams the most reflective settlement leader, compared the settlement resident to a devoted family physician and the house's working-class neighbors to patients. Like a physician, the settlement resident sought to draw upon the victims' recuperative capacity and alter their behavior, so they could overcome the pathologies with which they were afflicted and lead a healthier and more satisfying life.[29] Settlement workers and charity staff differed over important details of what I call the therapeutic approach, but such quibbling cannot be permitted to obscure their agreement on the basic method.

As the critical first step, an outside agent was supposed to establish a personal relationship with the members of the working-class family. Settlement residents held that the relationship would be most natural if it was truly voluntary; ideally, the first move should be made by the prospective clients. Charity organization staff found initial contact more problematic. Because they dealt with people in urgent need, the situation could hardly be regarded as unforced. And the relief worker was also charged with investigating fraud, a duty not readily conducive to intimacy. Nevertheless, no matter how the introduction was made, the caseworker next should cultivate mutual respect. Some resistance was to be expected from the male breadwinner who might sense a loss of his sovereignty over the family. So the female caseworker, continuing in the mode of the first friendly visitor, might use the link of shared gender experience to reach out to his spouse. Together they would then overcome his hostility. While family members were learning to trust the caseworker, she should begin to arrive at a specific diagnosis of their condition. Her full understanding of family problems would make it possible to formulate an appropriate remedial plan.[30]

Casework rested upon the belief that skillful, sustained contact could bring about a reconstruction of behavior. Since the caseworker had gained her clients' confidence, they would accept the therapeutic program of domestic instruction that she next introduced. If family mores and behavior seemed "functional"—that is, they contributed to the adjustment process—she was expected to reinforce them. But her educative guidance also was intended to discredit customs rendered obsolete by modern living conditions. For example, settlement workers counseled persistently against the ancient practice of midwifery.[31] In place of these customs, the caseworker sought to implant the latest bourgeois household management techniques. She might draw upon public kitchens, classes in domestic science and infant care, and visiting nurses.[32] Furthermore, to assist the family in sustaining the new ways, the caseworker would encourage her clients to make ongoing use of the network of educational, recreational, and cultural agencies that was beginning to take hold in the modern city.[33] And her efforts did not end there. Through her unobtrusive follow-up work, she would observe whether her clients had relapsed into destructive habits and practices. The other agencies to whom she had introduced her clients might also report any retrogression.

Although charity practices had provided some basis for therapeutic intervention, the model formulated by Progressive philanthropy represented an extraordinary accomplishment. The therapeutic design—contact, diagnosis, normalizing measures, ongoing contact with agencies, and continued oversight—went far beyond any intervention previously attempted, establishing the pattern for modern human services. In this ambitious design, the therapeutic approach suggested the possibility of vast power, at once subversive and constructive.[34] The caseworker selectively destroyed the family's behavioral patterns, even its cultural heritage, then provided substitute skills her clients needed to cope with their surroundings. If all went as planned, the working-class family emerged from the program with a thoroughly reordered lifestyle. Educative measures might give the father a more positive attitude toward his job or employment prospects, modernize the mother's practice of the domestic arts and household budgeting, and prepare the children for their future role in the work force or the home.[35]

Enlightened middle-class behavior set the standard for therapeutic adjustment. At the end of the nineteenth century the bourgeois home came willingly under the ministrations of domestic experts from such fields as home economics and medicine. The impetus was supplied not just by the specialists themselves but by women who appreciated that their status would be enhanced when it was finally recognized that efficient homemaking required sophisticated knowledge. Women active in philanthropy extended this outlook to their clients. In the philanthropic view, the working-class family would only function at an optimal level if it, too, came under the dominion of the modern social disciplines.[36] Of course, not all proper values changed with the times. Settlement houses promoted vocational education that, in addition to teaching job skills, sought to encourage a positive outlook on industrial labor among men and boys. Meanwhile, instruction in home and child care for women and their daughters communicated the message that tending to the home remained the highest role to which they should aspire.[37]

The soaring faith in the therapeutic approach that Progressive philanthropy expressed stemmed in part from its new evaluation of social marginality, at once more pessimistic and more hopeful than the verdict rendered by its predecessors. On one level, viewed through the lens of interdependence, the working-class family appeared more vulnerable. Distant social forces held the family in a vicelike grip, making plain that it did not control its own destiny. Yet, precisely because it was so readily acted upon by outside influences, it would be a fine "power receptor" for the more constructive intervention that philanthropy proposed. At the same time, the family seemed to retain a potential for contributing to its own rejuvenation that had not been appreciated before. Philanthropic activists previously had felt stymied by what they had perceived as its thorough degradation. Where its members had seemed so lacking in positive resources, philanthropy had found little with which to work. Now, in striking contrast, the working-class household appeared durable and resilient. If power is the capacity to make a new beginning, as Hannah Arendt said later in another context, the family was more than just a good object upon which to apply power—it was powerful in itself. Settlement house residents and charity operatives accordingly raised their expectations. From such material there seemed no limit to what might be accomplished.

Nonetheless, although clients were expected to make a significant contribution, philanthropy saw science as the key tool that assured the success of therapeutic intervention. In her project of family rehabilitation, the therapeutic caseworker made far greater use of scientific knowledge than had her charity predecessor. The working-class family could only master its situation by calling on the intellectual tools appropriate to a complex society. Problems of everyday life no longer lent themselves to solution by folk wisdom; they instead required the application of sociology, domestic science, child psychology, and other new disciplines. Since the family lacked scientific information, the caseworker had to function as a social technician, applying the latest findings in a practical setting. Expertise gave her the means to raise the quality of family relations or to enhance an individual's capacity to function in the modern world, and so became the decisive power resource.[38]

Something more needs to be said about the allure of science for philanthropic social personnel. The enthusiasm with which they embraced behavioral expertise makes it clear that the principal impact of science lay not in its instrumental value but in its ideological appeal. As an ideology, science gave rise to the conviction that objective knowledge could fundamentally reshape both society and individual human subjects. Such self-assurance—or, more accurately, hubris—was absent from nineteenth-century philanthropy, with its awareness of the corruption of the human soul. But Progressive charity workers, settlement residents, vocational counselors, and others celebrated the therapeutic enterprise as a triumph over earlier philanthropic ignorance, as the dawn of a new age. Here was

a worthy mission, something in which decent and well-educated bourgeois activists could fervently believe: to heal misery and distress, to make
wounded people whole again, without recourse to social upheaval. The
social technician assumed the vital duty to settle the social question once
and for all.

Not surprisingly, then, the therapeutic impulse spread into fields of
philanthropic activity where casework previously had made few inroads.
Child protection advocates, who had once preferred to separate children
from demoralized homes, began to see the value of intensive contact with
the families of abused and neglected children.[39] We find a parallel current
in institutional reform, too. Behavioral science became a source of inspiration to those in penology who hoped to instill a remedial mission in
prisons and juvenile reformatories. By using counseling and educative
techniques, it was claimed, institutions would be able to remold the attitudes and behavior of their inmates. Even those cast out by society would
thus be brought to forward-looking social norms.[40]

Yet, despite the eagerness with which certain asylum reformers
grasped onto adjustment methods, therapeutic discourse really served to
strengthen the hand of the growing number of philanthropic activists who
opposed the old emphasis on routine institutional care for marginal populations. The cost of asylums and their failure to rehabilitate their charges
left Progressive philanthropy increasingly disenchanted with confinement
as a corrective instrument. Child protection advocates were led to build
a foster care system so they would no longer have to rely on training
schools and sectarian orphanages.[41] As various philanthropic elements
challenged the hold of institutions in practice, so therapeutic doctrine
helped to discredit the asylum intellectually. Casework experiments appeared to demonstrate that many forms of maladjustment responded well
to normalizing intervention. Most confinement was therefore unnecessary. Indeed, because institutions separated clients from their home and
neighborhood, and so from the resources they needed to renew themselves, the carceral approach made the task of adjustment more difficult.
Philanthropy intended to normalize clients beyond institutional walls, not
to seal in maladjustment. Thrown onto the defensive, asylum interests
would have to settle for a more modest role.

Hidden Tensions

With so many high hopes for correcting maladjustment through casework methods, philanthropy understandably was not inclined to place its
approach under critical scrutiny. But since the early discourse of the
human services allows the logic of therapeutic intervention to emerge in

full candor, we should press the issues the Progressives did not address. The first involves what we might call the challenge of large-scale production. As social personnel nominated themselves for a major role in social reconstruction, few of them recognized that it might be difficult to reproduce positive results in a mass program. Charity workers like Mary E. Richmond eagerly set about to codify and formalize casework, a step they thought would make possible the use of normalizing techniques on a wider basis.[42] Only in the settlement houses do we find an awareness that what worked in a modest neighborhood program did not readily translate to a general service apparatus. Settlement residents disdained any rigid set of procedures, fearing that it would lead to mechanical dealings with clients and stagnation in the social agency.[43] Suspecting that only small organizations can maintain flexibility and informality, settlement residents were uneasy about the philanthropic plan to extend the therapeutic program. But Progressive philanthropy, seeing only the opportunity for itself, paid little attention to the problem of growth.

Philanthropy's unequivocal commitment to science raises more fundamental concerns. Once social personnel took scientific knowledge to be indispensable to modern family life, they linked the fate of the human services to the behavioral disciplines and to their own ability to put social research to effective use. At the time social science seemed extraordinarily promising, on the verge of duplicating the pattern of discoveries in the natural sciences. But if initial breakthroughs were to prove less productive than expected, social personnel could not look elsewhere for help, for to do so would call into doubt the very foundation of therapeutic power and the legitimacy of intervention. Instead failure would necessarily spark a relentless quest for new behavioral disciplines, with frustrated caseworkers putting all candidate theories to the test in their dealings with clients. Faith in science thus would force the unsuccessful normalizing agency to become a laboratory.[44] Furthermore, because social personnel esteemed science so highly, they regarded it as sufficient to correct all manner of family and personal pathology. They adopted a narrow, indeed, provincial view of the appropriate response to marginality. Approaches to maladjustment not predicated on scientific intervention would be unworthy of attention.[45]

Of basic importance, too, is philanthropy's skewed discussion of power. Although social personnel talked at length of the positive change they sought to bring about, they treated therapeutic power uncritically. This sets them apart in the American intellectual tradition. Power, in any form, has always excited suspicion. Certainly our own era shares the skeptical attitude that power exists to be abused. At the beginning of the twentieth century mistrust toward power was similarly widespread, clearly visible in movements like populism. Many of those active in philanthropy caught the tone and voiced hostility for the captains of industry or the bosses of political machines. Yet Progressive philanthropic discourse evinced no such reservations about the power it was promoting, despite the fact that therapeutic practice was designed to breach the inner recesses of human experience. This striking indifference to what was nothing less than an encroachment on personal sovereignty calls for discussion.

Such a casual attitude toward therapeutic power suggests first the impact of science-as-ideology. Power exercised under the mantle of science did not appear to be power at all: to Progressive social personnel, the term itself meant the use of coercion to compel surface compliance with arbitrary social norms. This they did indeed find highly objectionable. But it was a different matter when intervention derived its justification from scientific principles of right living and worked upon its subjects gradually, eliciting their willing cooperation. The caseworker arrived at a nonjudgmental diagnosis and offered expert advice that clients could readily see to be in their own interest. Precisely because social personnel were so attentive to the constructive uses of power—a sensibility that we have lost—they could not conceive of any darker possibilities.

I have contended that, along with social science, feminism played a major part in redefining philanthropy, and we must look here as well to explain the blithe acceptance of an approach that paid so little heed to the matter of privacy. Well-to-do women chose through philanthropy to make the quality of family life among marginal populations their special public concern. For some women activists, including Jane Addams and other settlement leaders, this manifested itself in the vigorous pursuit of social modernization and social provision. But these women also joined with others who were more narrowly concerned with private relief to frame the therapeutic approach and carry on the day-to-day work from which specific normalizing techniques emerged. They saw the therapeutic enterprise as a social expression of their deep concern with home and family, as a process based on mutual respect in which they merely shared the fruits of enlightened domesticity. How we depict power determines whether we will be alert to its full implications. In the formulations of the therapeutic project presented by women social personnel, power—let us understand it as the capacity to remold the desires and volitions of others—was so softened that it again no longer appeared as such.[46]

But far from sharing this relaxed view of therapeutic power, we ought to voice serious reservations about the very conception of the normalizing enterprise. Therapeutic intervention rests upon the premise that personal autonomy must be invaded in order to create a more desirable kind of autonomy. In a democratic society such a move must be regarded as suspect. I do not mean to suggest that we should reject out-of-hand all interference with personal choice. To take but the most obvious example, a democratic community rightly uses public schooling of minors to impart skills and mold civic values. However, the direct reach of the school is far more limited than the intrusive contact philanthropic activists contemplated. The relentless violation of autonomy they anticipated, then, must be carefully scrutinized. (I should add that their own successors have on occasion expressed some of the criticisms I pose here, as I shall discuss in subsequent chapters.)

An inability of persons to care for themselves might well justify some sort of protective intervention, but the notion of incompetence can reflect bias and self-interest. In therapeutic discourse we find both. Progressive philanthropy managed to convince itself that the ordinary working-class family could not function at the level required by modern conditions—it lacked the capacity to nurture its members. This assertion of incompetence reflected the drift of contemporary bourgeois discourse: it steadily inflated its expectations of healthful home life and domestic relations, so that the working-class family could not possibly keep pace with the advancing standard. So, although philanthropic testimony about the strength of family life among marginal populations highlighted an enduring capacity to cope with difficult circumstances, the family would have to yield its freedom to the social technicians. We must also remember that philanthropic activists, having devised a fascinating instrument in the technology of adjustment, were eager to put that instrument to use on a broad scale. Since a larger target population meant greater opportunities, there was every incentive to regard marginal groups as unable to fend for themselves. Once the concept of incompetence was corrupted, therapeutic discourse could not use it to legitimize the exercise of therapeutic power.

Troubling, too, is the refusal of Progressive social personnel to impose any limits upon that power, to declare any realm of their clients' private affairs beyond the caseworker's concern. The germ of social pathology might lie anywhere, therapeutic discourse held, so it was vital that casework diagnosis expose every facet of character, every quirk of behavior. Also, because clients could not cope with the complexity of their experience, they could not be left alone to define their own values and goals or to select their own activities. They must forgo their freedom to make unguided choices in favor of thorough instruction from the social expert. Only in this way could the caseworker assure their return to health. But the walls around family and individual serve a constructive purpose that therapeutic doctrine overlooked: they may frustrate an outsider's scheme for enlightenment, but they also act, as earlier skeptics about power understood, as a shield against many forms of social domination. In the drive to make clients well, they are rendered exceedingly vulnerable.

Finally, although intervention was supposed to culminate in restored independence, it is not clear that therapeutic logic would ever permit clients to regain full autonomy. The well-adjusted family was the one en-meshed in a web of organized activities. It was normal in the modern era, that is, to seek external support and instruction. Through this organized network, moreover, the caseworker could maintain contact with family members and step in again should evidence of dangerous tendencies re-surface. Thus, as philanthropy saw it, marginal populations had ex-changed their pernicious isolation for continued friendly surveillance and the prospect of recurrent helpful contact with social technicians. While this is merely hinted at in the early Progressive philanthropic discourse, a dangerous seed nevertheless had been sown.

The many risks embodied in therapeutic power might be tolerated if, by our rigid devotion to family autonomy, we are blinding ourselves to greater evils within the family itself. Feminists today have observed that the family cannot simply be treated as a unit with a single set of interests, but must be seen as an arena with its own set of historically unequal power relations. Men have benefited from laws and cultural norms that sustain their privileges, while women and children have been dependent on the income of male breadwinners. The abstract ideal of "family auton-omy" thus conceals the actual lack of autonomy of most family members. Given the weak position of women and children, any outside interven-tion, including normalizing casework, is to be welcomed, for it upsets male domination by setting a new form of power against traditional patri-archal authority. The collision between the external force and the hus-band/father, the feminist argument runs, yields an opening in which women and children can at last gain a measure of independence.[47]

Though the feminist critique of family power relations is compelling, we need to be skeptical about the liberating possibilities of the therapeutic approach. Intervention introduces new actors into the family equation, but they may not side with the weak. We should recall that feminists active in Progressive philanthropy, who themselves stepped outside of the confines of bourgeois domesticity, did not intend to promote a general assault on patriarchy. Quite the opposite: they regarded conventional gender roles as necessary to the effective functioning of the working-class household. Therapeutic discourse accordingly stressed the responsibility of working-class women to hold together their homes and comfort their husbands. Rather than find empowerment through normalizing agencies, women and children may discover that they have been made still more helpless.

Standard of Adjustment

Caught up in its zeal for the new technology of adjustment, Progressive philanthropy quickly linked normalization to the definition of the social living standard. It will be recalled that the content of the standard had been left open, defined only as what might be necessary for individual dignity and democratic citizenship. This could be expanded with little effort to incorporate an enlightened model of domestic adjustment. Accordingly, charity personnel and domestic science experts asserted that an adequate living standard should include not just material goods, but also a well-ordered domestic life. Only a program of therapeutic services could enhance the family's capacity to meet the full range of its members' psychic needs. Over time casework intervention created a basis for higher aspirations and for satisfying these new desires.[48]

It took but another short step to raise the therapeutic project to the status of a community responsibility. Because an adequate living standard was a matter of right rather than charity, therapeutic services became a basic component in the philanthropic conception of civic duty. If an enriched family life was a precondition for full citizenship, as philanthropy contended, it would be irresponsible not to make casework help available to all those suffering from some form of maladjustment. The working-class family was entitled to be free of domestic pathologies and, if it was unable to master its own deficiencies, the community was obligated to provide the appropriate adjustment support.[49]

Again because of their uncritical attitude toward therapeutic power, social personnel failed to notice that broadening the living standard to include normalization and making adjustment a community duty threatened to undermine citizenship itself. I have argued that therapeutic intervention necessarily compromised personal autonomy. We must also recognize that autonomy is a precondition for democratic citizenship: only people who enjoy a secure space have the capacity for political self-determination. What constitutes that space remains an important problem for democratic theory, but it must be defined in a way that permits mature adults to define for themselves what matters in the world and to make their own choices. However, left without any personal sanctuary, therapeutic clients lack a domain in which they can express who they are. They can no longer govern themselves, because the "self" is denied its voice. By proposing, in the name of citizenship, that casework intervention become a community responsibility for all who fell below its standard of adjustment, philanthropy in fact sought to deprive marginal persons of one foundation upon which effective citizenship rests.

A further implication of the living standard principle did not escape philanthropy's notice: in exchange for bestowing enhanced social rights upon the impoverished and incompetent, the community could demand that marginal populations conform to conventional behavioral norms. For the working-class family, the living standard meant, in Donzelot's apt term, "tutelage"—mandatory submission to instruction and surveillance by social personnel and, thus, the denial of the prerogative to freely choose habits, associates, and pleasures.[50] Edward T. Devine insisted, for example, that the dependent family had to submit to outside supervision over expenditures. If aid and counseling failed to normalize the marginal family, disciplinary steps were entirely justified. The family that refused to conform to budget guidelines should be subject to sanctions.[51] What to do in such cases? When educative steps had been exhausted, one social scientist told a charity conference, those who did not attain the behavioral standard ought to be placed under restrictive control.[52] Philanthropy in this way arrived at one new understanding of the place of the institution in the strategy to overcome maladjustment. Confinement remained a last resort for those clients, surely very few in number, who would fail to adjust themselves to the requirements for modern social living.

The utility of the living standard principle at last becomes fully clear. In the hands of philanthropy it proved to be a highly versatile doctrine. The social living standard emerged first as a liberating vision of society's material obligation to the laboring masses. Then, reflecting philanthropy's emphasis on casework with distressed families and individuals, the standard was embellished to require an elaborate therapeutic program. Marginal populations were entitled to the services required for full personal adjustment, even though these compromised their autonomy and circumscribed the space they needed to speak as citizens. Lastly, social personnel asserted that the claim to community support entailed responsibilities; as a condition of assistance, clients would be expected to meet the behavioral expectations set forth by social agencies. Social rights, in short, meant the abdication of other rights, including privacy. To this point such rights had been used to mask self-destructive conduct. The living standard justified tutelage by social agencies, with the prospect of coercive measures against any family that defied normalization.

For so long as therapeutic methods were confined to voluntary programs of modest scope, the implications of the social living standard would remain unexplored. But pursuit of the therapeutic agenda swiftly revealed to philanthropy the inadequacy of private efforts. To begin with, in this era before the advent of rationalized fund-raising mechanisms like community chests, private agencies obtained only irregular subsidies from middle-class and corporate donors. Therefore only a small fraction of those in distress could be reached, especially in times of economic crisis.[53] Experience with hostile or suspicious families also persuaded philanthropic field staff of the need for some greater enforcement power to back the caseworker's approach to the home. Visiting nurses, for example, found that lacking official status they could not gain entry to many tenement apartments.[54] And despite the proliferation of service agencies like settlement houses, many marginal families still eluded the reach of the normalizing apparatus or kept it at arm's length.[55]

Philanthropic activists soon appreciated that they needed the cooperation of the state on an unprecedented scale. Only the public sector commanded sufficient fiscal resources and disposed of the potent legal tools needed to embrace all marginal families in the therapeutic project.[56] Philanthropy in the preceding decades had tried to pave the way by articulating a conception of the state based on the goal of family preservation. However, notwithstanding this important theoretical foundation and the practical alliances with public institutions that philanthropy had forged, the state apparatus was very undeveloped. Earlier philanthropic efforts did no more than define appropriate avenues for the public response in fields like child protection. To fulfill the community obligation to provide a normalized living standard for the working class, state organization would have to be transformed. Family preservation in the Progressive era called for intervention by many public institutions capable of putting to use the new normalizing technology.

There were real obstacles to overcome, some the consequence of philanthropy's own prior actions. In the first place, as soon as philanthropic social personnel entered the public arena, they would lose monopoly control over their programs. Instead they would have to cope with outside partisan interference and public personnel who lacked the commitment to therapeutic methods. These problems had been the bane of earlier philanthropic leaders. For example, in the view of charity supporters after the Civil War, local party politics and poor administration necessarily tainted public outdoor relief. It had been alleged that public officials tried hard to please a variety of local constituencies and showed no aptitude for casework methods. In the Progressive era philanthropy still worried that the state lacked the capacity for expert normalizing intervention. Compounding the difficulty, the hostile response to public relief by organized charity in the 1870s and 1880s left Progressive philanthropic activists with an awkward intellectual legacy of opposition to public assistance. Because the coss had shunned public aid, moreover, few working relationships with public welfare agencies had been sustained.

To surmount the barriers and philanthropy's self-inflicted wounds, social personnel would have to push harder to make family adjustment the mission of the state. Where public service seemed to violate traditional philanthropic doctrine, a graceful reversal of position would be required. On a more practical level, it was necessary to equip the state for effective therapeutic service. Philanthropic methods and principles would have to be made the basis for new or remodeled public organizations. To these organizations philanthropy would transfer the normalizing technology it had so carefully developed in its own field laboratories.[57] Moreover, since public agencies had no competent social personnel of their own, experienced philanthropic cadre would themselves function as the first public caseworkers.[58] Their direct participation best assured that the state would understand its expanded mission—to elevate the working-class family to the standard of adjustment.

Part Two ─────────────────────────────

CREATING THE THERAPEUTIC STATE

Three

Models of Public Tutelage

PHILANTHROPIC activists and their allies during the Progressive era forged a link between therapeutic discourse and public authority that established the foundation for public human services in the welfare state. Political science today pays much attention to the activity of translating ideas into new programs, celebrating the practical talents of the protagonists by calling them "policy entrepreneurs." As we shall see in the next chapter, the term aptly describes what philanthropic leaders and various reformers accomplished. However, if the notion of policy entrepreneurship leads us to focus narrowly on concrete results, we seriously underestimate the contribution of the architects of the public therapeutic sector. They not only invented new institutions and programs but also grasped that public intervention introduced the possibility of more sweeping therapeutic power than even philanthropy had imagined.

We can best understand the theoretical vision behind public tutelage if we examine the discourse surrounding the creation of the juvenile court and the mothers'-aid program. The court idea presumed that therapeutic means and public authority would reinforce each other to normalize marginal children and their families. From a minor's initial contact with the institution through a period of judicial oversight that might continue for years, court social personnel were to apply normalizing casework techniques. Yet, because either the young offender or his parents might oppose advice and instruction, court intervention would also make use of the legal and coercive resources of the state.

Similarly, public assistance to widows with children was advocated as a program that would link adjustment techniques developed by philanthropy to the special capacities of a public agency. Here matters were complicated at first by a factional dispute within philanthropy itself, for private charity was slow to abandon its hostility to public relief. But since both the early public assistance supporters and their foes in the charity leadership accepted the new living standard doctrine, all could agree that the poor were entitled to help and that this assistance ought to incorporate normalizing casework. As mothers'-aid legislation was adopted, then, it was understood that the program represented another venture in public tutelage. Recipients and their families were to be succored with material aid but were to be integrated into the social mainstream through instruction and supervision. As in the juvenile court ideal, the model for agency-client relations closely followed that introduced by philanthropy. Yet public assistance was expected to have definite advantages over private charity. A public department would command a larger and more stable budget, its caseworkers would have a higher standing in the eyes of its recipients/clients, and public interventions were backed with the kind of sanctions private charitable agencies lacked.

In the juvenile court and mothers' aid alike, proponents saw that the use of the state would enhance the impact of casework techniques, and so create a second level of power effects beyond what philanthropy alone could produce. Public tutelage would capitalize on such attributes of a state apparatus as legitimacy and compulsion. With these added resources at their disposal, it was believed, caseworkers would become ever more omniscient and persuasive. Supporters of the therapeutic project looked forward to their triumph over the subtle obstacles that the working-class family had erected to deflect the agents of philanthropy.

Therapy as Juvenile Justice

The first attempt to join the normalizing technology developed by philanthropy to public authority came with the invention of the juvenile court. Most historical studies of the court properly stress that it was a radical departure in jurisprudence, intended to alter fundamentally the terms of judicial intervention in the life of problem juveniles.[1] I would go further to assert that the new institution in fact occupied a shadowy ground between legal tribunal and social agency. In its scope, proponents hoped, the court would reach beyond offenders to any child who might be deemed maladjusted. It would then treat the child and his family with the most advanced therapeutic methods. (I use the male pronoun throughout this section because the discourse on the court took male delinquency as the central problem.[2]) Normalizing intervention backed by the court promised results far superior to those attained by private child-protection groups. Historians also have not situated the court in the emerging therapeutic sector. As other public human services soon began to appear, court proponents saw that judicial tutelage would be able to enlist a range of adjustment tools to surround its clients with corrective influences.

The campaign to reorient juvenile justice to a therapeutic approach began in the early 1890s, well before any other Progressive philanthropic efforts to enlist the state in the expanding normalizing project. It was no accident that the quest for state support began here. In part the effort reflected fears among child-protection advocates and other philanthropic elements that grave harm was being done through judicial mismanagement of children's cases. Juveniles were allegedly treated with excessive leniency or brutality, and throughout the criminal justice system they had far too much contact with hardened adult criminals. Philanthropy worried, as it had since the Jacksonian era, that minors were being left to the easy corruption of the streets or were being initiated into the degraded values of the criminal stratum.[3]

On a more positive note, philanthropic activists had long placed a high value on cooperation with the judiciary. A court had seemed to be a neutral instrument, the essential fairness of which would not be questioned by its targets among the poor. In more practical terms, child-protection groups had developed ties to the judiciary that dated back several decades. Probation experiments in Massachusetts made use of philanthropic volunteers, field agents representing societies for the prevention of cruelty to children influenced judicial dispositions by reporting on a child's background, and sectarian child-placing agencies relied heavily on judicial authority.[4] Given the strong court-philanthropy linkages that had been forged, building public tutelage through the judiciary made good sense. And so a coalition formed, consisting of reform-minded judges, women's clubs, and the sectarian placement agencies, to redefine the judicial processing of cases that involved children.[5]

Through this court-philanthropy axis, the juvenile court emerged in 1899 to link judicial intervention to the therapeutic model. Jurists strained to find a coherent legal basis for the new institution.[6] But the court clearly owed more to the discourse of the human services than to traditional jurisprudence. Although the court incorporated earlier judicial innovations, its proponents correctly understood that it was not merely an incremental step to unify judicial child protection. Linking a court apparatus to philanthropy's larger normalizing project represented a great leap beyond the established judicial role into the exercise of the new therapeutic power under public auspices.[7]

That a therapeutic commitment guided the juvenile court movement can be seen first in its ideal conception of the institution's jurisdiction. The new court claimed an open-ended mandate, so broad that it included, besides children charged with infractions, those who were neglected, abused or exploited, "incorrigible," or likely to slip into one of these categories. All dangerous or endangered minors were to be brought by the juvenile court within reach of child-protection agencies. It thus would become an essential point of support for the social technicians determined to excise the pathologies of working-class family life.[8] By including in the court's domain conduct that would not be criminal if committed by an adult, social personnel would be able to address a situation in its earliest stages and thereby prevent more serious damage to the child.[9]

The therapeutic orientation, according to the movement model, similarly ran through the court's entire operating procedure. Each child called to official notice was to become an object of inquiry for diagnostic specialists. A probation officer contacted everyone who might know something about the case and then visited the home to interview the parents and weigh the domestic surroundings. Other court personnel studied the child for intellectual or medical deficiencies. By means of this initial evaluation the court would identify the family context and social setting that had precipitated deviant behavior or placed the minor at risk.[10] Significantly, it was hoped that, in cases in which a delinquent act had provoked judicial intervention, the assorted investigations and tests would push the specific offense into the background. The minor's antisocial behavior mattered only for its symptomatic value. Where the inquiry disclosed no support for the initial complaint but a pattern of poor social adjustment, the case certainly ought to be continued on other grounds.[11]

A hearing would follow that was supposed to more closely resemble a physician's examination than a criminal trial. The judge would use the diagnostic profile as well as other testimony to illuminate the child's entire milieu. What a minor had done, proponents reiterated, should count for much less than the parental care he had received, his morals, how his family related to its surroundings—anything and everything that made him what he was.[12] First the judge would interrogate the child to test his willingness to cooperate; a confession was seen as a vital demonstration that he was prepared to accept the court's overtures.[13] After this initial discussion, attention should shift to the larger issues of the child's environment, as the probation officer reported on the results of interviews and tests and gave his impressions of the family. The parents, too, might be given a chance to speak. But to the court they were already implicated by their manifest failure to teach proper norms. Court enthusiasts were confident that the parents, awed by this encounter with the law and struck by the obvious wisdom of the judge and his staff, would readily submit to censure and instruction.[14]

Using the hearing evidence as his guide, the judge would choose for the child a mode of treatment tailored to his individual needs. Whenever possible the juvenile court would order probation, a program of follow-up staff visits to the child in his own surroundings, to address his maladjustment at its source and restore him to a normal position in the community.[15] This aftercare would focus on the family as the unit of treatment, and was intended to tap the constructive possibility of therapeutic technology. With the child serving as the point of entry, the court would extend its influence over the entire household. Parents were the critical target, for, regardless of whether they had caused the child's difficulty, they appeared to be the means by which the court could have its greatest impact. Through the probation officer the juvenile court would make known to them its expectations: they must place the child under closer supervision, set a better example for him in matters of peer associations and sexual morals, cooperate with his teacher by insisting he attend school, and learn the elements of modern domestic hygiene, nutrition, and child health care.[16] The probationer's siblings also would be given advice, and the behavior of the entire family would come under official surveillance. Not until all family members had been rehabilitated was the court to relax its attention.[17]

To justify tutelage by the juvenile court, proponents characterized its adjudication as noncriminal and its dispositions as benign. The model procedures plainly disregarded a child's claim to due-process protections.[18] Yet while rhetoric about the prerogative of a caring community to impose discipline might satisfy social personnel, the legal establishment would ask what benefit the minor derived for surrendering his formal-legal rights.[19] It seemed useful, then, to depict the relationship between the court and the child as a kind of bargain. The child gave up recourse to ordinary judicial safeguards while the institution promised not to affix blame on him for his acts. Further, rather than punish him reflexively as it might a criminal, the court pledged to care for him as a unique individual.[20]

For the child to triumph over his maladjustment, it was soon realized, the court would need to apply the most advanced scientific knowledge. Only science, with its ability to fully grasp the plight of the troubled child, could restore the delinquent to a normal status.[21] We find here vivid evidence of the change that science-as-ideology had brought to the field of child protection. Court enthusiasts were confident of the institution's ability to make over the child's entire domestic environment. If no reliable science of delinquency yet existed, as had to be admitted, one would be generated. Accordingly, the juvenile court was to join forces with social and behavioral scientists, the institution providing cases so that the experts might test the latest theories. Within a decade the first juvenile psychopathic clinic was established to help the judge diagnose the child's condition.[22]

Some of these scientific resources would be drawn from the other social agencies upon which the probation officer would call to accomplish his adjustment tasks. Here we must consider, as the historians do not, the position that proponents expected the court to occupy in a web of normalizing services. The probation officer was to forge connections between the family and the other social agencies serving the neighborhood. As one social scientist insisted in a discussion of probation service, "Home conditions can be greatly modified by numerous modern ameliorative agencies, each one a boundless field for extension and improvement."[23] Public schools, municipal hospitals, and free clinics were beginning to incorporate the casework approach as an adjunct to their other operations. And several new public institutions like school and neighborhood centers were founded upon normalizing methods. Through a cooperative effort, the court and the emerging human service apparatus would penetrate the walls around the family. It would be seen as adjusted when it accepted permanent intervention by the human service network.[24]

But if the court hoped to adjust clients through the use of science, the movement appreciated that judicial tutelage also entailed the possibility of coercion. In its probation system the juvenile court would demonstrate that judicial authority could reinforce therapeutic technique. This was first brought home to the family in the preliminary investigation. The probation officer, in keeping with philanthropic practice, would hopefully gain the parents' confidence through a sympathetic approach. However, if they seemed hostile or secretive, they should be made to realize that his report might indict their fitness, leading the court to separate the child permanently from the home.[25]

Court proponents understood that the benefits of the court's coercive resources would be realized even more fully during the treatment phase of judicial intervention. While a probation officer was to try to gain the confidence of the minor and his family, the judge would reserve disciplinary sanctions that he could invoke at any time. One magistrate explained, "The discomfort of punishment affords in some cases an indispensable stimulus or moral tonic which cannot be supplied in any other way."[26] In effect the judge would suspend more severe measures, as Donzelot says, to create an opening in which educative remedies might take hold. The child was to be given his chance, so to speak, while the court maintained an ongoing surveillance.[27] Said one court supporter, "With probation he lives in fear for many weeks. The sword of Damocles is over his head, and his own effort must avert it." If either he or his family balked at the probation officer's instructions, harsher measures might be taken, including removal of the minor from the home or incarceration in an industrial school. Hence the critical value of probation: in place of a definitive judgment to resolve a case, the juvenile court would implicate child and family in a process of perpetual evaluation.[28]

Sometimes no choice would remain for the judge but to remove the child from his home. In certain types of cases, where the child was in immediate danger or posed a menace to others, probation had to be rejected because it promised only gradual results. Instead a child-protection group recognized by the court would promptly assume control over the child and arrange placement with another family or in an institution.[29] A role for established private child-protection organizations was thus assured at the founding of the therapeutic state. Also, court proponents acknowledged that a number of cases would fail to respond to mild educative techniques, because the damage to the minor had gone too far. For children who could not be adjusted through probation, the juvenile court fell back upon an apparatus of successively more restrictive institutions. Once again the court enlisted teachers and specialists, but in a closed environment. First in line came the new parental school, designed for chronic truants and youngsters too disruptive for an ordinary class-room.[30] The court would follow this brief incarceration with a test to determine whether the child could function in the community. If he failed, the court would eventually commit him to an industrial school or some other state facility. Judicial tutelage, then, drew upon yet another line of philanthropic endeavor, institutional care. Confinement was not intended to punish but to afford an alternative therapeutic setting. Isolation and strict discipline would erode the juvenile's obstinacy and persuade him to accept help in excising his deviant tendencies.[31]

Removal and confinement, it should be added, were to be prescribed more regularly for delinquent girls, especially when the court found evidence of sexual activity. Philanthropy had long seen female sexuality as a menace, a concern that continued into the Progressive era with the campaigns for moral purity. Since the immoral girl threatened to undermine fundamental social values, she had to be segregated from the community. Reform was still possible—normalizing intervention could address this form of degradation, too—but it would be more prudent to attempt adjustment in a restrictive setting. Probation was better suited to male delinquents who posed a less compelling public risk.[32]

Adversaries in a Common Cause

Philanthropy's drive to secure a decent living standard for the working-class family required other public initiatives besides the juvenile court. But the effort to put into place additional components of a therapeutic sector did not always proceed so smoothly. Not only might there be a lack of past associations with the state of the sort that characterized child protection, but, as I have commented, prior philanthropic deeds and words had left residual barriers to a positive public role. When Progressive philanthropy confronted this predicament in the field of public relief, during the debate over whether to establish public allowances or "pensions" for widows with children, sharp internal conflicts erupted. To resolve the disputes and move policy forward, philanthropy needed to reformulate its position toward public subsidy for the working-class family.[33]

The pension idea surfaced in the 1890s, at the very moment when Progressive philanthropy was revising its understanding of poverty and social obligation. Once regarded as degrading to recipients, relief came to be seen by charity leaders as part of the community obligation to the marginal working-class family. It not only brought economic victims through a desperate time and restored a minimum level of material well-being, but also, when combined with casework, helped renew their sense of self-worth.[34] The hostility toward relief softened first in the case of certain groups that seemed least able to care for themselves. Widowed mothers had always been an object of special solicitude in charity circles,[35] so charity agencies quite naturally identified them as entitled to material assistance.

However, even as philanthropy laid an intellectual foundation for public mothers' aid, some influential elements held back. To begin with, many child-protection groups had made a substantial investment in asylums and orphanages. These facilities were also the beneficiaries of lucrative public subsidies. Since outdoor aid would reduce the need for long-term placements, institutional interests resisted the allowance idea. However, as I have remarked, Progressive philanthropy adopted an anti-institutional posture. Asylum proponents by the beginning of the twentieth century had lost much of their prestige within philanthropic circles. The famous 1909 White House conference on children affirmed that home care was best for children, and thus signaled the eclipse of the institution.[36]

More formidable opposition to public allowances was mounted by the mainstream (predominantly East Coast) charity leadership. Inhibited by its old preoccupation with the dangers of public subsidies, it warned that public pensions would invite corruption and indiscriminate relief. Charity forces joined with child-protection agencies to turn back a proposal in New York in 1897 that would have permitted the use of public funds to support fatherless families.[37] Private charity, it was felt, could meet the community's obligation, and do so in a way that both subsidized and rehabilitated recipients. Charity groups then stepped up efforts to extend relief and tutelage to widows and half-orphaned children.[38] Thus the charity establishment staked its credibility upon its own capacity to help a sizeable group of families achieve the full living standard philanthropy had defined.

While organized charity struggled to reconcile its inherited wisdom with new doctrine, policy-making initiative was seized by other actors. A strong coalition emerged after 1900 to push for public pensions, consisting of women's clubs, miscellaneous journalists and reformers, settlement house residents, child-labor activists, and juvenile court judges.[39] This coalition suggests some of the forces that contributed to the elaboration of the therapeutic state. We should note, for example, that public allowances had become a feminist issue, as philanthropic women hoped to establish the principles that family life ought to be shielded from poverty and that mothers belonged in the home rather than in the factory. Of particular interest, too, is the role of juvenile court judges. Some, like

Merritt W. Pinckney in Chicago and E. E. Porterfield in Kansas City, became visible advocates of pension legislation. They complained that the normalizing mission of the court was thwarted when a family faced acute material distress.[40] In other words, the inadequacies of the early tutelary apparatus drove its operatives to demand its further development. The therapeutic state contained its own expansionist impulses.

As the pension coalition gathered its forces, the attempt by charity agencies to finance allowances from private contributions faltered. Some administrators of the voluntary programs freely conceded that because of insufficient funds many eligible widows had to be given inadequate grants or excluded altogether.[41] To make up for this, the agencies set up day nurseries to free the mothers for regular employment or helped them find piecework to take into the home. Yet, as both charity leaders and critics agreed, such arrangements resulted in the exploitation of the mothers' labor, poor childcare, and violations of child-labor restrictions.[42] With the widows reduced to desperation, they were forced at least temporarily to surrender custody of their children—exactly the outcome charity activists had pledged to prevent.[43] Organized charity found itself on the defensive.

Supporters of public allowances played upon the failures of private pensions. They argued that the community had special obligations to fatherless children and their widowed mother. The children, as future citizens, had a right to the kind of upbringing that prepared individuals for full and productive membership in the community;[44] their mother, for performing the service of training prospective citizens, was due some return from the community. "It is her right," proclaimed one pension advocate, "to expect compensation at the hand of society that ultimately and often immediately is the gainer by her maternal emotion."[45] Private charity, of course, had embraced this kind of thinking. So the implication drawn by the pension movement had a telling impact: since private effort did not suffice to discharge the community's responsibilities, a public program would be necessary.

Nevertheless, if pension advocates built their arguments upon the living standard idea, this doctrine could also be invoked by the opposition. The charity establishment warned that public relief officials had not incorporated in their work any of the elements that were now seen to comprise a therapeutic program: they did not accurately determine needs, they failed to develop remedial plans for each case, and they provided neither guidance nor supervision for recipients.[46] Aid without rehabilitative casework was self-defeating, because money alone could not raise the family to the standard of living philanthropic principles required. C. C. Carstens spoke for many charity activists when he insisted that aid to the widow required careful supervision "so that appropriate suggestions in regard to the health of mother and children, employment of older children, difficulties in discipline, an improved diet, and many other matters that come up in family life, besides advice on expenditures, may be made."[47] And it mattered little that pension advocates had sought to put to rest fears of public mismanagement by insisting upon an autonomous administrative structure for widows' pensions. For critics committed to normalization as a goal, no public agency had the capacity to fulfill therapeutic tasks.[48]

Just the same, the two sides were not so far apart as their rhetoric suggests. They shared a common discursive base—the commitment to the philanthropic concept of a living standard. On the one hand, as even pension foes conceded, the community was obliged to provide the fatherless family with basic material necessities. And the level of assistance should be sufficient to allow the mother to remain at home to raise her children, since that was her primary duty.[49] On the other hand, all parties to the debate agreed that, with the family entitled to a normalized living standard in the broad sense, the community obligation went beyond material aid. The value of family casework and supervision as adjuncts to public allowances was accepted, albeit grudgingly at first, within the pension movement.[50]

This common ground between pension supporters and their foes made accommodation possible. After the first public mothers'-aid programs were created, especially the Illinois program in 1911, both sides acknowledged the merit of the opposing position. More charity leaders agreed that public subsidy to maintain a material living standard was necessary.[51] At the same time, accepting the family-adjustment doctrine of Progressive philanthropy, pension proponents decided that the public department administering mothers' aid would adopt normalization as a policy goal. The report accompanying a legislative proposal in New York in 1914 made explicit the expanded pension agenda: "Public aid can be administered not as a handing out of money only, but for the rehabilitation of family life and for the constructive education in self-respect and self-reliance that is the aim of all relief work."[52]

Indeed, once mothers'-aid advocates began to think of the program as a therapeutic enterprise, they eagerly embraced the constructive use of power by the state. A public relief program, they asserted, would enjoy definite advantages over private charity in its capacity to adjust recipients. To begin with, widows receiving public aid would be more likely to accept casework by the state because they would see it as legitimate. Charity appeared to the poor as a class-based enterprise, an expression of elite generosity designed to appease the conscience of wealthy donors and bourgeois visitors, and recipients therefore rejected the advice of charity caseworkers. By contrast, since the state and the widow needed each other to raise a family properly, public assistance would operate on a more equal and democratic footing than private relief. The public social technician would not face the resentment that confronted charity agents, and would thus find it much easier to forge a therapeutic partnership.[53] In addition, given the nature of the relationship between the state and the mother, she would also accept more readily the demands placed upon her. The allowance would constitute wages for the service of childrearing, and the state, like any employer, could set standards for the quality of the work.[54] Proponents of mothers' aid predicted that a class-neutral state would reinforce the positive effects of class-neutral normalizing technology.

Of course, sound instruction might still fall on deaf ears. Another relative virtue of a public program lay in its access to a more persuasive disciplinary apparatus than private charity had at its command. If a private agency encountered a recalcitrant widow, it could do no more than withdraw aid, a step dangerous to the children. But a public mothers'-aid department need not retreat from difficult cases. Sometimes it would call upon other agencies to help supervise the family. When all else failed, rather than merely terminate benefits, the department would have the authority to arrange for the removal of the children from the home.[55] This possibility dramatically improved the prospects for successful intervention, because the implicit threat would not be lost on any mother.

The enthusiasm for tutelage by supporters of public allowances reflects the same uncritical attitude toward power that we found earlier in the discourse of Progressive philanthropy. As the mothers'-aid movement approached its moment of political triumph, public aid to the fatherless family was revamped, becoming an instrument that would join material support and adjustment methods to normalize an endangered home. Proponents accepted without question that the state would define good parenting, instruct mothers to reach its standards, and use coercion against those who resisted. Clearly, older limits upon the power of the state no longer mattered. To account for this willingness to expand the reach of public authority, we need only look back to philanthropic discourse itself. Philanthropy stressed the positive face of normalizing intervention to the exclusion of all else, what such power could do rather than what damage it might inflict. Proponents of public tutelage shaped their new enterprise exactly according to the philanthropic image.

One final step completed the reconciliation between the two philanthropic factions. Supporters of mothers' aid appreciated that therapeutic objectives would strain the administrative capacity of the responsible agency. The initial organization of a public pension department, they admitted, ought to be given over to those with appropriate experience in family diagnosis, treatment, and supervision. Thus charity activists, many of whom had opposed the very idea of public allowances, were called upon to fix the shape of the new public program. They responded positively to the invitation, and soon began to establish themselves at the center of mothers'-aid administration.[56]

Therapy as Public Assistance

In keeping with the terms by which the philanthropic dispute was settled, the mothers'-aid movement articulated a model for the program that united casework methods and public authority. This pension ideal was never presented overtly in manifestos; it emerges instead from the various studies of actual mothers'-aid programs conducted by agency administrators, social scientists, and proponents in the U.S. Children's Bureau.[57] These observers agreed that a public allowance would ease material distress while opening an avenue into the home that would be exploited by a trained caseworker. Continuing a pattern dating back to friendly visiting, the caseworker was presumed to be a middle-class woman. She would treat the mother and her children not just as "recipients" but as "clients." The procedure established for philanthropic casework—contact, planning, instruction, supervision, and integration into a network of normalizing agencies—would serve as the basis for all dealings with the family. But, much like the juvenile court probation officer, the mothers'-aid caseworker would have resources not available to private social technicians. The constructive possibility of aid for dependent children rested on the coercive support of the state as well as on the technology of adjustment.

Upon application by a widow for an allowance, the pension process would begin with a caseworker conducting a thorough social inquiry. It was necessary first to establish eligibility, in the broad sense: the mother should not only be in genuine need of aid but she should be a "suitable" candidate for normalization. The caseworker would visit the home to validate the mother's petition statements and to form an impression of the family. Then would come discreet inquiries to anyone who might be able to add to the picture of home conditions.[58] After the caseworker determined whether the family met the material eligibility criteria, she faced the more difficult task of deciding whether, if given an allowance, the mother could create an acceptable environment for the children. Pensions ought to be granted, the model suggested, only to mothers who demonstrated some competence in child care.[59]

To make this prospective evaluation, the caseworker was expected to consider family background, behavior patterns, and the applicant's attitude. Pension supporters felt that chronic domestic irregularities might subvert the therapeutic measures associated with the allowance. Appropriate grounds for rejection therefore included defective family heredity, a pattern of child neglect, or moral lapses by the applicant. The caseworker would hold the family to very strict standards, especially where the mother's sexual conduct was concerned. If she merely appeared to have compromised herself, the caseworker was supposed to recommend against a grant.[60] Furthermore, since successful rehabilitation depended upon the widow's collaboration, much weight should be attached to the attitude she had demonstrated during the preliminary inquiry. There would be good reason to anticipate future cooperation if, for example, she had agreed to account fully for how she had spent any insurance benefits or to support legal action against relatives for child support.[61]

The size of the monthly grant would depend upon specific family circumstances. To determine how much aid the family needed, the caseworker in consultation with the applicant would draw up a budget schedule. The schedule compared the widow's resources to her family's required expenses, the latter calculated by domestic science experts and codified in standardized tables covering food, shelter, and other necessities. By using the schedule, the pension authority would award an allowance just sufficient to assure the family of a Spartan but tolerable material standard of living.[62] Family eligibility and needs would be reviewed frequently, so that the agency might adjust or cancel the grant if conditions warranted. The mothers'-aid movement praised this flexibility as protection against the development of a complacent and rigid relationship between agency and family.[63]

However, of far greater significance, the contingency of the amount would serve to bring home to the recipient one truth about the nature of state power. Although the method for computing the allowance appeared entirely objective, changes in the size of the grant would remind her that public authority had a variable quality, so that her position remained fragile even when her rights had been expanded. Program supporters were confident that she would not become so presumptuous as to demand greater benefits. Mothers' aid accordingly would not be the start of a redistributive policy.[64] Moreover, because the widow's sense of vulnerability was heightened by the regular recertification of award levels, she would try harder to satisfy the caseworker and thus follow instructions with particular diligence. Flexibility would magnify the effectiveness of educative oversight.

This project of family rehabilitation would commence once the widow began to receive her grant. Supporters held that regular visits to the home, at least one per month, would give the caseworker an opportunity to strengthen the personal bond she had begun to develop during the preliminary inquiry. As a Pennsylvania manual for mothers'-aid personnel put it, "The first essential to effective supervision is real knowledge of the family; there is a great difference between familiarity and knowledge, and the latter does not come without effort and frequent visiting by the same person."[65] But the caseworker needed to do more than solidify a friendship, for the preparation of a plan for family adjustment rested upon detailed information about the mother's skills and behavior. The caseworker would secure a better understanding of the recipient/client by asking her at the outset to keep a detailed record of her expenses.

As a first remedial step the caseworker would reform the widow's haphazard management of family finances. Mothers'-aid proponents maintained that many working-class women lacked the ability to manage a budget and were prone to impulsive, extravagant, or uneconomical purchases.[66] They required guidance in their spending practices, lest their waste cause them to exceed the needs calculation of the pension agency. Now the expense report, which the mother was still obliged to file, became an educational tool; she would be taught how to live within her means, and the caseworker would point out changes in spending habits that might better stretch the family's resources.[67]

Instructing the widow on spending practices would necessarily implicate the caseworker in a far-reaching reconstructive effort. She would find, upon review of the expense forms, that her client remained unaware of recent advances in nutrition and personal health. Before the mother could be expected to make wise purchasing decisions, she had to learn about balanced diets, cooking techniques that maximized food values, home cleaning and ventilation, hygiene for herself and her children, proper sleep habits (including separate rooms for adolescent male and female children), and so forth. Casework intervention in the mothers'-aid ideal sought nothing less than a complete restructuring of the way in which the recipient/client ran her household. She would become the vehicle for raising family life to the higher standard of citizenship envisioned by philanthropy, a standard above that which she and her children had known before the loss of her husband.[68]

Because the present and future welfare of the children served as the justification for mothers' aid, they were also to be singled out for special attention. Philanthropic doctrine maintained that each client presented a unique set of problems and possibilities. It was the task of the mothers'-aid caseworker to distinguish the children according to their needs. One might require special medical care or counseling; another might show exceptional academic promise, in which instance the caseworker should intercede to extend the grant so the child might continue in school rather than find a job at the minimum age permitted by law.[69] By asserting herself in such situations, the caseworker would seek "to develop special gifts of personality, and to help bring the child to a healthy, normal adult life, in which his happy adjustment to his surroundings would insure his usefulness to society."[70] Individualized attention, along with improved home conditions, would serve as the means by which the state rescued children from poverty and raised them up to become contributing members of the community.

The pension movement did not expect the caseworker to accomplish her formidable tasks entirely on her own. Just as therapeutic discourse emphasized the role of a service network to surround the family, the model for mothers' aid directed that recipients/clients be brought into contact with a full array of normalizing agencies. The caseworker would call upon public health clinics, psychiatrists, teachers, and specialist social workers to address particular difficulties. The children would be encouraged to enroll in clubs at the local settlement house or school center. For the mother, too, these facilities provided educational programs in nutrition, household management and child care, and (where needed) English language skills.[71] Resources outside the human service apparatus might also have a therapeutic value. The Pennsylvania manual, positing an association between church membership and normal family life, urged that families in the program be counseled to attend religious services.[72]

It was also recognized that some time would pass before the program accomplished the sweeping results it sought. The widow and her children would have to accept the need for fundamental changes in their behavior and values. "Unless they can in the end be convinced of the desirability of the new order of things," one administrator observed, "the old regime will be re-established just as soon as the pressure from the relief giving agency is relaxed."[73] The caseworker would have to impress upon her clients that each suggestion she made was really in their best interest. For example, if a widow took offense at being required to report expenses, she should be told that the department only wanted to assure that she got full value for her money. Her protest would surely cease when she saw for herself the benefit of the advice.[74] Above all, the caseworker needed patience. Even with the support of other agencies, it might be months, perhaps longer, before progress was made in eliminating ignorance and superstition and restructuring how clients acted and thought.[75]

During this interval, while a verdict on the mother's fitness hung in the balance, the pension department also would use its openings to the family as a means of surveillance. The caseworker served again as the key agent. Her monthly visits to the home gave her an opportunity to take better measure of the mother's capacity than had been possible in the preliminary investigation and to assess improvements in domestic conditions.[76] The widow herself would facilitate oversight: her monthly expense forms would be examined to make sure she had grasped the various lessons the caseworker had been teaching her. Other social personnel, teachers, and even the family pastor would be asked to report on the mother and her children. When combined with the caseworker's impressions, this information would permit the pension agency to maintain a complete, dynamic family portrait.[77]

Pension supporters did not shy away from the implications of this ongoing domestic surveillance: however understanding the caseworker and her superiors were, the mother must be judged. She had been granted aid, it was often recalled, in exchange for meeting a standard of parenting, and she ought to be permitted to remain in the program only if she upheld her end of the bargain.[78] When the caseworker discovered dangerous or degrading behavior, a judgment might be reached quickly. For example, the widow who refused to obtain medical care for herself or her children was clearly unfit. In other cases the conclusion that the mother was incompetent would emerge only over time. She might persist in fiscal mismanagement and poor child care, or, after showing some improvement, she might regress into bad habits and indifference.[79] The widow who accepted a public allowance thus was supposed to face permanent scrutiny, a test she might fail at any time.

If the recipient/client did not respond to the positive exercise of normalizing power by the state, she would have to be made to confront the darker aspects of public tutelage. Once again the variability of public assistance played into the hands of the caseworker: just as the size of the grant could be adjusted, so, too, could an allowance be stayed and then reinstated. The pension model presumed that the caseworker would use this possibility to induce cooperation. When she found practices that put the children at risk, such as the presence in the home of a male boarder, she would immediately declare her intent to cancel the allowance. Usually the threat alone would suffice to jolt the widow back to her senses. The prospect of a loss of benefits might also be raised with her if she did not progress under supervision. And, as pension supporters had pointed out in their initial campaign, state power went beyond expulsion from the program. If the mother could not meet the standards for normal family life, she was unfit and her children were in jeopardy. It was the duty of the caseworker, then, to seek a judicial order for their removal from maternal custody. For a particularly recalcitrant mother, this would serve as the ultimate spur.[80]

The Amplification of Power

The models for the juvenile court and mothers'-aid program reflect the thoroughness with which Progressive social personnel approached the task of making normalizing intervention the mission of the state. They pondered in great detail how public agencies would use their adjustment technology to raise selected marginal populations to the living standard defined by philanthropy. As set forth in the models, the "irregular" family would be renovated—public social personnel would reorder its responsibilities and impose new functions so that it more closely resembled its bourgeois counterpart. Success in this enterprise would transform family members into enlightened citizens who shared bourgeois aspirations and who respected the rules of conduct necessary for functioning in an interdependent world. Thus we find displayed in the ideal of public tutelage the same fascination with the constructive possibilities of power that we observed in philanthropic discourse.

Still, if the philanthropic goal and method formed the starting point for public human services, proponents of the tutelary state saw it as an instrument with unprecedented capabilities. Philanthropy had invented a technique for remolding the working-class family, yet normalizing efforts had been blunted by the limits of voluntary action. The move to the state would allow social personnel to escape both the fiscal constraints that hampered philanthropic work and its embarrassing class associations. A public agency would reach a larger number of marginal clients who, because they were approached on what seemed to be a democratic basis, would welcome its help and be more willing to lay bare their lives to its representatives. At the same time, public social personnel would bring new resources to the therapeutic approach. They had access to better information about their clients, from those who treated the family and from the clients themselves, and so the public agency would proceed with a more accurate understanding of the consequences of its interventions. And for those clients who did not improve under educative measures, social personnel in the state apparatus could use public authority to break up a home or to order confinement of a delinquent. Thus, because of its wider scope, greater legitimacy, enhanced surveillance capacity, and various coercive options, public tutelage would dramatically amplify therapeutic power. The juvenile court and the mothers'-aid program were expected to achieve unparalleled positive results.

In the exercise of this remarkable power, public human service agencies would redefine the relationship between state and citizen. The liberal state in the American tradition encountered the family only sporadically, through tax collections, military service, and the provision of basic collective goods. Some years earlier philanthropy had pointed toward a new conception of the state based upon the principle of family preservation that would have enlisted public authority to correct the demoralization of marginal groups, but bourgeois activists had declined to follow the implications of this idea. In sharp contrast, Progressive movements for public tutelage set out to uncover new ways to use the state to invade the family's domestic sanctuary and compel its members to surrender their autonomy. Now those persons brought before the juvenile court or enrolled in a public-allowance program would find their most intimate behavior a matter of official concern and regulation. As clients of official normalizing agencies, they would be obliged to reveal their disreputable behaviors and personal weaknesses, and then be required to conform to any standard of conduct public caseworkers and probation officers might establish. Considering the depth and scope of intervention, public tutelage necessarily would become for its clients the dominant mode of "participation" in the political order.[81]

Amidst the general eagerness of social personnel to stretch the reach of therapeutic power, a voice of caution occasionally tried to make itself heard. The Pennsylvania mothers'-aid manual warned caseworkers that intervention had to be guided by a sense of the appropriate scope of instruction. "[W]e should always keep in mind that our object is not to destroy individual tastes but to ensure on as economical a basis as possible the fundamentals of physical and mental health upon which may be reared the manifold variations of personal and family differences." But the manual seems to express no principled objection to the aspirations behind the therapeutic project, for the reservation rested upon pragmatic concerns. "Our success depends too upon refraining from interference over nonessentials."[82] Recipients/clients could absorb only a finite amount of advice.

In their indifference to the question of how power should be limited, proponents of public tutelage merely reflected the attitude we observed among philanthropic activists. Therapeutic logic denied the distinction that the Pennsylvania manual tried to draw between conduct that mattered and "nonessentials." How could any behavior be regarded as trivial when it might be evidence of a serious underlying condition? To make absolutely certain that hidden sources of maladjustment were uprooted, social personnel were driven to trespass ever more deeply into the space around the individual. This held true whether normalization was sought under philanthropic auspices or by the state.

Therapeutic discourse, through its peculiar rhetoric, also served to ease any anxieties about the disciplinary tools available to the agencies of public tutelage. Although the state would make judgments about the fitness of its clients, social technicians spoke not of condemnation but of "diagnosis" and "evaluation," dispassionate scientific activities that sounded quite harmless. As for the coercion that was such a central feature of public tutelage, two maneuvers had placed discipline in a new light. First, given that philanthropy's living standard doctrine held that the working-class family had a duty to the community to attain a normal lifestyle, compulsion was justified when clients resisted tutelage. The juvenile court and mothers'-aid programs did no more than embody this view in an official setting. Second, the proponents of the therapeutic state attached a benign purpose to the use of sanctions. Where philanthropic activists endorsed coercion as punishment for stubborn clients, the models of the juvenile court and of mothers' aid treated disciplinary mechanisms as part of a continuum of remedial instruments. Coercion was regarded as but another constructive tool, wielded with scientific detachment, to bring about adjustment.

Although it is possible to explain the innocent worship of power characteristic of the first proponents of public tutelage, that ought not to exempt their attitude from critical scrutiny. They were oblivious to the dangerous implications of the union between public authority and normalizing technology, in much the same way that philanthropic activists declined to consider the risks entailed by the basic therapeutic approach they had devised. The invention of a new form of power carries with it the responsibility to reflect on its potential to do harm, which the protagonists in both cases abdicated in the first flush of success. As we did before, then, we must confront issues the Progressives overlooked. I will contend here that the very ideal of public tutelage is deeply flawed. For social personnel who accept educative adjustment as a goal, the alliance with the state would corrupt the therapeutic approach instead of strengthening it. More important, for those who stand outside therapeutic discourse, public authority would simply compound the worst features of the casework enterprise.

If we consider public tutelage from the perspective of social personnel themselves, it is plain that the use of coercion would compromise the therapeutic method. Progressive philanthropy had emphasized that the working-class family would have to choose when to initiate contact, that a real personal bond would then have to be forged by the caseworker, and that the success of educative measures depended upon willing emulation by clients. Although the models of public tutelage restated these principles, it was assumed that a therapeutic relationship could flourish when casework mixed with coercion. Adding compulsion to the therapeutic approach would mean, of course, that marginal families would not choose to participate and that public caseworkers would possess an authority that might make for a very skewed "partnership." Such deviations from the basic therapeutic model ought to have stimulated discussion. But enthusiasm for the cause seems to have stilled all doubts during the founding period. As we will see, problems caused by the fusion of adjustment techniques and coercion soon became a focus of concern among social personnel. Even then, however, the fault often was attributed to inept execution of casework methods by misguided officials, and supporters of institutions like the juvenile court were reluctant to admit that they faced an underlying contradiction in the therapeutic state.

When we distance ourselves from the therapeutic agenda, we can raise a more fundamental challenge to the models of public tutelage. Philanthropy's technology of adjustment, I argued earlier, threatened the autonomy and dignity of clients, and undermined the philanthropic quest for democratic citizenship. To the degree that intervention through public tutelage would intrude more deeply into the space around individuals, these risks would be magnified. The state would add an oppressive surveillance mechanism, in which various outside agents were to contribute to the dossier on the client; normalized behavior would be secured by intimidation rather than persuasion. We need merely recall the mother receiving a public allowance, constantly under observation, aware that her inadequacy or resistance could provoke legal moves to break up the home. Public tutelage when properly conducted would heighten the vulnerability of marginal families to a frightening degree. Moreover, in the name of higher standards, they would be expected to repudiate old values and interests—the very autonomous qualities that propel people to act as citizens. The therapeutic state, then, would obliterate the indigenous aspirations that form the basis for all real political self-determination. As state-sponsored human services more closely approximated the model for public tutelage, they would subvert more profoundly their original democratic intent.

Four

Practice against Theory

THE FIRST experiments in public tutelage during the Progressive era produced a mixed record, with important accomplishments matched by significant disappointments. Since we would not expect a policy innovation of this magnitude to achieve all its goals, the uneven performance of normalizing agencies is in itself quite unremarkable. But we still must examine the pattern of success and failure, for policy actors would later have to deal with the consequences of Progressive experiments in the human services. To the degree that early therapeutic activists put in place a normalizing apparatus and won acceptance of their approach in policy circles, future attempts to deal with marginal populations would continue along the same lines. At the same time, problems that beset the early ventures in state-sponsored casework would have to be addressed.

Considering the tasks that proponents of public tutelage set for themselves and the obstacles they faced, their achievements in the first two decades of the twentieth century were impressive. The juvenile court and mothers'-aid programs spread rapidly; other new human service programs appeared, especially with American entry into the First World War. Just as important, beyond these concrete programmatic gains, the therapeutic agenda attracted new supporters, including lawyers and public welfare officials. From this broader discursive movement emerged plans for further policy advances to realize the goal of a comprehensive therapeutic system. This progress in building a tutelary apparatus rested primarily upon the efforts of policy entrepreneurs, notably juvenile court judges, who pressed relentlessly to widen the domain of therapeutic practice. Their political success reflected a low-profile approach designed to sidestep controversy and to minimize confrontation with potential sources of opposition.

Nevertheless, although movement leaders took heart from the visible development of the therapeutic sector, they could not overlook the very serious problems that immediately came to light. The proliferation of agencies ostensibly committed to the therapeutic agenda did not conceal the fact that in practice such organizations failed to raise their clients to the social living standard philanthropy had defined. Though the political strategy selected by therapeutic activists served well at first, it yielded little long-term support and left public human services exposed to various hostile political influences. Local officials were given a large say in program design and administration, and through them community values were permitted to intrude upon and undermine the efforts of social personnel. Just as troubling to some proponents of the casework approach, client resistance and the refusal of mothers'-aid officials and juvenile court judges to make use of therapeutic expertise pointed to serious deficiencies in the scientific foundation of the therapeutic approach.

Establishing Public Tutelage

To translate the philanthropic vision of a tutelary state into reality was a daunting task, but significant positive steps were taken before the First World War and during the war period itself. This is particularly evident if we consider the juvenile court and the mothers'-aid program, the two innovations that gave rise to the model of public tutelage. Juvenile courts spread rapidly after the first one was created in Chicago; by 1915 enabling legislation had been adopted in forty-six states, and several hundred cities had established special courts to hear cases involving minors or had set aside time periods in existing courts exclusively for the same purpose.[1] A new population of minors accused of lesser infractions or "status offenses"—conduct deemed improper in a juvenile that would not be illegal if committed by an adult—was brought under legal discipline.[2] Legislative victories came swiftly, too, for the mothers'-aid campaign. Within a decade after the Illinois statute of 1911, some forty states had given approval to enabling laws. More than 130,000 dependent children were receiving assistance through mothers'-aid programs.[3] Studies conducted under the auspices of the U.S. Children's Bureau, an agency sympathetic to the program, reported that pension departments had begun to employ casework techniques, with impressive results as documented through the use of anecdotal case histories.[4]

Close on the heels of juvenile courts and mothers'-aid programs came a wave of local experiments in public therapeutic intervention. I have mentioned the school centers, clinics, and municipal hospitals that made use of social personnel. The successful development of new agencies devoted to casework methods moved proponents to look again at established public welfare programs. These presented a ripe field for the introduction of philanthropy's technology of adjustment. Once mothers' aid demonstrated the possibility of linking aid to casework under government auspices, it seemed only natural that all public relief should be given an educative purpose.[5] Social personnel were also pleased when a few cities merged their relief and human service activities into a single, casework-oriented public welfare department.[6] The basic therapeutic model, it will be recalled, held that family adjustment was best achieved through just this sort of coordinated approach. On another front, the principles of judicial tutelage that first inspired the juvenile court served as the foundation for further Progressive inventions. Courts of domestic relations and family courts sought to extend the therapeutic approach to an even broader clientele, so that family maladjustment might better be brought to the notice of some official body.[7] It seemed clear that a useful beginning had been made in the grand discursive project that sought to alter the relationship between the state and the working-class family.[8]

National mobilization for the First World War provided an opening for the expansion of the rudimentary human service network into new fields. To help families cope with the dislocations brought on by war preparations, the Red Cross developed its Home Service and drew heavily on trained social personnel. The program made casework services available to many rural communities for the first time.[9] Meanwhile, to contain the spread of immoral behavior and social disease, especially around military camps, the armed forces and public agencies embarked upon an ambitious campaign for social hygiene. Philanthropic activists had long regarded the regulation of sexual pleasure as a key objective of tutelage, so they welcomed this official support in their effort to direct biology "toward . . . wholesome personal affections."[10] Finally, faced with the need to restore disabled veterans to their place in the community, organizations like the Federal Board for Vocational Education chose to rely on casework techniques. Social personnel conducted family interviews to facilitate individual readjustment to civilian life and counseled the recipients of disability benefits on future vocational prospects.[11]

With the emergence of public social agencies, the therapeutic movement attracted additional supporters from beyond philanthropy itself. The juvenile court generated much favorable interest and publicity during its first decade. In a striking triumph of the therapeutic ideal, treatment-oriented jurisprudence won approval at the higher levels of the legal community. Progressive legal theorists like Roscoe Pound praised the court for examining the environmental influences on its clients' behavior, while at the same time treating each child as a unique individual who required carefully differentiated treatment.[12] Of greater practical significance, state appellate courts quickly affirmed the validity of judicial intervention premised upon a condition rather than an act.[13] Meanwhile, some local public welfare officials, brought under the influence of charity personnel in the recast relief agencies and public welfare departments, began to embrace therapeutic ideology. In his 1922 presidential address to the national meeting of social workers, Robert W. Kelso boasted that a new era had arrived in public agencies: "The public welfare departments are the seat of a great seismic disturbance. . . . Private agencies are being called in and their co-operation sought." The conference itself, he added, brought together the best representatives of social service, many of whom "are public social workers."[14] Public assistance for widows with children also gained backing from important public figures, including that paragon of Republican rectitude, Calvin Coolidge.[15]

Policy triumphs sometimes foster complacency, but here quite the reverse held true. The steps that had been taken toward creating a human service network around the marginal working-class family only stimulated the resolve of social personnel to push ahead. Examples of this intention abound in their discourse during the postwar years. Social hygiene advocates urged a community program to promote sex education; activists in vocational rehabilitation believed the field could expand beyond the military disabled to include the victims of industrial accident or disease; and the campaign for a "children's code," sponsored by social workers and encouraged by the Children's Bureau, raised the need for an enlarged child protection apparatus and preventive programs to secure the rights of children.[16] The Progressive therapeutic state represented but the first phase of what the movement hoped to accomplish.

To account for the proliferation of public social agencies during the Progressive era and the war years, we need to consider both the larger political climate and the particular efforts of therapeutic activists. American politics was being refashioned by the participation of newly mobilized groups and by broad changes in ideology. In the first place, the involvement of women in civic associations and other groups lent enormous impetus to the reform causes they supported. Just as they had taken an interest in philanthropy as a means to build upon their traditional concerns, so also did middle-class women back efforts to make the state an instrument for the preservation of home and family. As it became clear that organized women would command press attention and even influence election outcomes, politicians sought to secure the friendship of the female polity. Votes for mothers'-aid legislation and other therapeutic measures were seen as ways to acknowledge women's concerns.[17]

We might also speculate about the effects of the shifting debate over the role of the state in American life. During the last several decades of the nineteenth century, as the large business corporation had transformed the structure of economic life, intellectuals and populists had argued futilely that public power ought to be used to counterbalance that of private organizations. This position finally won widespread support in the years before the First World War.[18] Public human services often drew an endorsement from Progressive enthusiasts of "statism" as part of their general program for a more vigorous public sector. Of course, given the protracted struggle against the economic doctrine of laissez-faire, they directed greater attention to state intervention in the economy. Typically public tutelage was an afterthought, with juvenile courts and mothers' aid mentioned in passing. Just the same, the therapeutic program had taken hold in the Progressive imagination. On the other side of the coin, those who held out against statist doctrine were more likely to accept public human services than other components of the Progressive program. Conservatives could surely support an enterprise that sought to lessen class hostility by instilling personal and familial values they shared.

Feminist political pressure and the popularity of statist ideology thus eased the path for public human services, but concrete results depended upon the initiative of policy entrepreneurs. When such entrepreneurs do not occupy commanding positions in government, they need to win over political leaders. Therapeutic activists during the Progressive era courted support through vigorous promotion, appeals to politicians' interests, and cautious legislative maneuvering. Advocates of public tutelage began by overselling their programs, claiming extravagant results from, for example, the pilot efforts by the juvenile court.[19] When inflated promises did not suffice, normalization could be marketed as a prudent fiscal proposition. Juvenile court supporters represented their innovation to state legislatures as a device for realizing certain economies: by shifting juveniles out of state reformatories, probation promised to save the state treasury a significant sum.[20] Similarly, when mothers' aid came before the legislatures, it was advertised as an inexpensive alternative to public institutions for dependent children who had been removed from their homes. The first pension bills did not call for any state contribution to the program; the cost would be borne by counties or localities.[21] As a final tactic to secure legislative success, care was taken not to provoke potential centers of resistance. Social personnel realized that in many communities key political actors did not share their enthusiasm for the social living standard. Rather than confront this enemy at the outset and risk defeat, it seemed prudent to accommodate competing views by making statutes permissive. Again mothers' aid proves instructive, for localities were left free to choose whether to participate in the program and on what terms.[22]

On occasion therapeutic activists achieved a direct leadership role in shaping policy, whereupon they acted with haste to elaborate the therapeutic apparatus. The first juvenile court judges seem to have looked for inspiration to philanthropy rather than to the legal profession. From therapeutic discourse they adopted the vision of a comprehensive set of adjustment agencies. Being of an entrepreneurial bent, the judges determined to realize this vision through their own efforts. They capitalized on the prestige that the bench carries in local affairs to obtain additional resources for court-sponsored programs. Thus, whenever the juvenile court became aware of a gap in the local service apparatus, a substitute under the court's auspices was created.[23] If the judges could not meet a need on their own authority, they took it upon themselves to agitate in the legislative arena, where again their word was treated with deference. As I noted in the previous chapter, they played an important part in the campaign to establish mothers'-aid programs. This judicial lobbying was so persuasive in several states that the resulting statutes vested responsibility for administering the allowances in the juvenile court itself.[24]

Sometimes, too, larger events played into the hands of social personnel. In a recent study of social workers during this period, McClymer observes that they saw the war as an opportunity for broad-scale social renovation, a project in which their particular skills would be vital. Therapeutic practice became a kind of patriotic duty, and philanthropic leaders like Edward T. Devine assumed quasi-public positions to help recruit their peers for organizations like the Red Cross. Social personnel often assumed a dominant role in local service programs.[25] When the conflict ended, as I have remarked, they eagerly pursued further openings for their approach that emerged directly from their wartime work.

Flawed Instruments

Pleased though they were with the tangible development of public tutelage, movement leaders soon began to voice concern over the performance of the new social agencies. Progress could not be measured merely by counting the number of juvenile courts or tracing the rapid passage of mothers'-aid laws. It was also necessary, advocates understood, to look at what the tutelary apparatus had actually done. And despite high expectations and initial claims of astonishing results, the performance of the human services was a disappointment. Neither the juvenile court nor the mothers'-aid program proved to be the panacea for social maladjustment that supporters had predicted. By the early 1920s it was clear that something had gone badly awry.[26]

Disenchantment came first to backers of the juvenile court. In practice courts for children rarely adhered to the ideal of judicial tutelage. Every step in the process, from intake to disposition, was unsatisfactory. Rather than provide a complete diagnostic tool, the preliminary investigation amounted to nothing more than a disjointed compilation of hearsay, gossip, and trivia. Few courts could call on the services of a clinic, for only about a dozen had been established by 1918.[27] Further, when most judges conducted hearings, they ignored the child's condition and instead let the nature of his infraction determine the disposition. They thus repudiated the movement's assumption that the offense was a poor guide to a juvenile's needs.[28] Support from the legal elite counted for little when the everyday administration of the court rested in such hands. Just as unsatisfactory was the handling of the minor by the court after it had adjudicated the case. The institution did not exercise meaningful supervision and guidance over his everyday life. Because of low salaries for probation officers, trained social personnel shunned such positions, and those hired were unqualified to perform skilled casework. Making matters worse, judges and court staff, heeding the notion that a child's problems should never be ignored, were reluctant to dismiss cases outright, preferring instead to place many minors under "unofficial" supervision. Caseloads in most courts consequently averaged over one hundred per officer. Under such circumstances it was necessary to reduce "treatment" to an occasional office visit. Nor could the probation officers rely upon other social agencies in the community to ease the burden on the court. Private child protection groups wanted only certain types of cases, and those youngsters who did not fit the particular profile were not welcome.[29]

Court proponents were disturbed, too, by the response of the institution's clients. As the model of judicial tutelage anticipated, most came from a working-class background.[30] Yet where therapeutic discourse expected them to regard the juvenile court as an unbiased instrument of science, clients viewed it as a weapon they could use in their own family conflicts or as the unwelcome tool of an alien culture. Parents discovered that the court could be drawn into their disputes with a misbehaving or stubborn child; in particular, judicial hostility to female sexuality made it easy to report a problem daughter for immorality. For some impoverished parents, the court, through its dependency jurisdiction, represented relief from the heavy responsibility of child support. Children in turn found they could denounce their parents for neglect.[31] In short, while judicial intervention ought to have resolved tension within the family, the juvenile court was being made a participant in domestic strife. In other cases, clients went to the opposite extreme, maneuvering to keep the institution at arm's length. This was not difficult once minors and their parents discovered that court officials were strongly influenced by the pretense of cooperation. The court had no capacity to get beneath appearances.[32]

Undeterred by client subterfuges or its own superficiality, however, the court persisted in its agenda, with little to show for its efforts. It did establish its power over children and their parents. Recently Gordon has argued that the weaker family members, usually women and children, provoked intervention by courts and other social agencies, seeking thereby to alter the equation of family power.[33] Alas, though desperation may have driven people to the juvenile court, they did not find liberation when it acted. The court followed its own logic, which presumed that their very plea for help demonstrated a need for normalizing intervention. By denouncing each other, family members made it easy for the institution to identify new clients. More children and their parents found themselves under the harsh discipline of the court, made to conform to its behavioral conditions, and threatened with punishment. But if the juvenile court rapidly expanded its domain, the inability of the judge and his staff to see through clients' masks made it certain that judicial intervention would have no constructive impact on delinquency. Early claims that juveniles seen once by the court rarely returned gave way to the frank recognition that rates of recidivism remained as high as before its invention.[34] The court had failed to adjust the child or invest his family with more functional values.

Soon after this disturbing information surfaced about the juvenile court, supporters of mothers' aid likewise started to discover that their invention was not measuring up to their aspirations. The most pressing problems included poor coverage and the lack of adequate funding, quite the opposite of what they had predicted. As noted earlier, state lawmakers had left it up to county officials to decide whether to participate in the program and how much to appropriate for it. Many declined to set up pension departments at all, especially in the most impoverished areas; even where an agency was created, there was reluctance to set aside the necessary resources.[35] Lack of resources forced individual mothers'-aid departments to ignore statutory eligibility criteria and client needs. With too many qualified families seeking too little money, some means had to be devised by each department for controlling demand. Allowances went to those families that appeared most deserving, according to commonsense tests, so that, for example, a woman with only one child stood almost no chance of receiving a grant. Many applicants were consigned to waiting lists for years.[36] Moreover, for the families accepted by the department, the monthly grant rarely sufficed to cover basic living expenses. Officials, constrained by arbitrary grant ceilings or paltry appropriations, knowingly awarded allowances that fell short of what the budget schedule indicated was necessary.[37] The caseworker then was supposed to monitor the situation closely. Stated coldly, the family became the subject of an experiment by the department to see how little aid might be given before irreparable harm was done. Most mothers had no choice but to continue working; it fell to the caseworker to watch for signs of physical exhaustion or child neglect.[38] Any real improvement in the family's material living standard—a basic goal of proponents—was simply out of the question.

Although insufficient funding seemed the most urgent challenge, supporters also found that pension agencies performed little casework. Many mothers'-aid departments shunned any responsibility for raising their clients to a normal status. Studies placed part of the blame once again on inadequate appropriations. Compelled to get by on shoestring administrative budgets, pension officials allowed the caseload to rise above fifty families per worker, making intensive personal contact and supervision impossible. Little was learned about recipients; agency staff lacked the time to coordinate the intervention of other social agencies.[39] Yet the lack of money did not explain all the deviations from sound casework principles that had emerged. Some mothers'-aid executives failed to appreciate the value of casework skills when they hired staff. In other departments, administrators did not comprehend the normalizing purpose of the program and treated it instead as an extension of traditional outdoor relief.[40] There were instances, too, of what proponents regarded as misguided liberalism—mothers'-aid officials who deliberately rejected the idea that they were supposed to reshape recipients' behavior. According to one Children's Bureau report, the San Francisco pension department viewed casework as an intrusion upon the mothers' liberty and initiative. The agency therefore kept its distance unless recipients asked for service, even though, the report insisted, additional counseling and instruction would have been of enormous benefit to them.[41]

But social personnel had to admit to an uncomfortable truth about casework in public assistance: even proper therapeutic intervention could not reliably bring about adjustment to bourgeois norms. Studies by proponents suggested a disturbing parallel to the juvenile court, for in mothers'-aid programs, too, clients resented agency prying and stubbornly refused to accede to demands that they restructure their lives. Only rarely was the resistance overt, because mothers recognized the coercive power of pension agencies. Departments had acted with a heavy hand, initiating proceedings to remove children from the custody of unfit mothers, dropping others from the roles for various deviations from agency behavioral standards. Women in the program instead chose what one report termed "that more or less subtle attitude . . . which resents suggestions and insists on independence." They would seem to accept instructions and advice, but when the caseworker returned she would find things unchanged. Significantly, since passive resistance was found in the communities that mounted the most serious casework efforts, it could not be blamed, as were so many errors of practice, upon insufficient funds or the backwardness of certain program officials.[42]

Subversive Localism

When social personnel sought explanations for the vast gap between their models of tutelage and reality, they saw that much of the blame rested squarely on their own shoulders. They had pursued an entrepreneurial strategy designed to win legislative support without broad popular back-

ing.[43] We need only remember the appeal to the penuriousness of state
lawmakers made by proponents of both mothers' aid and the juvenile
courts and the decision to sidestep opposition by pushing permissive
rather than mandatory statutes. Thus programs were authorized with no
commitment of state funds and with much discretion left in local hands.
If this seemed at first a small price to pay for the significant achievement
of having established a foundation for the therapeutic sector, it quickly
became clear that the human services had been left in a precarious
position.

To begin with, the failure to gain state fiscal support at the outset continued to haunt public social agencies. County and local elected officials,
with only small revenue bases upon which to draw, were not eager to
assume additional obligations. The therapeutic apparatus at birth found
itself a fiscal orphan. Apart from the impact on public assistance grants
that I have described, this political abandonment sharply curtailed casework options. Localities resisted paying for trained social personnel for
mothers' aid and juvenile courts alike.[44] Program administrators and
their philanthropic allies accordingly returned to the state legislatures in
quest of subsidies. But having been told that public tutelage offered a way
to solve pressing problems while saving money for taxpayers, state lawmakers did not want to hear that the true dimensions of the task had been
underestimated. Since social personnel had not built a supporting coalition, moreover, they commanded few weapons of value in the legislative
arena. Elected state officials, who had looked positively upon public tutelage only insofar as it advanced their own agenda, saw little reason to
invest their political capital in programs so lacking in popular appeal.
Consequently, the movement found that further progress at the state level
was much more difficult than the opening victories.

Permissive statutes, meanwhile, fed a local political system that responded to the self-interest of key players rather than to the therapeutic
vision, defeating the movement ideal of a comprehensive and coordinated
service apparatus. Lawmakers thought it best to let communities choose
their own approach to juvenile justice and mothers' aid. This meant that
the actual instruments of public tutelage would be shaped by the distribution of political influence at the local level. In some places partisanship
made itself felt. When juvenile court activists fought to replace volunteer
probation service with paid professionals, they discovered that local
party leaders backed the change because it brought opportunities for patronage. It was also necessary to negotiate compromises with the established philanthropic groups, fearful lest the public apparatus displace
them completely. Sectarian child protection groups, for example, insisted
that their role in child placement be preserved.[45] With all the political
maneuvering and ad hoc concessions, social personnel could not preserve

the integrity of the therapeutic design, and normalizing intervention emerged in a form that was inefficient and incomplete. The situation was best illustrated by urban juvenile courts, supposedly the exemplars of enlightened judicial tutelage for their many service activities. It turned out that they had acquired their service apparatus not simply because of their enterprising judges but also because social personnel had not been able to establish other, more appropriate agencies to help problem youngsters or because existing agencies that should have stepped forward declined to do so. As one study by the Children's Bureau found, "In general the resources at the disposal of the court seem to have been developed in a haphazard manner and did not fit together to form a complete community program for the care of delinquent and dependent children."[46]

The decision to concede much authority to local officials opened the way for other potent if less organized influences to make themselves felt in the therapeutic sector. Juvenile court judges, city councilmen, and overseers of the poor adhered to an old conception of the proper exercise of power in a democratic society—they saw it as their task to uphold prevailing community moral standards. If the public thought that delinquent minors needed to be taught a lesson or that the poor needed to learn the discipline of hard work, then it was the duty of government to express those values. I use the term "localism" to denote the principle of representation to which such officials subscribed.

Although grassroots opinion on the problems of marginality varied considerably, certain sentiments tended to enjoy wide support. A generous outlook was sometimes found in the larger cities, where the notion that social forces were to blame for much human misery seems to have gained wide acceptance during the Progressive era. But on the whole, if the studies by social personnel are to be believed, the lay public remained traditional in its outlook, insisting that the poor and the delinquent be held responsible for their situation. And such views were held not only by local propertied elites, as we might anticipate, but also by the growing middle class and by many working people. The testimony of therapeutic activists indicates that they regarded the entire local electorate with misgiving.

Community skepticism about therapeutic assumptions worked in many cases to block the creation of human service agencies. Permissive state laws allowed local officials to decide whether to participate in an authorized program like mothers' aid. Proponents thus had to carry the struggle forward in each county, and they often stumbled when confronted by public hostility. Only in those places where philanthropic groups were well organized had the necessary groundwork been done to generate community acceptance. Social personnel could then coax elected officials into making full use of permissive statutes. Elsewhere, notably in rural areas, few friends could be enlisted to overcome the many local points of resistance. It was plain that therapeutic values had a much more narrow appeal than did the unfashionable ideology of individual responsibility.

In addition, even when social personnel managed to establish their programs in a community, the local political culture still intruded upon program administration. Let us take up first the case of mothers' aid. Local attitudes determined whether it was derided as but another "contemptible" form of outdoor relief or was regarded as a true social entitlement. Program executives defended this fidelity to community values as an expression of democracy.[47] But obedience to public opinion, complained therapeutic activists, made it impossible for a mothers'-aid department to pursue its mission of adjustment. Those in control preferred to select personnel who reflected the common wisdom of the community. Social technicians were thereby excluded. And without their expertise, it was necessary to resort to older methods for reforming clients. One Children's Bureau study of mothers' aid stressed that, lacking proper training in behavioral science, caseworkers were prone to "harsh judgments, undue punishments, and unwise recourse to the courts."[48] Responsiveness to the community meant betrayal of therapeutic ideals.

Popular values likewise made themselves felt in the juvenile court. On the face of it, here was the one institution in which social personnel might reasonably have expected to find respect for their methods and goals. The judicial branch, after all, is supposed to be relatively insulated from popular ideas. To this we might add the well-established pattern of cooperation between courts and philanthropy. Nevertheless, aside from a few celebrities, juvenile court judges did not share the therapeutic orientation. Instead they remained wedded to the conventions of the criminal court bench, from which they were usually recruited, often for only a brief term.[49] And criminal law as practiced in American communities has usually reflected the common sentiment that persons ought to be judged for their actions and punished when they transgress.

It was because they abided by these hallowed beliefs that juvenile court judges concerned themselves with the question of the minor's guilt rather than with his condition. They also depended more heavily than social personnel thought appropriate upon sanctions to reform behavior. Other court staff, added by judges in their own image, followed suit. Probation officers abandoned their neutral diagnostic role during hearings to condemn minors and their parents and later sought to render them docile by the use of blunt threats.[50]

Social personnel asserted that juvenile court judges and their staff, by giving vent to crude popular ideas of justice in an institution premised upon therapeutic principles, had compromised the legitimacy of judicial tutelage. Rather than using therapy and judicial power to reinforce each other, the court corrupted both elements. On one side, law enforcement values pervaded not only the court itself but also the associated casework procedures. When the family experienced the preliminary inquiry as a police-style investigation or when the child was confined in a "diagnostic" detention center as a warning, the court sacrificed any possibility that its intervention would be accepted as benign. Social personnel saw this excessive reliance on coercion, not coercion itself, as one cause of client resistance.[51] Conversely, by insisting upon certain therapeutic pretenses, the court lost its reputation as an instrument through which even the most humble could secure justice. Judges continued as a matter of convenience to recall its founders' claim that due-process formalities would hinder efforts to help the child. Yet once all procedural safeguards were discarded, the court could no longer persuade its clients of its commitment to fairness.[52] In sum, treatment and justice stood together or not at all.

The Knowledge Predicament

For many therapeutic activists, the mischief inflicted on the human services by politics and backward popular sentiment was acutely frustrating. Clinicians and social workers believed they possessed tools that could ease distress and bring marginal groups into the social mainstream, yet mothers'-aid officials and juvenile court judges were too parochial to make use of this expertise. The sin committed in the management of the juvenile court was perhaps most grievous, because, it was felt, scientific knowledge was so readily at hand. Important advances in the study of juvenile behavior had been made in the associated psychopathic institutes and clinics. Alas, the ordinary juvenile court magistrate lacked sufficient vision to introduce science into his courtroom; common sense or folk insight guided his work instead. Even the exceptional judge committed to a therapeutic approach blundered forward on his own, seeking to accomplish by sheer entrepreneurial spirit that which required the highest level of professional skill.[53]

However, if some social personnel felt slighted, others took a more sober view and conceded that responsibility lay as much with themselves. They had much less to offer the normalizing apparatus than they liked to admit, as certain episodes in the juvenile court showed. Here and there a judge enlisted the aid of social workers and behavioral scientists and tried to follow closely their advice. But the specialists produced simplistic diagnoses and arrived at only general or obvious prescriptions; in fact, recidivism among juvenile offenders subject to expert handling showed no appreciable decline.[54] This finding demonstrated that, though the state had been vested with major therapeutic functions, social personnel could not support it with the behavioral knowledge that normalization required. As one social worker concluded, "The social and biological sciences have not progressed sufficiently to aid us in understanding adequately human personality, motivation, social life, mental conflicts, and the interplay between the social situation and the genetic constitution of the individual."[55]

Casework practitioners willing to accept this disturbing conclusion appreciated that it called into doubt a basic premise of the therapeutic approach. The optimism of Progressive pioneers had been predicated on the conviction that the scientific tools of the social technician would permit the most intimate exercise of power. Minus the ability to lay bare the hidden roots of clients' maladjustment, however, casework could not begin to realize its vast constructive possibilities. It now seemed that, lacking the means to probe beneath appearances, social agencies would be stymied by surface acquiescence. J. Prentice Murphy cautioned the audience at the 1922 national meeting of social workers that "the outward expressions which we social workers so often catch are false indicators of the real life which is going on in the minds and hearts of those we are studying."[56] Science-as-ideology had carried the movement forward to the point at which doctrine could be tested as policy, and doctrine had shown itself unequal to the task.

The other actors making decisions within human service agencies, then, could hardly be faulted if they looked elsewhere for their cues. Responsibility for the conflict that emerged between therapeutic activists and other unenlightened local forces rested principally with the former. Once more the juvenile court served as the object lesson. Since the experts' recommendations yielded results no better than a judge's own intuition, he surely had little reason to accept their guidance. So, for want of anything better, judicial determinations were shaped by old homilies about the punishment fitting the crime. There was every reason to expect that the court's repressive and amateurish practices would continue so long as the human sciences remained in their primitive state.[57]

Prosperity and Reaction

Historical accounts of Progressivism have amply demonstrated that the 1920s were a dark era for reformers. This turn of events caught them by surprise. We have observed that many philanthropic leaders greeted American entry into the war with enthusiasm, believing that mobilization heralded the beginnings of a sweeping project of social reconstruction.

But with the end of the conflict and the postwar reaction, particularly the antiradical campaigns, the political climate abruptly became inhospitable. McClymer contends that philanthropic activists, convinced that expertise could trump any other power resource, had been too innocent. They were shunted aside from positions of leadership in community and national social programs by conservative business elites, then driven onto the defensive during the "red scares" of the early 1920s. Bright expectations of a national effort under philanthropic direction to heal the wounds of industrial conflict evaporated entirely. Even Chambers, who prefers to stress the positive achievements of reformers in this period, acknowledges that prosperity checked their ambition for further innovations.[58] The agenda for surviving Progressives became increasingly modest: to preserve what had already been won.

For public human services in particular, lay support declined. The public during the 1920s voiced no sympathy for the intellectual assumptions that had guided Progressive social personnel—marginal populations, so recently seen as "victims," reverted back to their earlier disgraced status. (To be more precise, the change occurred in cities; elsewhere, as I have argued, the ideas of Progressive philanthropy never gained a foothold.) We see the shift in the popular mood expressed most clearly in the common demands that juvenile delinquency be dealt with more sternly. Evidently, when judges resorted more readily to the use of their coercive resources, they were responding not only to their own deep-seated proclivities but to a ground swell in local sentiment.[59]

The currents of public opinion, of course, only served to compound the magnitude of the tasks facing therapeutic activists. They already confronted troubles of their own creation—a weak fiscal base, fragmented services, human service agencies which were too vulnerable to local interference, and a scientific arsenal that seemed impotent. Plainly, both in the political arena and in the agencies designed for normalizing practice, social personnel had not established the hegemony of the therapeutic approach. The political drift in the nation added to the obstacles in their path. They would have to attempt to squeeze more resources from elected officials without the benefit of grassroots support, possibly in the face of popular hostility. More important, there would be little outside backing as social personnel waged their struggle for internal control of the mothers'-aid departments and the juvenile courts.

Five

Strategies for Survival

ALTHOUGH PUBLIC tutelage faced many obstacles during the 1920s, participants in the movement never doubted the merits of their cause. Social personnel had too much invested in their enterprise to permit a graceful retreat or withdrawal. But more than self-interest was at work here. Practitioners convinced themselves that they had achieved some stirring results, enough to sustain their conviction that they were on the verge of tapping a vast, transformative power. When petty partisanship and reactionary judges blocked forward progress, therapeutic activists took the setbacks as a test of faith. Moreover, for the sake of their clients, they would not countenance a retreat from normalizing intervention. One need only contemplate, say, the situation of children in trouble. They must not be abandoned to parental neglect or abuse or to the brutality of their social environment. Hence, whatever the liabilities of an institution like the juvenile court, complete withdrawal from the problems of the working-class family seemed far worse.[1]

We should not be surprised by this pronounced tendency to cling to earlier assumptions and convictions, for it fits a pattern we have encountered before. I have contended that a discursive movement, upon its first sobering contact with reality, still pushes ahead along a path charted by its own past. Thus, Progressive philanthropy followed lines of activity set down by its nineteenth-century predecessor. In keeping with this pattern, therapeutic activists after the First World War sought to overcome the practical defects in public human services through the further pursuit of established movement strategies. This did not preclude innovation by social personnel. But sometimes their "new course of action" merely entailed borrowing from other ventures in Progressive reform, while other celebrated advances, especially in the area of casework techniques, reflected nothing more than the elaboration of conventional discursive categories. To put it simply, the attempt to redeem the therapeutic ideal was tightly constrained by what had come before.

Social personnel, determined to master the outside forces that were corrupting their institutions, pursued a two-pronged political strategy during the postwar decade. Serious damage had been inflicted upon the new social agencies by partisanship, organized interests, and popular community opposition. If normalizing methods were to be used properly and the coherence of the therapeutic sector restored, it would be necessary to contain and minimize such external interference. Accordingly, as the first arm of their strategy, movement leaders set out to rationalize the structure of public tutelage. They looked for inspiration to the Progressive public administration movement, which had articulated an ideal of a socially responsible and efficient state, free from the contamination of politics. Drawing on advances in public administration, therapeutic activists pushed to depoliticize human services and impose coherence upon the fragmented structure that had developed. Steps were taken to put in place administrative mechanisms, especially centralized bureaucracy, that would counter localism. In addition, because the politics-driven therapeutic sector had left many marginal families without service or had subjected them to inappropriate treatment, social personnel sought to reallocate tasks among agencies and shift the emphasis to those best fitted for educative intervention.

It was understood that top-down oversight and other rationalizing measures could be thwarted by local resistance if there were no reliable agents at the grassroots level to shepherd the reforms ahead. Hence, as the second leg of the campaign to suppress political interference, therapeutic activists looked to install additional trained social personnel in public welfare departments and juvenile courts. Again, we can see the influence of the past: when Progressive philanthropy had recognized the need for an alliance with the state, charity workers and others had decided to place themselves at key posts within the new human service agencies so their ideas would take hold. Now that the therapeutic sector had grown, there was a pressing need for a larger cadre of social technicians. The newly established social work schools were called upon to fill the need.

Important though such political countermeasures were to the fate of the therapeutic idea, several leading social personnel concluded that they could not hope to gain control of the therapeutic sector unless the weaknesses in the scientific foundation of their movement were remedied. Reaffirming their fundamental discursive commitment, they sought the solution to casework deficiencies in the therapeutic approach itself. Some suspected that too much diversity had arisen in practice, so they tried to formalize appropriate adjustment techniques. Others, notably the behavioral specialists, embarked upon an extended quest for a better science of adjustment, culminating by the late 1920s in mounting enthusiasm for Freudian psychoanalysis. Once their discursive house was in order, so to speak, movement leaders prepared to assert control over internal agency policy. Behavioral experts began to circulate more widely, making their latest discoveries available to public agencies heretofore untouched by therapeutic discourse.

The strategic course followed by the therapeutic movement brought the tutelary apparatus through its first crisis, but survival came at a price. The rationalizing measures and discursive advances complicated matters for social personnel: some political steps threatened to become self-defeating, while the introduction of a new methodological framework fragmented the discourse itself. In a very different vein, we need to establish again our critical distance from therapeutic discourse, and question the unspoken agenda that guided social personnel on the path that they chose in the 1920s. As they devised ways to enhance the power they exercised, they magnified the risks to the autonomy of marginal populations.

The Bureaucratic Imperative

The rationalizing impulse that propelled movement leaders after the First World War derived from two sources within the philanthropic tradition. As I discussed in chapter 1, advocates of institutional reform had settled upon the necessity for centralization in the period following the Civil War. Some form of state oversight, they had contended, would provide the needed antidote to local interference in the management of remedial asylums, and so assure that these would fulfill their moralizing mission. The drive to impose central control accelerated in the Progressive era, when state boards began to assume direct responsibility for secure facilities. Through state administration, institutions would be further sanitized of politics and, more important, the cardinal virtue of efficiency would be realized. At social work conferences, other activists heard of the many benefits that state control brought to the field of institutional service.[2] The contrast with the messy political world of mothers' aid and the juvenile court could hardly have been more obvious.

Still, since institutions represented but a peripheral component in the therapeutic apparatus, there was a need for more relevant examples of successful rationalization. Social personnel therefore were particularly encouraged by the developments in a second line of philanthropic activity, Progressive social modernization. I noted earlier that, unlike institutional reform, social modernization looked outward to the communities in which the working-class family lived, seeking to make over its everyday environment and assure that it achieved an adequate material standard of living. The need to find allies in this cause forced proponents to reach beyond the ranks of philanthropy, and they became part of a diverse coalition agitating for social legislation and public welfare programs. Here I must add that the coalition was strongly influenced by the contemporary belief that large-scale organization and modern management techniques could be used to remold social life—a belief that informed, to choose just two noteworthy examples, the political theory of Herbert Croly and the industrial time-and-motion studies conducted by Frederick W. Taylor. When the passion for social reform met the zeal for rational management, public administration emerged. Because this important discursive movement addressed itself directly to the problems of localism and partisanship, lessons that social personnel later took to heart, it calls for closer discussion.

Public administration embodied the guiding principles of both philanthropy and organization theory. Much as philanthropy expressed a desire to transcend class conflict, administrative reformers depicted their movement as a supraclass phenomenon that would rise above the particularities of social position. The connection with philanthropy can also be seen in the commitment of public administration to the social living standard: this discursive movement, too, intended to use power constructively to improve the living conditions of the urban masses. But the tools that public administration emphasized were the instruments of management rather than therapy. We might describe its ideal as Taylorism with a social conscience.

The reform coalition began with a critique of the narrow political outlook that characterized each of the major social groups involved in urban politics. It was said that business, the middle class, and the working class all entered politics to advance their own parochial interests. Businessmen allied themselves with party leaders to secure long-term control over utilities and transportation franchises and to circumvent regulations. So effective was this corporate strategy, bemoaned the Cleveland reformer Frederic Howe, that local government was reduced to a private agency responding to the corporate will. As a result the public was forced to pay inflated charges for basic services and working people were left exposed to dangerous conditions that city government did little to correct.[3] The city did not withstand these private aggressions because the other political constituencies pursued their own short-sighted agenda. Working-class voters supported a ward-based party organization that offered some personalized services, yet failed to put into practice any broader conception of public policy. Accordingly, the worst social problems were permitted to fester. Also of concern to devotees of modern scientific management was the reliance upon graft and corruption to grease the system, resulting in massive waste in municipal departments.[4] For its part, the middle class wanted only to keep taxes low and public services at an absolute minimum. It silently accepted the grip of corporate interests.[5]

The political approach favored by the middle class drew special comment because, from the vantage point of administrative reformers, it was at once praiseworthy and critically flawed. Weary of paying the cost of machine politics, middle-class voters backed campaigns to replace party government with "good government." They hoped thereby to install a new kind of official who would run the city according to modern business principles. Public administration had no quarrel with this; certainly greater efficiency in public services was a commendable goal. But, to the dismay of the movement, middle-class good government went no further. It protected only those interests that needed no protection. Government personnel, the critique continued, lacked any sense of the larger values that efficiency was supposed to advance. Toward the working class and its most urgent needs, for example, good-government regimes remained entirely indifferent.[6] Worse yet, they sometimes took backward steps in areas of utmost social importance. Thus, Henry Bruere, director of the famous New York Bureau of Municipal Research, reported that under the commission plan, a much-heralded reform that placed responsibility for running city agencies under an elected nonpartisan board, health services and city planning were badly neglected. Though a firm believer in the need for efficiency, he condemned commission government for its lack of a social welfare orientation.[7]

In contrast to the moral indifference that marked middle-class good government, public administration subscribed to the notion that public life should be conducted as a "community enterprise." A government that performed only routine housekeeping chores, Bruere insisted, must give way to one that provided what he termed the "simple prerogatives of citizenship"—everything from decent housing to parks to security against poverty. Howe endorsed the same proposals and added that the city should assume ownership of key franchises.[8] Through such recommendations, public administration tried to broaden the meaning of the concept of efficiency: the best city government sought to correct any condition that made its citizens less efficient contributors to their community.[9]

This commitment to a higher ideal of efficiency, reformers were quick to point out, did not imply that the state should retreat from managerial doctrine. Quite the opposite: the desire to do good was not a sufficient basis for public policy. "Always, getting the business of the city done," Bruere held, "depends on processes which in every field involve practical problems of administration." Proper management techniques made it possible for officials to eliminate waste, determine accurately the needs of citizens, and direct the expanded services where most needed. The day-to-day work of translating the social mission of the city into practice required the use of skilled personnel, chosen for their expertise rather than their political affiliation. Also, to assure the correct distribution of tasks and the maintenance of high standards of performance, these civil servants should operate under a bureaucratic form of organization. Public administration understood that the use of modern management tools served a political purpose, too. Competent management reassured the middle class that partisan interests no longer dominated the allocating process. But working people also received a wider range of benefits than had been provided by the government of ward politicians and spoilsmen.[10]

Although public administration tracts did not dwell on therapeutic programs, the two movements were so closely linked that social personnel eagerly fastened onto managerialism as an answer for their own political difficulties. The strong public administration/human service connection was forged by key philanthropic activists who participated in both efforts. Henry Bruere was a former settlement house resident, while settlement leaders like Jane Addams and Mary Kingsbury Simkhovitch backed both normalizing services and administrative reform. We also see cross-membership in the case of Frederic Howe: when he was not writing about or participating in "socialized" good government, he promoted mothers' aid.[11] Naturally enough, social personnel saw a parallel between the self-interested particularism that marred city politics and the localism that destroyed the coherence of their efforts. And it followed that what seemed to work in the former context—centralized control, rule-governed organization, merit personnel practices, and rational planning—might likewise suffice in the latter. Leading proponents of the human services turned to these modern managerial instruments to impose order on the chaos that confronted them.

Centralization and Casework

Proper administration appeared to require, as a first step, the clarification of agency goals and a clear statement of how these could best be reached. Then officials and staff would have some criteria against which to measure their efforts. Perhaps much of the disarray that marked the early practice of the human services stemmed from simple misunderstanding on the part of executives and judges of their new mission. Even if darker motives sometimes were at work, the formulation of optimal standards for agency operations might prove useful, for local activists could cite them when pressing for changes. Accordingly, soon after the First World War, the foremost advocates of therapeutic programs convened in special conferences to draft model operating guidelines. Supporters of the juvenile court put forward a design for the institution that they believed would eradicate the lingering traces of criminal jurisprudence, enshrine casework norms, and promote a high degree of professionalism among court staff. Meanwhile, standards for mothers' aid were set down by social personnel committed to both adequate relief and remedial casework.[12]

To the dismay of therapeutic activists who participated in these determined efforts to spread the word, the new administrative standards by themselves had a minimal impact. The Children's Bureau cooperated in disseminating them widely to officials, politicians, and private groups. It then sponsored follow-up studies by social workers to publicize successful examples of normalizing service by pension departments and juvenile courts.[13] All the same, the effort was seriously incomplete. Standards made for useful propaganda, yes, but it would take more than that to dislodge the entrenched local interests with which therapeutic activists had to contend. The guideline literature was filed away as soon as it arrived, and the many local officials and judges continued to practice their own peculiar versions of public tutelage as they did before. Social personnel, often placed in subordinate positions, lacked the leverage to impose their model of therapeutic intervention on their policy competitors.

Once again movement leaders turned to public administration. It suggested that political interference could be neutralized through authoritative control exercised from a central point. Where the campaign for standards amounted to an attempt to exhort from *without*, centralized supervision and management constituted the means to direct from *above*. Public administration texts meticulously detailed the appropriate organizational tools needed to produce specified policy outputs. Through the creation of state-level bureaucratic departments, therapeutic activists believed, it would be possible to project influence over even those local officials most inclined to defer to voter/taxpayer sentiment.[14]

First and foremost, the central agency would use the techniques of rational managerial control to impose therapeutic doctrine on local practice. Individual agencies would be pressured to adopt a uniform structure, follow regular procedures, hire trained caseworkers, and observe merit personnel practices. Everyday operations, then, could be gradually remolded to conform to the optimal standards for human service.[15] In the case of the juvenile court, proponents of a state probation agency hoped that such an instrument would promote merit selection and professionalism in probation departments, and so neutralize both partisanship and judicial mishandling of staff appointments.[16] Similarly, studies of mothers' aid called for state oversight to promote the virtues of adequate aid and constructive casework. State supervisory personnel would devote themselves to the education of local departments—county officials and juvenile court judges would be taught the true purposes of the program and local field staff would receive basic instruction in casework techniques.[17]

The state bureaucracy would also become a political force in its own right. It was hailed as an instrument for "interpreting" the therapeutic idea to the larger public, making human services more visible and intelligible. In the event of a direct showdown between an individual agency and reactionary interests in the community, local social personnel would know they could count on the backing of the state department.[18] Through the efforts of state bureaucrats, too, the problems afflicting the program, especially insufficient funds, would be brought to the notice of state leaders. They would learn that if they desired adequate administration, they would have to find a better way to pay for it.[19] Bureaucratization thus seemed an answer to the lack of resources that bedeviled the early human services.

Agitation by the therapeutic movement in favor of state bureaucratic control sometimes succeeded in overcoming strong localist opposition to administrative centralization. As was to be expected, resistance came from those policy actors who held the dominant position in the decentralized service network—juvenile court judges, county politicians, and poor-relief officials. The judges, able to play upon a tradition of judicial autonomy, warded off many attempts to subordinate the institution to state-level authority. Only where social personnel were well organized did they manage to create state agencies with the modest power to monitor probation. Court practice otherwise remained stubbornly resistant to change, especially in rural areas.[20] Poor-relief officials also fought against state direction of mothers' aid and other child-welfare programs. However, lacking the stature of judges, they often could do no more than delay initiatives to create state departments of public or child welfare. Such agencies emerged in most states by the late 1920s.[21]

Although state-level departments were hampered by their inability to impose administrative sanctions on uncooperative local officials, bureaucratic intervention seemed to yield the anticipated benefits. Social personnel affiliated with the state agencies used propaganda and persuasion aggressively, insisting that local bureaus follow merit personnel practices, calling upon county officials to preserve the integrity of mothers' aid through adherence to statutory eligibility standards and the award of adequate grants, and introducing the largely untrained local personnel to casework methods.[22] At the same time, state-level officials applied their influence to strengthen the legislative commitment to the program. It was found that in states with a central supervisory agency, state government more often agreed to share the cost of mothers' allowances and legislatures sometimes amended the program to make county participation mandatory.[23]

Beyond the immediate gains that bureaucratization brought to the field of public tutelage, the quest to centralize had implications that we must explore. The strategy drew together two modern sources of power, the therapeutic and the organizational, under public auspices. Philanthropy had known of both, but only now were they combined to reinforce each other.[24] Of particular significance, rational administration would be used to clear away political obstacles to the use of expert therapeutic skills: bureaucracy was the conscious antidote to democracy. Social personnel tried through state agencies to eliminate residency requirements for employment, a lingering vestige of prereform government that helped assure the expression of community values.[25] Furthermore, central supervision was regarded as a tool for reversing the gender hierarchy of the human services. Casework appeared to some social personnel to call for distinctively feminine qualities, yet local control clearly rested with male judges and overseers. The state agency would apply pressure on its subunits to employ women, so that public casework could be better feminized in practice.[26]

Division of Labor

As centralization in public welfare progressed, rationalization of the human services proceeded along a second track. Yet another lesson to be gleaned from public administration was that social efficiency depended upon the right organization of tasks. Managerial reformers, seeking to capitalize on the special competencies of particular agencies, insisted on the value of a correct division of labor in government operations. When therapeutic activists surveyed their early handiwork, they saw that they had been compelled to violate this principle. Political circumstances had forced social personnel into local improvisations, resulting often in confusion in the service network. Agencies duplicated each other's efforts, fought over turf, and offered services they were not competent to perform; many prospective clients were turned away, despite their pressing need for adjustment. Movement leaders realized the urgent need to make better use of available resources by imposing a coherent framework upon the makeshift local apparatus.

Modest improvements were achieved through the further exercise of state authority. Sometimes therapeutic activists managed to secure statutes that could be used in support of their push to bring greater uniformity to local service organizations. For example, in New York during the 1920s, counties were required by various laws to create separate juvenile courts with exclusive jurisdiction over children's cases and to establish a standardized public welfare organization that would cooperate with all public and private service providers. Elsewhere the support of the state public welfare agency was enlisted to make the most efficient use of available casework resources and to remedy the fragmentation among social agencies.[27]

All the same, despite helpful involvement from above, the problem of disorganization in the service network would not be resolved until the many competing normalizing agencies redefined their roles and redistributed their effort. As one step in this process, private and public agencies needed to clarify their roles in the emerging therapeutic sector. Social workers frequently asserted that private agencies were in a better position to press ahead with experimental projects; if public departments outpaced community opinion, they would place the entire public commitment to human services in jeopardy. Public agencies, it followed, were to assume responsibility for programs that had proven themselves.[28] In addition, clients in need of the most intensive casework services were to be referred to private agencies. These could limit their caseload, while public agencies faced enormous pressures to do something for all comers and therefore had to spread their resources too thinly. The high cost of maintaining long-term dependents, on the other hand, would exhaust the resources of private groups, so such cases were to be absorbed by the public budget.[29]

Besides differentiating between public and private agencies, the movement explored the proper distribution of tasks within the public tutelary apparatus. Much of the discussion centered on the juvenile court, which in many communities had assumed, either by default or design, a commanding position over the human services. The court's excessive use of coercion disturbed many of its proponents, who felt that its educative function had been compromised. Yet even the harshest critics were not prepared to recommend wholesale retreat from judicial intervention. Other human services had begun to depend on the court to sustain their normalizing program. If a family refused to submit to treatment recommended by social workers or specialists, the court stood ready to order compliance.[30] Judicial support also had brought managerial economy to the field of human services. In the juvenile court social agencies found a place to discard clients who responded poorly to voluntary therapeutic measures. Thus unburdened, the agencies conserved their resources for more suitable cases.[31] Whether one took a "humane" or pragmatic view, then, therapeutic child protection demanded that problems be addressed within the judicial framework.

Restoring the correct balance among public agencies seemed to require the removal of certain tasks from the juvenile court. This solution was put forward forcefully by Thomas D. Eliot as early as 1914. He argued, then and later, that when the court assumed various child protection and welfare functions, it exceeded its proper boundaries. Services were poorly performed and the stigma of a legal proceeding was inflicted unnecessarily on many children. As a judicial instrument the juvenile court was suited for adjudication, nothing more. Hence, it needed to be given a more modest role, and the responsibility for therapeutic work was to be transferred to noncoercive agencies like schools, clinics, and child welfare departments. Rather than encourage social personnel to initially refer all problem juveniles to its care, the juvenile court would urge voluntary intervention as a first resort.[32] Eliot's prescription reflected a chastened understanding of the limits of compulsion, but we must recognize the very limited nature of his critique. Although the scope of judicial action would be narrowed, he still presumed the need for judicial support in certain cases and hoped merely to disguise it by removing probation from the court's immediate auspices. Moreover, he was eager to extend the therapeutic project, witness his plans to bring casework methods into the schools. Use of the schools to normalize problem children would encourage the therapeutic sector to spill over into another part of the modern state apparatus.

Eliot's ideas soon received strong support from those outside the court, and some concrete steps were taken to circumscribe judicial responsibility in the human services. Judges and spokesmen for probation organizations predictably sought to dismiss Eliot.[33] Nevertheless, by the early 1920s a strong consensus emerged among social personnel that the court had taken on too many burdens. The critics of judicial overexpansion, following Eliot, took pains to indicate that they still saw a need to harness the coercive power of the state to the therapeutic mission. But to assure that marginal clients could receive adjustment services without stigma and that these services would be administered competently, they contended that purely educative and welfare functions ought to be removed to other agencies. Public assistance was often singled out as a program that did not belong in the legal-correctional orbit. Following through on this point, movement leaders successfully campaigned in several states during the postwar decade to sever mothers' aid from the jurisdiction of the court.[34]

The Cadre Strategy

To restore the integrity of the public tutelage, it was not enough to establish a state-level bureaucracy or formulate elegant designs for better apportioning tasks within the normalizing apparatus. Directives about how to manage a casework program would mean little if field personnel lacked mastery of casework techniques. Further, unless a strong commitment to the values of therapeutic practice could be instilled in judges, probation officers, and caseworkers, they would persist in deferring to community opinion. Naked compulsion would still characterize the juvenile court; in mothers' aid, practice would continue to reflect, depending upon local whims, excessive generosity or meanness. The situation called for an influx of skilled caseworkers to disseminate advanced normalizing methods and tout the merits of the therapeutic approach to a skeptical provincial audience. As yet, however, there were too few trained social personnel, and most chose to work in private family agencies.

Advocates of public tutelage accordingly called for a broad effort to encourage the staff of public departments to attend schools of social work. These professional schools multiplied rapidly during the postwar era, numbering more than forty by 1930. Within the schools, unlike most social agencies, therapeutic specialists faced no competition for control. Along with the technical knowledge students acquired, then, they received a full dose of social work ideology. It was hoped this would become the basis for a new professional identity for public social personnel. Various measures were proposed to induce public employees to enroll in social work educational programs. For example, a Children's Bureau study of mothers' aid recommended that staff compensation be tied to participation in courses and educational conferences. Steps to foster such in-service training were quickly introduced, helping to spread the casework method and philosophy in states like North Carolina where therapeutic ideas had scarcely made a mark.[35] Unfortunately, progress was slowed by the public workers themselves. Many decided upon completion of their studies that they could better pursue the therapeutic agenda by following the standard social work career path that led through the more prestigious and higher-paying private casework organizations. Yet, for all the loss of trained talent, the supply of professional cadre for the public human services gradually increased.

If the efforts of trained caseworkers in local agencies could be buttressed with outside support from the community, judges and county officials would more likely accept the wisdom of the therapeutic approach. Private family service agencies were enlisted, then, to provide a measure of grassroots leverage. Although public tutelage lacked the glamor of private social work, it was asserted that no wall should be erected between the two spheres. Private agency staff were to back their counterparts in the public departments as the latter struggled to sustain casework standards and overcome any drift toward routine casehandling. Therapeutic activists soon established many private advisory groups to cooperate with mothers'-aid departments and juvenile courts. In a few states, statutes mandated this kind of public consultation with private social personnel.[36]

Redemption through Science

The political strategy chosen by therapeutic activists seemed well-suited for bringing casework methods to the local outposts of the therapeutic sector. Still, confronted in the field by hostile actors who believed in traditional ways of shaping behavior, social personnel would prevail only by demonstrating that their new approach produced better results. And here leading proponents of the human services were troubled by doubts, for as we noted in the previous chapter casework outcomes had been disappointing. True understanding of the client's situation and condition eluded many social agencies. Social personnel, then, required more effective casework methods. Once they were properly armed, they could dislodge the representatives of unenlightened thinking and claim their rightful place at the helm of the human services.[37]

Certain social workers believed that deviations from proper casework procedures accounted for the poor results reported by many agencies. Amidst the rapid advances achieved by Progressive philanthropy, it was impossible to assure—if we may borrow another managerialist term— quality control. Practice became unduly eclectic, with many well-meaning executives and judges labeling their efforts as casework when these bore scant relation to the discursive model. Social workers were very defensive when Abraham Flexner, in a famous conference address in 1915, insisted that their field was not a profession, but they took the charge to heart. The time had come to impose order on the chaos of casework practice, to sort out acceptable procedures from ineffective, or worse, counterproductive ones. We might call the process the rationalization of method, for in spirit it closely resembled the administrative strategies I have described—the clutter generated by accidental circumstances would be replaced by uniformity and structure.[38]

The project to standardize casework owed much to the efforts of Mary E. Richmond. It will be recalled that she was among the original architects of the therapeutic approach in the 1890s. During the next two decades, most of which she spent working under the auspices of the Russell Sage Foundation, she remained committed to the further refinement of therapeutic power, publishing various case histories as a guide to practice. The war years found her engaged in the first systematic attempt to distill a single, consistent technique of normalizing casework. With the publication of two influential primers, *Social Diagnosis* (1917) and *What is Social Case Work?* (1922), she successfully codified what had until then been a disparate set of procedures. We do not need to review the volumes here; although they are sometimes credited as pathbreaking contributions, most of what they contained could have been gleaned from a close reading of earlier texts. What matters is that, upon their appearance, many social personnel believed that the exact tools needed to refashion clients' lives had been placed conveniently at the disposal of any casework practitioner.[39]

Yet there was still good reason to doubt that the mere formalization of existing procedures would suffice. Therapeutic intervention appeared to require a scientific discipline that generated valid diagnoses and adequate prescriptions for treatment, but the early forays by behavioral specialists had highlighted the lack of any such discipline. Clinicians continued to explore possibilities during the war years and immediately thereafter; social psychology and psychiatry thus attracted strong followings. Both approaches stressed the relationship between behavior and the environment, and therefore appealed to caseworkers of Progressive sensibility who thought that normalization depended upon changing clients' surroundings. Alas, treatment results obtained in child guidance clinics, mental hygiene clinics, and other settings remained discouraging. Despite diligent, highly competent intervention efforts, clients defied normalization. The flaw still seemed to lie with the scientific foundation (or "knowledge base") on which clinicians relied: social psychology and psychiatry, with their coarse diagnoses and recommendations for simple environmental correctives, merely skimmed the surface of behavioral irregularities.[40]

When psychoanalytic theory began to circulate in American intellectual circles in the late 1920s, then, social personnel were singularly receptive. Like other psychiatric approaches, Freudian doctrine lent itself to the individualized treatment that social agencies provided. But psychoanalysis also spoke directly to the conviction among clinicians and social workers that a science of human behavior ought not to rest on overly rationalistic assumptions—assumptions contradicted by the record of casework interventions. Child guidance clinics introduced psychoanalytic techniques, followed swiftly by family service agencies and other therapeutic organizations. Leaders hailed their new core discipline as the solution to the most vexing forms of personal difficulty.[41]

Incorporating psychoanalysis into the formal casework model set forth by Richmond posed no particular difficulty. The goal remained the forging of a therapeutic relationship. In psychoanalytic casework, as several historians have noted, the client's inner mental universe, rather than his environment, became the focus of diagnosis and treatment. Freudian techniques allowed a skilled practitioner to probe the unarticulated but real source of maladjustment. Failure to cope with the pressures of everyday living might stem from low self-esteem, distorted relationships within the family, grandiose ambitions, or some other hidden disorder. After analysis disclosed the cause of the difficulty, the client would be aided in reconciling himself to his situation. Casework lowered his hostility toward others and toward society and restored his capacity to choose activities in which he would find satisfaction. At the same time, the new approach better enabled the caseworker to understand her reaction to the client and the latter's response to her, including anger and emotional dependence. She would be able to keep her emotional distance from the situation, avoiding the deep frustration that afflicted many in the field. And because she would be less quick to judge, the client would feel that he was respected and respond more readily to her ministrations. Social personnel were convinced they would finally realize the constructive power of therapeutic intervention.[42]

Before they would arrive at that long-sought goal, of course, it would be necessary to make the leap from theoretical innovation to common practice. Most caseworkers in the field continued to fumble along, using the inefficient method of trial and error. If social personnel were to practice effectively, they would have to be educated in the latest theories and techniques. Again the schools of social work were expected to play a crucial role. Their curriculums would be sharply revised, shifting the emphasis from social science, that mundane staple of the liberal arts, to the new and more useful behavioral disciplines, psychoanalysis above all. Students would be exposed to the best in casework technique and carry this forward as they went into practice. As increased numbers of trained therapeutic cadre took up positions in social agencies, it followed, advanced scientific knowledge would be disseminated throughout the therapeutic sector.[43]

The renovation of therapeutic discourse seemed to set the stage for the triumph of social personnel within the human services. By virtue of their improved scientific instruments, they believed that they now possessed the means to gain the upper hand over their internal competitors, to create what Donzelot so aptly calls a "hierarchy of expertise." Well-drilled therapeutic practitioners would put to use psychoanalysis and other proven casework techniques to overcome client evasions, penetrate appearances, and generate positive conduct. Having demonstrated that they could deliver on the promise of family rehabilitation, social personnel confidently expected that other officials would defer to their wisdom.[44]

We find this enthusiasm most pronounced among therapeutic activists associated with the juvenile court. Theirs was an institution that had thus far resisted casework doctrine, leaving them to chafe beneath the judge's peremptory style. However, with the introduction of psychoanalytic methods, they would alter the reigning equation of forces. For the first time it would be possible to determine the true significance of a trivial offense—was it just youthful excess, as the judge guessed, or the first manifestation of serious unresolved family conflicts? Faced with such clearly superior understanding, the juvenile court judge would be overmatched. Treatment, too, would be revolutionized. When the child learned that the psychoanalytic professional listened without rushing to pass a crude judgment, he would be disarmed and won over. Social personnel would remove disposition from the judge's hands or, by confronting him with unassailable recommendations, dictate his choices.[45] Just as important, through cooperation with other child protection agencies and mothers'-aid departments, behavioral specialists would check the tendency to turn first to the court in difficult cases.[46] At each step in the process, therapeutic values would prevail over popular ones, and the expert would dislodge local lay opinion from its ruling position. The incipient scientific regime would thus tame the court's repressive tendencies.

In their push to elevate the role of scientific knowledge within their agencies, as in their other reform schemes, therapeutic activists by the late 1920s boasted of certain progress. Here, naturally, it is more difficult to support their claims with hard evidence. We do know that the philanthropic Commonwealth Fund in the early 1920s sponsored the creation of demonstration child guidance clinics to work closely with judges and probation staffs. The experiment was intended to make science available in many places where social technicians had not established a presence, and to do so in a language court officials could understand.[47] But this brief venture preceded the surge of interest in Freudian theory. Psychoanalytic techniques spread by a less orchestrated process, from the schools to the better private agencies and innovative clinics, thence to the most highly trained personnel in certain courts and child and public welfare departments. Toward the close of the decade, movement leaders and top behavioral experts reported that "a wider scientific spirit" had taken root in institutions like the juvenile court.[48]

The Solution Is the Problem

The therapeutic movement in the postwar decade assured the long-term survival of public human services. True enough, the support of program administrators, academics, and educators could not substitute for a mass constituency, so the rapid program expansion of the previous two decades was not sustained. But amidst a political reaction that otherwise sent Progressives into headlong retreat, it is striking that social personnel not only preserved what they had gained but even recorded important advances. Some success attended their efforts to neutralize political interference through centralization, merit personnel practices, and other rationalizing measures; trained caseworkers were found in growing numbers in public welfare departments and juvenile courts. Perhaps the best illustration of what therapeutic entrepreneurs could accomplish is provided by mothers' aid. Despite the hostile climate of opinion, the program did not contract; indeed, to the contrary, it enrolled more families each year, with the number of children receiving aid rising by Children's Bureau estimate from a daily average of 130,000 in 1923 to 200,000 in 1927.[49]

In weathering its initial test, the therapeutic sector also emerged as a permanent force in the field of social policy. The impact was especially pronounced in matters in which philanthropy had once been most active. As mothers'-aid departments extended their grip over relief for mothers and their children, private charity was permanently displaced; public support for certain types of fatherless families was treated as a given by the 1920s, no longer an issue to be debated in social work conferences. Public child welfare departments similarly assumed a substantial role in child protection, though they did not preempt their older private counterparts. At the same time, if therapeutic activists did not take immediate command over programs that had been traditionally left to local public control, they did manage to establish themselves as "players" in the local struggles for administrative supremacy and resources. Lawmakers, department heads, and judges henceforth would have to take account of public agencies and personnel committed to the therapeutic approach. The normalizing agenda might not have earned universal acceptance, but its widening circle of adherents guaranteed that it would shape subsequent policy innovation.

While social personnel assured the survival of public tutelage, however, their political and discursive strategies brought new tensions to the human services. To begin with, rationalization of casework agencies was more problematic than it first appeared. Amid the enthusiasm of therapeutic activists for public administration methods, a few dissenting voices warned that managerialism and large-scale organization might be incompatible with the therapeutic approach. What concerned the skeptics was the loss of flexibility that characterized bureaucratic institutions. Under the civil-service examination system, it was extremely difficult to make provision for the nonquantifiable human qualities that distinguished the successful caseworker; with businesslike fiscal controls, which brought aberrant case decisions under sharp scrutiny, public officials were deterred from recognizing the individual needs of their clients.[50] The doubters, it should be added, drew little support in therapeutic circles, where bureaucratic control was widely seen as an unmixed blessing. If the risks of this organizational form were addressed at all, they were dismissed. Thus, Ada Eliot Sheffield argued that it was the absence of rules, not their multiplication, that precluded good casework. Policies ought to be so fully detailed that all contingencies were covered. "The cure . . . for following hard and fast grooves of treatment is not to do without policies, but to have more of them."[51] In the therapeutic discourse of the 1920s, the answer to the problems of bureaucracy was more bureaucracy. Yet this blithe response scarcely masked the conflict between the ideal of an adaptive casework relationship as posited by the original therapeutic model and the rule-bound agency-client interaction the rationalizers desired.

Moreover, the antipathy for popular sentiment and its local representatives that therapeutic activists vented came back to haunt them, for they needed the cooperation of the very officials they dismissed. Social personnel made no attempt to appreciate community opinion. Local actors were hopelessly primitive in their outlook, it was felt, and their intent could only be evil. When the stakes in a dispute are raised to the level of a moral crusade, it is hard merely to understand the opposing camp's perspective, much less find some common ground. Local officials and the public at-large reciprocated the disdain. From their angle, caseworkers were prone to muddled thinking, confused by abstract doctrine about the need to "understand" the poor and the delinquent. So far as the community was concerned, enough was already known about these people; they simply had to be made to live up to the standards that applied to everyone else. The resulting polarization presented a special difficulty for social personnel. Their recent scientific innovations, notably the use of psychoanalytic casework techniques, required the intensive application of costly resources. Here lay the political trap. To obtain the means they required, social personnel would have to appeal to juvenile court judges, county lawmakers and the like, and these officials would never agree to ask local taxpayers to foot the bill.[52] Indeed, nothing could better demonstrate how far the therapeutic ideal stood from the concerns of the community than such extravagant requests. And so social personnel would find themselves caught between the voracious demands of their technology and the democratic politics it was supposed to replace.

Within the therapeutic movement itself, meanwhile, the advent of psychoanalysis did not bring about a consensus on casework technique but contributed instead to an insidious methodological pluralism. The Freudians called for the caseworker to adopt a detached and self-aware manner and to focus on the client's inner deficiencies. Such an approach could hardly be applauded by the many casework practitioners who still thought that environment weighed heavily or by those who wanted to restore to normalizing intervention the soft, feminized quality that had been lost under male-dominated agency hierarchies.[53] The psychoanalytic types failed to sweep aside competing methodological factions. Votaries of other approaches retained important footholds in the human services, as an examination of the proceedings from any contemporary social work conference reveals. In the human services, we can safely conclude, new theoretical perspectives never fully displace their predecessors, but rather become the next layer atop the existing intellectual edifice. Therapeutic discourse expanded to include the Freudian insights at the price of its own coherence. And once social personnel ceased to speak with a single voice, they would find it far more difficult to make the human services follow a single design.

Rationalization and Autonomy

For the targets of normalizing intervention, the strategies that social personnel pursued held modest promise and substantial risks. As centralization encouraged the broadening of mother's aid, some poor women and children gained a measure of choice they had not enjoyed before. An increasing number of widows who otherwise would have had to work and perhaps surrender their children to an orphanage were able to reduce their hours of outside employment and devote more time to their children. In addition, legislative reforms made more women eligible for assistance, including divorced, deserted, and (in a few instances) unmarried mothers. But we should not overstate the degree to which the pension programs empowered weaker family members. To maintain public support and stretch inadequate appropriations, program officials in practice disregarded the liberalized statutory eligibility standards and continued to restrict aid to those mothers who would be regarded in the community as most deserving. Often only widows received a grant. Thus a woman who might wish to leave her husband still found no solace at the local mothers'-aid office.

More important, although a handful of women and children may have reduced their exposure to arbitrary male authority, the steps taken by the therapeutic movement were intended to subdue the autonomy of these and other clients. Administrative rationalization sought to bring all marginal populations within the reach of the public tutelage, and thus ultimately sought to expose them to the full force of therapeutic power. Localism and inefficiency were attacked in part because they led to material suffering, but also because they shielded the working-class family from normalizing intervention. This concern lay behind the charge that mothers' aid was administered *too liberally* in some communities. Without due regard for its remedial function, public assistance would do nothing to remold recipients for the better. By the same token, when therapeutic activists complained about the chaos in local service networks, they feared that many maladjusted families were falling between the cracks and so were eluding their grasp. They intended that a proper allocation of responsibility among social agencies would close off such escape routes.

To the degree that social personnel would bring about a better division of labor within the therapeutic apparatus, it should be added, clients were less likely following intervention to recover their privacy. Poor coordination among agencies not only let marginal families avoid intervention but also helped those caught briefly in the grasp of social personnel to fade from sight. After all, an overloaded juvenile court could not follow most of its cases closely. But a well-ordered human service system would assign clients to an agency that had the capacity to maintain ongoing contact. With better cooperation between the agency and other community institutions like public schools and recreation programs, too, families would remain under steady if distant observation.

The desire to contain client autonomy likewise inspired the formalization of casework techniques and the exploration of the new behavioral disciplines. Where clients had preserved their independence behind a facade of cooperativeness with the normalizing agency, their true nature would be rendered visible by scientific progress. Reducing intervention to a definite set of procedures, as Mary Richmond attempted, assured that the amateurism of social personnel would no longer play into the hands of obtuse clients. And the appeal of a discipline like psychoanalysis lay in the claim that it alone could break down the walls that clients threw up around themselves. I have contended that in principle therapeutic discourse recognized no limits on the power it had invented. Fortunately, to this point social personnel had lacked an instrument that would let them get beneath appearances. If the scientific advances proved as useful as proponents claimed, however, the therapeutic practitioner would be able to penetrate to the very core of the human soul or (as we must say in deference to the inescapable terminology psychoanalysis has brought upon us) the personality. Clients would be left defenseless.

Six

The Paths to Social Membership

PROGRESSIVE PHILANTHROPY must be understood as a radical enterprise: despite its conservative goals, it was fascinated by approaches that called for the exercise of power at the most fundamental level of human experience. We have seen this in therapeutic discourse, with its drive to make over aspirations, desires, and modes of thought. Nor was normalizing casework the only radical approach to gain substantial backing among philanthropic activists. Under the inspiration of Robert A. Woods, the settlement leader, a segment of philanthropy urged the dramatic expansion of neighborhood self-government as a device for linking marginal populations to the social order. Early settlement experience suggested to Woods that working people should not be seen merely as individuals or family members, but also as political agents who, by drawing upon their own experiences and associations, were able to create community. If given real political autonomy, a social space in which to generate their own collective identity, they could bring themselves into the social mainstream. The approach Woods advocated sought to tap a power every bit as profound as that imagined by the proponents of the casework technology. And it should be noted that his ideas attracted a substantial following, beginning in the settlement movement but quickly extending beyond it. During the first two decades of the twentieth century, this group began to differentiate yet another line of philanthropic effort, "community organization," that sought to mobilize the self-renewing forces in the neighborhood.

Where the therapeutic approach accorded well with the prevailing intellectual ethos, however, Woods's participatory notions soon came to be seen as anomalous. On the face of it, other discourses linked to philanthropy, like social science and public administration, appeared to be committed to a strengthening of democracy. Yet closer inspection reveals that they dismissed citizen participation in any but the most routine form, and thus were deeply antipolitical. Moreover, within philanthropy itself, where the political approach of Woods and his allies had to coexist with the therapeutic model, the former fared badly. It was not well served by its friends. As they discovered that the neighborhood voice could be shrill and unpolished, they were only too eager to tamper with it. Political action was also devalued by therapeutic practitioners devoted to the new personality sciences. Finally, when philanthropic leaders during the period of the First World War tried to impose a rational structure on the clutter of the local agencies and neighborhood groups, grassroots political action was left without a place. Community organization then became a polite label for the subordination of indigenous neighborhood forces to the requirements of the human service apparatus.

The many-sided attack on neighborhood democracy matters for us because it narrowed significantly the possibilities for innovation in the subsequent development of social policy. Discursive actors, I have suggested, press ahead along a course delimited by their underlying assumptions and past practices. The political approach to social membership had pushed philanthropy down a new avenue, and thus had represented the possibility of broadening its agenda beyond the therapeutic. Community organization had arisen, we must note, at a moment when the outlines of social policy were in flux. I have also observed that the era of experimentation drew to a close after the war, with institutions taking hold that would condition all future policy reforms. It was at just this time that community organizers wavered in their support for political action; Woods himself questioned whether working people were prepared to build their own communal institutions. Hence, succeeding policy entrepreneurs would be housed not in a neighborhood government but in the human service apparatus, and when they contemplated how best to integrate marginal populations into the social fabric, public tutelage would be taken as the only acceptable approach.

Visions of the Neighborhood

In their earliest reports and commentaries on slum conditions, settlement house residents described the typical working-class district as being under siege. The factory system divided the city geographically along class lines, so that working people congregated in their own self-contained neighborhoods; immigration reinforced this separatist tendency by giving it an ethnic cast.[1] Yet, although the district's inhabitants sought security through their isolation, their haven was battered by the economic forces at work in the industrial economy. Frequent joblessness forced families to move repeatedly and encouraged wholesale population turnover. Neighbors became strangers, a tendency exacerbated by the pattern of ethnic succession.[2] We have noted, too, the common complaint that local politicians in the machine organization did nothing to promote neighborhood solidarity. Indeed, settlement residents felt the party structure discouraged popular involvement.[3] As a consequence, the district came to be made up of people with no local attachments, separated from each other by differences of ethnicity and religion, lacking common purpose.

Nevertheless, despite the forces arrayed against the neighborhood, settlement workers asserted that it contained important social resources for its own rejuvenation. On an informal basis, working people rose to the needs of those in distress with unflinching support. For example, in times of high unemployment, relatives and friends lent money or supplied food to the jobless, trying to shield them from the ignominy of charity.[4] A network of voluntary associations had also emerged, including fraternal lodges, political clubs, immigrant aid societies, youth gangs, and trade unions. Woods asserted that these groups had done more to organize the district than had all outside philanthropists and reformers. He and other settlement residents recognized, too, that the indigenous organizations performed an educational function, for through them members learned something about the art of self-government. In the most mundane associations, like the lodges, people discovered the need to tolerate each other, a prerequisite for neighborhood progress; at a more advanced level, the trade union demonstrated to workers that joint effort could address vital issues and gave them the opportunity to select their own leaders. This training in collective action broadened the social perspective of the participants.[5]

What marginal groups had accomplished on their own behalf suggested to Woods a simple but dramatic possibility for social reform. With limited tools, they had established various organizations to meet some of their most pressing needs. Imagine how much more the district could do for itself, he said, if it were granted political autonomy and entrusted with formal responsibility for administering certain public services. He urged measures that would return to the neighborhood its old village powers, with local representatives supervising such functions as education and public relief. These activities could be run through a district town hall, he noted, so that residents would also have a place of their own in which to meet.[6]

Woods championed neighborhood government less as a way to improve the quality of public services than as an instrument for civic education and as a vehicle to foster a sense of communal membership. The district was concrete and tangible in a way that any resident could feel and understand, being at once large enough to span the entire range of interests and attachments that develop outside the home, yet small enough to be comprehended as an entire city could not be. In this arena people could learn how to manage their own collective affairs.[7] More than that, through their involvement in neighborhood government, residents would begin to identify with their district and care about its future.

Woods contended that vigorous participation in such local political forums would lead to social membership. By engaging directly in public
deliberation and common action at this level, people would exercise
meaningful control over their shared destiny. They would then regard the
outcome as their own product, and appreciate that they had a real stake
in the social order they had helped to define.[8]

Important though neighborhood identity was, however, Woods did
not seek to promote neighborhood provincialism. He saw active involvement in district affairs as the path by which marginal groups would be
integrated into the mainstream of American life. The problem with larger
political units was that they were too remote to serve as the starting point
for political membership. Woods believed firmly that the sense of belonging could first be affirmed only at the neighborhood level. But he was also
convinced that once the neighborhood attachment had formed, the foundation would exist for membership in more extensive political communities. The initial affinity for the district would gradually broaden when the
residents came to recognize what they had in common with those on the
outside.[9]

In his enthusiasm for neighborhood activism Woods tended to roman-
ticize his approach, so he did not systematically elaborate upon its premises or its implications. I want to take up where he left off. Of particular
interest to us are the basic political concepts upon which he built his case
for neighborhood government. To begin with, for him the community
itself does not exist as a given, but instead must be constituted anew
through the constructive application of power. Woods construed power,
then, as the capacity to make a new beginning. In itself this notion, later
developed (independently) by Arendt, is radical: it implies an open-ended
process, one bounded solely by the imagination of the participants. And
going a step further, he suggested that the capacity to call forth a community exists among all groups, including the disenfranchised in the most
impoverished slums.[10] On the other hand, although political capacity
might be universal, people cannot take the first halting steps toward community unless they are secure in a social space entirely their own. For
without that measure of collective autonomy, established structures of
thought prevent them from finding their own voice, a voice they need if
they are to express the things that are central to their lives. Woods
thought, of course, that neighborhood government would provide the
necessary space. But the idea that people can forge their own community
does not presuppose this particular form of political organization, and
certainly other settings might do as well.

Once ordinary people start to use power to create community, Woods
also saw, they become not merely the subjects wielding power but also its
objects—they are transformed by what they have done. As they come to

feel themselves a part of the community they have invented, they cease to regard themselves as marginal figures in a world that takes no notice. What develops in place of this damaging self-image is a sense of solidarity, coupled with strong positive loyalties toward those with whom they have joined.[11] It follows that for Woods certain political attitudes must be regarded as the signs of successful social integration. The person who has risen to full membership in a democratic order displays a willingness to listen, grasps his responsibility to come to the aid of his fellows, and steps forward to uphold community standards. These sentiments in turn function as the building blocks of more sophisticated varieties of civic consciousness.

Thus elaborated, Woods's political approach to social membership differs profoundly from the program for integrating marginal populations defined by therapeutic discourse. Having reduced the problem of marginality to a condition of personal maladjustment, the therapeutic approach pursues membership through a process of individual and family instruction and counseling. Success is obtained, as we have seen, when clients internalize the domestic values and behavioral norms of the community and demonstrate the ability to sustain correct personal relationships. Political activities do not contribute to integration and political attitudes are not seen as the mark of proper adjustment. Furthermore, therapeutic discourse embodies very different assumptions about power, community, and autonomy. The therapeutic technician, like Woods, looks to the constructive use of power, but under therapeutic intervention it is used to mold private volitions and behavior. The standards are set from without, by an established social order that individuals are expected to join on its terms. As I have suggested, this leaves no role for autonomy; indeed, autonomy, individual and collective, represents a barrier to be overcome.

During the early decades of the twentieth century, Woods's views attracted a number of passionate adherents. Settlement leaders took up his call for expanding the democratic opportunities of the working class. Graham Taylor advocated the direct representation of the industrial masses in elective office and their participation in the administration of public affairs; George Bellamy, seeking to stimulate the latent self-governing resources of slum neighborhoods, proposed a variety of reforms to decentralize public recreation and cultural activities. The settlement movement, as part of its central mission, took up the responsibility for uncovering indigenous neighborhood associations, providing meeting places, and otherwise encouraging the surrounding district to organize itself.[12] Furthermore, in conjunction with settlement residents, other reformers and philanthropic activists promoted neighborhood and school centers under direct local control to establish a focal point for the many independent working-class associations. Through these efforts, community organization came to be differentiated as yet another line of philanthropic activity. It sought, in the words of John Collier from the People's Institute in New York City, to restore to the individual the "power to control his own destiny which had been taken away from him by . . . all the other power-building soul-corroding things incidental to our latter nineteenth century evolution."[13]

John Daniels offered perhaps the most forceful reiteration of the political approach to social membership. His 1920 study addressed a problem of much concern to philanthropy and other elite groups during the war period, the challenge of developing a common national identity among the mass of immigrants in American cities. Rejecting the blunt propagandizing approach favored by most official and philanthropic groups, he insisted that assimilation could be accomplished only by the immigrants themselves, as the end result of a long political evolution. This process Daniels laid out in elaborate detail. He took as his starting point the position, which he linked to de Tocqueville, that actual participation in social and public life is the best means to establish membership in a community.[14] Ample opportunities for participation could be found in the self-contained ethnic enclaves in which the newcomers took shelter. He, too, commented that neighborhoods gave rise to a multitude of voluntary organizations. Through involvement in these groups, which often dealt with community problems, immigrants gained their first significant political experience and began to shape local affairs. Daniels appreciated the need for broader social integration beyond the neighborhood. But, like Woods, he felt that progress toward this goal could only be promoted by certain neighborhood associations, including political clubs and consumer cooperatives, that linked the district to the surrounding community.[15] Thus, through neighborhood self-organization, ethnic groups made themselves a part of American life. Daniels advised those who wanted to foster this process to allow immigrants to control the programs intended for their benefit. Community organization must mean nothing less than a neighborhood that functioned "of itself," without constant interference.[16]

That an approach like community organizing could emerge beside normalizing intervention within Progressive philanthropy calls for some explanation. Casework fit well with the longstanding philanthropic interest in individual and family difficulties; the same cannot be said of efforts to tap the political capacity of marginal populations. Clearly, then, a discursive framework does not preclude participants from entertaining alternative problem formulations and practices. In this instance, the commitment of the settlement house residents to the modern social scientific norm of objective inquiry carried them beyond the analytical categories usually employed by philanthropy. But the discourse still influences even its deviant participants. Woods and most of his allies did not see any tension between their approach and the therapeutic, and they certainly did not repudiate the latter.

Expertise against Politics

While community organizers believed their moment had arrived, the drive for neighborhood activism and political autonomy ran against powerful intellectual and practical currents. If we begin outside the circle of Progressive philanthropy, several reformist discourses held that social integration depended upon the exercise of expert administrative skills rather than citizen action. Let us take as a first example sociology, the discipline within social science that enjoyed the closest relations with philanthropy. Sociologists strongly endorsed the emergence of public tutelage. Where traditional social control had weakened and the individual's own sense of restraint no longer checked destructive impulses, the molding of behavior by experts was essential to preserve order. State-sponsored normalizing intervention appeared to sociologists to provide the necessary artificial social control.[17] Their work is pertinent here because it repudiated popular action of the sort favored by Woods and his allies. Sociology, while professing its support for government responsiveness and accountability, mounted a strong attack on participation, condemning it as incompatible with the maintenance of social order under modern conditions. Given the association between sociology and philanthropy, this position necessarily colored philanthropic views of how best to deal with the collective efforts of marginal populations.

On the surface, to be sure, sociologists remained committed to democracy. Even as they eagerly promoted the direction of behavior by public social personnel, they insisted that the state be made answerable to the public. Edward A. Ross, for example, feared that social control might become so thorough that all unconventional doctrine would be submerged. He and his professional colleagues also feared the misuse of state power, its distortion by officials and experts into partisan class control. The checks proposed by sociologists included the development of autonomous social institutions, public debates and votes to establish the broad outlines of the public policy that the experts would enforce, public influence over the selection of experts through the setting of personnel standards, and the possibility of popular plebiscites as an ultimate formal restraint over administrative action.[18]

But the passion for order coexisted uneasily here with the faith in popular control, and the sociologists were more deeply wedded to the former. The voluntary groups that diluted state power also divided the individual's loyalty so that he did not identify with the entire community, and unscrupulous leaders manipulated his "tribal" feelings for their own purposes. The triumph of an all-inclusive community spirit, then, depended upon the elimination of the ties that bound people to sect or clan. It was necessary to do away with ethnic and other working-class organizations. At precisely the moment when ordinary citizens most needed a vehicle to express their concerns, sociology proposed to silence their collective voice.[19] By the same token, if experts were held directly accountable to the masses, social stability would be placed at risk. Prejudice and uninformed opinions, which sociologists like Luther Lee Bernard took to be the ruling force in a pure democracy, did not make for rational social control. Better that rule should devolve upon a scientific elite; at least it, unlike other dominant classes, would understand its social responsibility.[20]

At the most fundamental level, the sociological formulation left no space in which ordinary citizens might define their own future. With modern society increasingly interdependent, human action introduced a dangerous element of uncertainty, the risk of consequences the individual did not intend or foresee. Scientific administration would do away with action, Bernard promised, substituting in its place behavior guided by exact knowledge. Experts would instruct the individual on the social effects of his conduct, and even, should he be delinquent or defective, choose his activities for him.[21] As for action in its collective form, which merely multiplied uncertainty, this threat, too, would be contained by the social scientific regime. Experts would remove the social contradictions that generated friction among people, so that the motive force behind politics would disappear. Individuals who seek the same end and follow a path charted by social specialists find nothing to dispute or debate. In sum, sociology sought to depoliticize citizenship, trusting instead to expert stewardship to draw individuals, particularly members of marginal groups, into the community.

Popular action was also undermined by another important discursive movement linked to philanthropy, public administration. In the previous chapter I explored how therapeutic activists drew upon managerialist reform concepts for antidotes to the problems facing the human services. We return to administrative discourse now because, I suggest, it also challenged the logic of political participation. The administrative reformers spoke, using a rhetoric of democracy, of what government owed the common people, of new social rights, but went on to assume that the state's material outputs could provide the complete basis for political membership. The implicit redefinition of democracy stripped it of all vital political content. Again, when we recall the impact of administrative ideas on philanthropy, we can only conclude that this constricted view of politics would influence the thinking about community organization.

Beyond the material benefits produced by socially concerned public administration, advocates claimed, such a system led people to view their government in a new light. They no longer saw a corrupt or indifferent regime that stood apart from their aspirations. The public domain was now, in a very literal sense, a public household, providing all that a home could be expected to provide. Citizens in turn began to feel affection for their community, to take pride in its achievements. Through public services, in other words, the city generated civic identity.[22] It also inspired renewed interest in public affairs. Voter apathy reflected the irrelevance of municipal government to everyday problems. But the same attitude would not be found when government helped people to find work, looked after their health and cleanliness, transported them at low cost, and maintained parks for their recreation. Policies that touched them would inspire close popular scrutiny. As Mary Kingsbury Simkhovitch put it, where politics "becomes the community deciding its own destiny, indifferentism will disappear."[23]

Yet, in fact, public administration could find little for citizens to decide. Certainly government could be effective only if it possessed mechanisms that let officials determine public opinion; the failure of such mechanisms had contributed substantially to the breakdown of public accountability. For this reason administrative reformers recommended the use of citizen surveys to yield a more accurate picture of community needs. Some support also was expressed for instruments of direct democracy, like the initiative and the referendum, that would give people further opportunities to criticize policies and hold officials responsible.[24] Nevertheless, municipal government was supposed to express a vision articulated not by ordinary people but by city planners, engineers, public health professionals, and others with advanced training. Frederic Howe believed these experts could adequately represent the needs of an entire metropolis. On most policy questions, Henry Bruere remarked, proper administrative methods made citizen action quite unnecessary. Direct democracy really belonged to a bygone era, before officials had accepted their responsibility to join efficiency to a social program.[25] Government, it might be said, could serve its constituents better than they could hope to serve themselves.

Public administration thus entailed a curiously truncated understanding of political membership. Public services and benefits forged a strong link between the individual and the community. Meanwhile, policy making occurred within the closed circle formed by experts and department managers. They were expected to interpret the needs of constituents and to act in their interest, all without having to engage in the messy public deliberations that encouraged special pleading. But this approach to public welfare, which we can best label technocratic, deprived citizenship of active meaning: although the citizen acquired new material entitlements, he was assigned no corresponding tasks or obligations. He assumed the passive role of a recipient. For all the anticipation of renewed popular involvement, public administration accorded participation a most insignificant practical role. The citizen was called upon to do no more than express his general satisfaction with the bureaucratic outputs he had received.

Neighborhood Adjustment

These critiques of participation as a path to social membership were not the only significant challenges to neighborhood activism. Others came from within philanthropy itself. To begin with, community organizers set out to put their stamp upon the spontaneous political life of the district. The neighborhood's raw political potential, they believed, could be tapped most effectively with an assist from without. Existing groups were to be drawn into the orbit of the local settlement house or the school center; for segments of the community that lacked the opportunity to organize themselves, notably the women, organizers would take the lead in forming a new group.[26] The settlements quickly established a network of clubs linked together through house councils, while the first school center sponsored by the People's Institute worked to foster support for an elected neighborhood council.[27] Through these first attempts to strengthen local democracy by building upon latent or immature organizing tendencies, certain positive results were achieved: neighborhood groups found that access to settlement facilities made it easier to conduct their activities; leaders acquired valuable political skills; and the unorganized began to coalesce for the first time.

For most community organizers, it was not enough just to provide the instrument through which the neighborhood might organize itself. Popular activism had to be cultivated and given direction. Woods advised the settlement worker to sift through the neighborhood's organized activity, to learn not only how it might be stimulated but also how it might be directed toward "some better and worthier end."[28] Good-government reform ideals—the notion that politics should be a selfless activity, the principle that the public interest ought to guide public affairs, and so forth—shaped the community organization outlook on politics. While professing their sympathy for other forms of political expression, organizers were plainly irked by spontaneous strikes, ward politics, and anarchist and socialist street meetings.[29] A few settlement leaders dissented, arguing that working people must find their own voice, even if it struck outsiders as vulgar.[30] But this view was not widely shared, and practice was shaped by the dominant sentiment. The settlements and school centers accordingly promoted formalized debates on tense issues, instructed the locals on the fine points of parliamentary style, and preached the virtues of honest and efficient municipal government.[31]

By encouraging only acceptable forms of participation, community organizers subverted an important precondition for the self-constitution of community. They sought through their didactic measures to sanitize collective action. As the minority of organizers realized, however, the crude political vehicles that the settlements and school centers sought to displace served an essential purpose: people needed to vent their emotions, announce their grievances, and forcefully press their demands. The neighborhood voice, which ought to have been as raw and unrefined as everyday life, was prematurely modulated. If people are to place their confidence in collective action, it must permit the expression of authentic passions.

Therapeutic practitioners also helped to undermine support for political mobilization. In the initial flush of enthusiasm for neighborhood work, it is true, social personnel did pay greater attention to indigenous groups and to informal self-help arrangements in the districts they served. The private relief agencies, for example, made a serious effort to recruit visitors drawn from a working-class background.[32] However, as I pointed out above, the therapeutic and political approaches rest upon such different assumptions that they can be brought together only in unstable combinations. Once social personnel convinced themselves that advances in casework techniques had enhanced the constructive potential of therapeutic intervention, it was inevitable that they would begin to ignore political action as a means to secure social integration.

The definitive break came after the war, with the development of the new behavioral sciences. These indicated that casework sufficed to link together the individual and the community: through family and individual therapies, marginal clients not only exorcised their private demons but made their peace with the social order. Without such treatment, moreover, the disturbed person who engaged in political activism would remain maladjusted. Casework techniques were indispensable, but whether people shaped their collective destiny by deliberation and self-organization mattered not at all. As casework doctrine was disseminated during the 1920s, an increasing number of social personnel were exposed to this antipolitical stance.

If political action no longer counted in the scheme of normalization, community organizers would need a new mission. Mary E. Richmond, the casework theorist, proposed that the organizers' special skill lay in their ability to link together the expert services available to the neighborhood and to overcome its objections to external intervention.[33] This formulation, by casting the organizer in the role of a mediator between the district and the human-services apparatus, minimized the political role of the neighborhood itself, and so eviscerated the radicalism of collective initiative. Significantly, leading community organizers like Woods accepted their subordination to the therapeutic project.[34] Given that the neighborhood could not meet immediate crises like poverty and delinquency, he reasoned, it was necessary to call upon outside specialists and agencies. Woods took heart from their efforts to enlist neighborhood influences to sustain the progress clients had made: surveillance by the therapeutic apparatus would be that much more effective if it could capitalize on the "gossip of the tenements."[35]

The final blow against neighborhood mobilization was struck by the sweeping effort during and after the First World War to rationalize philanthropic programs and services. Worried about duplication and waste, local philanthropic leaders began to speak of the need to streamline the service apparatus. Neighborhood organizations were seen not as the vehicle of grassroots action but merely as a source of confusion and disarray in the human services. As part of the broader quest to achieve efficiency of effort, therefore, the indigenous associations had to be brought into proper working balance with each other and with the service professionals. This in turn required the development of a new organizational instrument that could impose direction on the many different social and neighborhood agencies. Initially many philanthropic activists backed the "social unit plan," which aimed to link neighborhood residents to social agencies through block councils. But when the first experiment in Cincinnati antagonized local elites and was abruptly terminated, enthusiasm waned.[36] An instrument more to the liking of the philanthropic establishment was found when it sought to mobilize support for the American war effort. In cities across the country philanthropic activists joined with local business and political leaders to establish community councils and war chests. These bodies, through their control of funds, dictated tasks to individual social and neighborhood agencies, and thus demonstrated that order could be brought to the service apparatus through large-scale, centralized federation.[37]

After the war period, when agencies might have returned to their independent ways, the federation movement continued to gather strength. Rather than fold, the war chests made themselves over into community chests. They proceeded to extend their reach, aided in no small measure by backing from local chambers of commerce, business leaders, and other wealthy patrons. Along the way, the federation movement arrived at its own definition of community organization: organization meant strict adherence by all voluntary groups to the local chest's service plan. By insisting that they must be free to use their staff expertise, the casework agencies were able to secure steady cash support without excessive federation interference in their operation. Settlement houses and neighborhood groups, however, felt heavy financial pressure to convert themselves into adjuncts of other service agencies.[38]

Federation and centralization confronted community organizers with a challenge. On the one hand, they had defended independent action by small neighborhood groups, while the community councils and chests threatened to suffocate the simpler associations originating within the neighborhood; on the other hand, like others in philanthropy, they were intrigued by the promise of efficiency. We can best follow how they understood and resolved this tension through the work of Eduard Lindeman, after the war a guiding figure in the field. In his estimation, the rationalization of neighborhood effort promised to be a mixed blessing. Contrary to the aims of community organization, social agencies, whether acting alone or through federated arrangements, did not reach out beyond their elite leadership to recruit popular support.[39] Still, whatever misgivings one harbored about the service machinery, certain points had to be noted in its defense. Social agencies, by supplying the essential services of specialists, brought to every community crucial resources. To this must be added the other benefits of administrative rationalization, such as the elimination of redundant services.[40] It was also necessary, Lindeman pointed out, to consider the alternatives. If the community chose instead to address its problems through political organizations, it would soon run aground on the weaknesses of mass democracy. Political bodies discounted the skills of the specialist, political leaders manipulated their uninformed constituents, and decisions were reached in haste, often without resolving the conflicts among groups. For a community trying to nurture in itself an organic social process, Lindeman concluded in a decisive break with Woods's early position, political action was inappropriate.[41]

Community organizers therefore needed to redefine their enterprise in a way that reconciled rationalization with local participation. Because no simple approach would meet these requirements, Lindeman urged a hybrid arrangement. Agencies with qualified staff ought to be encouraged to serve the community, and their coordinating chests and federations likewise ought to be promoted. But to protect against domination of local organized activities by this social machinery, the community also would have to establish formal links with the service apparatus. Clients and other interest groups in the district would be represented on agency and federation boards. Henceforth the service providers would subordinate themselves to direction by the entire community, thus assuring that their efforts reflected its collective interest. As the people came to see that they controlled vital local institutions, moreover, they would feel themselves empowered and develop a sense of membership.[42]

Lindeman regarded his solution as democratic, but it actually pointed to participation without politics. In his view, political conflict was resolved through brute strength, one group submerging another, to the detriment of the community. For its best interest, some mechanism had to be found to give recognition to all essential group concerns. The implication seemed to him plain enough: "This means community organization on a non-political basis."[43] When conflict arose, as it inevitably must, it would be resolved bloodlessly, through the application of rational procedure. The social service council or a similar body of citizens and experts would convene to hear the dispute, public comment would be solicited, the council would study the underlying problem, and the specialists would find the remedy.[44] Lindeman in principle reserved final authority for the community, yet he knew full well that the process lent itself to domination by the experts and the agencies. As he said, following the claims of the sociologists, science would settle most community disputes, making political parties, mass meetings, and majority votes an anachronism.[45] Hence, although the community movement may have stood in Lindeman's mind for the formal assertion of local control, he ultimately came down on the side of community management by the social agencies.

Retreat from Politics

The original proponent of popular activism regarded the mounting incursions of outside agents in the neighborhood with some foreboding. After the war, as Woods surveyed the accomplishments of various Progressive movements, he was disturbed by their impact on collective initiative. He and a colleague noted that although public administration brought greater efficiency to municipal departments and valuable services to the community, the gains came with a substantial cost. Government baffled and frustrated ordinary people; they encountered complex rules and rigid procedures, could not get comprehensible answers, and were forced to wander from office to office in search of help. At the same time, because centralization left the neighborhood without any real role to play, they were deprived of the opportunity to learn how to manage their own affairs.[46] Woods expressed misgivings, too, about the effects of the therapeutic movement. It was true that the new human services had attained a high level of technical proficiency and functioned well as a bulwark against corrosive social forces. Yet, where the settlements had enlisted their neighbors to help run programs, social agencies seemed disinterested in active local cooperation.[47]

However, if by Woods's own reasoning this depoliticization of neighborhood life demanded a repudiation, he now equivocated. Indigenous associations too frequently fell under the sway of the wrong elements; the settlement urged sensible reform policies only to discover that the neighborhood held back, ruled more by emotion than intellect. Clearly, though he wished to let the neighborhood govern itself, it did not yet possess the requisite leadership, maturity, or administrative capacity.[48] Reliance upon specialists was a necessary expedient. Woods still felt major institutions should be placed under neighborhood control, but he proposed to wait until the people of the district had cultivated better administrative and political skills. In the meantime social agencies and public departments should be challenged to do more for those in distress.[49]

John Daniels saw this "reappraisal" of neighborhood capacity for what it was—a full-fledged retreat from the political approach to social membership. Convinced that working people were not ready for serious responsibility, settlement residents and other community organizers made little effort to tap the inherent political capacity of the district, setting out instead to create new neighborhood organizations from scratch. Their self-proclaimed passion for democratic autonomy thus revealed itself as hollow. But their constituents did not care to be dismissed as underdeveloped. The people's reaction demonstrated that Woods had been right about them in the first place: precisely because they could run their own affairs, they took community tutelage as an affront to their dignity. The strained relations between the settlement and the men of the district actually bore out Woods's original point. Once people have forged their own collective instruments, they welcome no others. Rejection of the settlement was for Daniels not a sign of political incapacity but, to the contrary, clear evidence that the neighborhood already had discovered its own true collective voice. With the limited power available to them, the people had made a good start toward building a community of their own.[50]

Woods's flight from his earlier radical position requires some discussion. The move suggests both a profound lack of patience and a much more conditional commitment to autonomous politics than he had earlier admitted. We have seen that he believed that marginal groups would create community out of their own shared experiences. But when a people constitute themselves, the results of the process cannot be orchestrated. Support for democratic autonomy, then, cannot be reconciled with a demand for a particular outcome. Yet Woods expected community to emerge quickly, guided by the norms embodied in his own good-government ideal. When neighborhood politics proceeded more haltingly than he had anticipated, he found this deeply discouraging. Perhaps more important, when the collective initiative of the people living around the settlement did not live up to the noble standard he had imagined, he refused to see their efforts as steps forward.

In ceasing to conceive of political action as a vehicle to create social membership, community organizers inflicted a long-term wound on their own movement. Woods and his early allies, with their radical talk about self-creating communities, had stimulated an important discourse about power and citizenship. Now they flinched before its implications. It could, of course, be revived again, and we shall see that it has been on several conspicuous occasions. But each time someone took notice of what marginal groups could do through their own self-directed associations, the realization would be treated as a new discovery. Progressive community organizers did not found a tradition upon which others might build, did not bequeath to their successors a body of experiences that could be studied carefully for broader lessons.[51] Hence the first mistakes were fated to be repeated time and again.

Of even greater significance for our purposes, the failure by Woods, Lindeman, and company to sustain what they had begun had an enduring impact upon the future course of social policy. Their attempt to define an approach based on the political mobilization of marginal groups faltered at a pivotal moment. After more than two decades of dramatic change in social policy, marked by the emergence of a range of programs and agencies, policy activists during the postwar period turned to the preservation of the territory they had conquered. It followed that they would become settled in their understanding of marginality and in their choice of the means by which it would be addressed. At such a critical juncture, if the political approach were to survive, it required a base in institutions that embodied Woods's democratic principles. Such institutions—for example, organs of neighborhood self-government—might compete for policy influence with casework agencies and public bureaucracies. When community organizers stopped fighting for neighborhood autonomy and responsibility, however, the opportunity to create bastions of support for popular activism was lost. In contrast, proponents of the therapeutic model did not concede the terrain, and, as we have seen, their ideas found a relatively secure home in human service agencies and schools of social work.

The demise of the political approach also made itself felt within these organizations, in the form of a narrowing of vision. I noted that Woods and other settlement figures had pressed their philanthropic associates to make better use of neighborhood resources, and that caseworkers before the war had responded by looking for ways to encourage client mobilization. Here lay the seeds of a creative tension within social agencies. But, again, when community organizers abandoned the essential core of their doctrine, they left their sympathizers in charity organizations and public welfare departments with only platitudes about the virtues of popular involvement, not a real alternative. Meanwhile, personality sciences and casework methods were rising to new levels of sophistication. Social personnel welcomed an approach that seemed supremely sure of itself.

From that point forward, the political approach to social marginality faded from sight, and it did not continue to exercise a dynamic influence upon policy discussion. The therapeutic sector began to assert a practical monopoly over the field: since there were no vehicles through which people might manage things for themselves, programs could only be administered through the larger public and private social agencies. Once such agencies took firm hold, anyone wishing to foster a decentralized, neighborhood-based path to social membership would find them extraordinarily difficult to dislodge. Moreover, inside the agencies, now that efforts to mobilize the poor had unraveled, the neighborhood was seen as irrelevant, a corporate entity that was to be bypassed by programs targeted at individuals and families. At most, the neighborhood might make a convenient administrative unit; more likely, it represented a source of contamination, something to be overcome. Policy entrepreneurs shaped in this agency climate accordingly took it as a given that the integration of marginal populations required relentless normalizing interventions—not power used by autonomous citizens, but power used to overwhelm citizen autonomy.

Part Three

THE POLITICAL LIMITS OF EXPANSION

Seven

Nationalizing Public Tutelage

THE GREAT DEPRESSION gave rise to a new era of expansion in the therapeutic sector. Although the economic collapse sorely tested the human services, it also unleashed political forces that compelled elected officials to pursue broad revisions in public social policies. Therapeutic activists seized upon the opportunity provided by the New Deal to promote their doctrine at the federal level. They succeeded in putting into place minimal program structures, hardly a complete triumph but still a basis upon which it might be possible to make further incremental progress toward full realization of the therapeutic agenda. From then until the early 1960s, therapeutic activists pressed to secure more substantial federal resources for their ongoing efforts to normalize marginal populations.

A national therapeutic sector emerged initially in the 1930s through aggressive policy entrepreneurship by social personnel. During the Hoover administration and Roosevelt's first term, they pushed themselves into key administrative roles in public relief operations at the local, state, and national levels. Therapeutic doctrine also gained a toehold in the enlarged public relief mechanism when national emergency relief administrators forged a relationship with the schools of social work. Another opportunity to strengthen the therapeutic sector presented itself with the framing of legislation for a permanent social security program in 1935. Key therapeutic activists, especially those already in federal service, saw that they might press the case for federal support for Progressive human service programs like mothers' aid and public child welfare. But though the federal government was drawn into the therapeutic enterprise by the Social Security Act, other political actors imposed enough changes upon the legislation so as to render problematic its value for social personnel.

Even before the Act's weaknesses became clear, therapeutic activists realized that they had much work left to do. The Act at best provided a modest invitation for federally subsidized public tutelage. While federal money was funneled into public assistance and child welfare, no mention was made of adjustment as a goal or of casework as a method; further, the legislation did little to disturb existing impediments to good therapeutic practice, notably the vulnerability of social agencies to local opinion.

The prospects for public tutelage therefore rested on whether the federal bureaucracy could effectively disseminate therapeutic doctrine. Officials in the Children's Bureau and the Bureau of Public Assistance of the Social Security Board followed the two-sided political strategy that had been devised by movement leaders in the period following the First World War: state and local agencies were encouraged through pressure from above to adopt casework methods and objectives, and federal resources were committed in an effort to build up at the subnational level a core of personnel devoted to the therapeutic agenda.

Early returns on the Social Security Act and the bureaucratic drive to establish therapeutic principles as the working basis for local practice were decidedly uneven, but therapeutic activists had committed themselves. Localism defeated them more often than not. To this familiar pattern were added other ominous trends, in particular a splintering of the therapeutic effort and a narrowing of vision among various practitioners. Nevertheless, they pushed ahead after the Second World War along the same lines. If suasion alone did not yield a therapeutic outlook in assistance agencies or achieve service coordination in child welfare, surely the federal government could use additional resources to induce the desired behavior on the part of its subnational partners. Social personnel exploited new political openings in the 1950s and early 1960s—resurgent concerns about delinquency and dependency—to sell the idea of therapeutic intervention. In the end they were rewarded with legislation that explicitly embraced their approach and sought through better fiscal incentives and tougher sanctions to compel states and localities to do the same.

Crisis and Entrepreneurship

The economic collapse that began in 1929 confronted the modest human service apparatus with an extraordinary challenge. During the 1920s, social personnel had struggled to cope with a growing problem of poverty among certain groups bypassed by the general prosperity.[1] The combination of community chests and public relief agencies certainly had no extra capacity to cope with the misery brought on by mass unemployment. In short order, demands for relief exhausted the limited resources of private family welfare agencies and repeatedly forced public poor relief officials to seek additional funds from hard-pressed local and county governments.[2] As unemployed workers found themselves passed along from one office to another, sometimes given counseling instead of aid, their disenchantment and restiveness mounted. They vented their frustrations upon agency caseworkers. The caseworkers in turn began to complain about agency policies that degraded clients, to identify themselves less as professionals than as wage-labor employees. Before long this internal strife found an outlet in the larger cities in a growing rank-and-file movement. Its members called for a recasting of the profession with a new emphasis on more radical forms of social action.[3]

Much as a surge in joblessness forty years earlier had forced philanthropy to modify its assumptions, mainstream social workers were driven to reevaluate their discursive framework. Some concluded that, whatever the merits of casework in normal times, the method was unsuitable as a tool for dealing with mass unemployment. The people presenting themselves for help had managed on their own and had no special need of supervision.[4] Others retorted that a trained caseworker would treat applicants with compassion and respect. More than that, even in a general crisis casework skills could be used to sustain initiative among relief recipients and forestall the demoralization that sudden poverty might bring.[5] But it had to be conceded that many clients resented the suggestion that they needed any help beyond material assistance. The problem of client autonomy or "self-determination"—what the expert social technician should do when a person refused advice—thrust itself at last into the forefront of therapeutic discourse.

I have criticized the therapeutic movement for its initial failure to recognize this issue, for suggesting no limit on intervention, save for some vague wish to restore the client to a higher level of independent functioning. In fairness, it must be noted that casework theorists had begun to ponder the matter of autonomy in the 1920s, when Freudian doctrine first alerted them to the hidden dangers of manipulation in the worker-client relationship. But not until clients began asserting their autonomy in their routine dealings with relief agencies during the early Depression years did social workers agree that delineating the bounds of client self-determination was an urgent matter. A sharp debate ensued. One group, claiming for itself the label "democratic," held that as a matter of principle the caseworker was bound to address only those problems the client himself had identified.[6] This position was plainly unacceptable to practitioners of the Freudian persuasion who recognized the importance of denial and other psychological defense mechanisms. Yet even the psychoanalytic caseworker appreciated that, given the barrier posed by unconscious resistance, change could not be imposed on the client until he was prepared to accept it. As Gordon Hamilton put it, "Relationships are not taught, or forced, or directed, or managed—they are achieved." For prudential reasons, that is, it was necessary to respect client desires, at least in the short run.[7]

Clearly enough, then, the Depression brought turmoil and disarray upon the human services. But that is only part of the story, for many leading therapeutic activists recognized in the demise of the established welfare system a rare opportunity for policy entrepreneurship. They became convinced by the winter of 1930–31 of the need to dramatically expand public relief efforts. With private agencies running short of funds, public departments soon found themselves nearly alone in the relief field, a burden that taxed their limited administrative capability. Accordingly, a wave of social personnel made the jump from private to public auspices. While there were certainly other actors seeking to shape the program of the public departments, therapeutic activists saw an opening through which they might extend their influence.[8] They contended that public agencies ought to professionalize their staff, develop a diagnostic capability to identify cases needing intensive treatment, incorporate such techniques as family budget standards, and offer appropriate adjustment services.[9]

When it became apparent that local resources would not suffice to meet the rising tide of need, another opportunity presented itself. Social workers, along with many other groups, shifted their sights to the states as the next level of public authority. State governments could draw upon a broader tax base.[10] Beyond that obvious advantage, however, social personnel understood that the state represented the possibility of centralized leverage that could be used to overcome backward community attitudes in relief administration. The strategy, of course, was not new; what differed was the situation, which afforded the prospect of dramatically accelerating a transformation therapeutic activists had been pushing for a decade. State emergency relief organizations and enlarged public welfare departments required experienced personnel, and therefore sought to draw staff from the ranks of the private social agencies. Social workers recognized at once the logic of an alliance in which state administrators would support their drive to assert control from above over local practices and thus help introduce modern methods in the field.[11] In some states, notably New York with its Temporary Emergency Relief Administration in 1931, social workers assumed direct management responsibility for the emergency relief agency. They capitalized on this strong administrative position to establish statewide standards and to subsidize the placement of private agency caseworkers in local public relief, though communities still often did as they pleased.[12]

A similar pattern of entrepreneurship emerged on the national level, and seemed eventually to bear fruit, too. Early talk of a national relief effort was effectively sidetracked by the Hoover administration; even after state resources had been shown to be insufficient, the administration opposed relief loan legislation. Not until the approach of the 1932 election, with states veering toward bankruptcy, did the administration acquiesce in the creation of the Reconstruction Finance Corporation (RFC), which was vested with the authority to lend relief funds to the states. Social workers took up important positions in the RFC Relief Division. However, although they sought to repeat their strategy of top-down rationalization of relief administration, the statute left the federal agency without supervisory powers.[13] A more promising opportunity soon beckoned. In 1933 the new Roosevelt administration, recognizing the need to go beyond the RFC program, introduced several emergency relief measures. Social workers expressed special interest in the Federal Emergency Relief Administration (FERA). Modeled after the New York emergency relief agency, FERA was granted the sweeping control over state and local relief operations that the RFC had lacked. To head the new organization, moreover, the president chose Harry Hopkins. A social worker himself, Hopkins had encouraged the use of social personnel in the New York emergency program. Social workers welcomed him as one of their own and looked forward to a strengthened partnership between their enterprise and the national government.[14]

Far from representing a secure base for spreading the therapeutic vision, however, FERA became an arena in which all the conflicts that had surfaced in state and local relief politics played themselves out on the national level. Different factions grappled for control, each winning victories at a given point in the administrative hierarchy only to be confounded at another. Contrary to social workers' expectations, Hopkins declined to treat the program as an experiment in the application of casework techniques. The senior administrators he chose, only a few of whom were social workers, shared his skepticism about conventional casework and wanted only to assure a minimum material standard of living for the unemployed. He also ruled that public funds could only be spent at the subnational level by public agencies, thereby excluding the casework-oriented family service agencies that had been participating in public relief efforts.[15] FERA administration at the local level, meanwhile, reflected very different outlooks. Directors of the local offices were often businessmen or administrators with no background in the relief field. Through such persons the sentiments of local elites found convenient expression. On the other hand, in the larger cities where the unemployed were particularly militant, FERA offices faced considerable pressure from below; the rank-and-file movement drew much of its strength from FERA employees in the lowest rung of the local staff structure. With so many contrary elements at work, the tone of the program varied sharply from one place to another.[16]

Other elements may have preempted the top and bottom rungs of the FERA apparatus, but between them lay the vital levels of the state and regional organization. The FERA leadership viewed many permanent state welfare agencies as unduly partisan or hopelessly inefficient, so it moved to set up its own provisional state subsidiaries. Then, because the central staff was too small to exercise supervision over the states, FERA added a regional staff. Not only did the regional offices interpret Washington's policy to the field, but they also assumed responsibility for disseminating technical advice.[17] Social workers seized the chance to insinuate themselves into these middle levels of the national relief program. Hopkins and the core group encouraged the influx of therapeutic practitioners from private agencies as an antidote to localism. To the consternation of the national leadership, however, social workers made it clear that they had their own agenda, which embraced casework principles intended to realize their broader ideal of a social living standard.[18] Once inside FERA they exerted pressure to redirect agency policy along the lines suggested by their profession. It must be said that FERA never became a human service organization; social workers often lost the struggle to define state programs, and local offices found it easy to undermine standards sent down from above. But the senior officials around Hopkins recognized the validity of casework methods, even if emergency relief was not a normalizing program, and acknowledged the need for more administrators with casework skills at the subnational level.[19]

This admitted shortage led FERA to embark upon an initiative with lasting consequences. If too few professional social workers were available, more would have to be manufactured—in the American style, mass produced in the shortest possible time. Agency social workers at first went into the field to conduct training sessions, but the results were disappointing. FERA therefore set aside funds during its second year to send some one thousand administrators and field personnel to accredited schools of social work for a semester of formal graduate education. Presumably the national FERA leadership expected these students to absorb its own conception of social service with a minimal emphasis on casework. But the schools themselves still built their curriculum around the methodology of intensive casework and, while there was some adjustment to the federal sponsor's tastes, the FERA student cohort received a concentrated dose of therapeutic doctrine.[20] Beyond that, the federal government had forged an alliance with the social work education establishment, a lesson in cooperation that would be remembered.

By the time many of these students completed their studies, FERA itself was about to go out of existence. It was the victim in part of its chief's aggressiveness. Hopkins, determined to get money into the hands of the unemployed without favoritism or corruption, compelled the states to accept many of his demands for program management. State officials responded with sharp complaints about federal intrusiveness and learned to call his bluff—he was extremely reluctant for humanitarian reasons to withhold state allocations. In retrospect it can be seen that his willingness to circumvent existing relief entities, both public and private, entailed heavy political costs. The approach presupposed a national administrative capacity that did not exist and snubbed sources of political support vital for any program so inherently controversial. Congress was loathe to approve another relief or public welfare program that gave the responsible federal agency such discretion to trample upon its state and local counterparts.[21] When the Roosevelt administration shifted its focus to a permanent social welfare mechanism, the decision was reached to wind down FERA operations and fold up the organization.

During this concluding phase, the FERA leadership took an important step to assure a continuing place for the therapeutic movement in the forthcoming social security apparatus. Remaining administrative funds were allocated to the states to retain those supervisors who had completed the educational programs at the social work schools. FERA went so far as to advise the states that casework skills, though of limited value for emergency relief, would be particularly suited to permanent assistance programs. The states discharged nonprofessionals first.[22] Thus, while therapeutic practitioners could claim only modest success in bending FERA to their purposes, they alone endured the agency's demise, an administrative nucleus that would make its mark on what followed.

Human Services through Social Security

Most policymakers in the administration and in Congress gave little attention during the debates over social security to therapeutic programs like mother's aid. Believing he had addressed the immediate crisis during his first two years in office, Roosevelt hoped to set in place mechanisms that would assure ordinary citizens protection from future economic calamity. The cabinet-level Committee on Economic Security, which he established in June 1934, assumed that social insurance was the best instrument to provide that protection. Since the president held that the federal government ought to exit the relief field as soon as possible, the Committee proposed that care of residual groups—the unemployables not covered by social insurance—be shifted back to the states.[23] There were exceptions to this general principle, exceptions forced on the planners by pressures from below. As several historical studies stress, the Depression had unleashed powerful political insurgencies among the unemployed and the elderly that the administration could not afford to ignore.[24] The legislative package incorporated federal work relief and a grant-in-aid program to the states for public assistance for the elderly. No comparable constituencies had mobilized to demand federal support for public tutelage.

Still, by this stage of the Depression, therapeutic activists had come to look upon the federal government for their salvation. The human service apparatus had reached a crisis point. Public concern had centered on mass relief for the unemployed, not the problems of marginal groups. Existing normalizing programs had competed futilely for state and local funds against unemployment aid and old-age relief. So, for example, mothers'-aid programs, after expanding at the outset of the Depression, teetered now on the verge of collapse. Grants had been reduced and eligible mothers denied aid; in fact, many more fatherless families received help from FERA than from mother's aid.[25] Social personnel saw a real danger that the apparatus they had so laboriously pieced together over the previous decades would be completely undone. As one child welfare leader cautioned, "It is important that the particular gains made in more than twenty years through this type of legislation be not lost or swallowed up in the greater mass of unemployment relief now being distributed throughout the country." The importance of marginality had to be restored in the policy process. Even before the Committee on Economic Security convened, social workers had begun to speak of federal subsidies for components of the Progressive human service network.[26]

The framing of a permanent national social security structure presented an opening for proponents of the human services. As it happened, the agenda of therapeutic activists dovetailed neatly with that of the Committee on Economic Security: the former hoped to maintain distinct programs for marginal groups, with a strong casework orientation, while the latter intended that such groups receive care outside the basic social insurance scheme. The necessary institutional foundation was already in place in the form of child welfare and mothers'-aid departments, augmented by the FERA social work trainees. It would be a straightforward matter not only to maintain existing public social agencies but to broaden their coverage.[27] Creation of a national welfare state also might be the vehicle by which the therapeutic movement could pursue its other long-term goals. Even during the worst of the Depression, it never lost sight of the need to rationalize the human services or improve standards. Thus in the early 1930s the Children's Bureau, increasingly vexed by the failure of the juvenile court to function as a true social agency, began casting about for ways to circumvent judicial tutelage.[28] Federal resources could provide a wedge for reorganizing the division of responsibilities in the child welfare network so as to reduce the role of the court.

If all these aspirations were to be fulfilled in the absence of a mass constituency, a champion had to step forward. Enter the Children's Bureau and its leaders Katherine Lenroot and Martha Elliot. Aside from recognizing the need for federal resources in the human services, they saw the chance to expand the Bureau's responsibilities. Since its maternal and infant health care program had lapsed some five years earlier, the agency had been limited to research activities. New programs meant a return to direct operational authority, an organizational plum. With much to gain, Lenroot and Elliot adopted a vigorous entrepreneurial role during the deliberations of the Committee on Economic Security. Of particular interest to us, they persuaded the Committee of the value of federal subsidies for child welfare and mother's aid.[29]

The child welfare program was represented as a modest effort to demonstrate to the states the great value of coordinated local services, but Bureau leaders had in mind another purpose as well. Social personnel had drawn encouragement from a handful of pioneering efforts by public child welfare agencies at the county level. Through their comprehensive approach to children's needs, they addressed a range of problems, and did so without the liabilities of judicial tutelage. These agencies, then, seemed the best alternative to the juvenile court. As the program was designed, the Bureau would retain discretionary control over the funds, to permit it to insist upon the proper standards for participating agencies. By working with an autonomous local administrative structure, the federal government could make services available to *children*, not to the *court*. Court intervention might be preempted in all cases save the most serious incidents of delinquency.[30]

By comparison, the Children's Bureau contemplated no comparable organizational innovation under its plan for a federal grant-in-aid program, Aid to Dependent Children (ADC), to match a portion of state mothers'-aid expenditures. Experience gathered over several decades had established the most suitable organizational model—a state department exercising close leadership over local administrative units. With the Children's Bureau added to the line of authority, an unambiguous commitment to therapeutic principles would be assured.[31] A difficulty presented itself, of course, in those states that lacked a centralized public welfare apparatus. To prevent the program from fragmenting and falling prey to community pressures, the architects of the legislation decided to mandate that a single state agency assume responsibility for ADC. Other features of the draft legislation sought to assure more reliable and adequate payments, professional administration, and full statewide coverage so counties could no longer opt out of the program.

The human service proposals met no opposition within the Committee on Economic Security, but resistance surfaced as the legislation moved through review by the administration. In seeking to lay claim via ADC to a public assistance role, the Children's Bureau provoked interagency competition. The national FERA staff argued that it should retain control over all federal relief efforts and that mother's aid should be redefined so that it became available to a wider range of families, in effect a form of general relief. Although it is tempting to dismiss the FERA gambit as a desperate move by an agency due to expire, the dispute highlights two very different orientations to public assistance. The Children's Bureau accepted the need for cooperation with the states and represented the therapeutic agenda in its purest form; FERA, on the other hand, insisted on more centralized administration and spoke against a casework emphasis. Just before the social security package was submitted to Congress, the FERA faction prevailed, and the administration's draft bill placed ADC under FERA.[32]

Further political maneuverings reshaped both the ADC and child welfare titles as the bill made its way through Congress. Here, as within the administration, these parts of the legislation drew little attention. Yet such notice as they did receive sufficed to undo much of what the Children's Bureau and the FERA staff hoped to accomplish. In the first place, ADC was entrusted to neither FERA nor the Children's Bureau but to the new Social Security Board. (The Board also acquired the other federal assistance programs, Old Age Assistance and Aid to the Blind.)[33] At the same time, Congress deleted language that would have allowed the federal government to set minimum subsistence payments and professional employment standards for assistance personnel. The first of these changes came at the behest of Southern members; some have attributed their action to racist fears that a federal agency might use a minimum grant rule to give black women a viable alternative to low-wage labor. Other scholars contend the legislative amendments were a reaction to excessive national control brought on by the FERA experience. That Congress denied the federal government FERA-type personnel authority adds support to the latter interpretation.[34] Damage was also done to ADC through sheer Congressional indifference: when administration policymakers pointed out that the federal maximum for matching family grants allowed nothing for the caretaker, the Senate Finance Committee reportedly did not show enough interest to change the provision.[35] Meanwhile, the child welfare proposal ruffled feathers among Catholic child protection agencies, which feared that federal money would lead to government interference in their work. These sectarian groups were prepared to support the bill if the program were confined to rural areas, a deal the Children's Bureau readily accepted.[36]

When we seek to weigh the impact of the Social Security Act on the development of the therapeutic sector, two points stand out. First, the push by the Children's Bureau leadership and its professional allies to rationalize human services largely came to naught. Public assistance rested under the aegis of a new agency with no demonstrated commitment to casework doctrine, few means to contain localism, and no organizational link to child welfare. As for the child welfare program, though it remained in its natural bureaucratic home, the sponsors sacrificed much of the potential for assuring coordinated services in their compromise with the sectarian elements. Already the disjointed efforts of private, judicial, and local public actors had resulted in a service labyrinth.[37] According to the conventional wisdom of the therapeutic movement, such a situation called out for reorganization from above. Yet federal child welfare funds could not be put to use to counter the accumulating irrationalities of the urban child protection field.

Second, the Act both reflected and contributed to a fundamental redefinition of marginality, with far-reaching implications for the later course of welfare policy. The Progressive therapeutic movement had portrayed much of the working class as maladjusted; it followed that normalizing measures must be broadly targeted. But the Depression called into doubt the sweeping claim of maladjustment, thanks largely to agitation by popular movements. Even human service practitioners retreated from their grander ambitions so they might save programs targeted at the most marginal groups. In laying down the apparatus of a permanent welfare state, the Roosevelt administration accepted the narrowing of social marginality. Its particular contribution, expressing the President's own bias, was to make economic utility the decisive test: marginal persons were those who were economically superfluous. For the productive, social insurance would provide security; for the unemployable, there would be means-tested assistance and, if therapeutic activists had their way, casework services to help in the effort to cope. This bifurcation of welfare policy, as has often been remarked, could only sharpen the distinction between the two groups, a distinction Progressive philanthropy had never recognized.[38]

If we take a skeptical view of the merits of the therapeutic enterprise, this division between social insurance and public assistance appears as a mixed blessing. Critics of the insurance/assistance distinction point out that it has allowed the degrading treatment of assistance recipients. In a culture that values economic output as the supreme measure of individual merit, those with no place in the economy become the new unworthy poor. Such thinking gives rise to practices designed to make assistance as undesirable as possible.[39] More to the point here: from the perspective of social personnel, recipients cannot lay claim to the autonomy due (economically) contributing members of society. Recipients, by definition marginal, are seen as likely candidates for normalizing intervention, whether they desire it or not. On the other hand, with the inclusion of many workers in social insurance, the imperial ambitions of the therapeutic movement were checked. Some social workers urged that casework services be extended to include insurance beneficiaries, but the idea never caught on.[40] For the time being, at least, a point of access into the working class family had been closed off.

Institutionalizing Casework

As the dust settled, it was not clear what the Social Security Act meant for the therapeutic movement. The law seemed to offer little concrete support for public tutelage. Although a child welfare program was established, the initial appropriation of some $1.5 million was exceedingly modest. The public assistance titles made no mention of normalizing services or therapeutic goals. Social personnel understood this silence to reflect implicit support for their approach.[41] All the same, everything depended upon whether the responsible agencies shared their interpretation. How the Children's Bureau and Social Security Board defined their mission in implementing the Act would determine whether the therapeutic sector had found the vehicle to transcend its humble status.

The record of the Children's Bureau left no doubt that it would pursue the therapeutic agenda, and it did so aggressively as it introduced child welfare demonstration programs. From its inception the Bureau had regarded itself as an instrument to spread the therapeutic idea. Now that the Bureau had been given a direct role, it defined child welfare to include a strong emphasis on normalizing services. The Act also gave the administering agency certain means to assure that its conception of the program would be reflected in the field. State plans had to be reviewed by the Bureau. Through this plan-approval process, it moved swiftly to forge ties with state-level welfare administrators and persuade them of the value of a well-ordered therapeutic approach. Of value, too, was language unique to the child welfare title of the Act that retained for the Bureau the power to set personnel standards. It was thus possible to assure that participating agencies shared its commitment to professionalism. With trained social personnel in short supply, the agency reached out to the network of FERA workers who had received graduate training to form the nucleus for state child welfare departments. Program funds were released to more than thirty states during the first year.[42]

Although Children's Bureau officials and their allies liked to point to the progress achieved by the program, the early results were mixed at best. On the plus side of the ledger from the agency's view, child welfare services expanded in rural areas in which they had been in short supply, bringing therapeutic doctrine to bear in remote corners of American life. The rural departments, unobstructed by preexisting private or public agencies, also devised well-coordinated service networks.[43] Furthermore, appreciating the insufficient supply of child welfare specialists, the Bureau moved immediately to continue the FERA alliance with schools of social work. Use of federal administrative funds for educational leaves was encouraged so state and local personnel could obtain some graduate training. Through this they were introduced to casework methods and therapeutic philosophy, about both of which they were expected to proselytize upon their return to their agencies.[44] On the other side of the coin, the program's faults could not be denied, though Bureau leaders tended to soft-pedal problems as they tried to pry additional funds out of the states and Congress. Services in urban areas remained fragmented, wasteful, and incomplete. Nothing was done to dislodge the juvenile court from its central position.[45] Indeed, even in rural counties, the quest to generate an institutional counterweight to the court foundered on local political realities. Rural judges, powerful figures not lightly crossed, looked upon the child welfare worker as a rival who needed to be reduced to an adjunct of the juvenile court. The isolated worker frequently chose cooperation as the route to survival. In such instances the child welfare agency converted itself into the court's probation arm, thereby augmenting the resources available for judicial tutelage.[46]

Where it might have been predicted that the Children's Bureau would adopt a therapeutic orientation toward child welfare, public assistance under the Social Security Board presents a more interesting case. The Board, a new agency unbound by fixed habits or previous commitments, could chart its own path.[47] It chose to regard public assistance as a normalizing activity. ADC and the assistance programs for the aged and the blind were grouped together under the Bureau of Public Assistance (BPA), and Jane Hoey, an experienced social worker, was chosen as its first head. She proceeded to fill other key positions with her professional peers.[48] While this seemed to indicate a tilt toward the therapeutic approach, BPA operated in a far more complex environment than did the Children's Bureau. A few staff appointments by no means settled federal policy, much less the actual character of public assistance administration.

To begin with, the external political obstacles confronting the Social Security Board and BPA were formidable. Since the FERA model of top-down control had been deemed unsuitable, the cooperation of subnational governmental units would have to be induced by less coercive means. Yet states and localities had their own conceptions of federal public assistance grants. They were particularly eager to shift the cost burden to Washington, a desire bound to color their interpretation of eligibility standards under the new assistance titles. Demands for liberal distribution of aid to the elderly, which threatened to exhaust state and local relief budgets, added to the pressure to dump general relief cases into the categorical programs. Complicating matters for the Board in the late

1930s, localist sentiment had reasserted itself, taking the form of opposition to any outside interference, especially when it came from social workers in Washington.[49] There were also significant institutional barriers that would have to be overcome. The Social Security Act mandated that a single state agency assume responsibility for each aid category, and the Board preferred one agency for all three. In states with a history of decentralized administration under loose state oversight, however, such unification would be difficult to achieve. For instance, where mother's aid was still under the juvenile court, judges fought fiercely against ADC.[50] Nor did the Board have the luxury of time to cultivate friends and soothe bruised feelings: it faced intensive pressure to put programs into operation quickly, particularly Old Age Assistance (OAA). At a time when it seemed vital to build support for the agency, such pressure could not be ignored.[51]

BPA also had to pick its way delicately around heated disputes within the therapeutic movement over the nature of casework and client self-determination. Among social workers the arguments about these issues, which had begun in the early Depression years, prompted a split in the late 1930s between two schools of thought, the diagnostic and the functionalist. The controversy has been well documented elsewhere, and we need only consider the implications for public assistance.[52] Those on the functionalist side maintained that agency purpose rather than professional doctrine actually defined the caseworker's role. In public assistance the purpose was confined to meeting clients' expressed need for material assistance. From this perspective, casework patterned along therapeutic lines would be an unwarranted intrusion, a violation of the rights of citizens to make independent value choices.[53] The diagnostic view held that it was the professional responsibility of the trained caseworker to help clients cope with whatever problems beset them. This might include personality and behavioral difficulties they were not ready to acknowledge: "Does the physician treat only the illness which the patient is able to diagnose and accept as real?" Through ongoing normalizing service, clients might be brought to see that relief alone was not the complete answer, that they needed to make changes in themselves. Moreover, active intervention by a skilled professional might help move clients back to a position of self-support.[54] With much of the debate focused upon BPA programs, notably ADC, the agency could not help but be drawn into the fray.

To counter the political forces threatening disorder in the public assistance programs, the Social Security Board and the BPA leadership realized they would have to instill their conception of assistance in their administrative partners at the subnational level. The Social Security Act as adopted gave the federal government only weak tools to shape program design and administration in the states. Like the Children's Bureau in the case of child welfare grants, the Board did have to approve a state plan before funds would be made available. BPA used the plan-approval process creatively, often in ways Congress did not intend—for example, the Bureau insisted that plans assure objective personnel selection practices and professional staffing in the state welfare apparatus. But this mechanism only allowed federal officials to influence general program design, and left them with at best a limited impact on daily operations.[55] States could also be denied aid if their laws or administrative practices did not conform to federal law. As the Board appreciated from the experience of Hopkins at FERA, however, the exercise of such a prerogative would bring suffering upon recipients and poison intergovernmental relations. On balance, BPA and Board leaders concluded, the real solution would have to be found in the states.[56]

Seeing the state welfare department as the pivotal instrument under the grant-in-aid arrangement, federal officials did their best to support those state administrators who shared the BPA outlook. Responsibility in many states rested with a nucleus of experienced caseworkers inherited from mother's aid, backed by the FERA holdovers.[57] BPA, recognizing that Washington was too remote, moved first to establish intermediate agents in closer proximity to its state allies. The Social Security Board had decided to open regional offices to facilitate the work of all its subunits. While BPA agreed to make use of these, it asserted its own terms: BPA regional representatives would answer not to the regional directors but to the Bureau itself. It proceeded to recruit these representatives from mothers'-aid departments and private social agencies.[58] With the regional staff in place and technical specialists available from Washington, BPA began to coax state welfare administrators to aggressively supervise local operations, build a field staff to guide local offices, issue manuals of appropriate procedures, and set professional personnel standards.[59] It was the administrative command approach again, with a new layer superimposed upon the state bureaucracy.

BPA leaders quickly realized they would also need to continue the other leg of the old movement political strategy. Early returns showed that there were too few qualified social personnel for the state agencies, much less local offices. Although in-service training programs had some utility, it was felt that state administrators and field supervisors could acquire the proper outlook only through full professional training. Accordingly, BPA joined the Children's Bureau in approving the use of federal funds to send workers to accredited schools of social work—further confirmation that the school-government axis had attained permanent status.[60]

As for the discursive squabbles between functionalists and diagnosticians, BPA soon sided with the latter. This turn toward normalizing casework may have reflected the initial predisposition of the agency leaders, for Hoey and others from the beginning voiced support for an expansive notion of "services" that pointed in the direction of a therapeutic approach. In a 1939 article on ADC Hoey asserted, "Continuing service and guidance in helping families meet the many problems confronting them are equally essential if aid to dependent children is to fulfill its purposes."[61] Yet BPA also seriously entertained functionalist ideas. So it was that the agency published, without endorsement, a report by Grace Marcus that cautioned assistance agencies and workers to refrain from telling clients how to lead their lives.[62] We must explain, then, why BPA settled upon a more interventionist casework orientation. The answer lies in the internal dynamics of therapeutic movement and in the shifting composition of the relief clientele.

Among social workers the proponents of the diagnostic view always held the stronger hand, and they exploited it effectively in the early 1940s. The schools of social work, save for a few exceptions, remained bastions of therapeutic doctrine throughout the Depression. Through this dominant institutional position, the diagnosticians maneuvered to rephrase the debate in their own terms, stressing that the caseworker could only discharge her responsibility to her clients and society through intensive therapeutic methods. Just as important, functionalist discourse conceded much to the diagnostic opposition. Consider some functionalist postulates: recipients might indeed have problems they refused to acknowledge; caseworkers were supposed to be sensitive to needs that were not openly expressed; intensive services might still be appropriate, but these were best provided through referral to specialized agencies. A close reading of texts by Marcus and others reveals that their argument hinged less on a principled commitment to nonintervention than on the banal realization that public bureaucracies made poor casework agencies.[63] Thus, with the diagnosticians in command in the schools and the functionalists unable to articulate a cogent alternative, social personnel reaffirmed the therapeutic agenda.[64] Assistance officials on educational leave were exposed to the therapeutic gospel, only slightly leavened with democratic terminology.

The transformation of the public relief population during the Second World War also prompted renewed interest in educative tutelage. Industrial mobilization for war production after 1940 sharply reduced unemployment and the corresponding need for New Deal work relief programs. As such programs were terminated, a change in the relief clientele became visible at once; this group consisted of, in the jargon of the Social Security Board, the "unemployables."[65] The popular contention of the early 1930s that relief recipients were "no different from anyone else" ceased to be credible. Furthermore, through a statutory change in 1939, most widows with children were transferred from public assistance to social insurance. Until then state ADC programs, like their mothers'-aid precursors, overwhelmingly favored widows and half-orphans, attracting a luster through these indisputably worthy clients. Once open to families headed by divorced, deserted, and unmarried women, the dependent children category abruptly lost its elite veneer.[66] Popular sentiment and therapeutic discourse agreed upon the marginal status of the new public assistance recipients. And for social personnel, as always, marginality bespoke an urgent need for normalizing measures.[67]

In the BPA conception of assistance casework, then, the therapeutic predominated. Certainly we find a continuation of the new principles adopted by liberal relief agencies during the Depression: applicants were entitled to relief if they met eligibility requirements; aid should be adequate, based on a proper determination of needs through the use of budget standards; applicants and recipients should be treated with respect and the presumption of honesty; aid should be given in cash; and fair hearings should be assured to secure these values against local prejudices.[68] But these points had been accepted by diagnosticians as consistent with a therapeutic orientation. On the other hand, their view of public assistance as a full-fledged normalizing enterprise became the BPA credo. Although there were significant constraints on agency resources, the more treatable clients ought to receive casework support and supervision of a quality equal to that provided by the best private family service societies.[69]

Charlotte Towle, a leading casework theorist, laid out the therapeutic design most thoroughly in a 1945 BPA publication. She reminded assistance workers that material aid did not suffice for the many recipients who suffered from disordered family relationships, low self-esteem, and the "emotional discomfort" of poverty—and who, as psychoanalysis taught, were likely to respond to their plight with irrational behavior, denial, resistances, and regression to a childlike state. It was the first task of caseworkers to gain the trust of recipients, so they would be both more forthcoming (thereby aiding agency surveillance) and more receptive to normalizing intervention. Intervention itself should seek to encourage stronger family relations and healthy personality development. Since poverty may have left clients too wounded to seek help in these areas, Towle added, it was necessary sometimes to go beyond the problems they identified. Of course, services could not be forced upon clients. Their choice must be respected, not because of a right to self-determination, which was best realized after problems had been shared and explored, but because an authoritarian approach by the agency was bound to be counterproductive.[70]

In practical terms, even after it had resolved its theoretical stance, BPA made only halting progress in its effort to push state assistance agencies toward a therapeutic orientation. The Bureau was preoccupied at first with the mechanics of starting up a program that required revisions in state laws, new administrative divisions, and extensive personnel recruitment. Services in public assistance assumed secondary importance before 1940, though we should not confuse this concession to immediate circumstances with indifference to therapeutic objectives.[71] During the war years federal assistance officials began to promote therapeutic doctrine more actively in the states. New instruments were devised for this purpose: BPA announced that it would reimburse service costs as it did other administrative expenses and issued state letters—statements embodying agency policy interpretations of federal law—that encouraged a service approach by participating departments.[72] Yet, despite the shift in BPA emphasis and sunny optimism about the growing appreciation among assistance personnel of therapeutic methods and goals, it was difficult to find examples of state commitment to normalizing casework. Prospects for effective tutelage were undermined, as they had been under mother's aid, by restrictive eligibility tests, inadequate grant levels, and excessive caseloads.[73]

End of a Movement

The immediate results achieved by either BPA or the Children's Bureau, however, must count for less in our analysis than the larger trends we can discern during the first years of the Social Security programs. Therapeutic activists had reason to be pleased. While they might have hoped for more from state child welfare or public assistance departments, individual battles meant less than the grand campaign. Therapeutic doctrine took hold in new federal bastions and, through the cadre strategy, in the higher echelons in state social agencies. Social personnel thus secured valuable command positions for any subsequent human service initiatives. Federal administrative practices also made permanent the line of communication between public social agencies and the social work educational establishment. Finally, federal involvement brought swift program expansion, dramatically broadening the *potential* scope of the therapeutic apparatus. Where mother's aid had covered fewer than 300,000 children in 1934, by mid-1939 more that 700,000 children received benefits under ADC.[74] If normalizing services were extended to the many recipient families suffering from maladjustment, Therapeutic discourse was confident that the most positive results, such as reduced delinquency, would follow.[75]

On the other hand, any complete balance sheet from the therapeutic angle would have to recognize certain troubling patterns revealed by early experience under the Social Security Act. The steady push to aggregate power at the center failed to neutralize the power of local officials.

Juvenile court judges remained the pivotal actors in child welfare. And, although the single-agency provision was supposed to make public assistance administration more uniform, the impact of state supervision varied widely. Local relief offices often defied all efforts to impose common administrative practices.[76] Through these local agencies, community opinion made itself felt, displacing the BPA-state therapeutic agenda with one grounded in time-honored economic moralism. So it was that lay critics worried more about undeserving persons getting aid, especially in ADC, than about constructive measures to adjust recipients. This was most obvious in the South, where local (white) sentiment held that single black mothers ought to work, regardless of their statutory right to relief.[77] But the white poor faced community disdain, too. Such punitive local attitudes were a by-product of the decision by New Deal policymakers to separate contributory social insurance from means-tested public assistance. Assistance recipients suddenly found themselves isolated politically as well as programmatically. Set apart from, nay, set against the "employable" working class, they could call upon no allies as they faced the wrath of their neighbors.

To continue the entries that social personnel would record on the debit side of nationalized public tutelage, we must note a second tendency: bureaucratic logic began to fragment the therapeutic apparatus. Casework theory held that a family ought to be treated as a unit. But under the categorical approach, agencies were responsible only for individuals who fit their program definitions. The family did not exist; it was decomposed into discrete elements like needy children (ADC), impoverished grandparents (OAA), and an unemployed breadwinner (nonfederal general relief).[78] In theory, the child welfare program should have been more flexible, since it was not necessary to establish eligibility for its services through a means test. But clients were often poor, too. If they received ADC from another agency, as was typically the case, service coordination was entirely absent.[79] Federal money, in sum, visited a new kind of disorder upon the human services.

Possibly a coherent therapeutic movement would have resisted the centrifugal pressure brought on by categorical aid. Yet, though no one quite put it this way, the movement itself had begun to come apart at the seams—still another negative outcome in the wake of the Social Security Act. I noted in passing that social personnel in child welfare had distanced themselves from the juvenile court and then had split along public/sectarian lines. The New Deal and World War II unleashed other divisive forces in therapeutic circles. With the permanent assumption by government of the responsibility for aiding the poor, the old family service agencies vacated the relief field for good. The war brought abundant opportunities to serve clients in the social mainstream, and private social personnel settled into new missions.[80] Moreover, as federal funds and regulations fostered specialized state welfare agencies, bureaucratization destroyed the unifying ideal, so central to early therapeutic discourse, of an integrated approach to maladjustment. State and local therapeutic personnel fell prey to tunnel vision, seeing only their partial slice of a client's problems.[81] By the end of the war the Progressive therapeutic movement no longer existed. Its place was taken by clusters of policy advocates eager to defend their small piece of the human service turf.

A final loss in this formative period must be recorded, though again it was scarcely visible. These assorted policy groupings steadily dissipated the sense of urgency that had propelled the Progressive founders of the therapeutic movement. As the welfare state took hold, it devitalized therapeutic discourse. Where once marginality seemed to shake the foundations of the social order, the social insurance apparatus and the political integration of the working class into the Democratic party lowered the stakes. Social personnel were still moved by a sense of social injustice, by compassion for the poor, but they no longer construed maladjustment as a threat to social survival. It was instead a challenge to their discursive methods and the institutional framework they had created. The social question had been domesticated into a set of "policy problems."

Toward Consolidation

From the end of the Second World War through the early 1960s, therapeutic practitioners struggled against daunting political obstacles to expand upon their national footholds. It was not a propitious time for innovation in the human services. New Dealers were put on the defensive by the conservative swing in the public mood, and popular hostility toward the values embraced by social personnel mounted. A steady rise in juvenile delinquency cases prompted complaints about excessive judicial leniency and accompanying demands for a "get tough" posture.[82] Public assistance drew even sharper criticisms as the demographic makeup of recipients changed. With the ADC rolls increasingly coming to consist of deserted or unmarried women with children, the program was attacked for undermining the family.[83] At times the conservative tide threatened to undo whatever gains social personnel had made during the New Deal–World War II period. For example, BPA in the early 1950s found its influence over state and local practices reduced, following conservative attacks upon Jane Hoey and a showdown with the states over their punitive disclosure policies in which Congress sided against the federal bureaucrats.[85] Yet this popular disaffection also presented an opportunity, for politicians had unhappy constituents to mollify. If social personnel could sell their prescriptions as the best response to the public outcry, the therapeutic agenda could be advanced.

In the case of child welfare, public opinion played into the hands of those who wished to reorganize services to circumvent the juvenile court. To the Children's Bureau leaders and their allies, the irrationality of the urban child protection apparatus remained the chief obstacle to quality services for children at risk. Social agencies had proliferated, but they formed no coherent system; sectarian agencies fought to protect their domains; the influx of racial minorities made obvious the gaps in a service mechanism with a white ethnic basis. The juvenile court, as the centerpiece of this loose network and the gatekeeper for many services, came under fire again for its inability to impose administrative order and its refusal to shed tasks for which other organizations were better equipped.[86] In the decade after the war the Children's Bureau sought to broaden the coverage of federally supported child welfare programs to include cities. As before, however, these efforts were stymied by the Catholic child protection groups, still fearful that authorization of federal intervention would spell their demise. Here the general public, alarmed about delinquency and doubtful about the effectiveness of remedial agencies, became a decisive factor. The sectarian agencies were thrown onto the defensive. With something "new" to offer—the Depression-era concept of unified public agencies—the Children's Bureau found elected officials ready to listen. Modest initial progress was achieved in 1958, when Congress lifted the prohibition on federal support for urban child welfare programs.[87]

Matters proved more complicated in public assistance, in part because the problem of poverty assumed different proportions than anticipated. According to the thinking behind the two-tiered welfare state, the expansion of social insurance was supposed to reduce the need for public relief. The economic prosperity of the postwar era should have further lowered assistance rolls. But while some forms of dependency decreased as predicted, the ADC category not only refused to wither but actually grew, so that by 1957 ADC recipients outnumbered those in any other category.[88] Welfare officials understood that the broadening of social insurance would leave few "worthy" families in ADC. However, it was not clear why cases involving desertion and out-of-wedlock children were rising.[89] Such families further disturbed the welfare establishment because they were found by social personnel to be suffering from a range of difficulties that went far beyond a mere lack of adequate income. Among the troubles identified were "complex family disorganization and personality disturbance," parents ill-prepared to cope with their children's emotional and social needs, widespread demoralization, and the transmission of poverty and its pathologies from one generation to the next.[90]

This description, of course, has a familiar ring to us. In the swelling ranks of ADC recipients, therapeutic discourse rediscovered subjects in its own image, now relabeled "multiproblem families."[91] And once social personnel had cast the debate in their own terms, there was no doubt in their minds about what ought to be done. These cases had always been seen as needing normalizing intervention. So, again, did casework advocates in the late 1940s and the 1950s argue forcefully for a therapeutic approach. If combined with sufficient material relief, it was argued, skilled casework would bring the most disordered families to a level close to normal functioning, reinforce the parent-child bond, reduce delinquency among ADC children, and restore some recipients to a condition of self-support. Proponents further suggested that since many families were reluctant to seek help, it was the task of the agency to find them through aggressive outreach by social personnel.[92]

In the resurgent effort to promote normalizing casework, the intellectual hazards of allowing a single discursive tradition to dominate discussion in any policy area manifest themselves. Therapeutic discourse was isolated from the emerging academic policy disciplines. As a result, no force existed to check the expanding hubris of social personnel. We find them here expressing unbound ambition, pronouncing themselves ready to take on a clientele even more difficult than that which had faced their Progressive forerunners. After all, to that founding generation, it had seemed possible to help the working-class family because it had significant assets. The multiproblem family of the postwar era in contrast lacked even minimal resources for self-renewal. Hence, by the old standard, ADC recipients would seem to make unpromising targets for the exercise of therapeutic power. Yet the absence of resources did not give casework advocates pause. To the contrary, they took it as an intriguing technical challenge—if their methods had advanced with the introduction of psychoanalytic knowledge as much as they contended, the most severe maladjustment ought to give way under intensive normalizing services. Furthermore, no one questioned the flimsy evidence of the positive results that skilled assistance casework had supposedly achieved. Studies of pilot experiments suffered from such defects as poor definition of variables, spurious attempts to quantify subtle qualitative measures of progress, and "creaming" the assistance rolls for the most promising cases. But because the outcomes confirmed what therapeutic practitioners wanted to believe, they saw no reason to look more closely.[93]

The obstacles they did acknowledge lay not in the method itself but in its application by public agencies. Public welfare bureaucracies professed fidelity to the normalizing agenda, social personnel said, only to deal with recipients in a manner that made constructive relationships impossible. Front-line staff were compelled by agency policy to focus on eligibility and potential fraud; "suitable home" standards were enforced against mothers suspected of being unchaste yet who, with casework support, might still make decent parents; mothers were forced to swear out complaints against absent fathers, destroying prospects for family reconciliation; and grants were so small as to preclude a decent material living standard, long regarded as a precondition for casework. Many of these practices reflected the enduring commitment to localism and the influence of community opinion. Politicians in state legislatures and Congress thought of themselves as bearers of local values, in this case the mounting disenchantment with ADC, and insisted against the wishes of administrators on a harsh approach; individual assistance offices were particularly vulnerable to lay hostility toward the program.[94] In addition, even if local sentiments did not interfere with agency/client relations, the casework capacity of the typical public assistance department was extremely limited. Social personnel complained repeatedly that agency staffs lacked training. Because working conditions inhibited casework, the agencies could entice few skilled professionals to accept positions; many employees had not completed college.[95] Against these failings the federal government seemed helpless. BPA was supposed to throw its weight on the side of professional caseworkers, but as indicated earlier it had come under fire itself. Bureau officials judged it prudent to shy away from confrontations with local prejudice.[96]

Just the same, however hostile the public seemed toward assistance programs, this drift in opinion did provide social personnel with an opening. When BPA first proposed amendments to the Social Security Act in the late 1940s that would give statutory sanction for matching state casework expenditures, politicians had been indifferent. Indeed, they showed little interest in public assistance at all, for the field involved too many controversies and promised no credit. But by the mid-1950s, with public condemnation of welfare on the rise, elected officials were casting about for some way to reduce or prevent dependency.[97] Appreciating that the moment was ripe for a bit of entrepreneurship, proponents of the therapeutic approach stepped forward to fill the policy void. They contended that by augmenting the therapeutic component in public assistance, recipients would be enabled to care for themselves, function at a higher level, and return to a condition of self-support. To make the approach work, it was added, the federal government needed to assert vigorous leadership and give stronger incentives to subnational governments.[98]

The pitch for a service strategy was often couched in language intended to appeal to the popular alienation from public assistance. Although they paid lip service to helping recipients cope with the pain of poverty, social personnel hardly emphasized this humane objective. Instead they chose to sell casework as the best instrument to realize the moral values embodied in the ideology of political economy. If the community demanded reassurances that grant money would be well spent, caseworkers would instruct ADC mothers on money management, buying methods, and the like.[99] And if the public resented those who did not pull their own weight, caseworkers would boost the self-confidence of assistance recipients and encourage them to return to financial independence quickly. Assistance rolls and costs would then begin to decline.[100] We should note, however, that while it seemed expedient to cater to public hostility, this selling style provoked controversy within therapeutic ranks. Some warned that by stressing self-support as a major program goal, casework in practice would be reduced to a device to push ADC mothers with young children into the work force.[101]

The first significant initiative to reinvigorate the casework element in public assistance came in the form of the 1956 amendments to the Social Security Act. Placing the stamp of approval on longstanding BPA policy, the legislation called for federal reimbursement of one-half of the cost of services to facilitate self-care, strengthen family life, and promote self-support. In addition, the amendments mandated that state assistance plans indicate which services were available, authorized training grants to raise the level of staff casework competence (and solidify the tie between agencies and social work schools), and authorized grants for research on dependency and for demonstration projects designed to test innovative casework approaches.[102] The new law did not spell out what was meant by the notion of services; it fell to BPA to translate the concept into concrete operational terms. Since the nuances of therapeutic intervention defy ready description and since casework principles were supposed to be integrated throughout assistance administration, federal bureaucrats faced a daunting task. Elaborate guidelines were prepared for state and local agencies. BPA officials also did their best, through publications and speeches, to preach the merits of casework. It was confidently predicted by social personnel that with this push from above a service philosophy would finally permeate the public assistance field.[103]

Before long they were jolted back to reality. The amendments continued the old pattern of permissive legislation, for the states were not obliged to offer services. Congress evidently intended to make but a gesture. This became all too clear in the next few years when BPA found it impossible to secure appropriations for either training or research.[104] As for the states, precious little was accomplished. Here and there demonstration projects were launched, with great fanfare. More often, however, the states fell prey to the temptation to relabel as "services" their routine administrative activities, just to satisfy the federal requirement that services be described. At the same time, with the shift in program emphasis to normalization, simpler goals like assuring adequate aid were pushed into the background.[105]

We might expect to find therapeutic activists discouraged by the scant progress in both child welfare and public assistance. Yet, quite the contrary, they seemed not in the least deterred as the 1950s drew to a close. The casework approach, they told each other, was sound; to make it work, they merely required more substantial inputs from the federal government. Steiner has correctly observed that within such a closed policy community no other conclusion could emerge.[106] Meanwhile, circumstances were about to present the casework advocates with another golden opportunity. As ADC expanded, public disapproval rose, again placing politicians and responsible administrators on the defensive. Now, following the Democrats' triumph in the 1960 election, it became their turn to appease public opinion, and they, too, needed ideas in a hurry. Incoming Health, Education, and Welfare (HEW) Secretary Abraham Ribicoff, seeking policy guidance, accordingly rounded up the usual suspects—the administrators and social work educators who had urged the 1956 law. After recapitulating the therapeutic credo, they recommended stronger federal steps to bring about the needed reorientation of assistance and child welfare administration. In particular, social personnel called for more generous fiscal rewards and stricter penalties to induce cooperation from states and localities. To signal his staunch support, Ribicoff took the symbolic step of rechristening the Bureau of Public Assistance as the Bureau of Family Services.[107]

The 1962 amendments to the Social Security Act brought about the desired changes in federal policy. With all that has already been written about this legislation, I will address here only its contribution to the therapeutic project.[108] Turning first to public assistance, the amendments contained several measures intended to strengthen the federal commitment to tutelage. Social personnel especially welcomed the provision that established a higher rate of federal reimbursement for normalizing services than for routine administrative expenses (75% of the cost for the former versus 50% for the latter). In order to qualify for the higher rate, states were required to reduce the caseload per worker, supervise recipients more closely, develop service plans for *every* dependent child in the renamed Aid to Families with Dependent Children (AFDC) program and for other cases so in need, and offer certain services as prescribed by the HEW Secretary. Other amendments appeared to widen the reach of therapeutic intervention through public assistance: a temporary program that had made families with an unemployed breadwinner eligible for AFDC was extended, and states were permitted to offer services to those in danger of becoming dependent. Lastly, since professional caseworkers were presumed best able to perform service tasks, larger training grants were authorized.[109]

In the field of child welfare, the legislation attempted by a single stroke to broaden coverage and coordinate existing service elements. States were compelled to make public services for children available in all subdivisions by 1975, thereby assuring that the system at last became comprehensive.[110] Moreover, where before service priorities reflected rigid social agency and juvenile court boundaries, this provision was expected to lead to the long-sought rationalization of child protection. To fulfill their obligations to provide adequate services, states would have to create new public organizations. Social personnel believed these departments would embody the most advanced professional wisdom and be guided by children's needs rather than the entrenched patterns of agency behavior.[111] The renewed drive to transcend parochialism in the human services might also break down the barriers between child welfare and public assistance. While the two fields were not unified, states would be pushed to prepare joint plans integrating both sets of therapeutic activities.[112]

We may fairly regard the 1962 legislation as the culmination of a thirty year effort to make therapeutic discourse the cornerstone of national social policy. Beginning with the FERA experiment in federal public relief, social personnel had sought to enlist the national state to complete the therapeutic sector. For most of the period between passage of the Social Security Act and 1962, they had toiled in obscurity, using meager instruments of bureaucratic control to hold together a fragile intergovernmental alliance of therapeutic cadre. The 1962 amendments brought social workers into the public spotlight. Under the terms of the legislation, resources would flow into the human service network, lethargic state and local departments would be mobilized, skilled social technicians would be trained for public service, and gaps between agencies would be filled. Even with the splintering of the therapeutic movement, social personnel had preserved their vision of a casework apparatus encompassing all manner of services for marginal families.[113] The new law seemed to herald the realization of this vision.

Eight

Countervailing Forces

SOCIAL PERSONNEL have always had to struggle to gain control over the institutions they have created and the policy areas that concern them most directly. Invariably, because they have mustered only precarious political support, they have had to share power within organizational hierarchies, often occupying subordinate positions. Matters actually became worse for therapeutic practitioners in many agencies at the moment of their apparent triumph in the early 1960s. In the institutions where their hold was weakest, they withdrew and left the field to be fought over by other sets of actors. And even in settings where social personnel refused to retreat, they found themselves pushed aside rather than triumphant. Therapeutic discourse was rudely displaced from some of its important institutional bases. At the same time, policy questions that had once been the exclusive domain of social personnel came under the influence of the rising policy disciplines.

The process of discursive displacement began in the juvenile court, as legal discourse reasserted itself in the postwar era. We have observed that leading social personnel ceded the territory, turning their back on the court during the New Deal and choosing instead to pursue child protection through nonjudicial instruments. The void thus created was filled in the 1950s by the legal profession. It took new interest in the court, drawing it out of the shadows of the judicial system. Lawyers questioned the court's procedural irregularities and its punitive dispositions, and a few challenged the heretofore sacred moral foundation of the court movement. The judges saw their exclusive control over the courtroom challenged. State legislatures and higher courts, responding to the concerns raised by the legal profession, imposed certain due-process requirements during the 1960s. By bringing more lawyers into the juvenile court, these reforms have precipitated a new discursive tension. Now the conflict revolves around contrary notions of justice—whether help for a maladjusted minor can best be secured, as judges insist when they invoke Progressive catchphrases, by the exercise of judicial discretion or, as defense attorneys claim, by a strong commitment to formal rights.

Where social personnel chose not to flee an arena, they still found themselves under attack during the 1960s. Discontented voices from below were first drawn together through community action efforts. With support from the federal government, local militants promoted their own agencies that stressed advocacy and political action over casework. A welfare rights campaign emerged, too, to demand an end to many of the practices assistance caseworkers had used to normalize—and prescribe—recipient behavior. It is true that both movements were overwhelmed by the political forces they had opposed. Nonetheless, they brought chaos upon the therapeutic enterprise at every point at which they made their presence felt. To the protestors, casework was part of the problem, a tool used to deflect and lower popular hostility to the social order. The movements weakened the control that social personnel exercised over client contacts and left behind a new community leadership to contest for dominance in local agencies. With examples of grassroots opposition upon which to draw, moreover, feminists over the following decade established their own helping agencies outside the professional orbit of therapeutic practitioners.

Meanwhile, the service emphasis of the 1962 Social Security amendments fizzled in practice. Despite a determined push by federal bureaucrats, a number of factors combined to subvert the therapeutic project. Perhaps the most important of these was manipulation of the federal reimbursement scheme by the states. To this we should add the elements at work within public assistance departments that undermined professional casework. Recipients did receive services, even counseling, but such activity bore no relation to the model of therapeutic intervention. Public assistance cases continued to increase, contrary to what proponents of the service strategy had implied.

In the aftermath of this dismal experience, therapeutic activists could no longer retain their positions of influence in either higher policy circles or at the agency level. Political leaders in the late 1960s responded by forsaking therapeutic prescriptions, and grasped instead for other solutions to the welfare explosion. Local opinion was again allowed to assert itself, and continues to shape legislative initiatives to this day. We have witnessed, too, the ascent of policy intellectuals bred in such disciplines as economics. These actors substituted their own distinct assumptions about the poor and their own policy ideas for the therapeutic vision that had seemed so triumphant just a few years before. Further, completing the rout of social personnel, the mishandling of the services venture led to the conclusion that they were not equipped to run social agencies. Politicians and senior officials instead chose corporate-style managers and consultants to lead a drive for administrative improvements.

Counterrevolution in the Law

Through the first fifty years of the juvenile court's existence, it had attracted much less notice from lawyers than from social personnel. Occasional protest had been raised by the bar against the notion that the promise of treatment was a fair exchange for the surrender of procedural protections. But, as we have seen, early appellate decisions supporting the movement's claim that juvenile court proceedings were of a noncriminal nature defused resistance among lawyers. Just as crucial, for many years the court escaped scrutiny because of its low visibility and lack of prestige. The legal profession regarded the court as a career dead-end. Once the early judicial entrepreneurs had carved out their empires, leading jurists avoided serving on the juvenile court bench. And successful attorneys declined to practice in a setting in which they were made to feel superfluous and clients could not afford their fees.[1]

However, during the 1950s lawyers finally were provoked to take notice of the juvenile court both by the spread of some of its principles and by their own evolving norms. Therapeutic ideology had initially taken root only in courts dealing with family matters, but by mid-century it began to make itself felt in criminal courts, too. In one important example, an influential bar association group during the 1940s promoted the idea of a youth correctional authority to raise the age of criminal responsibility and extend to young adults the principle of treatment instead of punishment. As the doctrine behind the juvenile court exerted a wider sway, the institution could no longer be ignored.[2] Moreover, the legal profession had started to insist upon a high standard of due-process safeguards in nonfederal courts. When the juvenile court was established, its procedural latitude differed only in small degree from other local courts, but by the 1950s it appeared to be as primitive in its attention to due process as a star chamber.[3] In a different vein, the notion that the law should express a community's moral strictures regained a strong following among legal scholars. This idea had fallen from fashion in the Progressive jurisprudence that accompanied the rise of the juvenile court, a discourse that spoke only of what society owed the offender. Now the legal moralists asserted that it was proper for society to penalize those who refused to conform to its limits.[4] Prompted by these shifting values, then, lawyers scrutinized the court much more carefully than they had before.

They were most alarmed by its disregard for the juvenile's rights. In exchange for treatment, court movement theory had held, the minor agreed to surrender his due-process safeguards. Yet it was clear that the court did not assure that he would receive real adjustment services.

Rather, it engaged in a linguistic subterfuge: any disposition, no matter how punitive its effects, was labeled treatment. Meanwhile, the judge conducted his courtroom according to his whims, the minor faced adjudication and disposition without legal representation, and no record was kept that might give a basis for appeal.[5] Reiterating a charge some of the court's own proponents had made in the 1920s, the lawyers asserted that the institution's indifference to common judicial safeguards left a deep negative mark on its clients. Both the juvenile and his family felt wronged, and they questioned the legitimacy of the juvenile court and the law in general.[6]

Legal observers swiftly concluded that it was necessary, as in other courts, to place checks on judicial discretion and arbitrary power. Since the court had not delivered on its part of the rights-for-treatment bargain, the juvenile ought to have his full constitutional protections restored. This should include the right to counsel, time to prepare a defense, the opportunity to question witnesses against him, recorded hearings and rationales for dispositions so that he would have a basis for appeal, and more. Of particular interest, the lawyers rejected a favorite Progressive argument still advanced by judges that a confession was a vital first step in treatment and insisted that no minor be pressured to incriminate himself.[7]

As some members of the legal profession probed the status of the juvenile's rights in the court, others considered what might be termed the rights of the public. According to these legal moralists, any court must stand ready to validate the behavioral limits established by the community. One vital function of the judicial system, in short, was to declare clearly that an act was wrong. The social-agency ideal of the juvenile court completely overlooked this essential judicial responsibility. Social personnel in the court had urged the judge to base his decision not on what the child had done but rather on what he was. If the court followed the direction they favored, it abdicated its duty to utter the public's condemnation of the minor's act.[8] Interestingly enough, studies suggested that juvenile offenders and their families shared the moralist view that antisocial behavior ought to be censured. Adolescents knew full well that they had done wrong, and they voiced contempt for adults in the court who only sought to "explain" such behavior. Clients, too, wanted the juvenile court to act more like a court and less like a social agency.[9]

To ward off challenges from the legal profession, some judges fell back upon the social agency rationale of the court. Therapeutic activists may have repudiated the court, but the rhetoric of normalization could still be expropriated and put to use. The judges insisted that they needed extraordinary discretion if they were to aid the child, and warned that any procedural checks that interfered with their flexibility threatened not only the institution but the child himself. Moreover, in a return to the language of their Progressive counterparts, these judges asserted that a child's social rights ought to rank above mere formal-legal protections.[10]

Such invocations of the court's founding principles, however, could no longer persuade skeptical professional peers. State courts, rejecting the contention that the juvenile court only treated and did not punish, began to rule in the late 1950s that a child was entitled to full procedural safeguards. These decisions often were overturned on appeal, indicating that a segment of the judiciary remained convinced by the old movement ideology. But within a few years legislatures in New York, California, and other states passed statutes that made counsel available to some indigent juveniles.[11] Here policy entrepreneurship counted heavily again, though it was the initiative of a few legal aid attorneys, rather than that of social personnel, that spurred the legislative campaigns.[12] The United States Supreme Court also began to erode the constitutional foundation of the juvenile court, particularly in the 1967 *Gault* decision that affirmed a minor's due-process rights.[13]

On paper these legislative mandates and court rulings have threatened the judge's unique monopoly over the proceedings in his chamber. Defense lawyers have been grafted onto the court apparatus, expanding the circle of actors dealing with the juvenile offender. The minor now has a representative who, at least in theory, will speak on behalf of his constitutional rights and, if he is adjudicated delinquent, demand the treatment he needs. Since the child has an attorney, the state also requires one. The case against the juvenile offender may be argued today by a prosecutor rather than a probation officer.[14]

Alas, what actually happens in the juvenile court in the wake of its legal reformation is a different story. Let us take up first the supposed strengthening of due-process protections. Though the civil libertarians hoped to secure the procedural rights of the child, they have reason to be disappointed. During the late 1950s and the 1960s, before the addition of defense counsel to the court, the more conscientious judges became sensitive to the due-process issue and felt obliged to look after the juvenile's formal rights. Now it is assumed that the lawyer representing the minor will protect him. Some attorneys do work diligently to defend their young clients. But, because of a public unwillingness to provide resources, the court continues to attract low-caliber lawyers who feel more at ease taking the side of the court staff against their client. Since the juvenile himself regards his attorney as a part of the system, mutual hostility quickly surfaces. Representation in court therefore has not achieved what its legal advocates desired.[15]

When defense lawyers take seriously their client's due process rights, moreover, they find that judges cling fiercely to the old habits of thought.

The lawyers ask for much: attention to formal rights plus dispositions based upon a full understanding of the minor's needs and a commitment to do him the "least harm." We might fairly say that the defense agenda merges Progressive ideas and revisionist skepticism to produce a no-lose compound—the minor is owed both the safeguards due any accused person and the solicitude due any innocent victim. On the other side, many judges continue to insist discretionary power remains the best means to help a child and advance other social values. They try to run their courtroom much as before. Between these contrasting outlooks, then, the juvenile court finds itself once again beset with a polarizing discursive conflict. Prescott gives us a vivid picture of this antagonism in the post-*Gault* court. Defense lawyers object when the judge in disposing of a case fixes upon the gravity of the offense and slights their client's condition and treatment needs. Judges retort that for all the defense attorneys' rhetoric about how they want what is best for the minor, they merely seek to do for him what they would do for an adult criminal defendant—to beat the charge through any procedural device available or, failing that, to persuade the court to accept whatever disposition their client wants.[16]

Social personnel are still on hand in the courtroom, but no one maintains that they play more than a bit role. As in the past the probation department prepares a report on the child's condition, perhaps with the aid of a psychiatrist or other behavioral specialist. Now, however, this psycho-social study has become contested evidence: the child's representative fights to keep unfavorable background information out of the proceedings, the prosecutor uses it to construct the worst picture possible, and the judge permits himself to be swayed by the ugly social testimony even though there may be exculpatory evidence about the alleged violation itself. When the proceeding turns to disposition, another probation report, purporting to be a rehabilitative plan, is presented, but the judge and the attorneys pay no heed to the therapeutic verbiage. They see the disposition options, ranging from probation to placement in a secure facility, as gradations of punishment. The court's final determination depends not on profound analysis of the child's needs but on the defense lawyer's bargaining skills, the minor's prior record of offenses, and the availability of space in detention homes or training schools.[17] So, despite having been pushed to the institution's periphery, social personnel continue to facilitate a process that mocks the Progressive ideal of judicial tutelage.

Protest from Below

It has been said of social policy in the postwar era that the poor themselves exercised no influence.[18] Insofar as the claim refers to the higher levels of national policy formulation before the 1960s, this seems correct. Federal bureaucrats and their allies in the welfare establishment of state agencies and social work schools thought of themselves as sympathetic representatives of program beneficiaries and others in need. Accordingly, no effort was mounted to organize assistance recipients to speak out about inadequate grants, the degrading practices to which they were exposed, or their need for services. For example, in the hearings on the 1962 amendments to the Social Security Act, not a single recipient or representative of a neighborhood or grassroots organization spoke in support of the legislation.

Yet if national policy discussion on the human services did not include marginal populations, they were already making themselves heard in other arenas. Racial segregation was challenged in the late 1950s by the rise of the civil rights movement. Although welfare policy was not a central focus of the movement in its early days, the patently racist application of "suitable home" policies began to attract increasing notice.[19] Moreover, in a number of cities during the 1950s, vigorous grassroots opposition to the urban renewal program emerged. Local renewal agencies, through the technique of massive slum clearance, had obliterated whole neighborhoods. Officials had promised to relocate residents in housing of equal quality, but this pledge was not honored. After a few such episodes neighborhood activists started to fight back, condemning urban renewal as "Negro removal" and mounting publicity, political, and legal attacks on redevelopment plans.[20]

A handful of social workers, acting on a more modest scale, also took the first tentative steps to mobilize their clients for collective action. The statistical rise in juvenile delinquency served as the immediate catalyst. As I noted in the previous chapter, social personnel read these figures as evidence that existing programs had failed. While the professional mainstream asserted the need for unified child welfare services, others were not convinced that a therapeutic approach alone would suffice. They went outside the club for inspiration, turning to sociology and its new "opportunity structure" theory. As expressed most forcefully by Richard Cloward and Lloyd Ohlin, this theory held that delinquency was a normal response by young people whose access to legitimate social rewards was blocked by the institutions of modern urban life.[21] Demonstration projects were established to provide troubled adolescents with recreational outlets and employment training. But because such services did little to lift the structural barriers to opportunity, proponents believed that problem youth and other community residents needed to organize a political challenge to the dominant institutions shaping the slum environment. To Cloward and Ohlin and their followers in the field, the avenues of opportunity would only be opened through aggressive attempts to disturb complacent public and philanthropic social agencies.[22]

When the Kennedy administration assumed office, it embraced the mobilization strategy as a tool to combat delinquency. This support derived in part from an eagerness to test out new ideas—recall that the service strategy in public welfare captured Ribicoff's fancy because he was persuaded of its innovativeness. At the same time Kennedy staffers looked forward to applying rational managerial practices throughout the hidebound federal bureaucracy. In the area of delinquency control, where the federal effort was deeply fragmented, the managerial impulse led to the creation of an interagency group, the President's Committee on Juvenile Delinquency and Youth Crime, which might impose some coherence on policy. Ohlin himself was invited to help frame a new national initiative, and he naturally set out to sell his ideas. In this he seems to have been quite successful. The administration convinced Congress to back community-based antidelinquency measures, and some $8.2 million was placed at the disposal of the President's Committee in 1961 to fund research and demonstration projects that would test the utility of the Cloward-Ohlin approach.[23]

This modest subsidy for community action against delinquency amounted to little in itself, but the idea of popular mobilization as a tool of social policy had gained a following in high places and would shape what happened next. The administration came under pressure to take constructive steps to relieve poverty. For the first time the subject attracted serious study outside the narrow circle of social workers, and books like Michael Harrington's *The Other America* stimulated concern among journalists, academics, and other influential policy actors. The research suggested two very different directions for social policy. On one side, some accounts stressed structural economic causes of poverty like the displacement of agricultural labor in the South and the decline of low-skill employment, and so pointed to the need for more generous transfer programs and public investment in retraining surplus labor. On the other side, concern was expressed, sometimes in the same studies, about a "culture of poverty" that had taken root among the poor, so complex that mere broad-gauged social policy appeared insufficient. Fatalism, maladjustment, and other pathologies of poverty had to be confronted with a multi-pronged attack, the programs targeted directly at the most marginal populations.[24] The Kennedy administration began to reassess its earlier steps, and it quickly concluded that these, including the 1962 amendments, did not get to the heart of the problem. While little was done before the assassination of the president, the incoming Johnson administration also felt an urgent need to explore new approaches, and attention fastened upon the demonstration projects in delinquency control by the President's Committee on Juvenile Delinquency. Policymakers were so intrigued by the mobilization experiments that they threw their weight behind community action. It became a cornerstone of the great surge in social legislation in the 1964–65 period, embodied most fully in the Economic Opportunity Act of 1964.[25]

By that point, however, the concept itself had started to slip out of focus. Proponents agreed only on the failures of existing service agencies and city governments to respond to impoverished constituents, especially racial minorities. To some advocates of community action, marginal individuals needed to integrate themselves into the social mainstream through their own efforts so they might gain a sense of competency, and the neighborhood had to recover the capacity to solve its own problems. Thus the method was intended to promote a political approach to social membership, to restore local cohesion, very much along the lines suggested by the early Progressive notion of community organization. Yet to other supporters of the approach, its great virtue lay in its utility as a tool for rational planning. Professionals would use the new grassroots agencies to reorganize fragmented services along geographic lines, thereby bringing about better coordination. From the outset, then, community action was plagued by a dispute over whether control should rest with experts or ordinary citizens. In the rush to push ahead while Congress was receptive, there was no time to resolve the tension.[26] The Economic Opportunity Act mandated that the antipoverty programs it spawned seek the "maximum feasible participation" of those being served, but that famous and mischievous phrase merely begged the question. As the new Office of Economic Opportunity (OEO) moved to implement the Act, federal officials continued to wrestle with the proper scope of participation.

Local militants did their best to settle the issue by steering much of the community action effort into political mobilization. In a number of cities they seized control of the community action agencies (CAAs) established under the Act, rather than permit these to fall under the grip of politicians, service bureaucracies, or professional groups. OEO officials often acquiesced in such grassroots coups. Under the direction of neighborhood activists, the CAAs proceeded to set up autonomous service centers, bypassing the existing public/nonprofit service apparatus.[27] Residents were encouraged to join in the planning and administration of the CAA-run centers. For the first time minority groups could claim agencies of their own, and one effect became clear immediately—a new minority leadership cadre emerged.[28] But small-scale service centers provided at best a partial answer to sluggish public bureaucracies, unsympathetic leaders in city hall, and insulated redevelopment authorities. The CAAs therefore pressed for more direct political action and helped to organize neighborhood and client protests against these institutional adversaries.[29]

The exaggerated hopes raised by community action and the deliberate provocations aimed at powerful interests made for a volatile mix, and a reaction swiftly followed. To begin with, the lack of quick results, after so much had been promised, frustrated many of those involved. Proponents of community action had allowed their enthusiasm to get the best of them, failing to appreciate the formidable obstacles the CAAs would have to overcome. Conditions for indigenous local organization were far less propitious than they had been at the turn of the century. Although poor neighborhoods still contained some resources that the early settlement movement had identified as prerequisites for their rejuvenation, such as a network of small associations, there was less upon which to build. Urban renewal had devastated the local social ecology; services had become bureaucratized and could not readily be transferred into neighborhood hands. In economic terms, capital had fled and the shift to an urban service economy was well advanced, so job opportunities for low-skill labor were shrinking. Yet the federal government committed little new money to the antipoverty effort.[30] Under such circumstances a quick conquest of poverty was out of the question—indeed, even long-term victory must be seen as doubtful. Participants became disillusioned and parochial; community action degenerated into a struggle over the scanty crumbs previously allocated. Many local antipoverty agencies suffered from internecine disputes as competing factions fought to control the few dollars Washington had seen fit to provide.[31]

Meanwhile, the political actors who had been antagonized by grassroots militancy regrouped and launched their own counteroffensive. If various urban elites were divided in the American city of the early 1960s, as political science claimed, community action had the unintended effect of reunifying them in a defensive coalition.[32] CAA organizers derided urban service bureaucracies as the evil incarnation of vested interest, but failed to comprehend that such agencies, precisely because of their entrenched power, could not be lightly brushed aside. After being vilified the bureaucracies were bound to strike back. They resisted demands to provide better services to poor neighborhoods and fought off all but the tamest forms of decentralization. Joining the service bureaucracies in opposition to community action were state and local elected officials. From their perspective CAAs amounted to nothing more than a federally sponsored effort to promote unwelcome political competitors. Mayors demanded that the program funds be placed under their control. When they took their case to Washington, they discovered that there, too, community action had many enemies. The effort to mobilize the urban poor was seen as a partisan strategy to enhance the political base of the liberal wing of the Democratic party, and Republicans and conservative Democrats declined to cooperate in their own destruction. By 1967 they reduced the discretionary funds available to OEO and restored the authority of established local and state governments over community action programs within their jurisdiction.[33]

The demise of community action, however, did not put a stop to organized protest by marginal groups. A welfare rights movement stirred among AFDC recipients in 1966 and gathered a significant following over the next several years. Its appearance owed something to the civil rights movement, for the notion that the disenfranchised could assert their dignity and lay claim to basic prerogatives of citizenship proved highly contagious. Of more direct bearing on the welfare rights cause was the Johnson administration's War on Poverty. For example, the Economic Opportunity Act had funded, besides community action, a new program of legal services for the poor. A number of suits were launched by legal services attorneys against public assistance departments. Early victories gave concrete meaning to the idea that recipients enjoyed procedural rights and provided a foundation for further challenges to agency policies.[34]

The confrontation tactics favored by welfare rights activists quickly liberalized AFDC administration. Protestors challenged intrusive eligibility investigations and demeaning agency practices like "midnight raids"—unannounced, off-hours home visits that sought to prove an absent father had returned or some other man was cohabiting with the mother. Federal officials in the Bureau of Family Services (BFS) backed the movement with directives intended to assure the privacy of beneficiaries.[35] In addition, to increase assistance levels beyond the normal statutory cap, AFDC recipients pressured caseworkers to make full use of special grants.[36] These benefits, designed according to the therapeutic principle that each individual might present unique needs, had given caseworkers important discretionary control, a flexible instrument of the sort we have encountered before that makes clear to clients that leverage lies not with them but with the agency. By manipulating the provisions to their own advantage, recipients turned the variability of power against the state itself. AFDC roles surged upward dramatically during and after the period of welfare rights agitation, increasing from just over four million persons in 1965 to nearly eleven million in 1974. Though the causal connection between the rising caseload and the protests has remained a matter of dispute, it does seem clear that the demand to be treated with dignity helped remove the stigma attached to assistance. Where before many impoverished women with children had shunned public aid, by 1971 some 90% of those eligible were receiving AFDC grants.[37]

As in the case of community action, militancy also provoked a sharp reaction. The movement deliberately sought to overload the welfare system to provoke a crisis that would lead to its replacement. But this strategy underestimated the political forces that had been aroused in opposition to the demand for welfare rights and the capacity of public assistance mechanisms to absorb discontent. The broader public held fast to the belief that welfare mothers had engaged in immoral conduct and resented the increasing cost of the program. State legislatures blocked further increases in grant levels in the early 1970s and replaced the special grants provisions with fixed allowances.[38] Welfare rights activists were also confounded by the seeming openness of public assistance administrators. When Congress in 1967 mandated that welfare agencies involve the poor in planning and administration, it proved a simple matter to co-opt local movement leaders. They were drawn into sterile client advisory committees and "consulted" endlessly until their energy was dissipated.[39]

So ended the welfare rights protest, defeated like community action before accomplishing its broader goals. But for our purposes something more needs to be said about these grassroot movements: they sought, among other objectives, to remake the human services and so to transform the position of therapeutic practitioners. Public and philanthropic agencies were among the discredited bureaucracies that community action proposed to replace. Similarly in the case of public assistance, welfare rights activists took as their target the very components of program administration—individualized needs determinations and benefit levels, client supervision, and the like—that had been identified by social personnel as key tools for normalizing clients. We must examine further the demands made by militant clients of the human service apparatus and the impact of the upheaval upon agencies and their professional staff.

What clients wanted amounted to a repudiation of the therapeutic credo. The antitherapeutic impulse stands out especially when we consider community action. CAA leaders and community organizers charged that casework was irrelevant to the real problems facing the poor. If social personnel really meant to help, it was said, they would have to abandon their pose of therapeutic neutrality and their focus on personal adjustment. Poverty would only be defeated through committed advocacy and political action.[40] Moreover, because caseworkers came from outside the neighborhood, from what was indeed an alien culture, they were seen as unable to grasp their clients' experience and aspirations. Participation through advisory and planning mechanisms would do little to reshape practice unless local residents began to contribute to the day-to-day workings of the bureaucracy. CAAs accordingly insisted that social agencies create lower-skill staff positions that could be filled by applicants from the neighborhood. Not only would this bring in perspectives too often neglected by professionals, but it would create new career paths for the poor.[41] The welfare rights movement later incorporated similar calls for caseworker advocacy, an end to behavioral tests as a condition for aid, respect for client values, and the hiring of local paraprofessionals.

For a short time social personnel seemed willing to go along with this agenda for pragmatic reasons, though their working life became very uncomfortable. The uprising met with a sympathetic response from the various elements constituting the human service apparatus, not least because it advanced their respective aims. Senior officials welcomed the attempt to eliminate practices of which they themselves disapproved; private family agencies, acknowledging they had lost touch with clients, supported their participation; and caseworkers at the lowest rung hoped for an alliance with clients that would improve working conditions. In some large cities, public assistance employees joined recipients in staging disruptive protests.[42] Soon enough, however, social personnel began to feel themselves squeezed from all sides. The anger of clients, the charges of racism and insensitivity, and the sheer confusion of constantly changing policies made the climate within assistance agencies unbearable for field staff and administrators alike. All the while public hostility mounted, and it was directed not only at uppity clients but at caseworkers who seemed indifferent to community moral standards.

By the time social personnel realized that their precarious control over the setting of therapeutic practice had been badly compromised, it was too late to undo the damage completely. They gradually turned against client assertiveness, trying to appease public criticism and thereby husband whatever power they still retained.[43] But clients were no longer compliant and submissive. Moreover, although the new leaders generated by community action became less radical over time, they remained in place atop many social agencies, their skepticism about therapeutic nostrums intact. To battle these usurpers would also be politically counterproductive. By the early 1970s, with the broader public alienated by the chaos in the human services, they represented one of the few sources of political support upon which the apparatus might yet rely.

Grassroots challenges to therapeutic practice did not end with the demise of community action and welfare rights agitation. During the 1970s a resurgent feminism turned its anger upon the normalizing apparatus. Where Progressive feminists had supported intervention as a way to sustain traditional family values, their modern counterparts instead condemned the helping professions for seeking to preserve arbitrary patriarchal authority. Women activists held that social agencies had been so blinded by the alleged superiority of the two-parent family ideal that they encouraged poor women to remain dependent upon men who had shown themselves to be abusive and even violent. Appreciating the need to step outside the established therapeutic framework, feminists set out to create their own network of rape crisis hotlines, shelters for battered women, and nonprofessional counseling centers. This alternative caring system rejected the expert-dominated treatment design that has long been the cornerstone of therapeutic discourse.[44]

The Services Fiasco

Even as the first signs of client unrest appeared in the early 1960s, social personnel plowed ahead with their service strategy in public assistance. Their weapon, as we have seen, was the 1962 amendments to the Social Security Act, specifically the more generous reimbursement formula designed to induce states to expand service activities. Again it fell to federal bureaucrats in BFS to give the legislation operational meaning. Again they chose to define services very broadly, this time in terms of the problems or goals at which intervention would be directed, so that nearly any agency activity would qualify. In part the BFS approach reflected a sober recognition that state capabilities were limited: if liberal matching funds were permitted only for casework in its most pristine form, no agencies would meet the test, and the purpose of the statute would be foiled. The inclusive notion of services also followed from the therapeutic doctrine that invested nearly any contact with therapeutic significance.[45] Federal administrators set just a few specific minimal conditions for 75% reimbursement, such as a requirement that home visits be conducted at least once every three months. Further, states were permitted to phase in the service program gradually, to give them the opportunity to improve their agency staff.[46] It was expected that therapeutic cadre built up over the years in the state agencies and key local offices would use their command positions in the department hierarchies to coax others to adopt their outlook.

Things went awry from the start. First off, the liberalization of matching terms coupled with the broad definition of services proved too much of a temptation to the states. Faced with increasing demands on their own scarce resources, states were eager to find ways to ease their fiscal burden. They particularly wanted federal money. But while BFS officials hoped to engender certain behavior in exchange, the sweeping definition of services made it impossible to set meaningful performance standards. Since any family could be said to need intervention and since whatever was done for it could be depicted as a measure aimed at one of the federally identified target problems, the states passed off every administrative cost as a service.[47] Proponents of the service strategy should not have been surprised by this: recall that under the 1956 amendments the states had shown similar ingenuity, complying on paper with the mandate that they describe services by relabeling as such their routine administrative activities. Federal officials finally realized the need to tighten standards, but the process of cost shifting had gone too far to be easily reversed. In fact the revised 1967 service standards were even more vague.[48]

The 1962 amendments had also been devised to professionalize the human services, but on this front, too, events took another turn. Repeating the obstinacy it demonstrated after the 1956 amendments, Congress refused to appropriate training funds. BFS officials tried to circumvent the legislative recalcitrance by promulgating rules that would require a college degree for newly hired caseworkers and supervisors. Though this standard fell far below what social personnel deemed necessary, anything more rigorous was plainly unrealistic. It continued to be difficult to entice trained workers into assistance agencies because so much of the job involved tedious paper-processing to satisfy eligibility requirements.[49] The drive for professionalism was further hindered by the aforementioned push to employ the poor themselves in human service agencies. In truth, of course, many agencies, especially public assistance departments, had always settled for workers with scarcely more education than the people they served. Now that expedience was elevated to a mission, the quest to make the staff resemble the clientele accelerated.[50]

Patterns of bureaucratic development in public assistance agencies posed a more fundamental impediment to professional casework practice. When bureaucratization had first been proposed as the answer to localism, a few doubters cautioned that the strategy might be incompatible with the casework model. Forty years later the conflict suddenly became visible. All along social personnel had placed their confidence in the magical power of hierarchical control and formalized standards to elevate local practice. This line of thought culminated in the 1960s in a rules-and-more-rules fetish that infected all aspects of program administration.[51] Federal and state officials, seeing the decisions of field-level personnel as crucial to the service strategy, tried to overcome local prejudice and mold caseworker behavior by steadily adding guidelines and reporting requirements; the controversies over welfare rights led to further efforts to minimize discretion and to anticipate every contingency with more rules. Procedural manuals began to run to several volumes and thousands of pages. But this very effort to assert sound top-down control subverted the possibility of professional practice. Casework requires flexibility, yet skilled practitioners were constrained by the mounting red tape. Further, although the therapeutic model holds that a relationship with clients can be forged only through extensive contact, too much time was consumed by the paperwork needed to satisfy federal and state reporting requirements. As one study concluded about the service era in public assistance, the greatest change occurred not in the field but in what caseworkers "wrote down about their behavior toward recipients."[52]

Had social personnel embraced bureaucratic theory completely, they might have sidestepped some of the difficulty. Bureaucracy, in the classic Weberian formulation, rests not only upon hierarchy and rules but also upon specialization and a division of tasks within the organization. Specialization might have eased the dilemma of assistance caseworkers by freeing them from certain prosaic tasks that could be simplified and governed by rules. (As we shall see in the following chapter, social personnel finally came to see the wisdom of this solution.) However, precisely because therapeutic doctrine held that casework was unbounded, covering all aspects of client-agency relations, federal bureaucrats had emphasized the importance of channeling all dealings with a recipient through one employee. Thus it was not possible to differentiate a set of professional activities, in which discretion could be preserved, from routine and hence rule-guided agency practices.[53]

Surprisingly enough, notwithstanding state machinations, the lack of professionalism, and excessive bureaucratization, service activity actually did increase. But this can be misconstrued. Social personnel began to distinguish between two general types of services, "hard" forms that brought clients tangible benefits versus "soft" personal counseling. The latter, of course, constituted the tool through which the skilled caseworker was supposed to correct behavioral difficulties and other symptoms of maladjustment. Studies of public assistance services during the 1960s revealed a strong emphasis on the hard services—medical care, housing assistance, day care, and so forth. Little therapeutic casework was done. This bias partly reflected the increased availability of concrete benefits through the creation of new programs like Medicaid. More to the point, however, clients chose what they felt they needed, and they showed an overwhelming preference for the tangible kinds of help. Public assistance caseworkers also slipped into the role of "service finders," referring clients to other agencies that provided hard services.[54]

Such counseling as was performed, it must be added, could hardly be considered casework. Assistance caseworkers sought to do nothing more than have "a relatively infrequent, pleasant chat" with their clients. For fear of seeming overly intrusive, the caseworkers avoided sensitive personal matters and instead steered the conversation to safe subjects. Many recipients lived in socially isolating circumstances, so they welcomed the communication. Also, as they came to know one person in an otherwise faceless bureaucracy, they felt more comfortable about expressing special needs. (For their part, the caseworkers, because they could do little to help, were anxious to avoid discussion of any unusual requests!)[55] We should note that the shared personal characteristics of functionary and beneficiary fostered this friendly communication. Caseworkers hailed from extremely modest circumstances themselves; in addition, most were women, and so were intimately familiar with the problems of holding together a family under tough circumstances. It was only natural, then, that they disdained moralistic pronouncements about the virtues of chastity and encouraged their clients to have a social life. Class and gender solidarity humanized client-agency contact. Clients appreciated this and expressed approval of much of what caseworkers did.[56]

In sum, the service strategy when put to the test amounted to something far less dramatic than therapeutic discourse had envisioned. We might note that insofar as public assistance services were concerned, proponents and critics alike dwelled more on the theory than the reality. Both looked upon casework as an exercise of power, but the former saw intervention as a constructive instrument while the latter feared coercion and the destruction of client autonomy.[57] Let us set these assumptions against the lessons of practice. From the point of view of the service advocates, while any antidote to sterile program administration had to be applauded, a friendly conversation hardly amounted to the grand rehabilitative enterprise they had promised. Precisely because caseworkers avoided discussion of behavioral problems, which therapeutic discourse held to be among the precipitating factors in dependency, they were not doing their job.[58] As for the critics' warning that overbearing agency functionaries would dominate their clients, this concern likewise proved exaggerated. Here again it must be observed that, contrary to what the discourse stipulated, welfare caseworkers chose not to poke their noses into private matters. Similarly, they made little effort to supervise how grants were spent, a form of control the clients deeply resented. Besides the reluctance of caseworkers to satisfy the model job description, we should note that clients were shielded by the lack of resources for intervention. Excessive caseloads meant infrequent and superficial visits. Therefore it is not surprising that recipients rarely complained of agency intrusiveness or compulsion. Only when the caseworkers controlled access to some desired hard service did their clients feel obliged to accept their suggestions.[59]

Policy Competition, Old and New

Within several years after the passage of the 1962 amendments it became clear to all concerned that the service strategy had failed to bring about the results its advocates had promised. A few social workers had cautioned from the first against expecting too much from casework, especially as a device for limiting the rise in public assistance rolls.[60] When services were put to the test, this warning proved right on the mark: assistance cases, as we have seen, increased even more rapidly after 1962. Social personnel recognized the time had come to be candid about the value and limits of normalizing casework. It was conceded that amid poverty and despair services could not perform miracles. Rather, casework promised merely to ease some of the acute strains that otherwise threatened to overwhelm recipients. But the shift from calculated salesmanship to humane justification, however honest, did not satisfy members of Congress. They had been told the service approach would check dependency and contain public assistance costs and now felt betrayed.[61]

When the philosophy behind a program is discredited, the program itself is rendered vulnerable to colonization by some other ideological force. The failure of the service amendments called into doubt the entire therapeutic enterprise and so deprived the human services of their principal intellectual prop. Seeking some other basis upon which to organize social policy, elected officials in Washington began to listen again to the local voice. And what they heard were demands for a return to the moral code of individual responsibility and the strengthening of local discretion to cope with the problems of marginality.

Congress responded first with the 1967 amendments to the Social Security Act. The legislation created a new Work Incentive Program (WIN) to push public assistance recipients back into the labor market. Through WIN the federal government sought to confront marginality at its modern point of divergence from the mainstream, the breach between the employable and the unemployable. Services to recipients would be continued, but with a focus on their job skills rather than on their personal competence. The employment counselor would supplant the caseworker as the key agent of the assistance department. As for the recipients, some would be required to accept training and employment, and thus would face a new behavioral condition that would have to be satisfied if they wished to maintain their eligibility. (Hence the label "workfare" for this policy approach.) On the other hand, consistent with the morality of the marketplace, they would be rewarded by being permitted to retain a portion of their earnings without a corresponding reduction in their benefits.[62] State and local officials were given the authority to decide how stringently to apply the mandatory training and placement language. Through this device the legislation tried to assure that WIN administration would embody the particular wishes of each community.[63]

High expectations accompanied WIN, but the program fared no better in the field than had the therapeutic approach. Social personnel detested the 1967 legislation, condemning its provisions, WIN above all, as punitive and regressive.[64] I note in the following chapter that their control over the federal social welfare bureaucracy was eroding. Nevertheless, through the early 1970s they retained some influence, and they determined to exploit administrative discretion to nullify the will of Congress. The implementing HEW regulations exempted most recipients from mandatory participation in workfare. In addition, because the 1967 amendments did not openly disavow the service objectives of the 1962 legislation, the new regulations continued to stress the goal of strengthening family life.[65] At the state level WIN was further undermined. Federal administrators set the stage: with so many possible ends to meet, services naturally had to be defined in the broadest imaginable terms. Once again, given an open invitation to imbibe at the federal trough, the state assistance departments could not resist. They continued to describe everything they did in the terms needed to qualify for reimbursement at the highest rate. Very little new money went into the training that was supposed to move recipients off the dole and into the work force.[66] WIN did nothing to halt the increase in cases. Indeed, growth in the caseload following the 1967 legislation was far more rapid than during the so-called service era between 1962 and 1967.

Notwithstanding the tribulations of WIN, the intellectual reorientation that inspired the program has endured. Since 1967 the desire to put public assistance recipients to work has been a constant theme in welfare reform. Congress first decided, through the 1971 Talmadge amendments, to curtail the authority of federal bureaucrats to excuse recipients from required registration in the WIN program. In subsequent years other programs tried to encourage recipients to find jobs in the private sector, subsidized employment for those with minimal job skills, or guaranteed jobs for the participants in training sessions. Always the results were the same: program costs mounted as employment services became more complex, yet few recipients moved into the work force who would not otherwise have done so. Similar experiments at the state level generated better outcomes only because of "creaming"—the selection of clients clearly motivated to succeed. Despite this sorry record, the workfare idea has gathered steadily wider support, today spanning the political spectrum. The much-touted 1988 Family Security Act again stipulates that recipients work, and extends the requirement to mothers of preschool children.[67]

Apart from public assistance, too, national policymakers were eager by the late 1960s and early 1970s to establish additional vehicles through which community values might be expressed. The Great Society approach had irritated both local elites and ordinary voters. It did not suffice to tinker with certain federal programs like community action, these important political actors maintained, for the entire structure of national domestic policy rested on the presumption that Washington bureaucrats knew what was best for Main Street. Accordingly, once the Republicans returned to the White House in 1969, sweeping measures were introduced to reduce the role of the national government in the administration of public services and programs. Block grants grouped together many of the existing specific ("categorical") grant-in-aid programs, a move intended to permit state and local political choices to prevail over federal bureaucratic priorities; revenue sharing, another Nixon administration innovation, gave subnational elected officials even wider latitude in the use of federal monies.[68]

The new intergovernmental aid mechanisms were viewed by social personnel as a giant step backward. For forty years they had looked to the national state to rationalize the human services through its top-down direction. By turning policy responsibility back to the states, however, the federal government disavowed any further attempt to impose coherence on disjointed programs and agencies. The subsequent creation of Title XX in 1974, further broadening state discretion over services, confirmed the federal withdrawal from planning responsibility in the therapeutic sector. Title XX struck such an indulgent posture that states were even permitted to offer different services in different subdivisions, a practice not tolerated since the passage of the Social Security Act.[69] Of great concern, too, in the wake of the Nixon administration fiscal reforms, therapeutic activists would be dependent upon state government and city hall, arenas they had long distrusted. Title XX again solidified the unhappy new order of things: through a provision that mandated citizen participation in state service planning, the legislation appeared to play into the hands of well-organized interests and influential local constituencies, leaving the programs that served marginal groups at a disadvantage.[70] Social personnel pleaded during the 1970s for a return to tight federal control.[71]

But that era was over and would not be revived. Faith in localism thrives today, constrained only by fiscal prudence. States welcomed their release from the heavy hand of federal bureaucratic oversight; they have seen no reason to reshackle themselves. Hence they greeted without enthusiasm a later effort under President Carter to strengthen national control over public assistance, and helped to bury the scheme.[72] On the other hand, if subnational governments defend their autonomy in the name of democratic responsiveness, principle does not extend past the point where it might discommode taxpayers. The acute budget pressures under which these governments have labored for most of the past twenty years have left them determined to avoid any new fiscal obligations. They have declined to accept responsibility for a program if this would also mean assuming the burden of paying for it. Accordingly, a Reagan administration plan to return public assistance entirely to state control met with a cool reception from the states themselves. Under the proposal, they would have borne the full cost of public assistance (up from approximately 50% under the existing system), while the federal government in exchange would have absorbed the full cost of Medicaid. The states, however, only liked the latter half of the bargain.[73]

In tracing the revival of economic moralism and localist sentiments in policy circles, I do not mean to suggest that the failure of the 1962 amendments merely turned back the clock in social policy. To the contrary, the services charade also gave rise to a new configuration of policymakers, policy experts, and interest groups. Social policy, once a subject monopolized by social personnel, was seen as too important to be left to them alone. Where Congress had paid little attention to public assistance from the enactment of the Social Security Act through the early 1960s, the great surge in AFDC cases forced members to take a more active interest. They began to call upon experts schooled in other policy sciences for advice. From the late 1960s onward, when the economists and public policy specialists entered the process, social personnel have been pushed aside.[74] They played a very minor role during the early 1970s when Congress considered such important public assistance reforms as President Nixon's Family Assistance Plan (FAP) and Supplemental Security Income (SSI). Both proposals embodied the norms and methods of the recently summoned policy intellectuals, rather than therapeutic doctrine. Nor did political pressure by social personnel sway the outcome of congressional deliberations. The FAP scheme was defeated by opposition from both ends of the political spectrum—conservatives viewed the scheme as overly generous while liberals and welfare rights activists thought it not generous enough. SSI, which established minimum grant levels for certain assistance categories (the aged, blind, and disabled) at federal expense, prevailed because of lobbying by the states and by groups representing seniors, whose clout in national politics has always dwarfed that of caseworkers.[75]

The impact of the ascendant policy intellectuals in transforming social policy debate merits some discussion. As a first step, they discredited the fading coterie of social work academics and therapeutic activists by subjecting normalizing programs and casework to a vigorous critical reappraisal. Dissatisfied with the sort of anecdotal "happy family" stories that had so long passed for evidence of program success, evaluation experts insisted upon finding more verifiable criteria for rating service outcomes. This pursuit of empirical certainty met with resistance among social personnel who found the old methods quite congenial. But the evaluation people pressed ahead, and when they were done it was plain that the therapeutic emperor wore no clothes—casework intervention produced no significant results, no one had studied how clients fared after cases were closed, and clients were "creamed" to make programs look success-ful.[76] In part as a consequence of this evaluation research, the grandiose ambitions that had marked therapeutic initiatives gave way to a new sense of modesty in social policy.

Having established themselves at the center of policy debate, the new policy experts recast the terms for understanding marginality. Studies conducted during the late 1960s and the 1970s helped revise old ideas about poverty and the poor. Economists found that, contrary to sweeping generalizations about a permanent culture of poverty, many people suf-fered recurring but transient episodes of need. The research tended to confirm, too, that poverty owed more to structural economic patterns, notably the decline of working-class job opportunities, than to the trans-mission of values between generations.[77] (The culture-of-poverty view, however, has since been revived, as I will discuss in the next chapter.) Unfortunately, the economists' views of marginal populations were, if anything, more narrow and skewed than the conceptions that had in-formed earlier policy efforts. On the positive side, the poor were seen as rational economic actors who respond to conventional material incen-tives and rewards—just like everyone else.[78] Hence, their difficulties in coping appeared not as signs of abnormal behavioral pathologies, but as the common troubles of people who could not afford more of the com-modities with which to satisfy needs and desires. But the assumption of rationality oversimplifies human motivation and conduct, leading to a truncated understanding of behavior.

The policy measures that economists proposed reflected both the strengths and limitations of their basic premise. Rather than attempt to refashion values, their new wisdom held that the federal government ought to confine itself to establishing a base beneath income. This com-mon-sense realization contributed to the creation of ssi.[79] As part of the discussion about how best to set an income floor, research institutes and the federal government established large-scale pilot programs to test the impact of various income-maintenance approaches on recipients' work attitudes. For the first time an attempt was made to get at the truth behind popular beliefs, liberal and conservative alike, about whether recipients deliberately avoid work or would prefer to be employed if jobs were available. The experiments seemed to show that higher benefits discour-age work effort to a modest degree and produce an improved standard of living. To the surprise of many researchers, however, increased benefits meant greater family instability. What the rational-actor assumption overlooks is the reality of family power relations that feminists have grasped: given the wherewithal to survive on their own, poor women will choose to escape destructive domestic arrangements.[80]

When any discipline gains a monopoly of influence in policy circles, discussion suffers. This was evident in the heyday of the therapeutic activists before the 1962 amendments, and we see the risks again in the triumph of the economists and their allied policy analysts during the 1970s. In the latter period, as Katz says, poverty came to be redefined as the property of economists. Policy ideas derived from other disciplines or inspired by popular movements simply could not find an audience at the higher levels of government. For example, although sociologists and feminists continued to urge forms of community mobilization as a strategy to combat poverty, the political approach was never seriously considered during the 1970s. Certainly this can be explained in part by the recent painful experience with community action. But just as important, to the economists, with their single-minded focus on individual incentives, a policy based on collective action was incomprehensible.[81]

Meanwhile, at the field level, the collapse of the service strategy also resulted in a loss of influence for social personnel. We have seen that they had struggled steadfastly to professionalize social agencies, so that program administration might be shielded from community pressures. By the late 1960s the need for professional skills was widely acknowledged— but, to the chagrin of casework advocates, the skills in demand were not the kind they possessed. Rather, the chaos and lack of accountability in the service program pointed to the need for greater administrative control through the application of sophisticated managerial techniques. Managerial types increasingly dominated social agencies, often enlisting the help of efficiency consultants unfamiliar with therapeutic doctrine to guide the reorganization of programs and services.[82] We might remark upon the irony here: the very management science that social personnel had touted in the Progressive era as a key to rational therapeutic practice in the end drove them from command positions in the agencies they had sought to make their own.

Nine

The Tenacity of the Therapeutic

IN THE EARLY 1970s the survival of the therapeutic enterprise appeared very much in doubt. A wave of revisionist critics derided the benevolent pretenses of the human services and proclaimed the demise of rehabilitation as a policy objective.[1] Yet today we find the therapeutic sector very much alive—not thriving, perhaps, but certainly in no danger of extinction. In fact, social personnel have found new areas of practice. The remarkable persistence of the therapeutic enterprise, despite the clear evidence of its failure and unpopularity, rests in part on the determination of its proponents to make good on the promise of their mission. But fidelity to a creed would have counted for little had not social personnel shown themselves to be clever political actors. They have built upon their existing network of agencies, compromised principle to secure a role for themselves, capitalized on public concern about emerging social problems, and adapted their discourse to the tenor of the times.

The first steps in this recuperation occurred in the public organizations in which the therapeutic agenda seemed most corrupted. Social personnel by the late 1960s had seen themselves driven to the periphery of the juvenile justice system and public assistance. In a final effort to establish a place for their discursive values in both settings, they prescribed reforms that paralleled those favored by their precursors back in the 1920s. At that time, to assure the integrity of normalizing services, therapeutic activists had sought to redistribute tasks among the various human service agencies; proper intervention would then proceed untainted by, for example, the punitive approach of the courts. The notion that practice might be purified through the proper division of labor within the human services again seemed compelling forty years later. Accordingly, behavioral specialists and caseworkers, using the leverage provided by federal funds, pressed strongly to establish a niche for themselves. They have not done badly. Although the attempts to reorganize the therapeutic state have not panned out quite as they imagined, social personnel have secured new roles in the judicial and social welfare systems.

In addition, new opportunities for therapeutic practice have arisen. A great surge of social service spending in the early 1970s opened up for therapeutic practitioners the prospect of aiding less-marginal constituencies. As social agencies moved to fill this void, they gained substantial political clout. This has helped during the subsequent interval of fiscal stress and conservative retrenchment. Even a determined effort by the Reagan administration to withdraw federal support from the therapeutic sector could not dismantle the modern human services apparatus. New social issues have also stirred public interest over the past decade, a situation that invites policy entrepreneurship. Social personnel have been quick to seize the moment. So we find that they have claimed for themselves a leading position in the effort to cope with child abuse; there is every sign that they will repeat the coup when policy attention shifts to action on the phenomenon of "the underclass." Such willingness to defer to the vicissitudes of popular or elite attention has once again placed the agents of normalization in considerable demand.

With the multiplication of social agencies, however, the therapeutic sector has become more disorderly, necessitating yet another attempt to rationalize the system as a whole. The division of labor reflects interagency squabbles, policy fashions, and coalition politics. There is no discernible plan, no comprehensive approach to the problems of marginal populations. In the past social personnel had led the effort to rearrange service missions. But today the task has been assumed by public officials who use their control over private agency funding to impose their priorities on the sprawling network of service providers. And, to the dismay of social personnel, the conception of a rational service apparatus that guides government monitoring bodies emphasizes managerial values rather than therapeutic principles. Once more it appears that a victory has been won on someone else's terms.

Revival of the therapeutic in practice has been matched by a recovery in the discourse. The 1960s brought on a crisis of confidence among social personnel, but they have weathered the intellectual challenge to their enterprise. They have acknowledged a number of criticisms without abandoning their underlying faith in normalizing intervention through personal therapies. Even in the face of doubts within the field that casework can achieve the adjustments it seeks, social personnel continue to voice confidence that they have the necessary techniques—or that they are on the verge of developing such techniques—to help clients cope with the conditions that afflict them.

While social personnel have gained much since the nadir of the therapeutic enterprise two decades ago, we must be less sanguine about what recent developments mean for clients. The increased clumsiness and inefficiency of the entire tutelary mechanism permit many marginal families to elude intervention. However, with the expansion of certain forms of tutelage through the very innovations that have assured its survival, the therapeutic sector has become more menacing than before. It continues to inflict damage upon its supposed beneficiaries, and we are less likely to be able to defend them against its overtures.

Clean Hands in Dirty Systems

After their many setbacks during the 1960s, social personnel found themselves groping for ways to revive therapeutic practice. To cope with the demands of senior bureaucrats, clients, and recipients, frontline caseworkers devised various expedient measures such as rationing the benefits under their control. But these steps could do no more than make life bearable in otherwise hopeless work settings.[2] Social work educators and leading therapeutic activists instead stressed the need to establish autonomous institutions or divisions for their endeavors. We find this strategy in both public assistance and juvenile justice. In the former, social personnel urged a reorganization that would allow normalizing casework to stand apart from the more routine tasks of income maintenance. The juvenile court and its supporting institutions presented an even more difficult challenge, since punitive values so thoroughly dominated. Although the system might be beyond salvation, social personnel hoped to narrow its scope by preempting court intervention in many cases and by developing new disposition resources guided by therapeutic principles for others. Behavioral specialists would then assume responsibilities previously exercised by the court under conditions more conducive to effective adjustment.

In the public assistance field, the welfare establishment during the mid-1960s came to endorse the view that rehabilitative services ought to be separated from the administration of grants. A few social workers began to push for separation as early as the Kennedy years.[3] At the time they were plainly swimming against the tide, for the contrary assumption that aid and services ought to be linked had just been enshrined in the 1962 amendments to the Social Security Act. Amidst the ensuing service disaster, however, the separation idea quickly gained adherents in the federal bureaucracy, the professional association of welfare administrators, and the social work schools. Even those who had pressed for the explicit casework focus in assistance had to admit that the aid-service linkage had compromised the integrity of casework.[4]

The current service strategy, social personnel reflected, was based upon mistaken premises and was contributing to the erosion of their mission. In the first place, the 1962 amendments erred in the assumption that all assistance recipients suffered from problems for which services were appropriate. Though some recipients might require normalization, others did not; there was no inherent connection between a need for income maintenance and a need for casework intervention. Policies and administrative arrangements that presumed otherwise cast a shadow upon the entire assistance population. The sticky matter of client self-determination also had to be considered. Even recipients in need of services, this doctrine held, must be permitted to reject them. Yet, if assistance and services were provided through the same caseworker and office, recipients might feel pressured to submit to unwanted intervention.[5] As a matter of principle, then, separation was essential. At the same time, the more pragmatic case for reversing the service strategy could not be overlooked. The aid-service bond meant that skilled caseworkers had to devote too much of their time to clerical matters. Separation of the two functions would permit clients to choose freely whether they wished to receive services, let services stand in their own right, and allow the professionals to be professionals. Eligibility determinations and other mundane chores would be left to another category ("class" might be more apt) of agency employees, the eligibility technicians.[6]

Among social personnel concerned with juvenile delinquency, a parallel movement to establish autonomous settings emerged during the 1960s. This reflected, first, their further disenchantment with the juvenile court itself. It had become increasingly evident to them that fundamental tensions existed between therapeutic discourse and the juvenile court as an institution. A legalistic outlook warped the court's understanding of its clients: while science might disdain rigid categories and simple labels, a judicial institution found them indispensable.[7] Further, given that according to the therapeutic ideal a client had to participate voluntarily in the treatment relationship, it did not seem possible to treat youngsters under the court's direction.[8] Juvenile offenders certainly grasped the cold fact that they were subject to legal discipline. And this led them to dismiss clinicians associated with the court as an annoyance or to manipulate them to secure lenient treatment.[9] Finally, new research by social scientists suggested the great harm that might be done to young people through even unofficial contact with the court. Once they were identified as somehow deviant or maladjusted, they found it extremely difficult to shed the designation—and they tended to internalize it and behave accordingly. Better by far, it followed, to protect minors from such "labeling" by avoiding judicial intervention entirely.[10]

Significantly, lawyers agreed that where possible the court ought not to be involved in the lives of problem youngsters. Early in the postwar era legal experts had joined social personnel in an effort to narrow the court's jurisdiction over nondelinquency cases. But still the volume of court business rose; by 1959, more than a half million delinquency cases per year were being adjudicated or handled through unofficial dispositions.[11]

Many of these cases involved status offenses—the violations that would not be considered criminal if committed by an adult. Teenage girls were especially likely to be brought before the court on charges of defying parental authority or running away. However trivial such behavior might seem, judges and court personnel were reluctant to overlook it because they believed it would "escalate" into serious delinquent activity.[12] The due process reforms of the 1960s briefly encouraged legal critics of the court to believe that the institution's worst excesses would be curbed. But as it became evident that little had changed in actual court procedures, they took a renewed interest in reducing the number of minors moving through the system.[13] Because these lawyers commanded attention in their own circles and in state legislatures, their support for alternatives to judicial tutelage would be decisive.

Social personnel and their allies in the legal profession settled upon diversion as the best means to curtail the court. Under this innovation many status offenders and first-time violators would be kept out of the juvenile justice system. Instead, they would be referred, without a file ever being opened by the court, to noncorrectional normalizing agencies in the community. Diversion supporters still intended to intervene in the belief that action had to be taken to forestall escalation. Their technique can be seen as but the latest effort to realize Thomas Eliot's vision of a juvenile justice apparatus in which treatment was removed from the court itself. As in Eliot's model, the court in the diversion conception would act only as a last resort. But proponents still saw the court as a necessary backup, and so it would remain a part of the human service system for handling problem children and those at risk.[14]

Reducing the volume of cases coming to the court's attention did not address the plight of those juvenile offenders who passed through the court into its supporting network of training schools. Here social personnel drew their inspiration from the recent drive in the field of mental health to deinstitutionalize patients and place them in new community-based programs. Where confinement in state mental hospitals did far more harm than good, it would be possible in the less restrictive setting to foster a truly therapeutic milieu.[15] Since juvenile training schools also inflicted damage upon their charges, deinstitutionalization was urged for incarcerated minors, too. Proponents of the new approach intended to create a network of local treatment programs to assume the burden of adjusting severely troubled youth.[16] In these community programs, the behavioral specialists and caseworkers would occupy the leadership positions. Where before the bureaucrats and political appointees had stressed physical control rather than meaningful treatment, the needs of the youngsters would be defined in therapeutic terms.

A Place for Casework

In practice things have worked out rather differently than the purifiers anticipated, for they did not appreciate the political forces with which they would have to contend. It was easier to initiate the process of reform than to control its outcome or its consequences. At the outset the reform strategies appeared to make striking progress. Separation of aid and services became the policy of the Department of Health, Education, and Welfare (HEW) in 1967, with the states obliged to follow along several years later. Diversion and deinstitutionalization received federal support beginning at the same time, and more generous funding was made available in the following years in the hopes of prompting the states to accelerate their efforts in both areas. With the introduction of these measures, social personnel made certain that they would retain a place for themselves. Innovation, however, has also produced less happy effects. Therapeutic practitioners have established greater autonomy, yet they remain subordinate players who still lack the authority to direct their efforts where these seem most needed. Clients appear to have gained none of the promised benefits; indeed, for them things may now be worse. But because social personnel have acquired new roles for themselves, they have seen fit to accept this Faustian bargain.

The triumph of the separation idea in public assistance was assured when advocates secured the support of the welfare policy inner circle clustered around HEW. So there would be no doubt about the federal commitment to the new policy, the welfare bureaucracy was thoroughly restructured: the Bureau of Family Services (BFS) was eliminated; the service duties of all HEW subunits were placed under a new Social and Rehabilitation Service (SRS); and an Assistance Payments Administration was created within SRS to handle income maintenance.[17] Although the pro-therapeutic elements in SRS lost influence thereafter, they managed to promulgate regulations that required states by 1972 to separate their aid and service functions. In the resulting reorganization of social welfare departments, all those with casework skills, including assistance caseworkers and child protection personnel, were grouped together in a single office.[18] Soon the Republican leadership in HEW decided that the federal government ought not to dictate such administrative matters. Still, even after the federal government withdrew the regulations, most states opted to retain the separated structure.[19]

At first it appeared that enthusiasts of separation had gained what they wanted. Assistance caseworkers, recognized finally as professionals, were less burdened by paperwork and found themselves with the time to use their skills. Since some recipients would not choose services, caseloads would be brought down to an acceptable level. Along with bringing about better practice conditions, moreover, the reorganization was expected to improve professional-client relations. Those who opted for services, having done so of their own accord, would be most receptive to help. Social personnel predicted that agency caseworkers would develop with the new group of clients an authentic therapeutic bond, long regarded as a basic condition for constructive intervention.[20] Caseworkers also derived an important internal political benefit from the separation policy. They were concentrated in distinct units in which their professional ethos could be nurtured. Managerialism as the prevailing discourse in public assistance seemed to be checked at one point.

Nevertheless, because they expected a dramatic change in their dealings with recipients, caseworkers have had reason to be disappointed. Separation has not assured that "soft" counseling services, essential to therapeutic rehabilitation, would be given much emphasis. The choice of services remains with recipients, and they have continued to prefer concrete benefits like housing assistance. In addition, studies suggest that the recipients who request services from the public assistance department are not those who have, by the criteria of therapeutic discourse, the most serious needs.[21] The notion that a truly voluntary relationship would be possible, meanwhile, has been undermined by the continued fact of recipient dependency and by other assistance policies that incorporate mandatory services. When recipients feel the caseworker controls something vital to them, especially access to medical care or other hard services, they remain vulnerable to coercion. They also may be required to participate in such "service" activities as child-support collection or employment training. Refusal can result in the termination of their benefits.[22]

Once we abandon the perspective of the social personnel, moreover, the drawbacks of separation stand out more clearly. The policy had been justified as better for clients, but in fact they appear to have become its victims. Separation thoroughly bureaucratized relations between recipients and assistance agencies. When caseworkers were reassigned to the special units, recipients lost their only real human contact within the welfare department. Communication has been depersonalized, as each office visit means dealing with a different eligibility technician. One's life story must be retold time and again. Putting relations on a proper bureaucratic footing has also meant that no one in the agency attempts anymore to deal with recipients as whole persons. Before separation went into effect, they could present all their problems at one desk. Today, instead of responding to their experience in its full complexity, the specialized agency forces them to divide their problems to fit its categories.[23]

The impact of separation on recipients has been shaped, too, by the political context in which the policy has been implemented. By the early 1970s the casework concept in assistance had been discredited; the public and politicians were alarmed by the exponential increase in relief rolls and costs; and efficient, cost-conscious management became the order of the day, so much so that the federal government began to penalize states with a high rate of overpayments.[24] Senior officials at the state level recognized that separation could be exploited as a cost-control device. They correctly understood that the character of the interactions with clients would henceforth depend upon the frontline eligibility technicians. These nonprofessionals have accordingly been reconditioned. To assure that they pursue the managerial emphasis on holding down costs, their discretion to favor individual applicants with special needs has been reduced. Performance evaluation criteria also reward employees who do not make errors in favor of clients, thus stifling any natural tendency to feel sympathy for those who come in search of help.[25] At the same time, since the service doctrine in public assistance was out of fashion, management did not feel obliged to commit the agency's professional resources to counsel assistance recipients. Only during the first few years did caseworkers focus on the income maintenance population. Since then they have been treated by top officials as a kind of "fire brigade," to be reallocated to address whatever problem has captured public attention or seems likely to cause embarrassment to the organization.

In much the same manner, the diversion reform in juvenile justice began with bright hopes. Amidst popular skepticism about the effectiveness of the criminal justice system, the idea quickly developed a strong following, culminating in a 1967 endorsement by the President's Commission on Crime. Federal money to support youth service bureaus and other diversion programs became available over the next several years. With dollars floating around for those willing to enter the new field, private agencies discovered that it made sense to expand their operations to include delinquency prevention and treatment. Programs not directly under court auspices proliferated rapidly.[26] Because there was supposed to be little direct court involvement in any phase of intervention, social personnel expected to exercise greater control over case management than before. They seemed free to explore new diagnostic tools and treatment approaches.

Yet the net effect has been quite the opposite of what advocates wanted. Far from reducing the domain of the juvenile court, diversion has helped to expand it. By the early 1970s the system was processing more than one million delinquency cases per year, many involving minor violations of the type that the court had previously dismissed. Moreover, reports indicate that judicial tutelage has sometimes come to encompass the offender's siblings, even where they have committed no violation, and his parents.[27] It is plain that only an increase in resources would permit the institution to undertake such missions. And those augmented resources have come into the juvenile justice system under the auspices of diversion itself. The judges still function as the gatekeepers for services for children at risk.[28] Hence, minors can enter the new diversion programs only after being processed by the court or after it chooses temporarily to suspend its jurisdiction. Either way, its reach has been extended. We can conclude that the latest initiative by the court's foes to reduce its scope of operations has been confounded.

This contrary outcome came about primarily because the supporters of diversion underestimated the political obstacles they would have to overcome. First off, advocates of the plan should have realized that diversion is the sort of reform that popular sentiment will not abide. On several occasions, especially when delinquent conduct assumes a more violent form and lurid accounts appear in the press, the public has demanded a "get tough" posture toward problem juveniles. We have also witnessed a recent surge in public concern over runaway adolescents, with corresponding demands that official action be taken to return them to parental control.[29] This popular pressure, of course, plays directly into the hands of the juvenile court judges. Riding the crest of demands that public safety or family integrity be put first, they have forestalled efforts by reformers to limit the court's jurisdiction or soften dispositions. When social personnel complain that the court panders to the worst popular instincts, judges retort that they merely express the commonsense and legitimate position that citizens should not have to walk the streets in fear. Reformers have never managed to cultivate public backing to offset the popular mandate the judges can claim.

Even where public sentiment has not made itself felt, the judges have shown an ability to look after their institutional position. Lawyers who support diversion have encouraged the American Bar Association to endorse the policy. But the judges have resisted strongly. And because they sit atop the established institution defining the field of juvenile justice, their views command significant support within the legal profession. They have defeated a proposal that the ABA recommend stripping the court of its responsibility for status offenses.[30] In the political arena, too, juvenile court judges command enormous respect. State legislatures have approved diversion without substantially narrowing the scope of the court's jurisdiction. Statutes which appear to abolish the category of status offender nevertheless permit the court to adjudicate noncriminal behavior under other headings.[31]

Besides failing to anticipate the resistance they would face, diversion proponents made a key tactical error when they chose not to confront the entrenched power of the juvenile court directly. As so often in the earlier history of the human services, reformers opted for the path of least resistance. For example, diversion programs were created without doing battle with the judges over scarce resources. In the prosperous 1960s, it was unnecessary for policymakers to make real choices—they could subsidize both the court and the diversion alternatives. Since the court remained intact, it could proceed with business as usual. Indeed, it could do better than usual. Social personnel have learned they are not the only enterprising players in the system. When the federal government pumped more money into delinquency control, the judges and their probation departments moved aggressively to bring the funds under court control. Further, where reform was intended to steer status offenders away from the institution, juvenile court judges have pressed successfully in some states to bring under their authority entire families whose noncriminal behavior indicates a need for official supervision.[32] Diversion would have reduced judicial intervention only if reformers had put clear statutory bounds around the court's jurisdiction and choked off the flow of resources to the institution itself.

The political forces working to broaden judicial intervention have been augmented by pressures from marginal populations themselves. While many clients as before seek to rebuff the court, others continue to view it as a useful instrument to tilt the balance in family power struggles. Chesney-Lind observes that parents of teenage girls hold to the old behavioral standard that is far more tolerant of adolescent male rebelliousness and sexuality. To control defiant conduct by their daughters, such parents often have turned to the court, filing complaints under the various status offender headings. For their part, court officials have long seen it as their task to correct "immoral" female activity. Although diversion briefly delegitimized court intervention to check young women's sexuality, judges and probation officers found it hard to give up for good their past commitments. Hence, with increasing frequency during the 1980s, they have again permitted themselves to be used by the parents, accepting without challenge the reports of defiance or waywardness.[33]

Much the same sobering tale can be told of deinstitutionalization in juvenile justice. The federal government endorsed broadly the idea of community-based treatment, including the notion of "least restrictive placement" for juvenile offenders. To push the states in this direction during the 1970s, federal money was made available and regulations were issued that would encourage the development of treatment in open settings.[34] Nevertheless, placements in restrictive facilities appear to be as frequent as before. Although many state training schools have closed, they have been replaced by nontraditional institutions, including private correctional centers, nonprofit child welfare residences, and mental health facilities. Lerman shows that this trend toward reinstitutionalization has been spurred by the entrepreneurship of some social agencies and the organizational imperatives of others. On one side, as funds became available for community-based care, social personnel set out to secure every available dollar. New facilities were created and existing ones were adapted, all with an eye toward satisfying the letter of the regulations rather than producing genuinely open institutions. On the other side, institutional placement often becomes the easy way out for agencies with the burden of caring for problem youngsters. For example, child welfare officials, ill-prepared to handle the large volume of status offenders that diversion has brought to their doors, tend to label them as emotionally disturbed and to rely heavily on secure treatment facilities.[35]

If community-based treatment is not all that social personnel expected, they still have gained much under reinstitutionalization. In the private and nonprofit institutions, psycho-medical practitioners find themselves less restricted by the bureaucratic mentality that ruled the state carceral facilities. It is true that they are closely scrutinized by their neighbors, who fear having problem youth living in such close proximity. But this local mistrust can be neutralized through the careful selection of clients likely to be less dangerous or disruptive. As before, severely troubled youngsters, who are supposed to require the most intensive intervention, find themselves shunted to the remaining training schools where they are merely warehoused until their maturity. This rationing of clients accords better with the calculus of punishment than that of normalization. All the same, social personnel again have reason to go along.

For the youngsters themselves, the reshaping of confinement not only perpetuates the evils of incarceration but also encourages other insidious practices. The new generation of institutions functions out of the public view. When facilities describe themselves as "community-based" and "nonrestrictive," it is assumed they must offer enlightened care; the "homes" and centers are too obscure to attract much notice from journalists and too numerous for civil-liberties lawyers to exercise effective oversight. Behavioral specialists have a free hand, then, to test idiosyncratic treatment approaches. Nontraditional secure facilities tend to assume the character of laboratories, their inmates the unwilling subjects of experimental efforts to modify behavior and personality. And placements may last longer than those in training schools, to better permit an attack on the alleged underlying problem. Yet because this can be represented as treatment, it still appeals to therapeutic activists as less objectionable than straightforward punishment.[36] Furthermore, while much has been said about the harm that can be done by branding a minor with a negative label, this practice perversely has been encouraged under reinstitutionalization. Maximum federal reimbursement can be obtained for psychiatric services, so agencies have a powerful incentive to medicalize youth problems.[37] Juvenile offenders now risk carrying through life labels perhaps more destructive than that of being delinquent.

Broadening the Social State

The five years following the 1967 Social Security Amendments have been described by Derthick as a period of "uncontrollable spending" for social services. This spending surge did not come about through the agitation of social personnel, though we shall see that they have derived important benefits from it. Rather, expenditures were driven upward by the dynamics of intergovernmental relations and partisan politics. The 1967 legislation further loosened the terms under which the states could secure reimbursement, so that the legislation became a kind of fiscal relief for subnational governments. On the administrative front, a reorganization of the federal bureaucracy in 1967 also made it easier for the states to collect federal money. The new Social and Rehabilitation Service, placed under the control of vocational rehabilitation administrators, favored a more open definition of services than had the social worker-guided BFS. When the Nixon administration took office, partisan considerations caused federal bureaucrats to further relax the standards for matching state service expenditures. Republican appointees in HEW sought to bolster the political standing of Republican governors in key states like New York and California by approving any and all reimbursement requests. Under generous legislation and lenient administration, the states lined up again to dip into the federal till.[38]

Besides rising precipitously in the early 1970s, social service spending was redistributed to new constituencies. The 1962 amendments had established some precedent for services to persons not receiving public assistance, but very little was done along these lines. Five years later Congress made the working poor eligible, to encourage the states to offer services to potential assistance recipients; the implementing regulations issued by HEW stretched the language so the middle class might benefit, too.[39] Taken together, the legislative and administrative changes of the 1967–1971 period signaled the beginning of another kind of separation— that of services from assistance recipients. Over the following decade, particularly with the passage of the Title XX amendments in 1974, a steadily larger percentage of services went to the nonpoor.[40]

Social personnel welcomed this service reorientation as a sign that the therapeutic sector was emerging as a cornerstone of the affluent society. For some years, besides advocating normalizing intervention for marginal populations, they had proposed making services universally available. Services ought to be regarded, Alfred Kahn liked to say, as "social utilities" for all citizens who might need some help in coping with the profound stresses or even just the routine troubles of modern everyday life.[41] The concept recalled the Progressive doctrine of the social living standard, updated for an era in which psychological well-being had come to be defined as essential. Since every citizen had a right to the minimum standard of living, professional counseling attained the status of a basic entitlement.[42] It was time, then, to break the link between public normalizing services and the poor.[43] The social utilities concept pointed instead to an unbounded therapeutic sector, one indifferent to traditional notions of limited government. Therapeutic activists, of course, have never feared the power of the state.

Though social personnel took comfort from portraying their task as the fulfillment of a democratic calling, the real appeal of the social utilities ideal lay elsewhere. If a more respectable clientele arrived at the doors of the social agencies, therapeutic practitioners, especially the chronically insecure social workers, might rise on the professional ladder. Further, they might at last get to do what they liked best. When the poor sought help, they wanted immediate, concrete assistance—certainly useful, but not artistically stimulating to the caseworker. By comparison, the middle class seems to have an inexhaustible need for psycho-social counseling and mental health programs.[44] We might take this as a reflection of just how deeply Freudian insights about the neuroses of modern life had permeated the larger culture: even the middle class cannot be confident of its ability to attain full psychological self-awareness and adjustment, and so it seeks fulfillment through expert intervention by psychiatrists, psychologists, and other specialists. As social personnel set out to satisfy this new constituency, the tendency for hard services to crowd out all personal services was partially checked. While it is true that during the 1970s most public funds continued to pay for hard services, in absolute terms the therapeutic component of the service budget expanded.[45]

For all that the transformation of services meant to social personnel in professional terms, however, its greatest immediate effect on them was political. They had worried that Title XX would stimulate influential groups to seek services, preventing marginal clienteles from getting their fair share. Events bore out the prediction: the elderly and working-class parents of young children demanded services and, as noted, claimed an increasing proportion of the available funds.[46] But precisely because such

important constituencies backed service programs, elected officials supported appropriations at a level far above what therapeutic activists had
ever achieved through their own efforts. Social personnel had at last
begun to overcome their chronic weakness in the political arena. In addition, private social agencies became important advocates for public
spending on service activities. New regulations and statutes gave such
agencies a major role as service providers, leaving them increasingly dependent upon the steady flow of government monies.[47] With so much at
stake, the private agencies learned overnight to be effective lobbying
agents. Thus, when both Congress and HEW in the early 1970s sought to
roll back the clock by restricting service eligibility to assistance recipients
or those on the verge of dependency, they were thwarted by fierce opposition from the private providers and the constituent groups they
mobilized.[48]

This newfound political muscle proved indispensable during the next
decade when fiscal pressures threatened to crush the therapeutic sector.
The first test came during the Nixon years, as the states continued relentlessly to shift service costs to the federal treasury. Alarmed by the precip-
itous rise, Congress in 1972 imposed a $2.5 billion cap on service spend-
ing. This was carried forward in the Title XX legislation two years later.[49]
But if the cap halted the growth in expenditures, it also effectively stabi-
lized spending at a far higher level than during the previous decade. In
fact, the new ceiling doubled as a floor, because no elected official dared
to propose that Congress appropriate less than the maximum. The arrangement lasted until the arrival of the austerity-minded Reagan administration in 1981. It made the social services block grant (formerly Title
XX) an early target. Yet though the budget crisis gave a conservative
regime the opportunity to halt the surge in service spending, the level of
public expenditures has remained far higher than twenty years ago.[50] And
there are signs that service spending may climb again in the years to come.
We do not have to search hard for an explanation for the peculiar resil-
iency of the human services: the therapeutic apparatus has acquired
enough friends over the past twenty years to protect against attempts to
dismantle it. Thus, even though programs were slashed in Washington,
private providers and their well-organized constituents could prevail
within state legislatures.[51] The decentralization and grassroots politics
that were the bane of therapeutic entrepreneurs have of late shielded them
from the conservative tide.

Of course, I do not mean to suggest that retrenchment has been without effect. To the contrary, the poor and working poor have suffered,
many losing vital benefits. Access to income maintenance and hard services was first reduced in the 1970s through behind-the-scenes administra-

tive changes; during this period, too, the real value of AFDC benefits declined when grant levels remained frozen in a time of high inflation.[52] Under the 1981 Omnibus Budget Reconciliation Bill, the principle move in the Reagan retrenchment, some 500,000 families lost their eligibility for AFDC and another 300,000 had their benefits reduced. The practice of requiring disabled persons to obtain recertification of their incapacity likewise deprived thousands of Supplementary Social Insurance (SSI) benefits. Through such measures the state demonstrates that it has again learned how to use the variability of power. Marginal populations, having briefly turned this to their own purposes in the late 1960s, are coldly reminded of their acute dependence.[53] Austerity also has had an intellectual impact. The conservative attack on social services has exposed flaws in the social-utilities ideology so eagerly promoted by social personnel. Since this doctrine suggests no basis for ordering spending priorities when resources are scarce, there could be no intelligible alternative to the Reagan agenda. Social personnel, left to demand that every program be preserved, made themselves irrelevant. The human services have survived the conservative tide minus any sense of purpose appropriate to the fiscal realities of our era.[54]

Misery Means Opportunity

As the American body politic has noticed new social problems over the past decade, therapeutic practitioners once more find themselves with abundant opportunities. Certain miseries have become the object of heightened concern—I will speak here of child abuse and the growth of the urban underclass. Without denying the reality of the problems themselves, we must recognize that their identification as urgent issues works to the advantage of the helping professions. Since no other set of policy actors wishes to claim the terrain, an opening exists that social personnel can fill. Predictably, they have stepped forward with prescriptions for the broader application of their normalizing methods, and followed this with vigorous entrepreneurship to establish appropriate programs or reorganize existing ones. Where public departments have been drawn into the effort to address the problems of the moment, therapeutic activists have pressed to install themselves in key positions. All in all, they suddenly find themselves in greater demand than they have been since the early years of the Kennedy administration.

Few issues so arouse public compassion as child abuse and neglect. Although the field of child protection dates back to the nineteenth century, public concern has rarely reached the present level of intensity.

Shifting public norms account for some of this; ours is the era of nonviolent parenting. But we must also give credit for making child abuse a salient concern to pediatricians, who discovered how to put modern medical technology to use in detecting abuse, and to child welfare advocates. As a result of this newfound public alarm, the child welfare professionals find themselves in a thriving industry. Laws have been passed requiring all suspicious incidents to be reported; state legislatures have mandated the use of social service funds for child protection more often than for any other service; public social service departments have reallocated their casework personnel to emphasize child protection at the expense of services to assistance recipients.[55]

That therapeutic activists have achieved an iron grip over child protection policy becomes most evident when, as is too often the case, normalizing intervention fails. In larger American cities the media regularly report pathetic stories of children maimed or murdered by their parents or guardians. Frequently it emerges that the families were known to the child welfare department; indeed, some of the incidents involve foster placements arranged by its own caseworkers.[56] The embarrassed agency responds in two ways. First, to improve its public image, it cleanses itself through a ritual of bureaucratic human sacrifice: caseworkers are reprimanded, middle-level supervisors are transferred, and the senior official responsible for child protection resigns. Second, outside consultants are called in to review where the agency went wrong. Because these independent observers are themselves members of the child welfare network, they invariably recommend the same standard remedies for casework failures that have been prescribed since the Progressive era—better personnel training, greater professionalism, improved coordination of agency efforts, smaller caseloads, etc. Before long new episodes occur, and the pattern of agency self-correction repeats itself.

Another opportunity for social personnel to extend their influence, as yet largely unexplored, lies in the rediscovery of the underclass and the revival of the notion that it reproduces itself through a culture of poverty. Statistics indicate that among inner-city blacks there has been a sharp increase in the number of unmarried teenage mothers and unemployed young males. In these groups we find alarmingly high rates of drug use, child abuse and neglect, and crime.[57] While the demographics and social indicators are not in dispute, the same cannot be said for the other claims made about the underclass. Conservatives contend that its members are largely responsible for their own misfortune because of their self-destructive behaviors. Public social welfare policies are also blamed for the emergence of the underclass over the past two decades: whereas urban blacks once moved up the social ladder by the sweat of their brow, it is said, their children and grandchildren now depend on handouts.[58] Liberals dispute this causal reasoning, but they remain uncomfortable with the entire subject.[59] Not surprisingly, then, the Right continues to set the terms of the debate. Policy discussion focuses on how to inculcate greater regard for mainstream values about work and family.

Once the challenge of the underclass has been so framed, we have paved the way for casework by the therapeutic practitioner. Few other policy instruments have been designed to bring about changes on such an intimate level. Programs to promote economic development in inner-city neighborhoods do not confront personal behavior patterns directly; besides, such initiatives are out of style today. As another possibility, we might look here for a creative effort to pursue the political path to social membership. But this approach has never commanded sustained support among policy analysts and, in the wake of the community action turmoil of the 1960s, it receives scant attention today. There remains only normalizing intervention as defined by therapeutic discourse. If caseworkers have qualms about assuming this duty, we cannot forget that their techniques were invented for exactly such a purpose. Add, too, the promise of substantial funding that accompanies official interest in a social problem. It may be a sign for the future that some therapeutic activists have already indicated a willingness to enlist themselves in the cause of rehabilitating the underclass.[60]

Rationalization Redux

The measures that social personnel pursued to preserve a place for themselves and their vigorous entrepreneurship have resulted in a sharp increase in the number and variety of social agencies. Where a problem area has long been recognized, like juvenile antisocial behavior, many therapeutic activists dismissed existing agencies as a hindrance to good practice. Reformers concluded that it was necessary to create fresh structures. But the agencies that had claimed the problem for their own have not vanished from the scene. Interest in social problems of more recent vintage likewise has resulted in the multiplication of service providers. To address the issues that have arisen over the past fifteen years, some therapeutic entrepreneurs think it best to introduce new agencies. But established organizations, created to meet some other challenge, believe their experience better qualifies them for the role. As a result of recent policy reforms and innovations, we have witnessed the deposit of a new layer of agencies atop the organizational sediment accumulated through the Progressive, New Deal, and Great Society eras.

This relentless organizational proliferation has contributed to the incoherence of the entire human service mechanism. Although therapeutic activists have always insisted on the need to divide labor efficiently and purposefully, policy choices do not reflect their discursive logic. Instead, agencies have learned to see each other not as partners in a common enterprise but as competitors for resources, cooperating only when interagency backscratching advances particular interests. To further confuse matters, decisions are less likely to reflect professionals' views of service needs than the weight of interest group pressures and the whims of public attention. Additional dollars serve merely to further distend this system, so that coordination of the pieces becomes a more distant and elusive goal. The apparatus as it stands today has drifted farther away from the well-ordered form that therapeutic discourse has always identified as its ultimate institutional ideal.

We may take as an illustration the sorry case of child welfare and child protection. Services for children at risk, long dependent upon a maze of public, nonprofit, and parochial agencies, have become even more confused in the wake of diversion, deinstitutionalization, and the surge of concern about child abuse. Public funds have poured into the field. Yet social personnel worry that children often do not receive the services they need, for public and private agencies alike choose their young clients with great care. The organizations cannot afford a low success rate or public embarrassment if they hope to maintain their funding.[61]

Confronted by the mounting disarray that characterizes the therapeutic sector, some social personnel initially tried to make a virtue of necessity. They borrowed a page from the economists and announced that a lack of planning and overall control might be a blessing. Where once they worried about overlapping effort, duplication of services was suddenly praised for offering clients a choice between service providers.[62] But the market analogy works poorly here, for the system has not been driven by consumer preferences. "Product availability" has depended instead upon political factors—the clout wielded by coalitions of private agencies, calculations by public officials about which services will yield the highest electoral return, politicians' desires to dispense patronage or to pay off political friends, and the ability of agencies to negotiate successfully with public bureaucracies.[63] Service needs have gone unmet, however urgent social personnel might deem them, because this politicized decision mechanism has been indifferent to the priorities of therapeutic discourse.

As it became increasingly evident that public monies were contributing to chaos, the sponsoring government departments looked for some way to impose order. They quickly settled upon stronger centralized control, the technique favored by therapeutic activists since the 1920s. This quest for strict top-down oversight brought public officials onto sensitive terrain, because the many private agencies delivering services under contract were jealous of their autonomy. But providers, now heavily dependent on government support, could not afford to turn their backs on contract dollars. Knowing that private agencies have been reduced to supplicants, the funding departments have tried to close gaps in the service network by making it a condition of the contract that a provider take clients who would otherwise have been rejected.[64]

What results from such practices, however, is not rationalization as social personnel construe it. In the first place, the contract process is still deeply politicized—the ability of an agency to secure a contract depends heavily on political contacts and coalition politics, while the funding departments reallocate resources not because needs have been met but because public interest has shifted. Perhaps more disturbing to social personnel, agencies are forced by contract requirements to violate basic canons of the therapeutic enterprise. The well-ordered service apparatus envisioned by therapeutic discourse would find each agency treating the clients for which it was best equipped. To place marginal subjects in the wrong program plays havoc with sound casework principles; indeed, it is no better than denying them care entirely. Yet contracts mandate that programs accept referrals, however inappropriate, from public agencies or take clients on the basis of criteria that are unrelated to suitability. By the same token, where therapeutic discourse recognizes that clients will respond at different rates to normalizing intervention, public contracts fix the duration of services. This is not rationalization but uniformity. Finally, as providers struggle to conform to complex accountability guidelines, social personnel again find themselves shunted aside from leadership positions. Assuring compliance with the contract calls for the skills of the manager, not the caseworker.[65]

Bad as public monitoring of contract services makes things for social personnel, all is not lost. They also gain at the expense of their grassroots competitors. I pointed out in the previous chapter that feminists in the 1970s put in place their own network of programs, disdaining the use of helping professionals. But the feminist counterprograms also have come to depend on public funding, and with this they have been subject to contract monitoring. Public officials, though themselves management types rather than caseworkers, have accepted the claims of therapeutic activists that intervention requires expert skills gained through formal training in the normalizing disciplines. Of course, founded upon contrary principles, the feminist shelters and crisis centers did not meet this bureaucratic staffing standard. Official pressure accordingly has been applied to compel them to hire therapeutic practitioners with conventional credentials.[66]

An Adaptable Discourse

The many challenges that social personnel faced during the 1960s precip-itated a corresponding crisis in therapeutic discourse. We have seen that neighborhood militants condemned the preoccupation with the inner mental life of the poor. In this exercise of caseworker-bashing they were joined by "renegade" radical therapeutic practitioners and social work educators. External and internal critics alike chastised social personnel for the hidden political bias of their work, for functioning as agents of an oppressive social order.[67] Far from pursuing an objective standard of healthy adjustment, it was asserted, clinicians and caseworkers attempted to impose the tastes of their own social class on their marginal clients. Social personnel failed to see that the living arrangements of the poor were necessary adaptations to their circumstances.[68] Some community activists and their intellectual allies went further: if the minority poor shunned marriage and other signs of bourgeois propriety, theirs were le-gitimate value choices that white, middle-class caseworkers had no right to question.[69]

We can also distinguish a second line of attack that focused on the knowledge pretensions of therapeutic practitioners. Normalizing inter-vention had long been represented as an exercise of power grounded in the scientific understanding of human personality and psycho-social in-teractions. Where this contention had seemed to rest on a fragile founda-tion, social personnel had sought new disciplines around which to organ-ize their practice—hence the Freudian era. Despite all that had been expected of psychoanalysis, however, Freudian doctrine had come under attack from some of its own influential practitioners. Competing schools arose to challenge its dominance within the medico-psychiatric commu-nity; clinicians tried to sort their way through the confusion by superim-posing one approach atop another.[70] By the 1960s it was clear that social personnel still lacked behavioral knowledge that would allow reliable interventions. They remained unable to get beneath appearances, and continued to grope for answers to the complexities of personality and situation. Clinical intervention, it was acknowledged, did not obtain any better results than would be anticipated through natural healing processes.[71]

Where practice could not be guided by science, normalizing interven-tion ceased to be a constructive enterprise and degenerated into irrespon-sible tampering. Social personnel did not so much treat as experiment, with all the uncertainty that entailed.[72] In the worst instances, they pre-tended to be guided by science when in fact they sought to sell a new technique and thereby establish a professional reputation. Their subjects,

as critics were quick to point out, had no choice about whether to participate in such therapeutic adventures. Clients went along solely because
they had been ordered to cooperate or because social personnel controlled vital resources. And in cases in which intervention was voluntary,
treatment services were deliberately misrepresented to obtain client con-
sent.[73] Given these circumstances, it was most urgent to establish clients'
rights to reject intervention and to develop accountability mechanisms
that would force therapeutic practitioners to answer to the lay public.[74]

This intellectual thrashing threw social personnel off stride for a brief
time, but they have rebounded. The charges that they were agents of an
oppressive social order at first reduced them to a demoralized state.[75]
With the fading of the protests, however, outside voices, especially those
of clients, have once more been ignored.[76] Receptiveness to external challenge has given way to ritualistic pronouncements that practitioners must
sincerely consider how to mend their ways even as they continue to follow
their basic approach. In short, therapeutic discourse has settled back into
its established limits, and social personnel have again made peace with
what they do.

The political challenge to the casework approach has been neutralized
through a deft rhetorical strategy. Social personnel begin by acknowledging their role as instruments of elite domination and the limitations of
their method. Then, having admitted the truth of much of the criticism,
they proceed largely as though they never heard it at all. The refrain runs
something like this: Yes, casework only tries to fit people to an oppressive
order without changing conditions. Yes, for people without money or
medical care or decent housing, social justice is a more urgent concern
than individual counseling. Yes, neighborhood residents must be given a
say in agency operations. But we have tilted the balance too far away
from individual intervention under professional direction. We can see the
importance of personal counseling when we consider, for example, the
disorganized lives and the chaotic family relationships of the underclass.
And so we cannot be content with promoting access to hard services. The
lives of marginal citizens can be made more decent and worthwhile if we
guide them to the personal social services they really need and provide
those to which they are entitled.[77] By the same token, though we want our
agencies to be responsive to local wishes, we cannot "sacrifice the capacity for expertise and standards."[78]

Having glossed over the charges against them, social personnel go on
to contend that their accusers are callous about the fate of the very people
they claim they want to protect. Rights activists complain about the intrusiveness of the state, it is said, without offering a real alternative. They
have managed to expand the negative freedoms enjoyed by marginal
groups like mental patients because these rights cost taxpayers little. But
much less has been done to promote an ethic of social responsibility, with

the result that newly gained due-process protections are undone by public neglect of community-based care and basic material needs.[79] Social personnel go on to claim that the antitutelage posture, while avowedly liberal, resonates nicely with the conservative diatribe against big government. According to their indictment, leftist opponents of the human services failed to speak up for the disenfranchised when the Reagan administration set about to dismantle social programs.

Although this is a curious bill of particulars, it has served its purpose. Responsibility for the failure to develop community treatment resources must be assigned widely, not least to therapeutic practitioners. At the time of deinstitutionalization, after all, many social personnel renounced their obligation to their former patients. Remuneration in the new community mental health clinics was low, while an increasing number of middle-class patients could afford to pay higher fees, thanks largely to health insurance plans that agreed to reimburse subscribers for more forms of counseling.[80] As for the retrenchment in human services, to blame advocates of clients' rights and leftist critics is merely to condemn the messengers. They did not cause the abuses that had become routine in normalizing programs. And they are surely not responsible for the failure of such programs to bring about the results their sponsors promised or for the intellectual bankruptcy of therapeutic activists whose only response to that failure has been a call for more of the same. Nevertheless, by censuring their progressive foes for their supposed lack of compassion, social personnel have comforted themselves that all along they have occupied the moral high ground. From that vantage point, serious self-appraisal is quite unnecessary. It should be added that surveys of social workers document that they themselves feel no overriding obligation to help find solutions to compelling social issues like poverty.[81]

The scientific critique of therapeutic doctrine has not been answered so much as it has been dissipated. Over the past twenty years social work journals have featured innumerable articles proposing that social personnel redefine their field of practice so that it no longer rests upon unjustified assertions of scientific validity. Practitioners are abjured to identify themselves as advocates for the poor, specialists in long-term or personal care for the handicapped or disabled, or coordinators of hard services.[82] But the effect of these proposals is quite the opposite of what their framers intend. With so many alternative conceptions of practice available, social personnel can happily choose that which best fits their style or outlook. Those disaffected from the positivist paradigm accordingly cease to press for a discursive showdown. Intellectual pluralism means not having to make fundamental choices about the meaning of the enterprise.

Meanwhile, a solid core of clinicians and caseworkers continue to adhere to the notion that instrumental scientific knowledge can form the basis for normalizing intervention. Some maintain that practice knowledge is already sufficiently advanced to be applied effectively to prevent delinquency or correct it, to teach the poor to help themselves achieve self-sufficiency, to prevent teen pregnancies, and so forth.[83] We have encountered such assertions before. On close inspection, it still turns out that the evidence is drawn from pilot programs. Projecting from such demonstrations to more general applications is an exercise fraught with hazards. Even if we suspend disbelief and accept the claims of positive results, poor research design leaves us uncertain about which inputs produced the outcome.[84] And the benefits yielded by pilot projects under highly motivated researchers may well elude us under ordinary conditions in social agencies. Others in the field recognize that the promise of science has not been fulfilled, yet they are not discouraged. They contend that, as a by-product of the great volume of research in disciplines like psychology, a more mature understanding of behavior and motivation has been made possible. Once social personnel apply these research findings in their dealings with clients, adjustment and rehabilitation will be accomplished far more reliably.[85]

A reply to this contention would be pointless, for the discursive commitment to instrumental knowledge is not really open to debate. We are confronted here, as we have been since the beginning of the therapeutic movement, by science-as-ideology. True believers always cling to the notion that they are on the verge of triumph, that the next set of pilot studies will unlock the perverse mysteries of client behavior. After all, the priests—social-work educators and clinical researchers—continue to promise redemption. Like other faiths based on hope rather than reason, this one survives despite the overwhelming weight of contrary evidence.

The Pathologies of Durability

Throughout this study, I have suggested that it is not enough to evaluate the therapeutic enterprise according to the standards of its promoters. We also need to weigh the impact of therapeutic practice on its targets. Intervention, I have argued, threatens the autonomy of marginal families and individuals without compensating benefits. When we adopt this skeptical posture, we can derive comfort from some of the developments of the past fifteen years. Despite the attempt to rationalize the service apparatus, its component pieces still tend to work against each other. The enduring inefficiency of the therapeutic sector remains, from the standpoint of personal liberty, one of its few saving graces. Clients may brush up against the system as before without being absorbed against their will. Insufficient funds for referral and follow-up continue to allow service targets to fade from view. In addition, with the de-emphasis of services in public assistance, previously the largest component of the human service apparatus, people in need can receive some material support without having services thrust upon them.

But we should not overlook the danger that tutelage in its newer forms poses for anyone who comes to official notice. First off, with the turn to purchase-of-service arrangements in the therapeutic sector, normalizing intervention has increasingly been conducted under private auspices. We have been lulled by recent talk about privatization into the false confidence that private management represents merely a device to improve efficiency. In fact the drift to privatize the therapeutic marks a major step in the parcelling out of public authority that Lowi has decried. For example, private facilities for troubled adolescents deprive them of their liberty, sometimes for a longer period than juvenile offenders in state training schools.[86] Yet we have demanded almost no accounting of how such power is being used. Despite the vigorous attempt to monitor contract compliance, state officials rarely go beyond regulations governing financial management, staffing credentials, and physical space. No one, in short, looks at what actually happens in the private service sector.[87] The arbitrary and capricious decisions that brought so much shame upon public social agencies twenty years ago may be repeated, hidden from view, in the emergent contract-services apparatus.

When we examine the expanding public components of the therapeutic apparatus, too, we find cause for concern. The threat to privacy has been dramatically magnified, especially in the field of child protection. Thousands of families have been subjected to traumatizing state investigations. Often there is no evidence yet of abuse, but these families are labeled, as in the past, "at risk." This is done—we already hear the official assurances—only so that they may receive proper oversight from child welfare caseworkers. Were there any basis for confidence in the accuracy of the target identification, we might deem the assault on privacy an acceptable price to pay. But the ability of caseworkers to predict abuse or other behaviors is poor; child welfare agencies, afraid to miss any cases, compensate by over-predicting. Thus files are opened on many families merely because they share with known cases certain attributes, notably poverty. And, of course, despite promises of confidentiality, reputations are destroyed when caseworkers seek some evidence of abuse by questioning teachers, neighbors, and relatives.[88]

More is at stake in public intervention than loss of privacy or the destruction of one's good name. Increased funding for certain components of the apparatus has expanded public discipline of marginal families. In the juvenile justice system, we should recall, intervention in the wake of diversion has encompassed not only minors charged as status offenders but also their siblings and parents. Some of these siblings, without being accused of any violation, have been placed in the secure community-based residential facilities created under deinstitutionalization.[89] Expanded tutelage has also reinforced some of the uglier inequalities in family power relationships. I noted that parents use the juvenile court to preserve control over their adolescent daughters. Many of these girls, Chesney-Lind reports, complain they have been sexually abused at home; for them, running away is a survival strategy born of desperation. Yet the court ignores the abuse charge and intervenes to compel the girls to submit to parental authority; they may even be incarcerated if they persist in their attempts to escape. As diversion increases judicial involvement in status offenses, more young women will be pressured to stay home, vulnerable to male members of the household.[90]

Perhaps these incidents of unwarranted and overly intrusive intervention by the therapeutic sector are the exception. Even if that were the case, however, I see no grounds for complacency. The modern record confirms a lesson of the past—excessive intervention and the destruction of client autonomy are endemic to the social technician's normalizing enterprise. The risks are multiplied as the system expands and becomes more aggressive in seeking out clients. For this reason, there is much to fear in the reforms and innovations of the past fifteen years. They have made it more likely that marginal citizens will be brought face-to-face with therapeutic power.

Conclusion

Captive to the Past

PROGRESSIVE therapeutic activists set out to fashion a new kind of state, and in this they succeeded. The normalizing institutions they created have endured and many others have been introduced during later waves of reform. Today the marginal family or individual will likely have some contact with the caseworkers, clinicians, judges, probation officers, and counselors who staff the human service apparatus. For people who find it difficult to cope with the stresses of poverty or with the demands of everyday life, therapeutic mechanisms offer instruction, advice, and encouragement. And, as the Progressives envisioned, for those who cannot adjust to the social rules that normalizing casework aims to transmit, intervention can call upon ongoing surveillance and, as a last resort, formidable tools of coercion.

To a greater degree than we realize, we have come to accept the therapeutic sector, to rely upon it and view the world from the perspective of the social technician. When confronted by new forms of human misery, policymakers turn as if by reflex to the caseworkers. There is a measure of cynicism and resignation in this. We do not choose to invest in structural remedies to poverty; even if we had the will, we no longer have the confidence of the 1960s that we know how to solve the problems of homelessness, drug abuse, the underclass, family violence, and youth crime, to name but a few of the miseries that find their way into the newspaper headlines or the evening news. But we also look to the human services because we believe social personnel can help. Indeed, when we find evidence of deviant behavior or of an inability to cope, we feel a civic duty to call upon them. Good citizens, confronted with human misery, act appropriately—they report the situation to the responsible therapeutic agency. Our continuing faith in the ability of therapeutic practitioners to make damaged lives whole, despite innumerable counterexamples, reflects the degree to which we have absorbed therapeutic doctrine.[1]

Nevertheless, although therapeutic activists have put in place an array of public and private agencies, they have been thwarted in their larger agenda. When the therapeutic approach was first formulated in the Progressive charity organizations and settlement houses, proponents believed they had uncovered a new kind of power, one that would reach the innermost recesses of human experience and permit a thoroughgoing reconstruction of values, attitudes, behaviors, and relationships. But the positive power thought to be implicit in the technology of adjustment has never achieved the kind of results they anticipated. Despite endless refinements based upon new behavioral disciplines, therapeutic practitioners fail to make accurate assessments of clients' problems, condition, or needs, and agencies regularly mishandle corrective treatment.

Two factors best account for the inability of social personnel to make good on their convictions. First, they have suffered from their own hubris. Confident that the key to the mysteries of personality lies within their grasp, they have plunged boldly ahead in their quest to remold marginal populations. But the available knowledge has invariably turned out to be deficient; clients do not respond as expected. Hence the relentless quest for some scientific discipline that will work. Hubris also led early practitioners to overstate the eagerness with which the working-class family would respond to the caseworker. Instead clients have quickly learned that courts and other social agencies will be satisfied with the appearance of cooperation. Therapeutic practitioners still cannot pierce the defenses that clients erect around themselves, and so case reports contain large amounts of vacuous psychobabble. In other instances, clients manipulate the tutelary apparatus into inappropriate intervention, as when parents wish to assert control over adolescent girls displaying rebellious behavior.

Second, therapeutic activists have been confounded by the institutional and political settings in which they must operate. At every turn they have encountered discursive competition, especially from local publics demanding respect for traditional political-economy or legal-moralist standards of right conduct. Political arrangements, such as permissive state laws or election of juvenile court judges, have guaranteed that community sentiment will be heard. In addition, the ideology of localism—the belief among elected officials that they ought to express their constituents' values, no matter how parochial these may seem—has strengthened the influence of lay opinion over policy in the human services. Because social personnel have usually occupied subordinate positions within their own agencies, they have little leverage to use against either outside pressures or other actors within their organizations who do not subscribe to the therapeutic credo. To master this political environment, therapeutic activists have pursued various strategies—centralized bureaucratic control, service planning, the development of cadre, and, most recently, the invention of autonomous practice settings. Yet for all the effort invested in reform, the human services have merely become more bloated, and the quality of intervention remains unpredictable.

Having failed to secure the promised behavioral changes in marginal populations or to refashion the state, therapeutic discourse lives on today to serve other purposes. The social work schools require some justification for their existence; they cannot claim any exclusive responsibility for the study of social policy and community organization lacks professional cachet. In the perfection of therapeutic methods and the training of the next generation of therapeutic acolytes, the schools continue to find a core mission. If this is harmless enough, we cannot be so complacent about the other uses to which the therapeutic ideal is put. We find the doctrine employed to conceal the true nature of institutions, as when juvenile court judges invoked catchphrases about the need to consider each minor as a unique individual in their attempt to block due-process reforms or restraints on their discretion. Apart from such efforts to protect the interests of specific actors within the apparatus, moreover, therapeutic discourse has been enlisted to forestall more sweeping challenges to the entire normalizing enterprise. When critics speak out against caseworker intrusiveness in the name of a right to privacy, social personnel retort that the alternative is much worse. Would we prefer to leave clients alone to face the brutality of their existence?

The Dilemma of Marginality

Once the question has been posed, we recognize immediately why we have found it so difficult to escape from the policy universe framed by therapeutic discourse. On one level, the therapeutic embodies a global aspiration to bring the natural world under our conscious control. As other sciences give us instruments by which we can tame the physical environment, behavioral disciplines offer the promise that we shall tame the ugly impulses within us.[2] If we shun the quest for the scientific knowledge that would allow us to normalize behavior, we seem to deny this promise, and with that the fundamental modernist dream. Accordingly, the modernist in each of us cries out against romanticizing lower-class folk knowledge. We insist that the helping professionals better understand proper nutrition, budget management, sound mental hygiene, and enlightened child-rearing than do their clients. On another level, because the therapeutic has insinuated itself so deeply into how we view marginality, normalizing intervention has become a constitutive element in our ethic of care. Moral decency demands that we come to the aid of the vulnerable, that we safeguard their physical well-being and life-chances. Fulfilling our obligation means protection, treatment, supervision—in short, the therapeutic program. From this perspective, nonintervention is evil. To put the matter in stark terms, it appears that when we repudiate the caseworker, we embrace the child abuser.

I would reject certain solutions that have been put forward to resolve this predicament. Donzelot attempts to push it aside bodily by reformulating the problem. He notes that when we are faced with the choice between intervention and countenancing abuse or other deviant behaviors, we can only call for the social technicians. It is more important, he contends, to question the sort of power that is deployed through the mechanisms of tutelage. I have taken his cue and attempted to lay bare the logic of the therapeutic sector in the foregoing account. Yet, however necessary such a political inquiry is, the moral issue does not disappear once we have unmasked power. We must still come to grips with the very basic matter of our responsibility for our fellow citizens, especially the most innocent and helpless.

Others propose that we define away the dilemma of deviant behaviors by adopting a more tolerant moral pluralism. This position follows from the 1960s-era radical critiques of therapeutic discourse and more recent feminist analyses of patriarchal family structures. Rather than regard the middle-income, two-parent family as an ideal, it is said, we need to acknowledge the validity of many lifestyles and forms of family organization. I find much to commend in this line of argument. At the very least it should give us pause before we deem the adaptations of lower-class households to their precarious economic condition, such as the informal passing around of children in time of crisis, to be signs of pathological maladjustment. But how far are we prepared to carry our pluralism? If we push the idea to its limit, the most offensive and reprehensible conduct ceases to be deviant and becomes merely different. Any lifestyle is equally good, even if it includes indolence or family violence. Like most, I refuse to accept that we should not pass judgment on some behavioral choices.

However, where a finding that behavior is harmful immediately leads proponents of the therapeutic approach to prescribe intervention, I would reject that move out of hand. Our insistence that some behavior is unacceptable does not suffice to oblige us to act. We must also know that the tools we employ have a reasonable prospect of producing the outcome we seek and will not produce other negative consequences. Tutelage by the human services satisfies neither of these conditions. On the one hand, despite all we have invested in the technology of adjustment, we remain unable to bring about the rehabilitation of clients. On the other hand, when clients are stigmatized for life, when social personnel sustain brutal patterns of domination within the family, or when functioning marginal families are broken up, the harm we inflict is every bit as reprehensible as the behavior that prompted intervention. It would be better to utter our condemnation through due process of law and punish where appropriate than to torment clients in our therapeutic experiments. For that matter, we would cease to raise false expectations in the community that all can be made well again.

This is a pragmatic line of criticism, one that accepts the goal of behavioral adjustment while rejecting the method. But I would also reiterate a more principled objection to the therapeutic enterprise. Aside from the obvious damage done to clients through intervention, our reliance on the therapeutic approach slowly erodes the foundations for democratic citizenship. Personal autonomy, however flawed, is a prerequisite for membership in a democratic political community. Deviant behaviors represent a cry of pain and anger that should be heard, and our attention should be directed toward finding political outlets that will allow the anguish to find constructive expression. But therapeutic discourse has long regarded raw despair and frustration as evidence of individual maladjustment, devoid of collective meaning. Through normalizing intervention, clients can be led to see that such emotions are symptomatic of their refusal to accept reality. This assault on personal sovereignty is necessary, according to therapeutic discourse, to uncover any source of disfunction, with the assurance that ultimately autonomy will be strengthened. It is clear, however, that intervention often leads not to self-sufficiency but rather to ongoing surveillance and further episodes of tutelage. Marginal populations lose the space in which to define their problems in their own terms, one of the basic conditions for democratic politics.

Beyond the Therapeutic State?

Presuming we reject the therapeutic enterprise, then, it remains to be seen whether we can offer something better in response to the challenge of marginality. I have remarked favorably upon the political conception of social membership expressed in the Progressive settlement movement and in the community action programs of the 1960s. Both grasped the importance of allowing the dispossessed to define their own community through collective action. Yet we must acknowledge in all candor that we have little concrete evidence to support the proposition that political mobilization can integrate marginal groups into the social mainstream, much less bring about desirable behavioral changes at the individual level. As I indicated in chapter 6, the earliest ventures in community organization withered after the First World War. This pattern of short-lived experiments was repeated in the 1960s. Despite promising results at the outset, community control initiatives were stifled before a full judgment on their effects could be rendered. Accordingly, when we turn to a consideration of how we might pursue the political avenue to social membership, we embark upon an expedition of the imagination.

We must deal first with the problem of material want. As envisioned by both Progressives and modern community activists, the political approach presupposes a certain level of physical well-being. People who do not know whether they can keep a roof over their heads rarely participate in political life, and if they do their involvement is short-lived. While assurance of a minimum material standard of living does not create a sense of active membership, they would at least be able to think beyond immediate survival needs. Unfortunately, this material foundation for democratic citizenship has been eaten away during the past fifteen years by the steady decline in the value of public assistance grants and other measures that have denied benefits to the working poor. As a beginning, it would be necessary to reverse the recent policy drift. I would emphasize, of course, that we should not incorporate in public assistance the rest of the living standard ideal as it evolved under the influence of philanthropy—the commitment to behavioral norms and discipline. Income maintenance need not entail a therapeutic component.

In addressing the material preconditions for citizen mobilization, we also need to consider deprivation as a community phenomenon. Marginality is concentrated geographically. Since the beginning of the urban-industrial era the disadvantaged have tended to band together in particular city districts, but this pattern has become more pronounced of late. Middle-class elements have fled the inner-city neighborhoods. As the poorest remain behind, they find themselves bereft of the economic resources with which to bring about the rejuvenation of their community. Urban slums have always suffered from a lack of government and market investment; today public and private dollars for economic development continue to go elsewhere, chiefly into the downtown business districts or suburbs. With the departure of the successful families and the savings and purchasing power they represent, the capital problem assumes a more acute form. If there is to be any prospect for a rebirth of marginalized neighborhoods, they require a substantial infusion of economic resources.

Beyond material supports for individuals and neighborhoods, a political approach to social membership would require a far-reaching political reorganization, including sweeping decentralization and community control. I have in mind here an arrangement in which authority over a broad range of decisions would be vested in a "neighborhood government." To begin with, it would assume much of the responsibility for administration of routine public services, asserting independence from larger municipal bureaucracies. In earlier experiments with decentralization, chiefly during the 1960s, too little autonomy was conceded to neighborhood units. Meaningful local control entails a district-level government with the power to establish its own service priorities, purchase hard services from public and private providers, and hold these providers accountable. As outside capital for economic development was made available, furthermore, the neighborhood government would create its own enterprises to make investment choices. This would give it the economic tools that community action programs lacked. At the same time, however, the creation of a new layer of government "close to the people" would not in itself assure their active engagement. For this political reorganization to work as a mechanism for promoting a sense of membership, it would be necessary to encourage direct participation by community residents through frequent, accessible public meetings and diligent community mobilization.

We have no assurance, of course, that a neighborhood government would address the manifestations of social marginality that trouble us. Much would depend upon whether the new political structure sought creative solutions to urgent community problems. If it merely turned to established social agencies and helping professionals, it would effectively renounce its own premise. On the other hand, once the neighborhood government began to foster citizen activism among its marginal constituencies, it might be possible to introduce new mechanisms for helping people overcome the fear, hostility, and alienation that poverty brings in its wake. For example, where we now encourage intervention by the child welfare bureaucracy in suspected cases of child abuse or neglect, the emergence of vigorous block and tenant organizations or neighborhood women's groups might break down family isolation and make peer support more effective.[3]

As these innovative neighborhood efforts took hold, we would anticipate the rise of a different ethic of care, one no longer bound to the discourse of normalizing intervention. The emphasis might shift to the primacy of lay responsibility for recognizing aberrant behavior and taking it to task. I see, too, the possibility that caring might extend to an effort by peer organizations to right imbalances in family power relations. Battered women and abused daughters are most likely to find advocates and political allies among others similarly positioned. But a word of caution is in order: as is true whenever local sentiment is given scope to express itself, the behavioral norms that would be upheld would reflect the particular class and ethnic composition of each neighborhood.

This imaginary excursion, sad to say, cannot take us very far. Though I have suggested how the political path might displace the therapeutic, I must confess that I see precious little chance for making real the radical alternative. It is fashionable to close a critical study of an institution with a vague call for sweeping reform, leading readers to believe that the author thinks change is but a matter of mustering the needed enthusiasm. But I cannot pretend to an optimism that I know to be misplaced. The people who would have to make community control work may not be equipped for the task. More to the point, perhaps, this inquiry has made clear the accumulation of institutional forces within the therapeutic sector that virtually preclude any fundamental reconstruction of the human services.

Let us take up first the political weaknesses of the very poor. In inner-city slums, the lack of economic capital is matched by an absence of political skill and energy. Where Progressive community organizers like Robert Woods found residual organization and talent in marginalized neighborhoods, this reserve capacity seems today to be increasingly absent. I noted above the departure of the natural indigenous leadership. Because it has not been replaced, neighborhood government would rest upon the most disenfranchised—the broken families, the victims of drug abuse and alcohol dependency, the school dropouts. Burdened by the sense that they have no control over their destiny, they are hardest to mobilize for collective action and least likely to remain involved over time. They therefore seem unlikely to play an active part in community councils. Even if we committed ourselves to more adequate income support and established an ample public investment fund for urban neighborhoods, it is not certain that these political liabilities could be overcome.

When we add to this the institutional realities of the therapeutic state, prospects for a neighborhood-based political approach become more dismal still. In seeking the means to address urgent social problems, neighborhood governments would find themselves in direct competition with the public-private normalizing apparatus. It is difficult to imagine a more unequal contest. For while the new local organizations would be political novices, social agencies are savvy in the ways of building influence networks, cultivating favorable publicity, and undermining new entrants in the field. The therapeutic sector has used its political strengths to withstand formidable challenges, most recently the Reagan-era conservative efforts to dismantle the human services. Surely it would be child's play to ward off or co-opt neighborhood attempts to claim a share of the funds that now go to the service network. And though additional public resources may be committed to combat teen pregnancy, youth crime, drug abuse, and other problems of marginality, these dollars would likewise be cornered by the ever-eager therapeutic entrepreneurs.

Heeding the Other Voices

I prefer to close with a far more modest set of suggestions. Some good can be accomplished if we cultivate a skeptical posture toward the human services. Where we have been seduced by the proponents of new normalizing initiatives, who seem to offer answers to the miseries that trouble our conscience, we need to ask hard questions about the real benefits of intervention and the unseen costs. And where we have been intimidated by therapeutic activists, who equate criticism of their enterprise with callousness toward the poor, we must have greater confidence in our own judgments. I would hope that policymakers and opinion shapers learn to give their ear less readily to the therapeutic industry. But, as always in a political system where organized pressure counts most, policy shifts in the human services will become more likely when countervailing influences make themselves felt. So there is much work for ordinary citizens to do, particularly in the communities in which therapeutic facilities and social agencies are most heavily concentrated.

As a first step, we should encourage a broadening of the discourse about marginality beyond the narrow circle of therapeutic practitioners. Problems like delinquency, long-term dependency, and family violence cannot be left to the helping professions. The experts have demonstrated time and again that in this area any claim to exclusive wisdom is singularly suspect. Indeed, precisely because of the exaggerated claims social personnel made about the value of services in public assistance during the 1950s and 1960s, elected officials insisted upon the inclusion of other policy intellectuals. Though the economists were afflicted with their own blind spots, they did manage to introduce new perspectives in policy debates and break the stranglehold of the old gang of therapeutic agents in the Bureau of Public Assistance, the public welfare association, and the social work schools. We should seek now to draw into our social policy debates other participants, especially feminists, community activists, and grassroots organizers who work in the neighborhoods beset with the most serious problems. If we hope to devise solutions that do not fit the tired model of normalizing intervention, other perspectives must be given a serious hearing.

The involvement of local activists might allow us to restore to our policy discourse an element that has been largely lacking since the Progressive era. When the settlement house residents described conditions in the working-class slums, they were careful to note the strengths of the people and their neighborhoods. Soon enough, however, the focus in therapeutic discourse shifted, so that social personnel spoke of little besides deficiencies and weaknesses among their clients. Fifty years ago Richard C. Cabot, a pioneer in medical social work, told an audience of social personnel that this diagnostic model of intervention had put things backward. A constructive program should begin instead with a list of assets upon which to build.[4] I would argue that we have largely failed to follow Cabot's suggestion. In the current discussions about the underclass, for instance, we hear much about what is missing from the lives of the dispossessed and almost nothing about family or community resources. And I plead guilty myself to Cabot's charge, in my grim portrait of the difficulties that must be overcome today in the political mobilization of impoverished communities. We can offset our negative evaluation of marginality, however, by listening to those who have helped to organize welfare moth-

ers, tenant associations, "sweat equity" projects to rebuild decaying housing, block anticrime patrols, and other grassroots expressions of self-help.

Whether a broader dialogue about marginality can be stimulated depends in turn upon a resurgence of lay interest in the matters we have
permitted social personnel to claim for themselves. Policymakers will
heed popular dissatisfaction with the therapeutic approach. But ordinary
citizens have not stepped forward to voice their misgivings, save in isolated campaigns against facilities or programs in their own backyards.
We see from this public timidity that therapeutic discourse has succeeded
in mystifying its field of concern. Fixated on obscure behavioral sciences,
conducted in a jargon impenetrable to the uninitiated, the discourse does
not invite lay participation. Thus, while the problems of marginality are
painfully visible, policy formulation in the human services remains the
domain of a small network of social agencies, umbrella professional associations, and social work educators. Now that we have punctured the
image of technical competence that therapeutic activists have nurtured,
we need to shed our own habitual reliance upon the human services. The
tragedies that have provoked calls for more thorough casework should
instead inspire us to urge upon our elected officials a search for a better
approach.

In addition to pursuing a more open policy debate, we should seek
mechanisms that will hold specific human service programs accountable
to their clients. I do not refer here to the various reporting requirements
by which state-level bureaucrats impose managerial values on private
service providers. These devices do nothing to protect clients. Nor can we
put much faith in client advisory boards, common since the 1960s in both
public and private agencies. These have been as ineffective in shaping
practice in individual cases as they have been in defining general agency
policy. We need to find other means, then, that will force social personnel
to answer to the people they seek to treat. As a starting point, clients must
be supported in their right to reject intervention, the ultimate tool at their
disposal for protecting themselves against the caseworker. We can
strengthen this right in practice by insisting upon the use of lay advocates,
not affiliated with the social agencies, to explain proposed treatment to
prospective clients and by allowing clients to terminate interventions at
will. Where mandatory intervention appears necessary because of clear,
imminent harm, full due process, including representation by counsel,
should be assured. The standard of imminent harm itself should be drawn
much more narrowly than in the past.[5]

Defending clients' prerogative to reject intervention, it has been ob-
jected, reinforces intrafamily patterns of domination and exploitation. I
have noted the feminist argument that women sometimes call upon social

agencies in an attempt to change the terms of family conflict. For these women, a civil libertarian commitment to privacy translates into oppression at the hands of their mate, for he is the only one who gains from a hands-off posture by the state.[6] But as the feminists themselves admit, normalizing intervention has afforded such women and their children few opportunities for release. Unless they happen to be placed in the caseload of the rare caseworker who is nonjudgmental and enlightened, the mothers may be blamed for their difficulties and receive harsh treatment, including placement of the children in foster care or an institution. Recourse to a social agency, in sum, is a desperate gamble at long odds. Given this reality, I reject the feminist intervention fantasy that posits therapeutic power as a counterweight to male authority.

The vulnerability of weak family members needs to be addressed in a way that gives the disempowered real leverage. And the best strategy to accomplish this—or, to be accurate, the least-bad strategy—depends on a vigorous feminist movement that crosses class lines. This movement should press the case for adequate public assistance payments, because reasonable grants make it possible for women with children to escape from brutality at home. Feminists can also help to change the character of the tutelary apparatus. Among the more positive developments of the past twenty years was the emergence of an alternative caring network of women-run, nonprofessional shelters and crisis centers. Now that public officials have insisted upon installing therapeutic practitioners in these settings, the territory needs to be reclaimed. Furthermore, feminist groups should promote legal representation for women, adolescent girls, and children who become entangled with a child welfare agency or juvenile court. Due process is a more likely tool to neutralize male violence than a social agency that asks a woman what she did to bring such troubles upon herself.

Besides being held accountable to clients, social agencies should be forced to justify themselves to their hosts. Just as families and individuals have been made unwitting subjects of clinical experiments, so, too, has the therapeutic laboratory come to encompass the communities in which normalizing facilities are located. Policymakers and officials complain frequently today about the hostility of neighborhood activists toward human service programs for marginal groups. But if we recall the uncertain effects of intervention and the penchant for innovative methods that may clinch a sponsoring agency's reputation for being on the cutting edge of the field, then the community position seems entirely respectable. Local publics should also have the right to reject "nontraditional" institutions, innovative delinquency and drug abuse prevention programs, and other new therapeutic ventures.

Though experience suggests that therapeutic activists will accuse community opponents of cruelty and indifference, I would hope that the latter will trust their own hesitation. We need a large measure of caution about every new scheme put forward by social personnel. The time has come to shift the burden of proof to them, to demand that they explain in plain terms how their untested programs will work, to confront them with their past record of failure, to tell them that the suffering we see about us does not in and of itself compel us to follow their lead. Such opposition, I would be the first to admit, does nothing about social marginality itself. But the sad truth is that we face only poor choices. Popular refusal at least may check the further growth of the therapeutic state.

Notes

Abbreviations

AJS: American Journal of Sociology

Annals: Annals of the American Academy of Political and Social Science

JCL: Journal of Criminal Law

NCCC, *Proceedings*: Proceedings of the National Conference of Charities and Corrections

NCSW, *Proceedings*: Proceedings of the National Conference on Social Work

NYSCCC, *Proceedings*: Proceedings of the New York State Conference of Charities and Corrections

SSR: Social Service Review

SWF: Social Welfare Forum

Introduction

1. What I refer to as the human services are sometimes called personal social services or "soft" services. For a more sweeping use of the term that embraces all social policy, see Yeheskel Hasenfeld, "The Administration of Human Services," *Annals* 479 (May 1985): 68.

2. I do not mean to suggest that the therapeutic state is a uniquely American phenomenon. To the contrary, as I will indicate, this study was inspired in part by works that explore human services in other societies. In order to keep my inquiry within manageable bounds, however, I examine only the American situation.

3. Unfortunately, it is not possible to give an exact census of the clientele of the therapeutic sector. If the population of each program or service were added together, the total would be misleading, because there is a substantial overlap among programs. In addition, as I indicate below, some of those being served by social programs are not subject to the therapeutic approach; this is true today in public assistance.

4. For an example of a work that gives passing notice to normalizing intervention, see Michael Novak et al., *The New Consensus on Family and Welfare: A Community of Self-Reliance* (Washington, DC: American Enterprise Institute, 1987). The authors stress mandatory work as an answer to poverty, but mention educative services. See pp. 86, 102. The general tendency to focus on questions of economic incentives is noted in Nathan Glazer, "Reforming the American Welfare Family: 1969–1981," *Tocqueville Review* 6 (1984): 149–68.

Sometimes the therapeutic approach is given a central role in policy prescription. See Roger Wilkins, "The Black Poor Are Different," *New York Times*, 22 August 1989, p. A23; Lisbeth B. Schorr (with Daniel Schorr), *Within Our Reach: Breaking the Cycle of Disadvantage* (New York: Doubleday/Anchor, 1988).

5. The difficulty in locating the therapeutic sector stems, too, from the misguided academic habit of classifying political institutions into exclusive constitutional and functional categories. To choose but one example, we do not think of juvenile courts and income maintenance agencies as being of a piece with one another, because by tradition they fall under different branches of government and because the distribution of justice and the redistribution of wealth seem such dissimilar activities. But one of the notable features of the therapeutic sector is that it overlaps with other elements in the modern state structure. Indeed, there are few pure human service agencies, organizations that engage in only the therapeutic enterprise.

6. See especially Michel Foucault, *Power/Knowledge: Selected Interviews and Other Writings, 1972–1977*, ed. by Colin Gordon (New York: Pantheon, 1980).

7. Jacques Donzelot, *The Policing of Families* (New York: Pantheon, 1979).

8. See, for example, Stephen Skowronek, *Building a New American State: The Expansion of National Administrative Capacities, 1877–1920* (New York: Cambridge University Press, 1982); John Mollenkopf, *The Contested City* (Princeton, NJ: Princeton University Press, 1983). This approach has been applied to the study of social welfare by Katz. See Michael B. Katz, *In the Shadow of the Poorhouse: A Social History of Welfare in America* (New York: Basic Books, 1986).

9. See Linda Gordon, *Heroes of Their Own Lives: The Politics and History of Family Violence* (New York: Penguin Books, 1988); Katz, *In the Shadow of the Poorhouse*.

10. This is not a new observation. See Peter H. Rossi, "Power and Politics: A Road to Social Reform," ssr 35 (1961): 366, 368.

Chapter One
Moral Economy and Philanthropy

1. Benjamin J. Klebaner, "Poverty and Its Relief in American Thought, 1815–61," ssr 38 (1964): 382–86, 388–89; M. J. Heale, "Humanitarianism in the Early Republic: The Moral Reformers of New York, 1776–1825," *Journal of American Studies* 2 (1968): 175.

2. Joseph Tuckerman, *On the Elevation of the Poor: A Selection From His Reports as Minister at Large in Boston* (1874, reprint ed., New York: Arno, 1971), pp. 61, 79–80, 168; James D. McCabe, *Lights and Shadows of New York Life; Or, The Sights and Sensations of the Great City* (1872; reprint ed., New York: Farrar, Straus and Giroux, 1970), pp. 402, 523, 689, 697.

3. Tuckerman, *On the Elevation of the Poor*, pp. 111–12, 115, 117, 122, 169–70; McCabe, *Lights and Shadows of New York Life*, pp. 403, 696–97; Charles Loring Brace, *The Dangerous Classes of New York and Twenty Years' Work Among Them* (New York: Wynkoop and Hallenbeck, 1872), pp. 31, 41–42, 353–54.

4. On the shift in attitudes, see Raymond A. Mohl, *Poverty in New York, 1783–1825* (New York: Oxford University Press, 1971), pp. 22–23, 62, 159–64.

5. Bourgeois alienation from the city and the intellectual sources of this attitude have been described by Paul D. Boyer. I draw heavily on his work in this

section. See Boyer, *Urban Masses and Moral Order in America, 1820–1920* (Cambridge: Harvard University Press, 1978). The notion of a moral economy has been applied in a different context by E. P. Thompson. See Thompson, *The Making of the English Working Class* (New York: Vintage, 1966).

6. For representative statements, see Tuckerman, *On the Elevation of the Poor*, pp. 103–4; Amory Dwight Mayo, *Symbols of the Capital; Or, Civilization in New York* (New York: Thatcher and Hutchinson, 1859), pp. 16, 26–27; John Todd, *The Moral Influence, Dangers, and Duties, Connected with Great Cities* (Northhampton, MA: J. H. Butler, 1841), pp. 17, 80. It should be noted that during the first half of the nineteenth century, rural village culture was being transformed by the same economic forces that were remaking the cities. Proponents of the moral economy ideal cherished a communal structure that had largely ceased to exist.

7. Boyer, *Urban Masses and Moral Order in America*, p. 55; Edwin Hubbell Chapin, *Humanity in the City* (1854, reprint ed., New York: Arno, 1974), pp. 66, 76–77; Todd, *Moral Influence, Dangers, and Duties, Connected with Great Cities*, pp. 139, 141–42, 165.

8. Children's Aid Society [Charles Loring Brace], *Second Annual Report* (1855; reprint ed., New York: Arno, 1971), p. 3.

9. Tuckerman, *On the Elevation of the Poor*, p. 104; Children's Aid Society, *First Annual Report* (1854; reprint ed., New York: Arno, 1971), p. 4.

10. Josiah Strong, *Our Country* (1885, 1891; reprint ed., Cambridge: Harvard University Press, 1963), p. 53; McCabe, *Lights and Shadows of New York Life*, p. 640; Brace, *Dangerous Classes of New York*, pp. 34–35, 194. On the middle-class child-rearing norms in America, see Bernard Wishy, *The Child and the Republic* (Philadelphia: University of Pennsylvania Press, 1968). For a more general discussion of the bourgeois view of how working-class families raised children, see Jacques Donzelot, *The Policing of Families* (New York: Pantheon, 1979), esp. chap. 2.

11. Chapin, *Humanity in the City*, p. 189; Strong, *Our Country*, pp. 134, 140–41; Brace, *Dangerous Classes of New York*, p. 29; McCabe, *Lights and Shadows of New York Life*, p. 523.

12. Chapin, *Humanity in the City*, pp. 113–14; Strong, *Our Country*, p. 55; Children's Aid Society, *Second Annual Report*, p. 3; Brace, *Dangerous Classes of New York*, pp. 27–28. On the early political use of public outdoor relief, see Priscilla Ferguson Clement, *Welfare and the Poor in the Nineteenth Century City: Philadelphia, 1800–1854* (Rutherford, NJ: Fairleigh Dickinson University Press, 1985), pp. 53–54, 58–60.

13. For a short account of organizing efforts among the working class, see Thomas R. Brooks, *Toil and Trouble: A History of American Labor* (New York: Dell, 1964). The political content of this agitation, especially its republican component, has been the subject of several recent historical studies. See especially Sean Wilentz, *Chants Democratic: New York City and the Rise of the American Working Class* (New York: Oxford University Press, 1984). For the reaction among middle-class observers, see McCabe, *Lights and Shadows of New York Life*, p. 523; Strong, *Our Country*, p. 134.

14. Brace, *Dangerous Classes of New York*, p. 29.

15. For an excellent critical review, see the first several chapters in Boyer, *Urban Masses and Moral Order in America*.

16. Mohl, *Poverty in New York*, pp. 63, 116–18, 140–41, 148–49, 163–69, 241ff.; New York Society for the Prevention of Pauperism, *Report of a Committee on the Subject of Pauperism*, by John Griscom (New York: Samuel Woods & Sons, 1818); Clement, *Welfare and the Poor in the Nineteenth-Century City*, chap. 3; Heale, "Humanitarianism in the Early Republic," pp. 168, 171–72.

17. Michel Foucault, *Discipline and Punish: The Birth of the Prison* (New York: Vintage, 1979); Rothman, *The Discovery of the Asylum: Social Order and Disorder in the New Republic* (Boston: Little, Brown, 1971).

18. Frederick Law Olmsted, "Public Parks and the Enlargement of Towns," *Journal of Social Science* 3 (1871): 10–11, 21. For a useful discussion of Olmsted, though grounded in a different set of concerns, see Thomas Bender, *Toward an Urban Vision: Ideas and Institutions in Nineteenth-Century America* (Kentucky: University Press of Kentucky, 1975), pp. 161ff.

19. Robert H. Bremner, *The Public Good: Philanthropy and Welfare in the Civil War Era* (New York: Alfred A. Knopf, 1980), p. 34; Sam Bass Warner, Jr., *The Private City: Philadelphia in Three Periods of Its Growth* (Philadelphia: University of Pennsylvania Press, 1968, 1971), pp. 108–9.

20. Olmsted, "Public Parks and the Enlargement of Towns," pp. 17, 20; Bender, *Toward an Urban Vision*, pp. 169, 172, 176–77.

21. Isaac Parrish, "Report on the Sanitary Condition of Philadelphia," American Medical Association, *Transactions* 2 (1849): 479, quoted in Warner, *Private City*, pp. 109–10. Quoted passage from Sanitary Committee of the [Philadelphia] Board of Health, in Parrish.

22. Brace, *Dangerous Classes of New York*, pp. 55, 223; Roy Lubove, "The New York Association for Improving the Condition of the Poor: The Formative Years," *New York Historical Society Quarterly* (July 1959): 321–22.

23. Olmsted, "Public Parks and the Enlargement of Towns," pp. 25–30; Warner, *Private City*, pp. 108–9.

24. Brace, *Dangerous Classes of New York*. On the "arbitrary authority of the family," see Donzelot, *Policing of Families*, pp. 72, 83. On Brace, see Bender, *Toward an Urban Vision*; Bruce Bellingham, "The 'Unspeakable Blessing': Street Children, Reform Rhetoric, and Misery in Early Industrial Capitalism," *Politics and Society* 12 (1983): 303–30.

25. Brace, *Dangerous Classes of New York*, pp. 90–96, 182–84, 193, 231; Bender, *Toward an Urban Vision*, pp. 133–35, 143–48; Boyer, *Urban Masses and Moral Order in America*, pp. 97–98; Richard A. Meckel, "Protecting the Innocents: Age Segregation and the Early Child Welfare Movement," ssr 59 (1985): 464.

26. Joseph M. Hawes, *Children in Urban Society: Juvenile Delinquency in Nineteenth-Century America* (New York: Oxford University Press, 1971), chap. 8; Linda Gordon, *Heroes of Their Own Lives: The Politics and History of Family Violence* (New York: Penguin Books, 1988), pp. 27, 34, 41–43; Mason P. Thomas, Jr., "Child Abuse and Neglect. Part I: Historical Overview, Legal Matrix, and Social Perspectives," *North Carolina Law Review* 50 (1972): 307–8, 310–12.

27. Thomas, Jr., "Child Abuse and Neglect," p. 311; Gordon, *Heroes of Their Own Lives*, pp. 28, 49–51, 55.

28. For an explication of their thesis, see Francis Fox Piven and Richard A. Cloward, *Regulating the Poor: The Functions of Public Welfare* (New York: Vintage, 1972), chap. 1.

29. For a forceful contemporary statement, see Josephine Shaw Lowell, *Public Relief and Private Charity* (1884; reprint ed., New York: Arno, 1971). The views held by private relief leaders have been discussed at length by historians. See Walter I. Trattner, *From Poor Law to Welfare State: a History of Social Welfare in America*, 2d ed. (New York: Free Press, 1979), p. 78; Bremner, *Public Good*, p. 200; Robert H. Bremner, *From the Depths: The Discovery of Poverty in the United States* (New York: New York University Press, 1956), pp. 47–48; Blanche D. Coll, *Perspectives in Public Welfare: A History* (Washington, DC: U.S. Department of Health, Education, and Welfare, 1969), p. 43; Michael B. Katz, *In the Shadow of the Poorhouse: A Social History of Welfare in America* (New York: Basic Books, 1986), pp. 41–42.

30. Katz, *In the Shadow of the Poorhouse*, pp. 46–51; Coll, *Perspectives in Public Welfare*, pp. 43–44; Bremner, *Public Good*, pp. 200–201. Some smaller communities evidently followed suit. See Lowell, *Public Relief and Private Charity*, pp. 63–64.

31. Donzelot, *Policing of Families*, p. 55.

32. Trattner, *From Poor Law to Welfare State*, p. 80; Boyer, *Urban Masses and Moral Order in America*, pp. 144–46, 150; Bremner, *From the Depths*, p. 51; Bremner, *Public Good*, pp. 201–2; Julia B. Rauch, "Women in Social Work: Friendly Visitors in Philadelphia, 1880," *SSR* (1975): 244–45, 247–48.

33. Bremner, *From the Depths*, pp. 17, 51–52; Coll, *Perspectives in Public Welfare*, p. 54; Trattner, *From Poor Law to Welfare State*, pp. 82, 85; Boyer, *Urban Masses and Moral Order in America*, pp. 144, 151–52; Donzelot, *Policing of Families*, pp. 64–65, 69; Bender, *Toward an Urban Vision*, p. 153; Boyer, *Urban Masses and Moral Order in America*, p. 149.

34. The attempt to enforce family norms through the woman has been a focus of recent feminist historical scholarship. See Rauch, "Women in Social Work," pp. 244–45; Mimi Abramovitz, *Regulating the Lives of Women: Social Welfare Policy from Colonial Times to the Present* (Boston, MA: South End Press, 1988), pp. 37–39, 114–17. The threat to remove children was explicitly stated by Lowell. See *Public Relief and Private Charity*, pp. 104–7.

35. Steven L. Schlossman, *Love and the American Delinquent: The Theory and Practice of 'Progressive' Juvenile Justice, 1825–1920* (Chicago: University of Chicago Press, 1977), chaps. 3 and 6.

36. On the politics surrounding institutions, Katz's recent work is particularly useful. See Katz, *In the Shadow of the Poorhouse*, pp. 21–22, 25–27, 29. On the state boards, see Bremner, *Public Good*, pp. 152–56; Trattner, *From Poor Law to Welfare State*, pp. 75–76; Meckel, "Protecting the Innocents," pp. 465–66.

37. Lowell, *Public Relief and Private Charity*, pp. 68–69; Barbara J. Nelson, "Mothers' Aid, Pauper Laws, and Woman Suffrage: The Intersection of the Welfare State and Democratic Participation, 1913–1935" (Paper presented to the 1989 American Political Science Association Meeting, Atlanta, GA), pp. 17–18.

38. On the persistence of political and working-class opposition to philanthropy, see Katz, *In the Shadow of the Poorhouse*, pp. 52–57. On institutional reform and sectarian opposition to child protection, see Meckel, "Protecting the Innocents," pp. 464–66. On the efforts of SPCC clients to turn intervention to their own purposes, see Gordon, *Heroes of Their Own Lives*, pp. 38–39. For the views of philanthropic leaders, see the early volumes of the NCCC, *Proceedings*.

39. For the classic statement of this position, see William Graham Sumner, *What Social Classes Owe to Each Other* (New York: Harper Brothers, 1884). A great deal has been written on Social Darwinism in America. See, for example, Richard Hofstadter, *Social Darwinism in American Thought, 1860–1915* (1944).

40. Barry J. Kaplan, "Reformers and Charity: The Abolition of Public Outdoor Relief in New York City, 1870–1898," *SSR* 52 (1978): 203–4; Rauch, "Women in Social Work," pp. 253–54.

41. On the limited appeal of Social Darwinism among the middle and upper classes, see Robert H. Wiebe, *The Search for Order, 1877–1890* (New York: Hill and Wang, 1967), pp. 134ff.

42. On the weakness of the early American state, see Stephen Skowronek, *Building a New American State: The Expansion of National Administrative Capacities, 1877–1920* (New York: Cambridge University Press, 1982), chap. 2; Charles C. Bright, "The State in the United States During the Nineteenth Century," in Charles C. Bright and Susan Harding, eds., *Statemaking and Social Movements: Essays in History and Theory* (Ann Arbor: University of Michigan Press, 1984), pp. 121–58; Morton Keller, "Social Policy in Nineteenth-Century America," in Donald T. Critchlow and Ellis W. Hawley, *Federal Social Policy: The Historical Dimension* (University Park: Pennsylvania State University Press, 1988), pp. 99–115.

43. Thomas, Jr., "Child Abuse and Neglect," pp. 293–94, 299, 301.

44. Gordon has also remarked upon this. See *Heroes of Their Own Lives*, p. 57.

45. Sheldon S. Wolin, "Democracy and the Welfare State: The Political and Theoretical Connections between Staatsrason and Wohlfahrtsstaatsrason," *Political Theory* 15 (1987): 477–80. As Piven and Cloward argue, the poor are therefore more likely to accept the discipline of wage labor on almost any terms. See *Regulating the Poor*, chap. 1.

Chapter Two
The Discourse of the Human Services

1. Thomas L. Haskell, *The Emergence of Professional Social Science: The American Social Science Association and the Nineteenth-Century Crisis of Authority* (Urbana, IL: University of Illinois Press, 1977), pp. 145ff.

2. Edward A. Ross, *Social Control: A Survey of the Foundations of Order* (New York: Macmillan, 1901), pp. 13, 18–19, 87.

3. Christopher Lasch, *Haven in a Heartless World: The Family Besieged* (New York: Basic Books, 1977, 1979), p. xxii. Haskell notes that interdependence implies mutual dependence without exploring the significance of this theme. Haskell, *Emergence of Professional Social Science*, p. 13.

4. Washington Gladden, *Social Salvation* (Boston and New York: Houghton Mifflin 1902), pp. 3–6.

5. For typical descriptions of the social scientific orientation of the settlement houses, see Robert A. Woods, "University Settlements as Laboratories in Social Science," [1893] in Woods, *The Neighborhood in Nation-Building* (1923; reprint ed., New York: Arno, 1970), pp. 35–36; Jane Addams, "A Function of the Social Settlement," [1899] in Christopher Lasch, ed., *The Social Thought of Jane Addams* (Indianapolis: Bobbs-Merrill, 1965) [cited hereafter as *Social Thought*], pp. 186–87; Jane Addams, *Twenty Years at Hull House* (1910; reprint ed., New York: New American Library, 1961), p. 136.

6. Addams, "Function of the Social Settlement," pp. 186–87; Woods, "University Settlements as Laboratories," p. 31; Herman F. Hegner, "Scientific Value of the Social Settlements," *AJS* 3 (1897): 175, 178. See also Christopher Lasch, *The New Radicalism in America (1889–1963): The Intellectual as a Social Type* (New York: Alfred Knopf, 1966), p. 64.

7. On the exclusion of women from politics and public welfare, see Julia B. Rauch, "Women in Social Work: Friendly Visitors in Philadelphia, 1880," *SSR* 49 (1975): 245. On the mobilization of women during the Progressive era, see Sheila M. Rothman, *Woman's Proper Place: A History of Changing Ideals and Practices, 1870 to the Present* (New York: Basic Books, 1978), chap. 3; Theda Skocpol, "Protecting Soldiers and Mothers: The Politics of Social Provision in the United States, 1870s-1920s," in preparation. Chambers has prepared a useful review of the literature on the record of women in early social work. See Clarke E. Chambers, "Women in the Creation of the Profession of Social Work," *SSR* 60 (1986): 1–33.

8. The degree of male control over the COS has been the subject of debate. Rauch argues that women visitors waged a long struggle within the Philadelphia agency for administrative power, gradually gaining access to some supervisory posts. But policy-making board positions remained in the hands of men. Chambers suggests men and women played an equal part in shaping social work, yet he notes that men held administrative power. See Rauch, "Women in Social Work," pp. 254–56; Chambers, "Women in the Creation of the Profession of Social Work," pp. 5–6.

9. Most recent accounts of Progressive philanthropy make this point. See, for example, John F. McClymer, *War and Welfare: Social Engineering in America, 1890–1925* (Westport, CT: Greenwood Press, 1980), chap. 1; Michael B. Katz, *In the Shadow of the Poorhouse: A Social History of Welfare in America* (New York: Basic Books, 1986), pp. 169–70.

10. For contemporary statements, see Jane Addams, "Why Women Should Vote" [1910] in *Social Thought*, p. 144; Jane Addams, "The Larger Aspects of the Women's Movement" [1914] in *Social Thought*, pp. 154–55.

11. Addams, *Twenty Years at Hull House*, p. 162; Robert A. Woods, ed., *The City Wilderness* (Boston: Houghton Mifflin, 1899), p. 92.

12. For examples of the settlement movement attack upon organized charity, see Jane Addams, *Democracy and Social Ethics* (New York: Macmillan, 1902), pp. 13–16, 18–19, 22–23, 26–30; Robert A. Woods and Albert J. Kennedy, *The Settlement Horizon: A National Estimate* (New York: Russell Sage Foundation,

1922), p. 71; Mary Kingsbury Simkhovitch, "Friendship and Politics," *Political Science Quarterly* 17 (1902): 195.

13. John Graham Brooks, "The Future Problem of Charity and the Unemployed," *Annals* 5 (1894): 11–12; Mary Conyngton, *How to Help: A Manual of Practical Charity* (New York: Macmillan, 1909), pp. 11–12, 15, 18; Edward T. Devine, *Misery and Its Causes* (New York: Macmillan, 1909), pp. 3, 11–12. For a discussion of the new view of poverty, which, however, overstates the rupture with earlier philanthropic thought, see Robert H. Bremner, *From the Depths: The Discovery of Poverty in the United States* (New York: New York University Press, 1956, 1972), esp. chaps. 2 and 8.

14. For an elaborate statement of this view, see Robert Hunter, *Poverty: Social Conscience in the Progressive Era* (1904; reprint ed., New York: Harper and Row, 1965). See also the discussion of the Pittsburgh Survey in McClymer, *War and Welfare.*

15. Lee K. Frankel, "The Relation Between Standards of Living and Standards of Compensation," NYSCCC, *Proceedings* 7 (1906): 23, 30. See also Lee K. Frankel, "Report of the Committee on Needy Families in Their Homes," NYSCCC, *Proceedings* 6 (1905): 24–26; Edward T. Devine, *The Principles of Relief* (New York: Macmillan, 1904), pp. 151–52; Mary Kingsbury Simkhovitch, *The City Worker's World in America* (1917; reprint ed., New York: Arno, 1971), pp. 85, 168.

16. Jane Addams, *The Spirit of Youth and the City Streets* (1909; reprint ed., Urbana, IL: University of Illinois Press, 1972), p. 31; Addams, *Twenty Years at Hull House,* pp. 128–29; Woods, ed., *City Wilderness,* p. 289.

17. Addams, *Twenty Years at Hull House,* pp. 130, 170, 202–11; Simkhovitch, "Friendship and Politics," p. 191. See also the various writings by Lee Frankel and Edward Devine in note 15 above.

18. Conyngton, *How to Help,* pp. 164–71; S. E. Forman, "Standards of Living," NCCC, *Proceedings* 33 (1906, 2d ed.): 342–49; Simkhovitch, *City Worker's World in America,* pp. 27–28, 43, 168–69; Devine, *Principles of Relief,* pp. 29–33.

19. John A. Ryan, "A Minimum Wage and Minimum Wage Boards," NCCC, *Proceedings* 37 (1910): 461; J. A. Ryan, "The Standard of Living and the Problem of Dependency," NCCC, *Proceedings* 34 (1907): 343.

20. Simkhovitch, *City Worker's World in America,* pp. 20, 48–49, 170–71, 176; Jane Addams, "Charity and Social Justice," President's Address, NCCC, *Proceedings* 37 (1910): 2–3.

21. Devine, *Principles of Relief,* p. 21; Conyngton, *How to Help,* pp. 18–19.

22. Simkhovitch, *City Worker's World in America,* pp. 50–51; Frederic Almy, "The Ethics of Too Low a Standard of Living," NYSCCC, *Proceedings* 9 (1908): 44; Ryan, "Standard of Living and the Problem of Dependency," pp. 344–45.

23. Brooks, "Future Problem of Charity and the Unemployed," pp. 2–3, 9–10, 15; Gladden, *Social Salvation*; Jane Addams, "The Subjective Necessity for Social Settlements," [1892] in *Social Thought,* pp. 30–31.

24. Addams, *Twenty Years at Hull House,* chap. 14; Robert A. Woods, "The University Settlement Idea," in Jane Addams et al., *Philanthropy and Social Progress* (New York: Thomas Y. Crowell, 1892), pp. 86–87; Devine, *Principles of*

Relief, pp. 36–39, 42, 46, 69. cos leaders also figured prominently in these efforts. See Kathleen D. McCarthy, *Noblesse Oblige: Charity and Cultural Philanthropy in Chicago, 1849–1929* (Chicago: University of Chicago Press, 1982), pp. 130–31.

25. On the reform coalition, see Martin J. Schiesel, *The Politics of Efficiency: Municipal Administration and Reform in America, 1880–1920* (Berkeley: University of California Press, 1977). Chambers speculates that these modernization measures were an expression of a feminist agenda for "civic housekeeping." However, though the women identified as "social feminists" gave important support to the public administration agenda, it had vigorous backing from male reformers, too. See Chambers, "Women in the Creation of the Profession of Social Work," p. 13.

26. Allen F. Davis, *Spearheads for Reform: The Social Settlements and the Progressive Movement, 1890–1914* (New York: Oxford University Press, 1967, 1976), pp. 61–65, 123–32; Linda Gordon, *Heroes of Their Own Lives: The Politics and History of Family Violence* (New York: Penguin Books, 1988), p. 64.

27. Mary Kingsbury Simkhovitch, "The Case Work Plane," nccc, *Proceedings* 36 (1909): 141–42; Woods, ed., *City Wilderness*, pp. 273–74. The continuity in philanthropy is suggested by Donzelot. See Jacques Donzelot, *The Policing of Families* (New York: Pantheon, 1979).

28. For a discussion of settlement activities, see Davis, *Spearheads for Reform*, pp. 41–50.

29. Robert A. Woods, "University Settlements: Their Point and Drift," [1899] in Woods, *Neighborhood in Nation-Building*, p. 50; Woods, ed., *City Wilderness*, p. 248; Woods, "University Settlement Idea," pp. 83, 92. See also Addams, *Twenty Years at Hull House*, p. 144.

30. Addams, *Democracy and Social Ethics*, pp. 66, 143–44, 146, 151–52; Woods, ed., *City Wilderness*, pp. 265, 275; Simkhovitch, "Case Work Plane," p. 144; Devine, *Principles of Relief*, pp. 18, 23, 171–74; Conyngton, *How to Help*, pp. 42, 44–49; Mary E. Richmond, *Friendly Visiting Among the Poor: A Handbook for Charity Workers* (1899; reprint ed., Montclair, NJ: Patterson Smith, 1969), pp. 154–57.

31. Addams, *Twenty Years at Hull House*, pp. 208–9, 211–12; Lilian D. Wald, *The House on Henry Street* (New York: Henry Holt, 1915), p. 58; Woods and Kennedy, *Settlement Horizon*, pp. 250–56.

32. Woods and Kennedy, *Settlement Horizon*, pp. 241, 251; Wald, *House on Henry Street*, pp. 55–57; Simkhovitch, *City Worker's World in America*, p. 157.

33. Woods and Kennedy, *Settlement Horizon*, p. 311; Addams, *Spirit of Youth and the City Streets*, p. 47.

34. Foucault contends that social analysis must pay closer attention to the positive effects of power. See Michel Foucault, *Power/Knowledge: Selected Interviews and Other Writings, 1972–1977* (New York: Pantheon, 1980), chap. 6.

35. Addams, *Twenty Years at Hull House*, pp. 208–9; Wald, *House on Henry Street*, pp. 55–58; Woods and Kennedy, *Settlement Horizon*, pp. 241, 250–51, 256; Simkhovitch, *City Worker's World in America*, p. 19–20, 61, 157; Devine, *Misery and Its Causes*, p. 74; Richmond, *Friendly Visiting Among the Poor*, pp. 191–92.

36. Donzelot, *Policing of Families*; Rothman, *Woman's Proper Place*, chap. 3.

37. Davis, *Spearheads for Reform*, pp. 46–47, 50–54; Chambers, "Women in the Creation of the Profession of Social Work," p. 14.

38. Davis, *Spearheads for Reform*, pp. 34–35; Woods, "University Settlements as Laboratories," p. 43; South End House, *Fifteenth Annual Report* (Boston: 1907), p. 4.

39. C. C. Carstens, "The Development of Social Work for Child Protection," *Annals* 98 (November 1921): 137–38, 140; Gordon, *Heroes of Their Own Lives*, pp. 63–64, 70, 72–73.

40. David J. Rothman, *Conscience and Convenience: The Asylum and Its Alternatives in Progressive America* (Boston: Little, Brown, 1980), chap. 2.

41. Richard A. Meckel, "Protecting the Innocents: Age Segregation and the Early Child Welfare Movement," *ssr* 59 (1985): 470–71.

42. See Richmond, *Friendly Visiting Among the Poor*; Conyngton, *How to Help*.

43. Woods, "University Settlement Idea," p. 68; Addams, *Twenty Years at Hull House*, p. 98; William Horace Noyes, "Institutional Peril of the Settlements," [1899] in Lorene M. Pacey, ed., *Readings in the Development of Settlement Work* (New York: Association Press, 1950), pp. 62–63.

44. Interestingly, the laboratory analogy was popular among settlement workers, though they seemed untroubled by the implications. See Hegner, "Scientific Value of the Social Settlements," p. 176; Woods, "University Settlements as Laboratories," p. 41.

45. For a suggestive critique of science as basis for intervention, see Richard Korn, "The Private Citizen, the Social Expert, and the Social Problem: An Excursion Through an Unacknowledged Utopia," in Bernard Rosenberg, Israel Gerver, and F. William Howton, eds., *Mass Society in Crisis: Social Problems and Social Pathology* (New York: Macmillan, 1964), pp. 578, 581–82.

46. Nisbet also refers to the softening of power, but offers very different explanations for the phenomenon. See Robert A. Nisbet, "The New Despotism," in Kenneth S. Templeton, Jr., ed., *The Politicization of Society* (Indianapolis: Liberty Press, 1979), pp. 197–207.

47. See especially Linda Gordon, "Child Abuse, Gender, and the Myth of Family Independence: A Historical Critique," *Child Welfare* 64 (1985): 219–21; Gordon, *Heroes of Their Own Lives*, chap. 9.

48. Devine, *Principles of Relief*, pp. 10–11; Edward T. Devine, "Remedies for Too Low a Standard of Living," NYSCCC, *Proceedings* 9 (1908): 63; Samuel G. Smith, "Social Standards," President's Address, NCCC, *Proceedings* 32 (1905): 8; Thomas G. Riley, "A Sociological View of Poverty," NYSCCC, *Proceedings* 14 (1913); Conyngton, *How to Help*, p. 13; Richmond, *Friendly Visiting Among the Poor*, pp. 6, 8–9.

49. Richmond, *Friendly Visiting Among the Poor*, pp. 191–92; Simkhovitch, *City Worker's World in America*, pp. 19–20.

50. Donzelot, *Policing of Families*, p. xxi.

51. Devine, *Principles of Relief*, pp. 19, 22–23.

52. Frank A. Fetter in "Discussion of 'Ethics of Too Low a Standard of Living,'" NYSCCC, *Proceedings* 9 (1908): 62. See also Brooks, "Future Problem

of Charity and the Unemployed," pp. 24, 27; Charles E. Faulkner, "Twentieth Century Alignments for the Promotion of the Social Order," NCCC *Proceedings* 27 (1900): 7–8.

53. Robert A. Woods, *Americans in Process: A Settlement Study* (Boston: Houghton Mifflin, 1902), p. 7.

54. Wald, *House on Henry Street*, p. 44. See also Addams, *Twenty Years at Hull House*, pp. 146, 211–12; Gordon, *Heroes of Their Own Lives*, p. 77.

55. Simkhovitch, *City Worker's World in America*, p. 67; William I. Cole, *Motives and Results of the Social Settlement Movement* (Cambridge, MA: Harvard University Department of Social Ethics, 1908), p. 16.

56. Woods, ed., *City Wilderness*, pp. 290–304; Robert A. Woods, "Settlement Houses and City Politics," [1900] in Woods, *Neighborhood in Nation-Building*, p. 68; Addams, *Twenty Years at Hull House*, p. 238; Gertrude Vaile, "The Principles and Methods of Outdoor Relief," NCCC, *Proceedings* 42 (1915): 479.

57. Vaile, "Principles and Methods of Outdoor Relief," p. 480.

58. Wald, *House on Henry Street*, pp. 60, 261; Addams, "Function of the Social Settlement," p. 197.

Chapter Three
Models of Public Tutelage

1. See Sanford J. Fox, "Juvenile Justice Reform: An Historical Perspective," *Stanford Law Review* 22 (June 1970): 1187–1239; Anthony M. Platt, *The Child Savers: The Invention of Delinquency*, 2d ed. (Chicago: University of Chicago Press, 1977); David J. Rothman, *Conscience and Convenience: The Asylum and its Alternatives in Progressive America* (Boston: Little, Brown, 1980); Ellen Ryerson, *The Best-Laid Plans: America's Juvenile Court Experiment* (New York: Hill and Wang, 1978); Steven L. Schlossman, *Love and the American Delinquent: The Theory and Practice of "Progressive" Juvenile Justice, 1825–1920* (Chicago: University of Chicago Press, 1977).

2. On the hidden gender content of delinquency research and its implications, see Meda Chesney-Lind, "Girls' Crime and Woman's Place: Toward a Feminist Model of Female Delinquency," *Crime and Delinquency* 35 (1989): 5–29.

3. Joseph M. Hawes, *Children in Urban Society: Juvenile Delinquency in Nineteenth-Century America* (New York: Oxford University Press, 1971), p. 162; Karl Kelsey, "The Juvenile Court of Chicago and Its Work," *Annals* 17 (1901): 298; Richard S. Tuthill, "The Juvenile Court Law," National Prison Association Annual Congress, *Proceedings* (1902): 119; Edith I. Clarke, "Juvenile Delinquency and Dependency: Report of Inquiry at Chicago," *The Commons* 5 (February 1901): 2; Platt, *Child Savers*, pp. xxvii–xxviii.

4. Ryerson, *Best-Laid Plans*, pp. 19–20, 35; Thomas D. Eliot, *The Juvenile Court and the Community* (New York: Macmillan, 1914), pp. 122–24.

5. The dynamics of this coalition were explored some years later by its participants. See the various essays in Jane Addams et al., *The Child, the Clinic and the Court* (1925; reprint ed., New York: Johnson Reprint Corporation, 1970). Fox overstates the role of sectarian child protection organizations in producing the

1899 Illinois Juvenile Court Act and misunderstands its emphasis when he claims it was primarily intended to upgrade institutional conditions. See Fox, "Juvenile Justice Reform," pp. 1222–23, 1226–27. For a more balanced account based on the Wisconsin experience see Schlossman, *Love and the American Delinquent*, pp. 133–37.

6. On the legal rationales for the court, see Schlossman, *Love and the American Delinquent*, chap. 1; Bernard Flexner, "The Juvenile Court—Its Legal Aspects," *Annals* 36 (1910): 51–52.

7. For a vivid early account of the therapeutic orientation of the court, see Harvey H. Baker, "Procedure of the Boston Juvenile Court," *The Survey* 23 (5 February 1910): 643–52. Fox asserts that the juvenile court should be seen as merely an incremental reform because it continued a pattern of procedural informality in juvenile justice. See Fox, "Juvenile Justice Reform," pp. 1221–22. It is clear from court movement writings, however, that informality was but an adjunct to the full therapeutic revolution that proponents intended.

8. Sophonisba Breckinridge and Edith Abbott, *The Delinquent Child and the Home* (New York: Russell Sage Foundation, Charities Publication Committee, 1912), p. 105. On the scope of juvenile court jurisdiction and its connection to philanthropic strategy, see Jacques Donzelot, *The Policing of Families* (New York: Pantheon, 1979), pp. 87–88, 109–10. Fox also stresses the value of the court for philanthropic intervention. See Fox, "Juvenile Justice Reform," p. 1227.

9. Ryerson, *Best-Laid Plans*, pp. 43–47.

10. Donzelot, *Policing of Families*, pp. 119–20, 122–24; Rothman, *Conscience and Convenience*, pp. 215, 218; Annie Ramsey, "Work of the Probation Officer Preliminary to the Trial," NCCC, *Proceedings* 33 (1906, 2d edition): 132–35; Bernard Flexner, "The Juvenile Court as a Social Institution," *The Survey* 23 (5 February 1910): 628.

11. Ramsey, "Work of Probation Officer Preliminary to Trial," p. 134; Donzelot, *Policing of Families*, pp. 110–11.

12. Baker, "Procedure of Boston Juvenile Court," p. 649; Tuthill, "Juvenile Court Law," p. 121; Donzelot, *Policing of Families*, p. 111; Rothman, *Conscience and Convenience*, pp. 215–16.

13. Donzelot, *Policing of Families*, p. 108; Baker, "Procedure of Boston Juvenile Court," pp. 646–48; "Testimony of Judge Merritt W. Pinckney," in Breckinridge and Abbott, *Delinquent Child and the Home*, pp. 227–28.

14. Breckinridge and Abbott, *Delinquent Child and the Home*, pp. 230–32; Ryerson, *Best-Laid Plans*, p. 43; Donzelot, *Policing of Families*, p. 108; Richard S. Tuthill, "How the Juvenile-Court Law is Working," *The Commons* 5 (February 1901): 7; Hastings L. Hart, "Distinctive Features of the Juvenile Court," *Annals* 36 (1910): 58.

15. Frederic Almy, "Juvenile Courts and Juvenile Probation," NYSCCC, *Proceedings* 2 (1901): 284; Donzelot, *Policing of Families*, pp. 103–4. On individualized treatment of deviants during the Progressive era, see Rothman, *Conscience and Convenience*, pp. 5–6, 43, 50.

16. Tuthill, "How the Juvenile-Court Law is Working," p. 7; Eliot, *Juvenile Court and the Community*, p. 169; Carrie Weaver Smith, "The Elimination of the Reformatory," NCSW, *Proceedings* 48 (1921): 130; Donzelot, *Policing of Fami-*

lies, pp. 45–47; Rothman, *Conscience and Convenience*, pp. 219, 221–22; Schlossman, *Love and the American Delinquent*, p. 190.

17. Breckinridge and Abbott, *Delinquent Child and the Home*, p. 170; Ryerson, *Best-Laid Plans*, pp. 50–52.

18. For example, the model left little room for lawyers to represent the child; if a family brought an attorney, the judge would instruct him on his proper role. He should be made an ally of the court, so that he might apply pressure on the minor and his parents to cooperate. Baker, "Procedure of Boston Juvenile Court," p. 649; Bernard Flexner and Roger Baldwin, *Juvenile Courts and Probation* (New York: Century, 1914, 1916), p. 64; Rothman, *Conscience and Convenience*, p. 216.

19. For a penetrating legal critique from this period see Edward Lindsey, "The Juvenile Court Movement From a Lawyer's Standpoint," *Annals* 52 (1914): 141–44. Even within the court movement questions arose over the procedural latitude granted the institution. See Flexner, "Juvenile Court as a Social Institution," pp. 637–38.

20. These views were frequently expressed by Julian Mack, the second Chicago juvenile court judge. See Mack, "The Juvenile Court; The Judge and the Probation Officer," NCCC, *Proceedings* 33 (1906, 2d ed.): 123–31; Mack, "Juvenile Courts as Part of the School System of the Country," NCCC, *Proceedings* 35 (1908): 369–83; Mack, "The Law and the Child," *The Survey* 23 (5 February 1910): 638–43. See also Ryerson, *Best-Laid Plans*, pp. 76–77.

21. Carl Kelsey, "The Juvenile Court of Chicago and Its Work," *Annals* 17 (1901): 299; Charles T. Walker, "The Work of the Juvenile Protective Association," Child Conference for Research and Welfare, *Proceedings* 1 (1909): 60. Ryerson contends that the need to put the court's work on a scientific footing was recognized only later, but these early statements demonstrate that a scientific foundation was sought from the outset. See Ryerson, *Best-Laid Plans*, pp. 100ff.

22. "Testimony of Judge Merritt W. Pinckney," pp. 234–35; Addams et al., *Child, the Clinic and the Court*.

23. Mabel Carter Rhoades, "A Case Study of Delinquent Boys in the Juvenile Court of Chicago," AJS 13 (1907): 77. See also Henry Thurston, "Some Phases of the Probation Work of the Juvenile Court," NCCC, *Proceedings* 32 (1905): 180–82; Flexner, "Juvenile Court as a Social Institution," pp. 630, 632.

24. George W. Kirchway, "Social Work and the Law: Forms of Cooperation Between Law and Social Work," NCSW, *Proceedings* 53 (1926): 182; Flexner and Baldwin, *Juvenile Courts and Probation*, pp. 80–81; H. F. Bretthauer, "The Social Service Aspects of the Juvenile Court," NCSW, *Proceedings* 47 (1920): 173; Donzelot, *Policing of Families*.

25. See sources in note 10 above.

26. Baker, "Procedure of Boston Juvenile Court," p. 650. See also Thomas Murphy, "The Juvenile Court of Buffalo," NYSCCC, *Proceedings* 3 (1902): 137–38; Mrs. Helen W. Rogers, "The Probation System of the Juvenile Court of Indianapolis," NCCC, *Proceedings* 31 (1904): 376.

27. Donzelot, *Policing of Families*, pp. 108–9.

28. Almy, "Juvenile Courts and Juvenile Probation," pp. 288–89; Donzelot, *Policing of Families*, pp. 110–11.

29. Clarke, "Juvenile Delinquency and Dependency," p. 3; Breckinridge and Abbott, *Delinquent Child and the Home*, p. 114. Sexually active girls were regarded by court proponents as a source of "moral infection" who should be removed from the home, an attitude that reflected traditional philanthropic rejection of sensual pleasures. See Vida Hunt Francis, "The Delinquent Girl," NCCC, *Proceedings* 33 (1906, 2d ed.): 142.

30. Peter A. Mortenson, "The Chicago Parental School," in Breckinridge, ed., *Child in the City*, pp. 156–66.

31. Rothman, *Conscience and Convenience*, pp. 220–21.

32. Chesney-Lind, "Girls' Crime and Woman's Place," pp. 14–17.

33. On the campaign for mothers' aid, see Mark H. Leff, "Consensus for Reform: The Mothers' Pension Movement in the Progressive Era," SSR 47 (1973): 397–417; Anthony R. Travis, "The Origin of Mothers' Pensions in Illinois," *Journal of the Illinois State Historical Society* 68 (1975): 421–28; Hace Sorel Tishler, *Self-Reliance and Social Security, 1870–1917* (Port Washington, NY: Kennikat Press, National University Publications, 1971), pp. 141–58; Roy Lubove, *The Struggle for Social Security, 1900–1935* (Cambridge, MA: Harvard University Press, 1968), pp. 91–112; Frank J. Weed, "Bureaucratization as Reform: The Case of the Public Welfare Movement, 1900–1929," *Social Science Journal* 16 (1979): 79–89.

The split that mothers' aid provoked in philanthropy was not, as some historical accounts make it appear, between forces of "reaction" and "reform." According to this view, old-line charity leaders resisted the public-aid scheme advanced by more radical philanthropic elements like the settlement house residents. It has also been argued that, as a result of subversive efforts by the former, the program lost sight of its original purpose and became tainted with traditional charity values. Such claims seriously misrepresent the issues dividing philanthropy and the meaning of the outcome. As I demonstrate here, both pension proponents and the charity leaders who opposed them based their arguments on the new philanthropic concept of the social living standard. It makes no sense, then, to characterize either side as "reactionary." And since the use of casework in pension programs was entirely consistent with living standard doctrine, we cannot regard the introduction of a normalizing approach as evidence that charity activists distorted the program. The errors in the historical view, it is clear, stem from a failure to understand the discourse of Progressive philanthropy. I exempt from this criticism Leff and Tishler, who recognize that both sides in the pension debate accepted common premises.

34. Mary E. Richmond, *Friendly Visiting Among the Poor: A Handbook for Charity Workers* (1899; reprint ed., Montclair, NJ: Patterson Smith, 1969), p. 141; Nathan Bijur, "Report of the Committee on the Care and Relief of Needy Families in Their Homes," NYSCCC, *Proceedings* 4 (1903): 55–58; Frederick Almy, "The Ethics of Too Low a Standard of Living," NYSCCC, *Proceedings* 9 (1908): 44; J. A. Ryan, "The Standard of Living and the Problem of Dependency," NCCC, *Proceedings* 34 (1907): 344–45.

35. On early charity efforts for widows, see Raymond A. Mohl, *Poverty in New York, 1783–1825* (New York: Oxford University Press, 1971), pp. 147–48; Priscilla Ferguson Clement, *Welfare and the Poor in the Nineteenth-Century*

City: Philadelphia, 1800–1854 (Rutherford, NJ: Fairleigh Dickinson University Press, 1985), p. 144.

36. Conference on the Care of Dependent Children, *Proceedings* (Washington, DC: Government Printing Office, 1909) [cited hereafter as 1909 White House Conference, *Proceedings*].

37. David M. Schneider and Albert Deutsch, *The History of Public Welfare in New York State, 1867–1940* (1941; reprint ed., Montclair, NJ: Patterson Smith, 1969), pp. 181–82; Richard A. Meckel, "Protecting the Innocents: Age Segregation and the Early Child Welfare Movement," *SSR* 59 (1985): 472.

38. Richmond, *Friendly Visiting Among the Poor*, pp. 73–74; Leff, "Consensus for Reform," p. 399.

39. Leff, "Consensus for Reform," pp. 397, 399–400, 402–3, 405–10; John Clayton Drew, "The Abolition of Child Labor and the Origins of Child-Centered Welfare Programs: A Comparison with the Modernization Thesis for the Case of Mothers' Pensions" (paper presented at the 1985 American Political Science Association Annual Meeting, Washington, DC); Theda Skocpol, "Protecting Mothers and Soldiers: The Politics of Social Provision in the United States, 1870s–1920s" (in preparation), chap. 7.

40. Sophonisba P. Breckinridge, "Neglected Widowhood in the Juvenile Court," *AJS* 16 (1910): 53–87; Merritt W. Pinckney, "Public Pensions to Widows. Experiences and Observations Which Lead Me to Favor Such a Law," NCCC, *Proceedings* 39 (1912): 473–80.

41. Mrs. William [Hannah B.] Einstein, "Pensions for Widows as a Means of Securing for Dependent Children the Benefits of Home Training and Influence," NYSCCC, *Proceedings* 11 (1910): 225; Schneider and Deutsch, *History of Public Welfare in New York State*, p. 185.

42. Edward T. Devine, *The Principles of Relief* (New York: Macmillan, 1904), pp. 94–95; Mrs. William Einstein, "The Keeping Together of Families," NYCityCCC, *Proceedings* 3 (1912): 61–62; Florence Kelley, "Governmental Aid for Dependent Women and Children," NYCityCCC, *Proceedings* 3 (1912): 77–78.

43. Einstein, "Pensions for Widowed Mothers as a Means," pp. 224–25; Edward T. Devine in 1909 White House Conference, *Proceedings*, pp. 47–48.

44. Benjamin J. Shove, "The Duty of the State to Support Destitute and Neglected Children," NYSCCC, *Proceedings* 9 (1908): 171–72; Alice L. Higgins and Florence Windom, "Helping Widows to Bring Up Citizens," NCCC *Proceedings* 37 (1910): 138.

45. Emil G. Hirsch, "The Home Versus the Institution," in 1909 White House Conference, *Proceedings*, p. 90. See similarly Mabel Potter Daggett, "The City as a Mother," *World's Work* 25 (November 1912): 113; Frederick C. Howe and Marie Jeeney Howe, "Pensioning the Widow and the Fatherless," in Edna D. Bullock, ed., *Selected Articles on Mother's Pensions* (New York: H. W. Wilson, 1915), p. 126.

46. Frederic Almy, "Public Pensions to Widows. Experiences and Observations Which Lead Me to Oppose Such a Law," NCCC, *Proceedings* 39 (1912): 482–84; Mary Conyngton, *How to Help: A Manual of Practical Charity* (New York: Macmillan, 1909), pp. 192–93.

47. C. C. Carstens, *Public Pensions to Widows With Children: A Study of Their Administration in Several American Cities* (New York: Russell Sage Foundation, Charity Organization Department Publication No. 31, 1913), p. 17. See similarly James F. Jackson in 1909 White House Conference, *Proceedings*, p. 44; Anna B. Fox in "Discussion of 'Case Work—Adequate Treatment and Adequate Relief,'" NYSCCC, *Proceedings* 13 (1912): 246–47.

48. Almy, "Public Pensions to Widows," p. 482; Tishler, *Self-Reliance and Social Security*, pp. 146–49.

49. Almy, "Public Pensions to Widows," pp. 481–82, 485. See also the discussion accompanying the Pinckney-Almy exchange at the 1912 NCCC meeting.

50. *Report of the New York State Commission on Relief for Widowed Mothers* (Albany: 1914), p. 7; Pinckney, "Public Pensions to Widows," pp. 476–77, 479; Leff, "Consensus for Reform," p. 412.

51. Robert W. Hebberd, "Public Outdoor Relief," NYSCCC, *Proceedings* 12 (1911): 56–58; Schneider and Deutsch, *History of Public Welfare in New York State*, p. 187n.

52. Richard M. Neustadt, "Home Conservation—A Step in Social Conservation," in *Report of the New York State Commission*, p. 141.

53. Ibid., pp. 50, 92, 113, 136, 141, 147–48, 154–55.

54. Jane Addams, "Charity and Social Justice," President's Address, NCCC, *Proceedings* 33 (1906, 2d ed.): 7; Albert Jay Nock, "Motherhood and the State," *Atlantic* 114 (August 1914): 159.

55. Neustadt, "Home Conservation," pp. 148–49.

56. Julia Lathrop in "Discussion of 'Public Pensions to Widows,'" NCCC, *Proceedings* 39 (1912): 488; Einstein, "Pensions to Widowed Mothers as a Means," p. 231; Tishler, *Self-Reliance and Social Security*, pp. 153–54; Linda Gordon, *Heroes of Their Own Lives: The Politics and History of Family Violence* (New York: Penguin Books, 1988), p. 64.

57. See especially Edith Abbott and Sophonisba P. Breckinridge, *The Administration of the Aid-to-Mothers Law in Illinois*, Children's Bureau Legal Series No. 7 (Washington, DC: Government Printing Office, 1921); *Proceedings of the Conference on Mothers' Pensions*, Children's Bureau Publication No. 109 (Washington, DC: Government Printing Office, 1922); Florence Nesbitt, *Standards of Public Aid to Children in Their Own Homes*, Children's Bureau Publication No. 118 (Washington, DC: Government Printing Office, 1923); Emma O. Lundberg, *Public Aid to Mothers With Dependent Children: Extent and Fundamental Principles*, Children's Bureau Publication No. 162 (Washington, DC: Government Printing Office, 1926); Mary F. Bogue, *Administration of Mothers' Aid in Ten Localities: With Special Reference to Health, Housing, Education, and Recreation*, Children's Bureau Publication No. 184 (Washington, DC: Government Printing Office, 1928).

58. Abbott and Breckinridge, *Administration of Aid-to-Mothers Law in Illinois*, pp. 19–22; Higgins and Windom, "Helping Widows to Bring Up Citizens," pp. 139–40; Bogue, *Administration of Mothers' Aid in Ten Localities*, p. 6.

59. *Report of the New York State Commission*, p. 10; Lundberg, *Public Aid to Mothers With Dependent Children*, p. 6.

60. As the list of factors to be considered makes clear, "suitability" in pension

discourse covered many aspects of the family condition. If, in the subsequent development of public assistance, maternal sexual behavior became the dominant preoccupation, such behavior was treated by the Progressive mothers'-aid movement as but one element among several that a caseworker should examine. See Higgins and Windom, "Helping Widows to Bring Up Citizens," p. 139; Bogue, *Administration of Mothers' Aid in Ten Localities*, p. 6; Abbott and Breckinridge, *Administration of Aid-to-Mothers Law in Illinois*, pp. 77–78.

61. Abbott and Breckinridge, *Administration of Aid-to-Mothers Law in Illinois*, pp. 19–21.

62. Florence Nesbitt, "The Family Budget and Its Supervision," NCSW, *Proceedings* 45 (1918): 360–62; Nesbitt, *Standards of Public Aid to Children in Their Own Homes*, pp. 6–7, 11, 13; Mary F. Bogue, "Recommendations of the Committee," in *Proceedings of the Conference on Mother's Pensions*, pp. 14–15.

63. Neustadt, "Home Conservation," pp. 177–78.

64. Ibid., pp. 131–32.

65. Pennsylvania Department of Public Welfare, *Manual of the Mothers' Assistance Fund*, Bulletin No. 1 (Harrisburg, PA: J.L.L. Kuhn, 1922), p. 43. See also Abbott and Breckinridge, *Administration of Aid-to-Mothers Law in Illinois*, p. 28.

66. Nesbitt, "Family Budget and Its Supervision," p. 363; Nesbitt, *Standards of Public Aid to Children in Their Own Homes*, p. 32.

67. Frank W. Goodhue, "Analysis of Budget Questionnaire Returns in *Proceedings of the Conference on Mother's Pensions*, p. 9; Bogue, "Recommendations of the Committee," p. 15; Nesbitt, "Family Budget and Its Supervision," p. 364.

68. Nesbitt, "Family Budget and Its Supervision," pp. 363–64; Nesbitt, *Standards of Public Aid to Children in Their Own Homes*, p. 35; Abbott and Breckinridge, *Administration of Aid-to-Mothers Law in Illinois*, p. 28; Bogue, "Recommendations of the Committee," p. 14; Pennsylvania Department of Public Welfare, *Manual of the Mothers' Assistance Fund*, pp. 31–33; Ada E. Sheffield, "Public Agencies as Public Carriers of Ideas," NCSW, *Proceedings* 49 (1922): 88.

69. Mary F. Bogue, "The Greater Economy of Adequate Grants," NCSW, *Proceedings* 46 (1919): 304; Nesbitt, *Standards of Public Aid to Children in Their Own Homes*, pp. 31, 34; Bogue, *Administration of Mothers' Aid in Ten Localities*, pp. 11–12, 14, 16–18; Pennsylvania Department of Public Welfare, *Manual of the Mothers' Assistance Fund*, p. 33.

70. Nesbitt, *Standards of Public Aid to Children in Their Own Homes*, pp. 33–35. See similarly Abbott and Breckinridge, *Administration of Aid-to-Mothers Law in Illinois*, pp. 29–30.

71. Bogue, *Administration of Mothers' Aid in Ten Localities*, pp. 22–24; Elizabeth F. Moloney, "The Family Budget and Adequacy of Relief," NCSW, *Proceedings* 46 (1919): 302; Pennsylvania Department of Public Welfare, *Manual of the Mothers' Assistance Fund*, p. 44.

72. Pennsylvania Department of Public Welfare, *Manual of the Mothers' Assistance Fund*, p. 36. See similarly Higgins and Windom, "Helping Widows to Bring Up Citizens," p. 140.

73. Nesbitt, "Family Budget and Its Supervision," p. 364.

74. Pennsylvania Department of Public Welfare, *Manual of the Mothers' Assistance Fund*, pp. 43–44; Bogue, *Administration of Mothers' Aid in Ten Localities*, p. 55; Mrs. Daniel Ancona in "General Discussion," *Proceedings of the Conference on Mother's Pensions*, p. 17.

75. Bogue, *Administration of Mothers' Aid in Ten Localities*, p. 103.

76. Edward E. Porterfield, "How the Widow's Allowance Operates," *Child-Welfare Magazine* 7 (1913): 210; Abbott and Breckinridge, *Administration of Aid-to-Mothers Law in Illinois*, p. 43.

77. Bogue, *Administration of Mothers' Aid in Ten Localities*, pp. 16–18, 25, 64–65; Pennsylvania Department of Public Welfare, *Manual of the Mothers' Assistance Fund*, pp. 23, 25.

78. Ancona in "General Discussion," pp. 16–17; William Hodson in "General Discussion," *Proceedings of the Conference on Mother's Pensions*, p. 24. Leff seems to regard the insistence upon a standard of child care as a deviation from the original principles of the mothers'-aid movement. See Leff, "Consensus for Reform," p. 413. But the expectation that the mother would have to demonstrate satisfactory homemaking was clearly stated when pension supporters likened the allowance to wages.

79. Abbott and Breckinridge, *Administration of Aid-to-Mothers Law in Illinois*, pp. 38–42; Bogue, *Administration of Mothers' Aid in Ten Localities*, pp. 12–13, 15, 42.

80. Abbott and Breckinridge, *Administration of Aid-to-Mothers Law in Illinois*, pp. 38–42.

81. On the importance of client status as a form of participation, see Barbara J. Nelson, "Client Evaluations of Social Programs," in Charles T. Goodsell, ed., *The Public Encounter: Where State and Citizen Meet* (Bloomington, IN: Indiana University Press, 1981), p. 39; Barbara J. Nelson, "Women's Poverty and Women's Citizenship: Some Political Consequences of Economic Marginality," *Signs* 10 (1984): 210.

82. Pennsylvania Department of Public Welfare, *Manual of the Mothers' Assistance Fund*, p. 42.

Chapter Four
Practice against Theory

1. Ellen Ryerson, *The Best-Laid Plans: America's Juvenile Court Experiment* (New York: Hill and Wang, 1978), p. 61; David J. Rothman, *Conscience and Convenience: The Asylum and its Alternatives in Progressive America* (Boston: Little, Brown, 1980), p. 237; Joseph M. Hawes, *Children in Urban Society: Juvenile Delinquency in Nineteenth-Century America* (New York: Oxford University Press, 1971), p. 246.

2. By the Second World War over 65,000 children each year were placed on probation. Lowell Julliard Carr, *Delinquency Control* (New York: Harper, 1941), p. 135. On the expansion of judicial intervention, see Rothman, *Conscience and Convenience*, pp. 251–52.

3. Figures for the number of children in mothers'-aid programs vary; sometimes the same expert cited very different totals. For example, Emma O. Lundberg

of the Children's Bureau reported in 1921 that 200,000 children were receiving assistance, while in 1926 she gave a figure of 130,000. The discrepancy arose, it seems, because the first total was based on an extrapolation from an unrepresentative sample of agencies. See Lundberg, "Aid to Mothers With Dependent Children," *Annals* 98 (November 1921): 100–101; Lundberg, *Public Aid to Mothers With Dependent Children: Extent and Fundamental Principles*, Children's Bureau Publication No. 162 (Washington, DC: Government Printing Office, 1926), p. 16.

4. Edith Abbott and Sophonisba P. Breckinridge, *The Administration of the Aid-to-Mothers Law in Illinois*, Children's Bureau Legal Series No. 7 (Washington, DC: Government Printing Office, 1921), pp. 29–30, 33–39; Florence Nesbitt, *Standards of Public Aid to Children in Their Own Homes*, Children's Bureau Publication No. 118 (Washington, DC: Government Printing Office, 1923), pp. 64, 66, 79, 96–97, 126; Mary F. Bogue, *Administration of Mothers' Aid in Ten Localities*, Children's Bureau Publication No. 184 (Washington, DC: Government Printing Office, 1928).

5. Jeffrey R. Brackett, "Public Outdoor Relief in the United States," NCCC, *Proceedings* 42 (1915): 450; A. W. MacDougall, "New Jersey Experiments in the Field of Public Social Service," NCSW, *Proceedings* 46 (1919): 341; Francis H. McLean, "National and Local Social Agencies Rendering Services to the Home and Family," *Annals* 105 (January 1923): 52.

6. Gertrude Vaile, "Principles and Methods of Outdoor Relief," NCCC, *Proceedings* 42 (1915): 480–81; J. L. Gillin, "The Public Welfare Movement and Democracy," *Annals* 105 (January 1923): 13; Robert W. Kelso, "The Transition From Charities and Corrections to Public Welfare," *Annals* 105 (January 1923): 24.

7. Charles N. Goodnow, "The Chicago Court of Domestic Relations," in Sophonisba P. Breckinridge, ed., *The Child in the City* (Chicago: Chicago School of Civics and Philanthropy, 1912), pp. 330–40; Edward F. Waite, "The Outlook for the Juvenile Court," *Annals* 105 (January 1923): 240.

8. George Elliott Howard, "Social Control of the Domestic Relations," AJS 16 (1911): 805–17.

9. John F. McClymer, *War and Welfare: Social Engineering in America, 1890–1925* (Westport, CT: Greenwood Press, 1980), pp. 162–64. Rural county agents had earlier engaged in some of the educative measures characteristic of the philanthropic method, but this seems to have been an incidental aspect of their work. See E. C. Lindeman, "Organization of Rural Social Forces," NCSW, *Proceedings* 48 (1921): 16.

10. Valeria Parker, "Social Hygiene and the Child," *Annals* 121 (September 1925): 46–52; McClymer, *War and Welfare*, pp. 167–69.

11. David Helm Holbrook, "The Twilight Zone Between Vocational Re-Education and Social Service," NCSW, *Proceedings* 46 (1919): 347–48; Joanna C. Colcord, "What Is the Immediate Future of the Family?" NCSW, *Proceedings* 46 (1919): 316.

12. Waite, "Outlook for the Juvenile Court," p. 234; Roscoe Pound, "Forward," in Pauline V. Young, *Social Treatment in Probation and Delinquency* (New York: McGraw-Hill, 1937), pp. xxv, xxviii.

13. Julian W. Mack, "Legal Problems Involved in the Establishment of the Juvenile Court," in Sophonisba P. Breckinridge and Edith Abbott, *The Delinquent Child and the Home* (New York: Russell Sage Foundation, Charities Publication Committee, 1912), pp. 190–91; Ryerson, *Best-Laid Plans*, pp. 67–68.

14. Robert W. Kelso, "Changing Fundamentals of Social Work," Presidential Address, NCSW, *Proceedings* 49 (1922): 11. See also Jesse Frederick Steiner, "Professional Training for Public Welfare," *Annals* 105 (January 1923): 165. These trends in public welfare have not been sufficiently appreciated in some historical studies of social work. Lubove, for example, asserts that social workers through the 1920s dismissed public welfare personnel out of hand. Any balanced reading of conference proceedings and other publications shows that his contention is simply not correct. See Roy Lubove, *The Professional Altruist: The Emergence of Social Work as a Career, 1880–1930* (1965; reprint ed., New York: Atheneum, 1980), pp. 52–54. For a better treatment of the relationship between private caseworkers and their public counterparts, see Stanley Wenocur and Michael Reisch, *From Charity to Enterprise: The Development of American Social Work in a Market Economy* (Urbana: University of Illinois Press, 1989), pp. 70–71.

15. Mark H. Leff, "Consensus for Reform: The Mothers' Pension Movement in the Progressive Era," SSR 47 (1973): 405–6.

16. Valeria H. Parker, "The Social Worker in a Sound Social Hygiene Program," NCSW, *Proceedings* 48 (1921): 120–21; Parker, "Social Hygiene and the Child," p. 49; Holbrook, "Twilight Zone Between Vocational Re-Education and Social Service," pp. 350–51; Edward N. Clopper, "The Development of the Children's Code," *Annals* 98 (November 1921): 154–59; Mary S. Larabee, "Problems of Children as a Public Agency Sees Them," *Annals* 121 (September 1925): 126–27.

17. On the response of the political system to women, see Theda Skocpol, "Protecting Soldiers and Mothers: The Politics of Social Provision in the United States, 1870s-1920s," in preparation.

18. On the shift, see, for example, Sidney Fine, *Laissez Faire and the General Welfare State: A Study of Conflict in American Thought, 1865–1901* (Ann Arbor: University of Michigan Press, 1956, 1978).

19. See, for example, Edith I. Clarke, "Juvenile Delinquency and Dependency: Report of Inquiry at Chicago," *The Commons* 5 (February 1901): 4.

20. Steven L. Schlossman, *Love and the American Delinquent: The Theory and Practice of "Progressive" Juvenile Justice, 1825–1920* (Chicago: The University of Chicago Press, 1977), pp. 62–63, 66; Sanford J. Fox, "Juvenile Justice Reform: An Historical Perspective," *Stanford Law Review* 22 (1970): 1224.

21. Edith Abbott, "The Experimental Period of Widow's Pension Legislation," NCSW, *Proceedings* 44 (1917): 154; Leff, "Consensus for Reform," pp. 397, 404–5.

22. Abbott, "Experimental Period of Widow's Pension Legislation," pp. 154–55; Lundberg, *Public Aid to Mothers With Dependent Children*, pp. 2–3.

23. Thomas D. Eliot, *The Juvenile Court and the Community* (New York: Macmillan, 1914), pp. 13–14, 16; Pound, "Forward," pp. xxviii–xxix; Alice Scott Nutt, "The Future of the Juvenile Court as a Case-Work Agency," NCSW, *Proceedings* 66 (1939): 371.

24. Lundberg, *Public Aid to Mothers With Dependent Children*, pp. 9–10.

25. McClymer, *War and Welfare*, pp. 154ff.

26. Historians sometimes claim that proponents of tutelary programs paid no attention to the way they operated. See Schlossman, *Love and the American Delinquent*, pp. 126–27; Leff, "Consensus for Reform," p. 414. But as I demonstrate in this section and the ones that follow, the performance of social agencies was the subject of much contemporary discussion.

27. Roger Baldwin, "The Presentation of the Case," in Breckinridge, ed., *Child in the City*, pp. 341–44, 347; Bernard Flexner and Roger N. Baldwin, *Juvenile Courts and Probation* (New York: Century, 1914, 1916), pp. 44–45, 51; Katherine F. Lenroot and Emma O. Lundberg, *Juvenile Courts at Work: A Study of the Organization and Methods of Ten Courts*, Children's Bureau Publication No. 141 (Washington, DC: Government Printing Office, 1925), pp. 94, 100–101; Douglas P. Falconer, "Making the Child Safe for the Community," NCSW, *Proceedings* 53 (1926): 165.

28. Bernard Flexner, "The Juvenile Court—Its Legal Aspects," *Annals* 36 (1910): 53, 55; Julian Mack, "The Law and the Child," *The Survey* 23 (5 February 1910): 640; Flexner and Baldwin, *Juvenile Courts and Probation*, pp. 75, 77.

29. Flexner, "Juvenile Court as a Social Institution," pp. 614–17, 620–21, 636–37; "Testimony of Judge Merritt W. Pinckney," in Breckinridge and Abbott, *Delinquent Child and the Home*, pp. 207–8; Henry Thurston, "Some Phases of the Probation Work of the Juvenile Court," NCCC, *Proceedings* 32 (1905): 178–79; Eliot, *Juvenile Court and the Community*, pp. 22, 25; Pound, "Forward," p. xxx; Rothman, *Conscience and Convenience*, pp. 244, 249–50; Ryerson, *Best-Laid Plans*, pp. 89–92.

30. Breckinridge and Abbott, *Delinquent Child and the Home*, pp. 56–57, 61, 70, 160.

31. Clarke, "Juvenile Delinquency and Dependency," p. 3; Linda Gordon, *Heroes of Their Own Lives: The Politics and History of Family Violence* (New York: Penguin, 1988), pp. 190–92; Meda Chesney-Lind, "Girls' Crime and Woman's Place: Toward a Feminist Model of Female Delinquency," *Crime and Delinquency* 35 (1989): 20–21.

32. Breckinridge and Abbott, *Delinquent Child and the Home*, pp. 170–71, 173–74; Nutt, "Future of Juvenile Court as a Case-Work Agency," p. 373; Lenroot and Lundberg, *Juvenile Courts at Work*, pp. 111, 195.

33. Gordon, *Heroes of Their Own Lives*.

34. For discussions of the early findings on recidivism, see Carr, *Delinquency Control*, pp. 173–80; Grace Abbott, "The Juvenile Court and a Community Program for Treating and Preventing Delinquency," SSR 10 (1936): 233–34.

35. Emma O. Lundberg, "The Present Status of Mothers' Pension Administration," NCSW, *Proceedings* 48 (1921): 239; William Hodson in "General Discussion," in *Proceedings of the Conference on Mothers' Pensions*, Children's Bureau Publication No. 109 (Washington, DC: Government Printing Office, 1922), p. 23; Abbott and Breckinridge, *Administration of the Aid-to-Mothers Law in Illinois*.

36. Abbott and Breckinridge, *Administration of the Aid-to-Mothers Law in Illinois*, pp. 11–12, 14–15, 114; Bogue, *Administration of Mothers' Aid in Ten*

Localities, pp. 33, 68, 112–13; Jane Grey Potter, "Mothers' Pensions—Graft, Charity or Justice," *Outlook* 112 (1916): 523; Pennsylvania Department of Public Welfare, *Manual of the Mothers' Assistance Fund,* Bulletin No. 1 (Harrisburg, PA: J.L.L. Kuhn, 1922), pp. 11–12, 23.

37. Helen Glenn Tyson, "Measuring Our Results in Securing the Essentials of Family Life: Some Suggestions Based on a Review of Mother's Assistance in Pennsylvania," NCSW, *Proceedings* 53 (1926): 296–98; Bogue, *Administration of Mothers' Aid in Ten Localities,* pp. 6–7; Nesbitt, *Standards of Public Aid to Children in Their Own Homes,* pp. 16, 22; Lundberg, *Public Aid to Mothers With Dependent Children,* p. 16.

38. Nesbitt, *Standards of Public Aid to Children in Their Own Homes,* pp. 16–21; Florence Nesbitt, "Study of Standards of Aid," in *Proceedings of the Conference on Mothers' Pensions,* p. 11; Bogue, *Administration of Mothers' Aid in Ten Localities,* pp. 6–7.

39. Bogue, *Administration of Mothers' Aid in Ten Localities,* pp. 9, 12–13, 112–13, 131–32; Nesbitt, "Study of Standards of Aid," p. 11.

40. Bogue, *Administration of Mothers' Aid in Ten Localities,* pp. 68–69, 113–14, 129–31, 145, 147; Abbott and Breckinridge, *Administration of the Aid-to-Mothers Law in Illinois,* pp. 40, 128, 136–66.

41. Bogue, *Administration of Mothers' Aid in Ten Localities,* pp. 160–61; See also Mary F. Bogue, "The Greater Economy of Adequate Grants," NCSW, *Proceedings* 46 (1919): 303–4.

42. Abbott and Breckinridge, *Administration of the Aid-to-Mothers Law in Illinois,* pp. 19–20, 40–41, 77. See also Bogue, *Administration of Mothers' Aid in Ten Localities,* pp. 42, 178.

43. Abbott, "Experimental Period of Widows' Pension Administration," p. 154.

44. Abbott and Breckinridge, *Administration of the Aid-to-Mothers Law in Illinois,* pp. 43–44; "Testimony of Judge Merritt W. Pinckney," p. 222; Eliot, *Juvenile Court and the Community,* pp. 138–39; Lenroot and Lundberg, *Juvenile Courts at Work,* pp. 159–60.

45. Bogue, *Administration of Mothers' Aid in Ten Localities,* pp. 25–26. Schlossman suggests that communication with clients on probation may actually have improved under the patronage system, because political appointees were more likely to share a common class background with those families brought into court. See *Love and the American Delinquent,* pp. 140–41. Contemporary supporters of the court did not entertain this view.

46. Lenroot and Lundberg, *Juvenile Courts at Work,* pp. 160, 194, 225, 228, 245.

47. Gillin, "Public Welfare Movement and Democracy," p. 14; Amy D. Steinhart in "Discussion" of Lundberg, "Present Status of Mothers' Pension Administration," p. 241. On the efforts of public welfare officials to justify themselves, see Michael B. Katz, *In the Shadow of the Poorhouse: A Social History of Welfare in America* (New York: Basic Books, 1986), pp. 167–68.

48. Bogue, *Administration of Mothers' Aid in Ten Localities,* p. 14.

49. Francis H. Hiller, "The Juvenile Court as a Case Working Agency: Its

Limitations and Its Possibilities," NCSW, *Proceedings* 53 (1926): 142–43; Mack, "The Law and the Child," p. 642; Eliot, *Juvenile Court and the Community*, pp. 23–24; Pound, "Forward," p. xxvi; Ryerson, *Best-Laid Plans*, pp. 85–86.

50. Nutt, "Future of Juvenile Court as a Case-Work Agency," p. 374; Baldwin, "Presentation of the Case," pp. 347–48; Eliot, *Juvenile Court and the Community*, pp. 32–33; Willard E. Hotchkiss, "The Juvenile Court as It Is Today," NCCC, *Proceedings* 39 (1912): 456–57; Bernard Flexner, "A Decade of the Juvenile Court," NCCC, *Proceedings* 37 (1910): 108, 110–11; Young, *Social Treatment in Probation and Delinquency*, pp. 14–15; Nutt, "Future of Juvenile Court as a Case-Work Agency," p. 374. This aspect of juvenile court development has been much discussed by historians. See, for example, Rothman, *Conscience and Convenience*, pp. 261–63.

51. George W. Kirchway, "Social Work and the Law: Forms of Cooperation Between Law and Social Work," NCSW, *Proceedings* 53 (1926): 182; Katherine F. Lenroot, "Progressive Methods of Care of Children Pending Juvenile Court Hearing," NCSW, *Proceedings* 53 (1926): 141–42; Abbott, "Juvenile Court and a Community Program for Treating and Preventing Delinquency," p. 237; William Healy and Augusta F. Bronner, *New Light on Delinquency and Its Treatment* (New Haven: Yale University Press, 1936, 1950), pp. 147, 205, 222.

52. Herbert M. Baker, "The Court and the Delinquent Child," *AJS* 26 (1920): 178; Flexner, "Juvenile Court as a Social Institution," p. 637; Pound, "Forward," p. xxvii.

53. Jesse Taft, "Problems of Social Case Work with Children," NCSW, *Proceedings* 47 (1920): 379; William Healy, "The Psychology of the Situation: A Fundamental for Understanding and Treatment of Delinquency," in Jane Addams et al., *The Child, the Clinic and the Court* (1925; reprint ed., New York: Johnson Reprint, 1970), p. 48; Henry S. Hulbert, "Probation," in Addams et al., *Child, the Clinic and the Court*, pp. 239, 241, 243–44; Young, *Social Treatment in Probation and Delinquency*, p. 605; Carr, *Delinquency Control*, pp. 4, 18–19, 158.

54. Sheldon Glueck and Eleanor T. Glueck, *One Thousand Juvenile Delinquents: Their Treatment by Court and Clinic* (Cambridge, MA: Harvard University Press, 1934); Abbott, "Juvenile Court and a Community Program for Treating and Preventing Delinquency," pp. 233–234. For a discussion of Glueck and Glueck, see Rothman, *Conscience and Convenience*, pp. 245–48.

55. Young, *Social Treatment in Probation and Delinquency*, pp. 25–26, 126, 132, 292.

56. J. Prentice Murphy, "The Superficial Character of Child Caring Work," NCSW, *Proceedings* 49 (1922): 32.

57. Young, *Social Treatment in Probation and Delinquency*, pp. 603–4; Baker, "Court and Delinquent Child," p. 177; Carr, *Delinquency Control*, pp. 198–99.

58. McClymer, *War and Welfare*, pp. 176ff; Clarke A. Chambers, *Seedtime of Reform: American Social Service and Social Action, 1918–1933* (Minneapolis: University of Minnesota Press, 1963). On the retreat of social feminism in this period, see J. Stanley Lemons, *The Woman Citizen: Social Feminism in the 1920s* (Urbana: University of Illinois Press, 1973), p. 228.

59. Eliot, *Juvenile Court and the Community*, p. ix; Justin Miller, "Introduction," in Young, *Social Treatment in Probation and Delinquency*, p. xxxiv; Ryerson, *Best-Laid Plans*, pp. 78–79.

Chapter Five
Strategies for Survival

1. Ruth I. Workum, "The Relationship Between the Functions of the Juvenile Court and Those of the General Child-Caring Agencies," NCSW, *Proceedings* 49 (1922): 142; Willard E. Hotchkiss, "The Juvenile Court as It Is Today," NCC, *Proceedings* 39 (1912): 450, 455; Edward Lindsey, "The Juvenile Court Movement From a Lawyer's Standpoint," *Annals* 52 (1914): 147–48. See also Jacques Donzelot, *The Policing of Families* (New York: Pantheon, 1980), p. 98.

2. A. W. MacDougall, "New Jersey Experiments in the Field of Public Welfare," NCSW, *Proceedings* 46 (1919): 342, 345; Robert W. Kelso, "The Transition From Charities and Corrections to Public Welfare," *Annals* 105 (1923): 21–22; Sophonisba P. Breckinridge, "Summary of the Present State Systems for the Organization and Administration of Public Welfare," *Annals* 105 (1923): 95–97.

3. Frederic C. Howe, *The City: The Hope of Democracy* (1905; reprint ed., Seattle: University of Washington Press, 1967), pp. vii–viii, 32–33, 63, 77, 86–87, 90, 216–17.

4. Mary Kingsbury Simkhovitch, *The City Worker's World in America* (1917; reprint ed., New York: Arno Press, 1971), pp. 30, 182, 185; Mary Kingsbury Simkhovitch, "Friendship and Politics," *Political Science Quarterly* 17 (1902): 195–96.

5. Howe, *City: Hope of Democracy*, pp. 1–2, 46, 116–17.

6. Simkhovitch, *City Worker's World in America*, pp. 184, 199–200; Jane Addams, *Democracy and Social Ethics* (New York: Macmillan, 1902), pp. 222–23, 265–66, 270.

7. Henry Bruere, *The New City Government: A Discussion Based on a Survey of Ten Commission Governed Cities* (New York: D. Appleton and Company, 1912, 1916), pp. 87–88, 242–44, 314.

8. Ibid., pp. 1–5, 102–3; Frederic C. Howe, *The Confessions of a Reformer* (1925; reprint ed., New York: Quadrangle Books, 1967), p. 113; Howe, *City: Hope of Democracy*, pp. 26, 54, 119, 128–29, 202–4, 211–12, 219, 286–87.

9. Bruere, *New City Government*, p. 8; Simkhovitch, *City Worker's World in America*, p. 183.

10. Bruere, *New City Government*, pp. 5–6, 12, 86; Frederic C. Howe, *The Modern City and Its Problems* (New York: Charles Scribner's Sons, 1915), p. 229; Howe, *City: Hope of Democracy*, pp. 135, 303; Howe, *Confessions of a Reformer*, pp. 180–81.

11. See Frederic C. Howe and Marie Jenney Howe, "Pensioning the Widow and the Fatherless," *Good Housekeeping* 57 (September 1913): 282–91. On Bruere's association with the settlement houses, see Allen F. Davis, *Spearheads for Reform: The Social Settlements and the Progressive Movement, 1890–1914* (New York: Oxford University Press, 1967), pp. 185–86.

12. *Juvenile-Court Standards*, Children's Bureau Publication No. 121 (Wash-

ington, DC: Government Printing Office, 1923); *Proceedings of Conference on Mothers' Pensions*, Children's Bureau Publication No. 109 (Washington, DC: Government Printing Office, 1922); Emma O. Lundberg, *Public Aid to Mothers With Dependent Children: Extent and Fundamental Principles*, Children's Bureau Publication No. 162 (Washington, DC: Government Printing Office, 1926), pp. 3–4. For a discussion of the work on the juvenile court, see Marguerite Rosenthal, "The Children's Bureau and the Juvenile Court: Delinquency Policy, 1912–1940," *ssr* 60 (June 1986): 306–7.

13. On the role of the Children's Bureau in promoting the social agency model of the juvenile court, see H. Warren Dunham, "The Juvenile Court: Contradictory Orientations in Processing Offenders," *Law and Contemporary Problems* 23 (1958): 513–14; Rosenthal, "Children's Bureau and the Juvenile Court," p. 307. For an example of a promotional (but still critical) follow-up study, see Katherine F. Lenroot and Emma O. Lundberg, *Juvenile Courts at Work: A Study of the Organization and Methods of Ten Courts*, Children's Bureau Publication No. 141 (Washington, DC: Government Printing Office, 1925).

14. Joel D. Hunter, "Mothers' Pensions: Problems of Administration," ncsw, *Proceedings* 48 (1921): 234; Edith Abbott and Sophonisba P. Breckinridge, *The Administration of the Aid-to-Mothers Law in Illinois*, Children's Bureau Legal Series No. 7 (Washington, DC: Government Printing Office, 1921), p. 170.

15. Howard W. Odum, "Attainable Standards for State Departments of Public Welfare," *Annals* 105 (January 1923): 137–43; Grace Abbott, "Public Protection of Children," Presidential Address, ncsw, *Proceedings* 51 (1924): 8, 11.

16. Emma O. Lundberg, "The Juvenile Court as a Constructive Social Agency," ncsw, *Proceedings* 49 (1922): 159–60; Katherine F. Lenroot, "The Evolution of the Juvenile Court," *Annals* 105 (January 1923): 221; Francis H. Hiller, "The Juvenile Court as a Case Working Agency: Its Limitations and Its Possibilities," ncsw, *Proceedings* 53 (1926): 146–48.

17. Abbott and Breckinridge, *Administration of the Aid-to-Mothers Law in Illinois*, p. 170; William Hodson in "General Discussion" in *Proceedings of Conference on Mothers' Pensions*, p. 24; Mary F. Bogue, *Administration of Mothers' Aid in Ten Localities: With Special Reference to Health, Housing, Education, and Recreation*, Children's Bureau Publication No. 184 (Washington, DC: Government Printing Office, 1928), p. 25.

18. Ellen C. Potter, "The Bureau System," ncsw, *Proceedings* 51 (1924): 565; Abbott, "Public Protection of Widows," p. 8.

19. Hunter, "Mothers' Pensions: Problems of Administration," p. 235; Abbott and Breckinridge, *Administration of the Aid-to-Mothers Law in Illinois*, pp. 167, 171.

20. Herbert H. Lou, *Juvenile Courts in the United States* (Chapel Hill: University of North Carolina Press, 1927), pp. 195–96; David M. Schneider and Albert Deutsch, *The History of Public Welfare in New York State, 1867–1940* (1941; reprint ed., Montclair, NJ: Patterson Smith, 1969), pp. 257–58; Nutt, "Future of Juvenile Court as a Case-Work Agency," pp. 377–78.

21. For examples of effective delaying tactics, see Schneider and Deutsch, *History of Public Welfare in New York State*, pp. 257, 277, 285–86.

22. *Proceedings of Conference on Mothers' Pensions*, pp. 12, 19–20, 22–23;

Mary F. Bogue in "Discussion of 'Problems of Organization in Smaller Communities,'" NCSW, *Proceedings* 48 (1921): 267–68; Rose Porter, "The Cost of Maintaining Good Case Work in a Public Agency," NCSW, *Proceedings* 52 (1925): 240. On state centralization, see also Michael B. Katz, *In the Shadow of the Poorhouse: A Social History of Welfare in America* (New York: Basic Books, 1986), p. 208.

23. Lundberg, *Public Aid to Mothers With Dependent Children*, pp. 14–15.

24. For a clear statement indicating the awareness that organization meant power, see Edward N. Clopper, "The Articulation of Service of Juvenile Courts, Compulsory Attendance and Child Labor Laws, Training Schools, Placing Agencies, and Other Bodies, under a Controlling and Directing State Department," NCSW, *Proceedings* 48 (1921): 210.

25. Hiller, "Juvenile Court as a Case Working Agency," pp. 146–47; Schneider and Deutsch, *History of Public Welfare in New York State*, p. 285; Henry L. Lurie, "The Role of Professional Standards in Public Social Work," NCSW, *Proceedings* 56 (1929): 614–15.

26. Ada Eliot Sheffield, "Public Relief Officials," NCSW, *Proceedings* 51 (1924): 540–41.

27. Grace Abbott, "Public Protection of Children," Presidential Address, NCSW, *Proceedings* 51 (1924): 8; Schneider and Deutsch, *History of Public Welfare in New York State*, pp. 258, 285, 287–88; Potter, "Bureau System," pp. 564–65.

28. Hiller, "Juvenile Court as a Case Working Agency," p. 143; Charles H. Johnson, "The Correlation of Public and Private Social Service," NCSW, *Proceedings* 51 (1924): 30; Robert W. Kelso, "Is There a Dividing Line Between the Cases Which the Public Agency Should Take Over, and Those Which Should Be Handled by Private Social Agencies," NCSW, *Proceedings* 48 (1921): 217.

29. Frank R. Johnson, "The Division of Family Case Work Between Public and Private Agencies," NCSW, *Proceedings* 46 (1919): 339–40; Kelso, "Is There a Dividing Line Between the Cases . . . ," p. 217. This distinction is sometimes associated with the turn toward psychoanalytic methods in private casework. See Roy Lubove, *The Professional Altruist: The Emergence of Social Work as a Profession, 1880–1930* (1965; reprint ed., New York: Atheneum, 1980), pp. 114–15. However, social personnel began to stress the capacity of a private agency to perform more intensive casework before they were captivated by Freudian doctrine.

Not all advocates of public tutelage accepted the division of labor described here. It was sometimes claimed that the advantages of private agencies were overstated or the result of temporary conditions. See Frank J. Bruno, "The Integration of Effort in Theory and Practice by Private and Public Agencies for the Common Good," NCSW, *Proceedings* 54 (1927): 244–45. A few went so far as to assert that the public role should expand without limit until government had absorbed all social welfare responsibilities. See Leyton E. Carter, "Governmental Responsibility in the Field of Social Work," NCSW, *Proceedings* 53 (1926): 459. But this remained very much a minority view.

30. Thomas D. Eliot, *The Juvenile Court and the Community* (Macmillan, 1914), pp. 73–74, 116–17, 151–54; Workum, "Relationship Between the Func-

tions of the Juvenile Court and Those of the General Child-Caring Agencies," p. 142; Johnson, "Division of Family Case Work Between Public and Private Agencies," p. 340.

31. Pauline V. Young, *Social Treatment in Probation and Delinquency* (New York: McGraw-Hill, 1937), p. 28; David J. Rothman, *Conscience and Convenience: The Asylum and its Alternatives in Progressive America* (Boston: Little, Brown, 1980), p. 247; Donzelot, *Policing of Families*, pp. 112, 124–25.

32. Eliot, *Juvenile Court and the Community*, esp. pp. x-xi, 20–21, 50–52, 124–26. See also Eliot, "The Trend of the Juvenile Court," *Annals* 52 (1914): 149–58; Eliot, "The Project-Problem Method as Applied in Indeterminate Sentence, Probation, and Other Reeducational Treatment," in Jane Addams et al., *The Child, the Clinic and the Court* (1925; reprint ed., New York: Johnson Reprint, 1970), pp. 102–7.

33. Charles L. Chute, "Juvenile Probation," *Annals* 105 (1923): 227; Edward F. Waite, "The Outlook for the Juvenile Court," *Annals* 105 (1923): 231, 237.

34. Herbert M. Baker, "The Court and the Delinquent Child," *AJS* 26 (1920): 178; Workum, "Relationship Between the Functions of the Juvenile Court and Those of the General Child-Caring Agencies," pp. 141, 143; Carrie Weaver Smith, "The Elimination of the Reformatory," NCSW, *Proceedings* 48 (1921): 130; Abbott and Breckinridge, *Administration of the Aid-to-Mothers Law in Illinois*, p. 6; Hunter, "Mothers' Pensions: Problems of Administration," pp. 235–36.

35. Jesse Frederick Steiner, "Professional Training for Public Welfare," *Annals* 105 (1923): 170–71; Lurie, "Role of Professional Standards in Public Social Work," p. 618; Bogue, *Administration of Mothers' Aid in Ten Localities*, pp. 9–10; Howard W. Odum, "The County Unit as Basis of Social Work and Public Welfare in North Carolina," NCSW, *Proceedings* 53 (1926): 463.

36. MacDougall, "New Jersey Experiments in the Field of Public Social Service," p. 346; William Hodson, "A State Program for Child Welfare," *Annals* 98 (November 1921): 166; Johnson, "Correlation of Public and Private Social Service," p. 31; Bruno, "Integration of Effort in Theory and Practice by Private and Public Agencies," pp. 241–44; Ruth Taylor, "The Integration of Effort in Theory and Practice by Private and Public Family Agencies for the Common Good," NCSW, *Proceedings* 54 (1927): 251.

37. William Healy, "The Psychology of the Situation: A Fundamental for Understanding and Treatment of Delinquency," in Addams et al., *Child, the Clinic and the Court*, pp. 47–48; Herman M. Adler, "Our Responsibility for the Future," in Addams et al., *Child, the Clinic and the Court*, p. 66; William Healy and Augusta F. Bronner, *New Light on Delinquency and Its Treatment* (New Haven: Yale University Press, 1936, 1950), pp. 141, 146–47, 220–22; Lowell Julliard Carr, *Delinquency Control* (New York: Harper, 1941), p. 283.

38. See Abraham Flexner, "Is Social Work a Profession?" NCCC, *Proceedings* 42 (1915): 576–90. The interpretation of discursive rationalization that I offer here differs from that suggested by Lubove and Ehrenreich. They contend that the effort to formalize casework reflected a determination to secure a professional status for social work by defining a unique set of skills. Although I agree that a "status anxiety" motive figured in the intellectual ferment of the 1920s among

social workers, we should not overlook the clear parallel to administrative rationalization. And, in a larger sense, an excessive emphasis on status uncertainty obscures the political, as opposed to narrowly professional, motives of therapeutic activists. They sought not merely social status but a controlling position in the tutelary apparatus. Wenocur and Reisch better appreciate the political drive to secure agency control. See Lubove, *Professional Altruist*, chap. 5; John H. Ehrenreich, *The Altruistic Imagination: A History of Social Work and Social Policy in the United States* (Ithaca, NY: Cornell University Press, 1985), pp. 53–56; Stanley Wenocur and Michael Reisch, *From Charity to Enterprise: The Development of American Social Work in a Market Economy* (Urbana: University of Illinois Press, 1989), parts 2 and 3.

39. For a particularly insightful discussion of Richmond's role and the contribution of Russell Sage, see Wenocur and Reisch, *From Charity to Enterprise*, pp. 49–50, 56–67, 94–95.

40. Lubove, *Professional Altruist*, pp. 73–77; Ehrenreich, *Altruistic Imagination*, pp. 64–65, 71–72; Donzelot, *Policing of Families*, pp. 137–41.

41. Bronner, "The Contribution of Science to a Program for Treatment of Juvenile Delinquency," in Addams et al., *Child, the Clinic and the Court*, pp. 82–83; Ehrenreich, *Altruistic Imagination*, p. 52; Lubove, *Professional Altruist*, pp. 89, 91–93, 96–97, 99, 100–102, 108–10.

42. Lubove, *Professional Altruist*, pp. 89–121; Ehrenreich, *Professional Altruist*, pp. 72–73, 117–18. For contemporary statements reflecting these ideas, see Healy and Bronner, *New Light on Delinquency*, pp. 141–42; Young, *Social Treatment in Probation and Delinquency*, pp. 289–90.

43. Kenneth L. M. Pray, "Some Reasons for the Development of the Professional School," *Annals* 121 (1925): 169–71; Steiner, "Professional Training for Public Welfare," pp. 165–66, 168; Lubove, *Professional Altruist*, pp. 19–20, chap. 5. Lubove notes that Flexner's speech haunted social workers: he had asserted that the professional was set apart by distinctive skills acquired through special training, yet the best caseworkers learned on the job and pursued an approach much like that of the volunteer. Through formal education in the most sophisticated methods, social workers would not only become more effective but also transcend their image as mere do-gooders, and so attain a professional status they craved.

44. Donzelot, *Policing of Families*, pp. 97, 107–8, 118–19, 134–35.

45. Bronner, "Contribution of Science to a Program for Treatment of Juvenile Delinquency," p. 79; George W. Kirchway, "Social Work and the Law: Forms of Cooperation Between Law and Social Work," NCSW, *Proceedings* 53 (1926): 185–86; Lou, *Juvenile Courts in the United States*, pp. 201–3; Young, *Social Treatment in Probation and Delinquency*, pp. 320, 324–28, 330–31; Ellen Ryerson, *The Best-Laid Plans: America's Juvenile Court Experiment* (New York: Hill and Wang, 1978), pp. 110–11; Donzelot, *Policing of Families*, chap. 5, esp. pp. 143–45, 148–50, 170.

46. Bogue, *Administration of Mothers' Aid in Ten Localities*, p. 14; Douglas P. Falconer, "Making the Child Safe for the Community," NCSW, *Proceedings* 53 (1926): 166.

47. Barry C. Smith, "The Commonwealth Fund Program for the Prevention of

Delinquency," NCSW, *Proceedings* 49 (1922): 168–74; Lou, *Juvenile Courts in the United States*, p. 200.

48. Lou, *Juvenile Courts in the United States*, p. 203. See also the essays in Addams et al., *Child, the Clinic and the Court*. Psychiatric casework evidently gained a foothold most readily in certain agencies that were on the periphery of the medical apparatus. See Wenocur and Reisch, *From Charity to Enterprise*, p. 103.

49. Bogue, *Administration of Mothers' Aid in Ten Localities*, p. 1n. It seems appropriate here to take issue with the thesis, advanced most forcefully by Piven and Cloward, that public relief necessarily contracts in the absence of a strong working-class constituency. See Francis Fox Piven and Richard A. Cloward, *Regulating the Poor: The Functions of Public Welfare* (New York: Vintage, 1972). Although working-class support for mothers' aid was at best sporadic, grant levels rose, state reimbursement was liberalized, and eligibility for the program was broadened. Even if we assume that the growth in mothers'-aid cases represented a gradual shift from other public relief programs (an assumption for which we lack evidence), historians have documented a broader pattern of increasing public welfare expenditures during the 1920s. See Katz, *In the Shadow of the Poorhouse*, pp. 208–9.

50. Johnson, "The Division of Family Case Work Between Public and Private Agencies," NCSW, *Proceedings* 46 (1919): 338; Ruth Taylor, "The Integration of Effort in Theory and Practice by Private and Public Family Agencies for the Common Good," NCSW, *Proceedings* 54 (1927): 248–49.

51. Sheffield, "Public Relief Officials," pp. 542–43. Weed seems to suggest that bureaucratization was widely seen as antithetical to high professional standards. See Frank J. Weed, "Bureaucratization as Reform: The Case of the Public Welfare Movement, 1900–1929," *Social Science Journal* 16 (1979): 79–89. However, for most social personnel during the 1920s, quite the reverse held true: expertise and bureaucracy went together. Only a handful appreciated that bureaucracy threatened the exercise of professional skills.

52. Sheffield, "Public Relief Officials," pp. 539–40; Grace Abbott, "Case Work Responsibility of Juvenile Courts," NCSW, *Proceedings* 56 (1929): 154; Ryerson, *Best-Laid Plans*, pp. 104–5.

53. On the tension between science and empathy in social work, see Clarke E. Chambers, "Women in the Creation of the Profession of Social Work," *SSR* 60 (1986): 12, 16–17.

Chapter Six
The Paths to Social Membership

1. James B. Reynolds, "The Need and Value of Settlement Work, NYSCCC, *Proceedings* 1 (1900): 50; Lilian D. Wald, *The House on Henry Street* (New York: Henry Holt, 1915), pp. 286, 293, 300.

2. Graham Taylor, "The Neighborhood and the Municipality," NCCC, *Proceedings* 36 (1909): 157; Jane Addams, "The Subjective Necessity for Social Settlements," [1892] in Christopher Lasch, ed., *The Social Thought of Jane Addams* (Indianapolis: Bobbs-Merrill, 1965)[cited hereafter as *Social Thought*], p. 31.

3. Robert A. Woods, ed., *Americans in Process: A Settlement Study* (Boston: Houghton Mifflin, 1902), p. 163.

4. Taylor, "Neighborhood and the Municipality," p. 159; Wald, *House on Henry Street*, p. 17; Woods, ed., *Americans in Process*, p. 129; Mary Kingsbury Simkhovitch, *The City Worker's World in America* (1917; reprint ed., New York: Arno, 1971), p. 78; Jane Addams, "Why the Ward Boss Rules," [1898] in *Social Thought*, p. 126.

5. Robert A. Woods, ed., *The City Wilderness* (Boston: Houghton Mifflin, 1902), pp. 301–2; Taylor, "Neighborhood and the Municipality," pp. 159–60; Simkhovitch, *City Worker's World*, pp. 88, 114–15, 119–21; Mary Kingsbury Simkhovitch, "Friendship and Politics," *Political Science Quarterly* 17 (1902): 192, 201.

6. Woods, ed., *City Wilderness*, p. 307; Woods, ed., *Americans in Process*, pp. 365–66.

7. Robert A. Woods, "The Neighborhood and the Nation," NCCC, *Proceedings* 36 (1909): 102, 104; Robert A. Woods, "The Neighborhood in Social Reconstruction," [1914] in Woods, *The Neighborhood in Nation-Building* (1923; reprint ed., New York: Arno, 1970), pp. 148–49.

8. Woods, ed., *City Wilderness*, p. 307; Woods, ed., *Americans in Process*, p. 367; Woods, "Neighborhood and the Nation," pp. 103–4.

9. Woods, "Neighborhood in Social Reconstruction," p. 149.

10. Robert A. Woods, "The Recovery of the Parish," in Woods, *The Neighborhood in Nation-Building*, p. 135; Woods, "Neighborhood and the Nation," pp. 102–3.

11. Robert A. Woods, "Democracy A New Unfolding of Human Power," in *Studies in Philosophy and Psychology, by Former Students of Charles Edward Garman* (Boston: Houghton Mifflin, 1906), p. 94; Woods, ed., *Americans in Process*, pp. 382–83.

12. Graham Taylor, "Development in Municipal Activities Tending to Neighborhood Improvement," NCCC, *Proceedings* 31 (1904): 491; Taylor, "Neighborhood and the Municipality," p. 160; George A. Bellamy, "The Culture of the Family from the Standpoint of Recreation," in Lorene M. Pacey, *Readings in the Development of Settlement Work* (New York: Association Press, 1950), pp. 102–3, 106; Jane Addams, "The Objective Value of a Social Settlement," [1892] in *Social Thought*, p. 61; Mary Kingsbury Simkhovitch, "The Settlement and Religion," in Pacey, *Readings in the Development of Settlement Work*, pp. 136–37.

13. Clarence Arthur Perry, "The School as a Factor in Neighborhood Development," NCCC, *Proceedings* 41 (1914): 385–93; John Collier, "The Organized Laity and the Social Expert: The Meaning of Public Community Centers," NCSW, *Proceedings* 44 (1917): 468–69; John Collier, "Community Councils—What Have They Done and What Is Their Future?" NCSW, *Proceedings* 46 (1919): 476–77; Roy Lubove, *The Professional Altruist: The Emergence of Social Work as a Career, 1880–1930* (1965; reprint ed., New York: Atheneum, 1980), p. 173; Robert Fisher, "Community Organizing and Citizen Participation: The Efforts of the People's Institute in New York City, 1910–1920," SSR 51 (1977): 474–90.

Beyond the ranks of philanthropy, too, the neighborhood movement claimed a measure of support. Philosophical pluralists seized upon the neighborhood as the critical instrument for linking together the multitude of associations that characterized modern social life. Mary Parker Follett contended, with more optimism than accuracy, that neighborhoods sustained real social intercourse by mixing people without regard to class or status. Only the neighborhood could overcome the particularity of narrow groups to generate civic consciousness, so it represented the ideal political unit around which to organize a new participatory democracy. Mary Parker Follett, *The New State: Group Organization the Solution of Popular Government* (1918; reprint ed., Gloucester, MA: Peter Smith, 1965), chap. 22.

14. John Daniels, *America via the Neighborhood* (New York: Harper and Brothers, 1920), pp. 7–15.

15. Ibid., chaps. 3–5, 10–12.

16. Ibid., pp. 459–62.

17. Edward A. Ross, *Social Control: A Survey of the Foundations of Order* (New York: Macmillan, 1901), pp. 111, 426–27; Edward A. Ross, *Sin and Society: An Analysis of Latter-Day Iniquity* (Boston: Houghton Mifflin, 1907), pp. 41–42; Luther Lee Bernard, "The Transition to an Objective Standard of Social Control," *AJS* 16 (1910–11): 531, 533–35; George Elliott Howard, "Social Control of the Domestic Relations," *AJS* 16 (1911): 805–17.

18. Ross, *Social Control*, pp. 178–79, 370; Ross, *Sin and Society*, pp. 143–46, 160–64; Robert A. Kern, "The Supervision of the Social Order II," *AJS* 24 (1918–19): 435–38, 452; Bernard, "Transition to an Objective Standard of Social Control," pp. 532, 534–35.

19. Ross, *Social Control*, p. 52; Ross, *Sin and Society*, pp. 54–59, 66–67, 86–87, 114–16.

20. Bernard, "Transition to an Objective Standard of Social Control," pp. 533–34.

21. Ibid., pp. 533–34. On Bernard's hostility to action, see R. Jeffrey Lustig, *Corporate Liberalism: The Origins of Modern American Political Theory, 1890–1920* (Berkeley: University of California Press, 1982), p. 184.

22. Frederic C. Howe, *The City: The Hope of Democracy* (1905; reprint ed., Seattle: University of Washington Press, 1967), pp. 175–76, 292, 302, 312.

23. Ibid., pp. 118, 120, 123–24; Simkhovitch, *City Worker's World*, pp. 207–8.

24. Henry Bruere, *The New City Government: A Discussion Based on a Survey of Ten Commission Governed Cities* (New York: D. Appleton and Company, 1912, 1916), pp. 109, 378–79; Howe, *City: The Hope of Democracy*, pp. 171–74; Frederic C. Howe, *The Confessions of a Reformer* (1925; reprint ed., New York: Quadrangle Books, 1967), pp. 177–78.

25. Howe, *Confessions of a Reformer*, pp. 180–81; Howe, *City: The Hope of Democracy*, pp. 135, 303; Bruere, *New City Government*, pp. 377–78.

26. Simkhovitch, *City Worker's World*, pp. 128–29; Woods, "Neighborhood and the Nation," p. 104.

27. On the People's Institute neighborhood council, see Fisher, "Community Organizing and Citizen Participation," pp. 476–77.

28. Robert A. Woods, "University Settlements as Laboratories in Social Science," [1893] in Woods, *Neighborhood in Nation-Building*, pp. 37–38; Woods, ed., *Americans in Process*, p. 376.

29. See, for example, Robert A. Woods and Albert J. Kennedy, *The Settlement*

Horizon: A National Estimate (New York: Russell Sage Foundation, 1922), p. 174. For a discussion of these attitudes, see Fisher, "Community Organizing and Citizen Participation," p. 477.

30. For a passionate statement of this position, see Simkhovitch, *City Worker's World*, p. 34.

31. Woods, ed., *Americans in Process*, p. 367; Woods and Kennedy, *Settlement Horizon*, pp. 165, 219.

32. Charles F. Weller, "Charity, the Family, and the Modern Social Movement," NCCC, *Proceedings* 39 (1912): 102–9; Daniels, *America via the Neighborhood*, pp. 134–36, 166–68, 295–97.

33. Mary E. Richmond, "The Inter-Relation of Social Movements," NCCC, *Proceedings* 37 (1910): 217.

34. Woods and Kennedy, *Settlement Horizon*, p. 344; Stanley Wenocur and Michael Reisch, *From Charity to Enterprise: The Development of American Social Work in a Market Economy* (Urbana, IL: University of Illinois Press, 1989), pp. 72–73. See also John L. Gillin, "Economic Aspects of the Community that Determine the Nature and Extent of Comprehensive Democratic Organization," NCSW, *Proceedings* 52 (1925): 355.

35. Woods, "Neighborhood in Social Reconstruction," pp. 155, 157; Robert A. Woods, "The City and Its Local Community Life," [1917] in Woods, *Neighborhood in Nation-Building*, pp. 192, 194.

36. Anatole Shaffer, "The Cincinnati Social Unit Experiment: 1917–1919," SSR 45 (1971): 159–72.

37. Collier, "Community Councils," pp. 476–78; Eduard C. Lindeman, *The Community: An Introduction to the Study of Community Leadership and Organization* (New York: Association Press, 1921), pp. 68–70; Daniels, *America via the Neighborhood*, pp. 302–5; Lubove, *Professional Altruist*, pp. 178, 181–82.

38. Lubove, *Professional Altruist*, pp. 173–74, 180–81, 183–84, 187–88, 201–2; William J. Norton, "Community Organization," NCSW, *Proceedings* 46 (1919): 666–69; C. M. Bookman, "The Relation between Neighborhood Work and Financial Federations," NCSW, *Proceedings* 51 (1924): 394–95; Wenocur and Reisch, *From Charity to Enterprise*, p. 143.

39. Lindeman, *Community*, pp. 102, 106, 114–16, 147–48.

40. Ibid., pp. vii, 100, 145–47.

41. Ibid., pp. 126–33, 137, 143–44. See also E. C. Lindeman, "Aspects of Community Organization in Relation to Public Policy," *Annals* 105 (January 1923): 83.

42. Lindeman, *Community*, pp. 113–14, 139–40, 143–49, 164–68, 172–74.

43. Ibid., p. 137.

44. Ibid., pp. 175–78, 184–85, 201.

45. Ibid., pp. 85–86, 132–33, 137.

46. Woods and Kennedy, *Settlement Horizon*, pp. 316–17, 360.

47. Woods, "City and Its Local Community Life," pp. 192, 194; Robert A. Woods, "The Settlement Reconsidered in Relation to Other Neighborhood Agencies," [1921] in Woods, *Neighborhood in Nation-Building*, pp. 270–72, 279. See also Woods and Kennedy, *Settlement Horizon*, pp. 311, 315, 318–19.

48. Woods and Kennedy, *Settlement Horizon*, pp. 72, 155, 355, 360.

49. Ibid., pp. 356, 398.

50. Daniels, *America via the Neighborhood*, pp. 219–20, 221–23, 230–31.

51. The failure to sustain a commitment to popular mobilization is also noted by Shaffer. See Shaffer, "Cincinnati Social Unit Experiment," pp. 170–71.

Chapter Seven
Nationalizing Public Tutelage

1. On poverty during the 1920s, see James T. Patterson, *America's Struggle Against Poverty, 1900–1980* (Cambridge: Harvard University Press, 1981), pp. 38–39, 40–41.

2. Josephine Chapin Brown, *Public Relief, 1929–1939* (New York: Henry Holt, 1940), chap. 3; Harry L. Lurie, "Developments in the Public Welfare Program," NCSW, *Proceedings* 59 (1932): 261.

3. John H. Ehrenreich, *The Altruistic Imagination: A History of Social Work and Social Policy in the United States* (Ithaca, NY: Cornell University Press, 1985), pp. 102–4, 110–14; Rick Spano, *The Rank and File Movement in Social Work* (Washington, DC: University Press of America, 1982).

4. Harry J. Lurie, "The Drift to Public Relief," NCSW, *Proceedings* 58 (1931): 218–19; Homer Folks, "Public Relief as a Social Problem," NCSW, *Proceedings* 60 (1933): 54; Homer Folks, "Making Relief Respectable," *Annals* 176 (November 1934): 158–60.

5. Paul L. Benjamin, "The Family Society and the Depression," *Annals* 160 (March 1932): 137–38, 142–43; Elizabeth McCord, "A Cooperative Experiment Between Public and Private Agencies," NCSW, *Proceedings* 59 (1932): 274; Gordon Hamilton, "Case-Work Responsibility in the Unemployment Relief Agency," NCSW, *Proceedings* 61 (1934): 390–94.

6. Brown, *Public Relief, 1929–1939*, pp. 226–28.

7. Gordon Hamilton, "Refocusing Family Case Work," NCSW, *Proceedings* 58 (1931): 178; Grace Marcus, "The Status of Social Case Work Today," NCSW, *Proceedings* 62 (1935): 134, 138.

8. Stanley P. Davies, "Working Toward One Professional Standard—Public and Private," SSR 6 (1932): 437–38, 449.

9. Hamilton, "Refocusing Family Case Work," pp. 177–78; Linton B. Swift, "The Future of Public Social Work in America: From the Point of View of the Private Agency," NCSW, *Proceedings* 58 (1931): 453; Lurie, "Drift to Public Relief," pp. 217–18.

10. Lurie, "Drift to Public Relief," p. 221; Brown, *Public Relief, 1929–1939*, p. 77.

11. Davies, "Working Toward One Professional Standard," pp. 440–41.

12. Ibid., pp. 439–40, 442–43; Brown, *Public Relief, 1929–1939*, pp. 91–94; Bruce D. Blumell, *The Development of Public Assistance in the State of Washington During the Great Depression* (New York: Garland Publishing, 1984), pp. 48–50, 76–78, 83, 85.

13. Brown, *Public Relief, 1929–1939*, pp. 101–2, 124–25, 129–30. Colcord took issue with Brown's contention that social workers came only belatedly to see

the need for federal aid. See Joanna C. Colcord, "Social Work and the First Federal Relief Programs," NCSW, *Proceedings* 70 (1943): 382–94.

14. Brown, *Public Relief, 1929–1939*, pp. 147, 150, 172.

15. Ibid., pp. 153–54, 183–84, 245, 274. For an example of the leadership view that expresses the commitment to a material living standard, see Aubrey Williams, "Standards of Living and Government Responsibility," *Annals* 176 (November 1934): 37–39. Williams was the FERA Assistant Administrator. My interpretation of the place of social workers in FERA differs sharply from that suggested by Wenocur and Reisch. They believe social workers exercised commanding influence in the organization. See Stanley Wenocur and Michael Reisch, *From Charity to Enterprise: The Development of American Social Work in a Market Economy* (Urbana: University of Illinois Press, 1989), pp. 172–73.

16. Brown, *Public Relief, 1929–1939*, pp. 295–98; Grace Abbott, "How Secure Administrative Skill with Professional Competence for State and Local Public Welfare Service?" NCSW, *Proceedings* 63 (1936): 499–500; Ehrenreich, *The Altruistic Imagination*, pp. 110–12.

17. Brown, *Public Relief, 1929–1939*, pp. 176, 179–83, 188–89, 199–201.

18. Joanna C. Colcord, "Report of the Committee on Current Relief Program," NCSW, *Proceedings* 61 (1934): 126; Kenneth L. M. Pray, "Relative Responsibilities of Public and Private Social Work," NCSW, *Proceedings* 61 (1934): 211–12.

19. Brown, *Public Relief, 1929–1939*, pp. 221, 229–30, 233, 274.

20. Ibid., pp. 280–91; Mary Lois Pyles, "Learning with Our FERA's," *The Family* 16 (1936): 281–84.

21. Brown, *Public Relief, 1929–1939*, pp. 183–84, 210–11, 213–14; Edith Abbott, "Public Welfare and Politics," *SSR* 10 (1936): 406; Michael B. Katz, *In the Shadow of the Poorhouse: A Social History of Welfare in America* (New York: Basic Books, 1986), pp. 218–19. Wenocur and Reisch exaggerate Hopkins's power over the states. See Wenocur and Reisch, *From Charity to Enterprise*, p. 172.

22. Brown, *Public Relief, 1929–1939*, pp. 292–95, 317–20.

23. Arthur J. Altmeyer, *The Formative Years of Social Security* (Madison: University of Wisconsin Press, 1966), pp. 3, 11–12, 16; Patterson, *America's Struggle Against Poverty, 1900–1980*, pp. 59–60, 70.

24. Patterson, *America's Struggle Against Poverty, 1900–1980*, pp. 52–53; Ehrenreich, *The Altruistic Imagination*, pp. 86–87, 91–92, 94, 98; Francis Fox Piven and Richard A. Cloward, *Regulating the Poor: The Functions of Public Welfare* (New York: Vintage, 1971), part 1.

25. Grace Abbott, "The Government and Youth in a Troubled World," NCSW, *Proceedings* 60 (1933): 297; Grace Abbott, "Recent Trends in Mothers' Aid," *SSR* 8 (1934): 198–201, 205–8; C. W. Areson, "Federal and State Aid to Children," *Child Welfare* 13 (March–April 1934): 1, 4; Winifred Bell, *Aid to Dependent Children* (New York: Columbia University Press, 1965), p. 25.

26. J. Prentice Murphy, "Children in the New Deal," *Annals* 176 (November 1934): 125–7, 129–30. Some social workers, especially those in the FERA leadership, rejected separate categorical programs, preferring instead a federal subsidy for a unified general relief program. Brown, *Public Relief, 1929–1939*, pp. 304–

5; Homer Folks, "Making Relief Respectable," *Annals* 176 (November 1934): 154.

27. Abbott, "Recent Trends in Mothers' Aid," p. 210; Murphy, "Children in the New Deal," pp. 126–27.

28. Marguerite Rosenthal, "The Children's Bureau and the Juvenile Court: Delinquency Policy, 1912–1940," *SSR* 60 (1986): 310–12.

29. Ibid., pp. 312–13; Edwin E. Witte, *The Development of the Social Security Act* (Madison: University of Wisconsin Press, 1962), pp. 32, 162.

30. Rosenthal, "Children's Bureau and the Juvenile Court," pp. 309–10, 313.

31. Brown, *Public Relief, 1929–1939*, pp. 311, 467.

32. Witte, *Development of the Social Security Act*, p. 162. Brown's account of these events differs slightly, colored perhaps by her own participation in the FERA coup attempt. See Brown, *Public Relief, 1929–1939*, pp. 309–11.

33. The House Ways and Means Committee refused to permit FERA administration of either ADC or Old Age Assistance, reasoning that permanent programs did not belong in a temporary agency, especially one with as many political enemies as FERA. But the Children's Bureau was in the Labor Department, and Secretary Frances Perkins had her own foes on Capitol Hill. Hence the House settled upon the Social Security Board, and held fast to this position in final conference with the Senate. Witte, *Development of the Social Security Act*, pp. 162–63; Altmeyer, *Formative Years of Social Security*, pp. 36–37, 41–42.

34. Brown, *Public Relief, 1929–1939*, pp. 307–8; "Federal Grants-in-Aid and Federal Standards," *SSR* 9 (1935): 317–18; Patterson, *America's Struggle Against Poverty, 1900–1980*, pp. 69–71; Martha Derthick, *The Influence of Federal Grants: Public Assistance in Massachusetts* (Cambridge: Harvard University Press, 1970), pp. 43–45.

35. Witte, *Development of the Social Security Act*, p. 164.

36. Ibid., pp. 168–70; Rosenthal, "Children's Bureau and the Juvenile Court," p. 317n.

37. Alice Scott Nutt, "The Juvenile Court in Relation to the Community," *SSR* 17 (March 1943): 5–6.

38. On the two-tier welfare state, see Katz, *In the Shadow of the Poorhouse*, pp. 180–81, 238; Theda Skocpol, "America's Incomplete Welfare State: The Limits of New Deal Reforms and the Origins of the Present Crisis," in Martin Rein, Gosta Esping-Andersen, and Lee Rainwater, eds., *Stagnation and Renewal in Social Policy: The Rise and Fall of Policy Regimes* (London and Armonk, NY: M. E. Sharpe, 1987), pp. 38–39.

39. Patterson, *America's Struggle Against Poverty, 1900–1980*, p. 76.

40. Russell H. Kurtz, "Social Case Work in a National Program of Social Security," NCSW, *Proceedings* 62 (1935): 227.

41. Ibid., p. 230. Whether Congress intended that its silence be taken this way is another matter. A Senate amendment to authorize federal funds for services to the blind was deleted in conference, allegedly out of resentment toward social workers. Wilbur J. Cohen, "Factors Influencing the Content of Federal Public Welfare Legislation," *SWF* 81 (1954): 213–14.

42. Mary Irene Atkinson, "Organizing for Child Welfare Grants-in-Aid," *SSR* 10 (1936): 465–71; Katherine F. Lenroot, "The Federal Government and Desir-

able Standards of State and Local Administration," NCSW, *Proceedings* 64 (1937): 434.

43. Sophonisba P. Breckinridge, "Government's Role in Child Welfare," *Annals* 212 (November 1940): 47–48; Alice Scott Nutt, "The Future of the Juvenile Court as a Case-Work Agency," NCSW, *Proceedings* 66 (1939): 377–78.

44. Atkinson, "Organizing for Child Welfare Grants-in-Aid," pp. 475–76; Mary Irene Atkinson, "Child Welfare Work in Rural Communities," *Annals* 212 (November 1940): 214; Benjamin Youngdahl, "The Effect of Administrative Procedures on Case Work in a Rural Setting," NCSW, *Proceedings* 67 (1940): 286–87.

45. Nutt, "Juvenile Court in Relation to the Community," pp. 2–3.

46. Rosenthal, "Children's Bureau and the Juvenile Court," p. 313; Nutt, "Future of the Juvenile Court as a Case-Work Agency," p. 378. For early statements that remain blissfully unaware of the risks of absorption by the court while documenting the trend, see Andrew F. Juras and Verl Lewis, "Child Welfare Services and the County Court," *SSR* 17 (1943): 175–87; Anne Sory, "Child Welfare Services in Rural Tennessee," *SSR* 18 (1944): 224–43.

47. Brian Balogh, "Securing Support: The Emergence of the Social Security Board as a Political Actor, 1935–1939," in Donald T. Critchlow and Ellis W. Hawley, eds., *Federal Social Policy: The Historical Dimension* (University Park, PA: Pennsylvania State University Press, 1988), p. 56.

48. Brown, *Public Relief, 1929–1939*, pp. 346–47; "Staff for the Administration of the Social Security Act," *SSR* 10 (1936): 142; Charles McKinley and Robert W. Frase, *Launching Social Security: A Capture-and-Record Account, 1935–37* (Madison: University of Wisconsin Press, 1970), pp. 164–65. We should note in passing that BPA in 1936 had to fight one brush war within the Board against the accounting division to establish its control over the assistance programs. McKinley and Frase, *Launching Social Security*, pp. 31, 197–98, 215–16. Hoey may have been appointed in part because of a long friendship with the Roosevelts. Susan Ware, *Beyond Suffrage: Women in the New Deal* (Cambridge: Harvard University Press, 1981), p. 55.

49. Brown, *Public Relief, 1929–1939*, p. 320; Frederick Dewhurst and Margaret Grant Schneider, "Objectives and Social Effects of the Public Assistance and Old Age Provisions of the Social Security Act," NCSW, *Proceedings* 63 (1936): 394–95; Harry Greenstein, "Problems Confronting State Welfare Administrations in Accepting Grants-in-Aid," NCSW, *Proceedings* 63 (1936): 278–80; Ruth Taylor, "Problems Created by Assistance Categories," NCSW, *Proceedings* 67 (1940): 201–2. For a discussion of the SSB concerns about Old Age Assistance, see Jerry R. Cates, *Insuring Inequality: Administrative Leadership in Social Security, 1935–1954* (Ann Arbor: University of Michigan Press, 1983), p. 105

50. Brown, *Public Relief, 1929–1939*, pp. 320–21; William Haber and Herman M. Somers, "The Administration of Public Assistance in Massachusetts," *SSR* 12 (1938): 397–98; "Delay in Acceptance of Federal Old Age and Mothers' Aid Grants-in-Aid," *SSR* 10 (1936): 346–47; Marcia H. Dancey, "Mothers' Pensions and the Aid to Dependent Children Program in Michigan," *SSR* 13 (1939): 634, 637.

51. McKinley and Frase, *Launching Social Security*, p. 145.

52. For a more complete discussion, see Ehrenreich, *The Altruistic Imagination*, pp. 123–35.

53. Grace F. Marcus, "Changes in the Theory of Relief Giving," NCSW, *Proceedings* 68 (1941): 267–79.

54. Helen E. Hayden, "Case Work Possibilities in a Public Assistance Program," NCSW, *Proceedings* 71 (1944): 326–34. See also Rosemary Reynolds, "Do We Still Believe Case Work Is Needed in a Public Relief Agency?" *The Family* 19 (1938): 171, 173, 175–76; Donald S. Howard, "Who Shall Be Granted Public Aid? How Much? In What Form?" in Russell H. Kurtz, ed., *The Public Assistance Worker: His Responsibility to the Applicant, the Community, and Himself* (New York: Russell Sage Foundation, 1938), pp. 74, 88–89; Margaret E. Rich, "Dealing with People in Need," in ibid., pp. 100–130.

55. Jane M. Hoey, "The Federal Government and Desirable Standards of State and Local Administration," NCSW, *Proceedings* 64 (1937): 440–42; McKinley and Frase, *Launching Social Security*, pp. 163–64, 180–81. Cates argues that the plan approval process was used by the Board to limit the appeal of public assistance, which it saw as a threat to its favored social insurance program. See Cates, *Insuring Inequality*, pp. 108–10.

56. Altmeyer, *Formative Years of Social Security*, pp. 53–54; Jane M. Hoey, "Aid to Families with Dependent Children," *Annals* 202 (March 1939): 75.

57. Hoey, "Aid to Families with Dependent Children," p. 81; Brown, *Public Relief, 1929–1939*, pp. 400–401. In the opinion of some leading therapeutic activists, the FERA people were far less qualified than mothers'-aid caseworkers and so represented a second-best solution. See Paul T. Beisser, "Appraisal of Social Security Provisions Affecting Children," *Annals* 202 (March 1939): 90.

58. Robert T. Lansdale, "Federal and State Organization of Tax-Supported Social Work," NCSW, *Proceedings* 63 (1936): 327–28; McKinley and Frase, *Launching Social Security*, pp. 104–5, 117–18, 132–33.

59. McKinley and Frase, *Launching Social Security*, pp. 181–82, 194–95; Lansdale, "Federal and State Supervision of Tax-Supported Social Work," pp. 331–32; Edith Foster, "Constructive Federal-State Relationships: II. From the Federal Viewpoint," NCSW, *Proceedings* 71 (1944): 313–17.

60. Russell H. Kurtz, "Public Assistance and Social Work," in Kurtz, ed., *Public Assistance Worker*, pp. 207–8; Agnes Van Driel, "Staff Development in the Public Assistance Programs," SSR 14 (1940): 227–30; Brown, *Public Relief, 1929–1939*, p. 403.

61. Hoey, "Aid to Families with Dependent Children," pp. 78, 81. See also Jane M. Hoey, "Our Common Stake in the Development of the Social Security Program," *The Family* 18 (1938): 295, 297; Agnes Van Driel, "Personnel in Social Security," SSR 11 (1937): 434, 436, 439–40.

62. Grace F. Marcus, *The Nature of Service in Public Assistance Administration*, Public Assistance Report No. 10, Federal Security Agency (Washington, DC: Government Printing Office, 1946). See especially pp. 2–3, 5, 17–18.

63. Ibid., pp. 20, 25, 28–29; Dorothy Bird Daly, *Case Work Practice in Public Assistance Administration* (Chicago: American Public Welfare Association, 1942), pp. 16, 24, 85–87, 91–92; Elizabeth H. Dexter, "Has Case Work a Place in the Administration of Public Relief?" *The Family* 16 (1935): 136.

64. On the decline of functionalism, see Ehrenreich, *The Altruistic Imagination*, pp. 135–37. For a statement reflecting a therapeutic approach to public assistance, see Marjorie J. Smith, "Social Case Work in Public Assistance," NCSW, *Proceedings* 71 (1944): 319–25.

65. Donald S. Howard, "American Social Work and World War II," *Annals* 229 (September 1943): 138.

66. Hoey, "Aid to Families with Dependent Children," pp. 76–77; Helen Glenn Tyson, "Care of Dependent Children," *Annals* 212 (November 1940): 170–71; Dorothy C. Kahn, "Conserving Human Values in Public Welfare Programs," NCSW, *Proceedings* 68 (1941): 311; Mildred Arnold, "What Are Some of the Weaknesses of the Social Security Program at This Time?" *Child Welfare* 19 (April 1940): 9; Bell, *Aid to Dependent Children*, pp. 27–28, 33–35.

67. For early statements of how public welfare agencies should deal with the new clientele, see Mary S. Larabee, "Unmarried Parenthood Under the Social Security Act," NCSW, *Proceedings* 66 (1939): 446; Gertrude Vaile, "Tying in with the Community," in Kurtz, ed., *Public Assistance Worker*, p. 173.

68. Brown, *Public Relief, 1929–1939*, pp. 368–70; Foster, "Constructive Federal-State Relationships," pp. 316–17; Altmeyer, *Formative Years of Social Security*, p. 81; Charlotte Towle, *Common Human Needs* (1945; reprint ed., New York: American Association of Social Workers, 1953), pp. vii–ix, 24. To pursue these liberal policies, BPA had to fight the Social Security Board. See Cates, *Insuring Inequality*, pp. 118ff.

69. Eileen Blackey, "Case Work Services in an A.D.C. Program," *The Family* 23 (July 1942): 185–91.

70. Towle, *Common Human Needs*, pp. 10–13, 19, 22–23, 28–29, 32–34, 56.

71. Hoey, "Aid to Families with Dependent Children," pp. 78–79. This gap between theory and practice leads some scholars to the erroneous view that BPA adopted the service orientation only later, after the war. See Gilbert Y. Steiner, *Social Insecurity: The Politics of Welfare* (Chicago: Rand McNally, 1966), p. 257; Derthick, *Influence of Federal Grants*, p. 129; Patterson, *America's Struggle Against Poverty, 1900–1980*, p. 76.

72. Derthick, *Influence of Federal Grants*, p. 130; Charles E. Gilbert, "Policy-Making in Public Welfare: The 1962 Amendments," *Political Science Quarterly* 81 (1966): 201.

73. Arnold, "What Are Some of the Weaknesses of the Social Security Program?" p. 2; Maude T. Barrett, "Public Assistance Features of the Social Security Act," NCSW, *Proceedings* 69 (1942): 330; Carol Goldstein, "Case-Work Services in the Aid to Dependent Children Program: A Study in Cook County," SSR 18 (1944): 480.

74. Breckinridge, "Government's Role in Child Welfare," p. 47.

75. Foster, "Constructive Federal-State Relationships," pp. 317–18.

76. For example, in Massachusetts earlier efforts at state supervision had accepted a measure of town autonomy, and local officials resisted all efforts to impose administrative standards under the federal grant-in-aid program. See Derthick, *Influence of Federal Grants*, pp. 25–28, 36–37, 101–4.

77. For a contemporary statement of the problem, see Larabee, "Unmarried

Parenthood Under the Social Security Act," p. 454. The issue is discussed most fully by Bell, *Aid to Dependent Children*, chap. 3.

78. Youngdahl, "Effect of Administrative Procedures on Case Work in a Rural Setting," pp. 282–84; Ruth Taylor, "Problems Created by Assistance Categories," NCSW, *Proceedings* 67 (1940): 199–201, 203–4.

79. Blackey, "Case Work Services in an A.D.C. Program," p. 187; Goldstein, "Case-Work Services in the Aid to Dependent Children Program," pp. 494–95.

80. Howard, "American Social Work and World War II," pp. 140–3; Harold L. Wilensky and Charles N. Lebeaux, *Industrial Society and Social Welfare* (1958; revised ed., New York: Free Press, 1965), pp. 168–69, 175–77.

81. One view, favored by sociologists, is that this fragmentation of effort and outlook is an inevitable by-product of modern organizational life. See Wilensky and Lebeaux, *Industrial Society and Social Welfare*, pp. 231–32. However, we find a much stronger sense of common enterprise among social personnel before the New Deal. I therefore prefer to treat the dispersal of the therapeutic movement as a political outcome. Federal policy, by encouraging specialization, clearly amplified any inherent tendency toward parochialism.

82. Justine Wise Polier, "Social Work, Social Problems, and Community Values," SSR 29 (1955): 260–66.

83. It should be added that during this period many middle-class women sought work outside the home. Thus the notion that a mother should devote herself exclusively to child-rearing conformed less well to the reality of middle-class life. Since this notion was basic to ADC, support for the program flagged. Val M. Keating, "ADC Demands Our Study," *Child Welfare* 31 (March 1952): 9; Ernest F. Witte, "Children in the Public Assistance Family," *Child Welfare* 38 (January 1959): 21; Eveline M. Burns, "The Role of Government in Social Welfare," SWF 81 (1954): 81; Kermit T. Wiltse, "Social Casework and Public Assistance," SSR 32 (1958): 47.

84. Patterson, *America's Struggle Against Poverty, 1900–1980*, p. 90; Bell, *Aid to Dependent Children*, esp. chaps. 5 and 6; Derthick, *Influence of Federal Grants*, pp. 76–80, 85–86; Steiner, *Social Insecurity*, pp. 91–92.

85. Steiner, *Social Insecurity*, pp. 82, 97–98, 114–15, 163–64; Altmeyer, *Formative Years of Social Security*, pp. 190–91.

86. Roman L. Haremski, "More on 'Administrative Reorganization of Child Welfare,'" *Child Welfare* 35 (July 1956): 12; Maurice O. Hunt, "Issues in Child Welfare Administration," SWF 85 (1958): 93–96; Arlien Johnson, "Public Funds for Voluntary Agencies," SWF 86 (1959): 87–88, 92–94; Nutt, "Juvenile Court in Relation to the Community," pp. 6–7; Alan Keith-Lucas, "Social Work and the Court in the Protection of Children," *Child Welfare* 28 (July 1949): 3–4.

87. Steiner, *Social Insecurity*, pp. 13–14; Johnson, "Public Funds for Voluntary Agencies," p. 86.

88. Steiner, *Social Insecurity*, pp. 21–23, 28, 31. For a typical expression of the official view that public assistance would recede in importance, see Jane M. Hoey, "Next Steps in Public Assistance," NCSW, *Proceedings* 72 (1945): 149–50, 158.

89. Ellen Winston, "The Future of Public Assistance," SWF 86 (1959): 72–73; Marion B. Folsom, "Our Challenge in Social Welfare," SWF 83 (1956): 104–5.

Program administrators and social personnel acknowledged the general changes in American family life. (See note 83 above.) But their analysis largely ignored broader patterns of economic change, including the mechanization of southern agriculture and the decline of urban industry, which had significant if less direct impacts. Piven and Cloward, *Regulating the Poor*, chap. 7.

90. For descriptions of family difficulties, see Alfred J. Kahn, "Child Welfare: Trends and Directions," *Child Welfare* 41 (December 1962): 462; Phyllis R. Osborn, "Aid to Dependent Children—Realities and Possibilities," *ssr* 28 (1954): 161; Witte, "Children in the Public Assistance Family," pp. 20, 23. For recognition of these problems by federal officials, see Folsom, "Our Challenge in Social Welfare," pp. 103–4; Jay L. Roney, "Taking Stock and Looking Ahead in Public Assistance," *swf* 85 (1958): 79–81.

91. The connection with the past was sometimes explicitly recognized. See Wilensky and Lebeaux, *Industrial Society and Social Welfare*, p. 172. Only later was it noticed that the increase in multiproblem families may have been an artifact of the method used to identify such cases. They were found through their contacts with social agencies. As the number of agencies rose, the likelihood that a given family would come into contact with more than one agency increased, and thus the likelihood that it would be counted as having multiple problems. By this logic, too, communities with more services were bound to have more "hardcore" families. See especially Irving F. Lukoff and Samuel Mencher, "A Critique of the Conceptual Foundation of Community Research Associates," *ssr* 36 (1962): 437–38.

92. Helen Harris Perlman, "Case-Work Services in Public Welfare," *ssr* 21 (1947): 191; Osborn, "Aid to Dependent Children—Realities and Possibilities," pp. 164–65; Kermit T. Wiltse, "Social Casework Services in the Aid to Dependent Children Program," *ssr* 28 (1954): 174, 176–78; Corinne H. Wolfe, "A Ten-Year Plan for Improving Public Assistance," *swf* 83 (1956): 123; Witte, "Children in the Public Assistance Family," pp. 22–23. It should be noted that a few social workers remained skeptical of the casework approach in the assistance context. See Wilensky and Lebeaux, *Industrial Society and Social Welfare*, p. 174.

93. Some criticisms of the research are suggested by Lukoff and Mencher, "A Critique of the Conceptual Foundation of Community Research Associates," pp. 438–39; Gilbert, "Policy-Making in Public Welfare," pp. 214–15; Steiner, *Social Insecurity*, pp. 142, 146, 190–91. Examples of vague definitions and poor research evaluation can be found in Wiltse, "Social Casework Services in the Aid to Dependent Children Program," pp. 178, 182–84; Jack L. Roach, "Public Welfare and the ADC Program in New York State," *Child Welfare* 39 (October 1960): 19. For an example of deliberate selection of easier cases, see Carol K. Goldstein, "Services in the Aid to Dependent Children Program in Illinois," *ssr* 22 (1948): 482. Assistance officials readily swallowed these results. See Jane M. Hoey, "Public Welfare—Burden or Opportunity?" *ssr* 27 (1953): 379–80.

94. Bell, *Aid to Dependent Children*, pp. 61–63, 80–81, 88–89; Derthick, *Influence of Federal Grants*, pp. 74, 78–80; Altmeyer, *Formative Years of Social Security*, pp. 188, 190–91; Steiner, *Social Insecurity*, pp. 91–93, 114–17; Cohen, "Factors Influencing the Content of Federal Public Welfare Legislation," pp. 201–2.

95. Carol K. Goldstein, "Services in the Aid to Dependent Children Program

in Illinois," p. 481; Osborn, "Aid to Dependent Children—Realities and Possibilities," pp. 155, 166–67; Arthur H. Kruse, "Implications for Voluntary Agencies," *SWF* 84 (1957): 109–11; Witte, "Children in the Public Assistance Family," p. 22; Bell, *Aid to Dependent Children*, p. 160; Steiner, *Social Insecurity*, pp. 183, 188–89.

96. For examples, see Bell, *Aid to Dependent Children*, pp. 79–81.

97. Gilbert, "Policy-Making in Public Welfare," p. 202; Derthick, *Influence of Federal Grants*, pp. 130–31; Steiner, *Social Insecurity*, pp. 48–49.

98. Phyllis Osborn, "Establishing Confidence in Our Social Welfare Programs," *SWF* 79 (1952): 125; Hoey, "Public Welfare—Burden or Opportunity?" p. 383; Derthick, *Influence of Federal Grants*, pp. 131–32.

99. George K. Wyman, *A Report for the Secretary of Health, Education, and Welfare*, in Committee on Ways and Means, *Public Welfare Amendments of 1962*, 87th Congress, 2d Session (Washington, DC: U.S. Government Printing Office, 1962), p. 135.

100. Winifred Bell, "The Practical Value of Social Work Service: Preliminary Report on 10 Demonstration Projects in Public Assistance," in Committee on Ways and Means, *Public Welfare Amendments of 1962*, pp. 371–76. This attitude among social workers is discussed in Eveline M. Burns, "What's Wrong with Public Welfare?" *SSR* 36 (1962): 116.

101. Osborn, "Aid to Dependent Children—Realities and Possibilities," pp. 165–66; "Public Assistance: Straws in the Wind," *SSR* 30 (1956): 75.

102. The amendments are discussed most thoroughly in Jacobus tenBroek, "The 1956 Amendments to the Social Security Act: After the New Look—the First Thought," *Journal of Public Law* 6 (1957): 123–62.

103. On the difficulty of defining services, see Derthick, *Influence of Federal Grants*, pp. 133–34. On BPA efforts, see Gilbert, "Policy-Making in Public Welfare," pp. 202–3. For an example of BPA promotional material, see Helen B. Foster, *Services in Public Assistance: The Role of the Caseworker*, Public Assistance Report No. 30 (Washington, DC: U.S. Department of Health, Education, and Welfare, 1957, 1965). The optimism is reflected in Winston, "Future of Public Assistance" pp. 80–81; Loula Dunn, "Potentialities for State and Local Public Welfare," *SWF* 84 (1957): 100.

104. Gilbert, "Policy-Making in Public Welfare," pp. 202–3; Steiner, *Social Insecurity*, pp. 41–42.

105. These points were expressed most forcefully by Marguerite Galloway, "The Essential Service in Public Assistance," *SWF* 84 (1957): 127–32.

106. Steiner, *Social Insecurity*, pp. 171–73.

107. For a full account of the formulation of policy in the new administration, see Steiner, *Social Insecurity*, pp. 35–39, 46–47, 143–147, 164, 173–74; Gilbert, "Policy-Making in Public Welfare," pp. 204–5, 207–9. For contemporary statements on the urgent need to promote services, see *Report of the Ad Hoc Committee on Public Welfare* in Committee on Ways and Means, *Public Welfare Amendments of 1962*, pp. 65–105; Wyman, *A Report for the Secretary of Health, Education, and Welfare*, pp. 113, 134–37, 142.

108. Besides the accounts in Steiner, *Social Insecurity*, and Gilbert, "Policy-Making in Public Welfare," see, for example, Wilbur J. Cohen and Robert M.

Ball, "The Public Welfare Amendments of 1962," *Public Welfare* 20 (1962): 191–98, 227–33.

109. Cohen and Ball, "Public Welfare Amendments of 1962," pp. 191–92, 194–95; Bell, *Aid to Dependent Children*, pp. 170–71; Gilbert, "Policy-Making in Public Welfare," pp. 210–11.

110. Cohen and Ball, "Public Welfare Amendments of 1962," p. 196.

111. Frank Newgent, "Issues for Child Welfare in the 1962 Public Welfare Amendments," *Child Welfare* 42 (1963): 439–40; Kahn, "Child Welfare," p. 472.

112. Kahn, "Child Welfare," pp. 470, 475–76; Gilbert, "Policy-Making in Public Welfare," p. 199. Unification was resisted by the Children's Bureau and by child welfare activists. Both feared that their programs would be lost within the larger public assistance administration. See Kahn, "Child Welfare," p. 463; Newgent, "Issues for Child Welfare in the 1962 Public Welfare Amendments," p. 438.

113. For a good statement in the postwar era, see Donald S. Howard, "The Social Services and the Maintenance of Optimum Standards of Living," NCSW, *Proceedings* 74 (1947): 114–21.

Chapter Eight
Countervailing Forces

1. Frederick W. Killian, "The Juvenile Court as an Institution," *Annals* 261 (January 1949): 93; Lewis Yablonsky, "The Role of Law and Social Science in the Juvenile Court," *JCL* 53 (December 1962): 427, 429.

2. John Forbes Perkins, "Indeterminate Control of Offenders: Arbitrary and Discriminatory," *Law and Contemporary Problems* 9 (1942): 624–34; Yablonsky, "Role of Law and Social Science in Juvenile Court," p. 435.

3. Ellen Ryerson, *The Best-Laid Plans: America's Juvenile Court Experiment* (New York: Hill and Wang, 1978), pp. 57–59, 61. The comparison with the star chamber was first advanced by Roscoe Pound in the 1930s. See Pound, "Forward," in Pauline V. Young, *Social Treatment in Probation and Delinquency* (New York: McGraw-Hill, 1937), p. xxvii.

4. Anthony M. Platt, *The Child Savers: The Invention of Delinquency*, 2d ed. (Chicago: University of Chicago Press, 1977), pp. 152–55.

5. Francis A. Allen, "The Borderland of the Criminal Law: Problems of 'Socializing' Criminal Justice," *SSR* 32 (1958): 116; H. Warren Dunham, "The Juvenile Court: Contradictory Orientations in Processing Offenders," *Law and Contemporary Problems* 23 (1958): 516–17, 519; Paul W. Tappan, "Judicial and Administrative Approaches to Children with Problems," in Margaret Keeney Rosenheim, ed., *Justice for the Child: The Juvenile Court in Transition* (New York: Free Press, 1962) pp. 149, 159; Robert G. Caldwell, "The Juvenile Court: Its Development and Some Major Problems," *JCL* 51 (1961): 504–6; Yablonsky, "Role of Law and Social Science in Juvenile Court," pp. 431–33; Henry Nunberg, "Problems in the Structure of the Juvenile Court," *JCL* 48 (1958): 502.

6. John F. Perkins, "Common Sense and Bad Boys," *Atlantic Monthly* 173

(May 1944): 47; Allen, "Borderland of the Criminal Law," p. 117; Eileen L. Younghusband, "The Dilemma of the Juvenile Court," *ssr* 33 (1959): 15–17; Elliot Studt, "The Client's Image of the Juvenile Court," in Rosenheim, ed., *Justice for the Child*, p. 204; Ryerson, *Best-Laid Plans*, pp. 132–35.

7. Sol Rubin, "Protecting the Child in the Juvenile Court," *jcl* 43 (1952): 427; Caldwell, "Juvenile Court: Its Development and Some Major Problems," p. 507; Yablonsky, "Role of Law and Social Science in Juvenile Court," p. 431. See also Allen, "Borderland of the Criminal Law," pp. 118–19; Bernard C. Fisher, "Juvenile Court: Purpose, Promise, and Problems," *ssr* 34 (1960): 78–79; Howard E. Fradkin, "Disposition Dilemmas of American Juvenile Courts," in Rosenheim, ed., *Justice for the Child*, p. 121.

8. Caldwell, "Juvenile Court: Its Development and Some Major Problems," pp. 507–9; Tappan, "Judicial and Administrative Approaches to Children with Problems," pp. 147–48, 151, 154–55. For an early statement of this position, see John H. Wigmore, "Juvenile Court vs. Criminal Court," *Illinois Law Review* 21 (1926): 375–77.

9. Dunham, "Juvenile Court: Contradictory Orientations in Processing Offenders," pp. 520–21; Younghusband, "Dilemma of the Juvenile Court," p. 17; Studt, "Client's Image of the Juvenile Court," pp. 209–10; Nunberg, "Problems in the Structure of the Juvenile Court," pp. 502–3.

10. Gustav L. Schramm, "Philosophy of the Juvenile Court," *Annals* 261 (January 1949): 102–3; Orman W. Ketcham, "The Unfulfilled Promise of the Juvenile Court," in Rosenheim, ed., *Justice for the Child*, pp. 25–28; Paul W. Alexander, "Constitutional Rights in the Juvenile Court," in Rosenheim, ed., *Justice for the Child*, pp. 84–85, 87–90, 92. The manipulation of the rhetoric of rehabilitation to conceal punitive activities is noted by Allen, though not with specific reference to the juvenile court. Francis A. Allen, *The Decline of the Rehabilitative Ideal: Penal Policy and Social Purpose* (New Haven: Yale University Press, 1981), pp. 53–54. The deft use of Progressive rhetoric by juvenile court judges has misled some otherwise astute analysts. For example, though Lerman displays a healthy skepticism about most actors in the child welfare system, he takes judges at face value when they claim that due process obstructs them in their attempt to assure treatment. See Paul Lerman, "Child Welfare, the Private Sector, and Community-Based Corrections," *Crime and Delinquency* 30 (1984): 29, 33.

11. Alexander, "Constitutional Rights in Juvenile Court," pp. 83–84, 92; Sanford J. Fox, "Juvenile Justice Reform: An Historical Perspective," *Stanford Law Review* 22 (June 1970): 1235; Peter S. Prescott, *The Child Savers: Juvenile Justice Observed* (New York: Alfred A. Knopf, 1981), pp. 7, 63–64.

12. Prescott, *The Child Savers*, pp. 51, 59–61.

13. *In re Gault*, 387 U.S. 1 (1967). For a discussion of the Court's reasoning and decision, see Ryerson, *Best-Laid Plans*, pp. 147ff.

14. Prescott, *Child Savers*, pp. 65, 219.

15. Fox, "Juvenile Justice Reform," p. 1237; Platt, *Child Savers*, pp. 164–69; Prescott, *Child Savers*, pp. 5, 18–19, 102.

16. Prescott, *Child Savers*. This account is based upon the New York City courts.

17. Ibid.

18. Gilbert Y. Steiner, *Social Insecurity: The Politics of Welfare* (Chicago: Rand McNally, 1966), p. 3.

19. In 1960 Louisiana abruptly dropped more than 22,000 children from its ADC rolls, primarily because they were illegitimate and therefore could not by definition receive adequate care from their mothers. Some 95% of the children were black. See Winifred Bell, *Aid to Dependent Children* (New York: Columbia University Press, 1965), chap. 9.

20. There is a substantial literature on urban renewal and the accompanying protest. For a discussion of national policy and its local manifestations in two cities, Boston and San Francisco, see John H. Mollenkopf, *The Contested City* (Princeton, NJ: Princeton University Press, 1983). A vivid account of the impact of renewal may be found in Robert A. Caro, *Power Broker: Robert Moses and the Fall of New York* (New York: Random House, 1978).

21. Richard A. Cloward and Lloyd E. Ohlin, *Delinquency and Opportunity: A Theory of Delinquent Gangs* (New York: Free Press, 1960). For a discussion of the impact of this work on social personnel, see Alfred J. Kahn, "Social Work and the Control of Delinquency: Theory and Strategy," *Social Work* 10 (April 1965): 6–7.

22. Irving A. Spergel, "Community-based Delinquency Prevention Programs: An Overview," *SSR* 47 (1973): 24–25; Alvin L. Schorr, "The Tasks for Voluntarism in the Next Decade," *Child Welfare* 49 (1970): 429–30.

23. Peter Marris and Martin Rein, *Dilemmas of Social Reform: Poverty and Community Action in the United States*, 2d ed. (Chicago: University of Chicago Press, 1973, 1982), pp. 20–23; "Grants for Juvenile Delinquency Projects," *SSR* 35 (1961): 436.

24. For analysis of the two positions, see James T. Patterson, *America's Struggle Against Poverty, 1900–1980* (Cambridge, MA: Harvard University Press, 1981), pp. 99–101, 111–12, 115–20. The "culture of poverty" research and its policy implications are thoroughly discussed in Michael B. Katz, *The Undeserving Poor: From the War on Poverty to the War on Welfare* (New York: Pantheon, 1989), pp. 16ff. See also John H. Ehrenreich, *The Altruistic Imagination: A History of Social Work and Social Policy in the United States* (Ithaca, NY: Cornell University Press, 1985), pp. 166–67.

25. Patterson, *America's Struggle Against Poverty*, pp. 127–28, 134–36; Theodore J. Lowi, *The End of Liberalism: The Second Republic of the United States*, 2d ed. (New York: Norton, 1979), pp. 210–11.

26. For the political view of community action, see Morris Janowitz, *Social Control of the Welfare State* (Chicago: University of Chicago Press, 1976), p. 127; Ehrenreich, *The Altruistic Imagination*, pp. 172–73. On the tension between the two camps, see Marris and Rein, *Dilemmas of Social Reform*, chap. 1; Katz, *Undeserving Poor*, pp. 99–100. Lowi takes a different view of what community action sought to accomplish, arguing that it represented an attempt to create new interest groups so the poor would be properly represented in the universe of American pluralism. Lowi, *End of Liberalism*, p. 212.

27. Ehrenreich, *The Altruistic Imagination*, pp. 170–71; Patterson, *America's Struggle Against Poverty*, pp. 145–47; Sidney E. Zimbalist, "Research in the Ser-

vice of a Cause: The Changing Context of Community Welfare Research," *SSR* 38 (1964): 134.

28. Alfred J. Kahn, "Service Delivery at the Neighborhood Level: Experience, Theory, and Fads," *SSR* 50 (1976): 30–31; Michael B. Katz, *In the Shadow of the Poorhouse: A Social History of Welfare in America* (New York: Basic Books, 1986), pp. 254–55. For a critical view that recognizes the appearance of new leadership but attributes it to general civil rights ferment, see Lowi, *End of Liberalism*, pp. 222–23.

29. Ehrenreich, *The Altruistic Imagination*, pp. 173–74.

30. On the lack of local resources and the inadequacy of the federal fiscal commitment, see Patterson, *America's Struggle Against Poverty*, pp. 150–52. Katz discusses some of the research on the decline of community resources. See Katz, *Undeserving Poor*, pp. 168–71.

31. Lowi, *End of Liberalism*, pp. 216–18, 233.

32. Ibid., p. 234.

33. Lillian B. Rubin, "Maximum Feasible Participation: The Origins, Implications, and Present Status," *Annals* 385 (September 1969): 24–27; Patterson, *America's Struggle Against Poverty*, p. 147. As Katz points out, the OEO programs were particularly vulnerable because they had been established outside of the regular federal line agencies. Katz, *Undeserving Poor*, p. 89.

34. George Hoshino, "Money and Morality: Income Security and Personal Social Services," *Social Work* 16 (April 1971): 20; Frances Fox Piven and Richard A. Cloward, *Regulating the Poor: The Functions of Public Welfare* (New York: Vintage, 1971), chap. 10.

35. Joel F. Handler, *Reforming the Poor: Welfare Policy, Federalism, and Morality* (New York: Basic Books, 1972), p. 34; Martha Derthick, *The Influence of Federal Grants: Public Assistance in Massachusetts* (Cambridge: Harvard University Press, 1970), pp. 75, 94–95.

36. Piven and Cloward, *Regulating the Poor*, p. 324.

37. The controversy centers on the claim by Piven and Cloward that mass unrest by the poor led to the welfare explosion. See ibid. For summary statements of other factors that may have contributed to the "welfare explosion," see Katz, *In the Shadow of the Poorhouse*, p. 267; Patterson, *America's Struggle Against Poverty*, pp. 178–79. On the increased willingness of eligible women to assert their rights, see Daniel P. Moynihan, "The Crises in Welfare," *Public Interest* 10 (Winter 1968): 22. For the eligibility figures, see Patterson, *America's Struggle Against Poverty*, p. 179.

38. Moynihan, "Crises in Welfare," pp. 19–22; Piven and Cloward, *Regulating the Poor*, p. 325.

39. Bell notes the participation requirement without appreciating its limits. See Winifred Bell, "Services for People: An Appraisal," *Social Work* 15 (July 1970): 6.

40. Aleanor Merrifield, "Implications of the Poverty Program: the Caseworker's View," *SSR* 39 (1965): 294–95; John B. Turner, "In Response to Change: Social Work at the Crossroad," *Social Work* 13 (July 1968): 7–9.

41. Arthur Pearl and Frank Riessman, *New Careers for the Poor: The Non-Professional in Human Services* (New York: Free Press, 1965).

42. Derthick, *The Influence of Federal Grants*, pp. 237–38; Piven and Cloward, *Regulating the Poor*, pp. 328–29; Charles R. Morris, *The Cost of Good Intentions: New York City and the Liberal Experiment, 1960–1975* (New York: Norton, 1980), pp. 69–71.

43. This pattern of agency response appears to be quite general in service agencies. Clarence N. Stone, "Whither the Welfare State? Professionalization, Bureaucracy, and the Market Alternative," *Ethics* 93 (April 1983): 592–93. On the enduring anger that service workers feel for their clients, see Ann Withorn, *The Circle Game: Services for the Poor in Massachusetts, 1966–1978* (Amherst: University of Massachusetts Press, 1982), pp. 89–90, 139.

44. Linda Gordon, *Heroes of Their Own Lives: The Politics and History of Family Violence* (New York: Penguin Books, 1988), pp. 25, 282–85.

45. Derthick, *The Influence of Federal Grants*, pp. 135–36; Eveline M. Burns, "What's Wrong with Public Welfare?" *SSR* 36 (1962): 113–14. Burns sharply challenged the doctrine that all client contact was of therapeutic value.

46. Derthick, *The Influence of Federal Grants*, p. 137.

47. Ibid., p. 156; George Hoshino, "Separating Maintenance from Social Services," *Public Welfare* 30 (Spring 1972): 56; Glenn Jacobs, "The Reification of the Notion of Subculture in Public Welfare," *Social Casework* 49 (1968): 531; Handler, *Reforming the Poor*, p. 52.

48. Derthick, *The Influence of Federal Grants*, pp. 154–55.

49. Bell, *Aid to Dependent Children*, p. 171; Derthick, *The Influence of Federal Grants*, p. 172; Hoshino, "Money and Morality," p. 20.

50. On the success—and limits—of the "new careers" movement, see Paul A. Kurzman, "The New Careers Movement and Social Change," *Social Casework* 51 (1970): 22–27.

51. Derthick, *The Influence of Federal Grants*, p. 217.

52. Ibid., p. 151. See also Hoshino, "Money and Morality," p. 20. Lowi contends that welfare programs were insufficiently bureaucratized, rather than overly so. A "perfect bureaucracy," fully rule-governed, would maximize services to those eligible. See Lowi, *End of Liberalism*, p. 204. However, given the nature of casework in the therapeutic model, further rule specification would only have undermined the activity more completely.

53. For an early statement recognizing this problem, see Burns, "What's Wrong with Public Welfare?" pp. 116–17.

54. Davis McEntire and Joanne Haworth, "The Two Functions of Public Welfare: Income Maintenance and Social Services," *Social Work* 12 (January 1967): 30; Joel F. Handler and Ellen Jane Hollingsworth, "The Administration of Social Services and the Structure of Dependency," *SSR* 43 (1969): 408–10.

55. Handler and Hollingsworth, "Administration of Social Services and the Structure of Dependency," pp. 407–8, 410, 413–14; Handler, *Reforming the Poor*, p. 54.

56. Handler and Hollingsworth, "Administration of Social Services and the Structure of Dependency," pp. 408–9, 411. For similar findings from a later period, see Hrasura Rubenstein and Mary H. Bloch, "Helping Clients Who Are Poor: Worker and Client Perceptions of Problems, Activities, and Outcomes," *SSR* 52 (1978): 80. Nelson suggests we ought to be skeptical about reported client

satisfaction, which may reflect low expectations and the tendency of clients to adopt a dependent role posture. Barbara J. Nelson, "Client Evaluations of Social Programs," in Charles T. Goodsell, ed., *The Public Encounter: Where State and Citizen Meet* (Bloomington: Indiana University Press, 1981), pp. 37–38.

57. For statements of the critics' position, see McEntire and Haworth, "Two Functions of Public Welfare," p. 28.

58. Handler and Hollingsworth, "Administration of Social Services and the Structure of Dependency," p. 414; Handler, *Reforming the Poor*, pp. 54–55. Agency staff with professional training admitted the failing. They believed clients suffered from personal difficulties that made any return to self-sufficiency or significant improvement in basic functioning unlikely. But clients denied these problems and rejected personal counseling. Thus, although caseworkers were glad to provide tangible aid, they felt they were doing little to help the family over the long haul. See Rubenstein and Bloch, "Helping Clients Who Are Poor," pp. 73–74, 76–80.

59. Handler and Hollingsworth, "Administration of Social Services and the Structure of Dependency," pp. 410–11, 414; Handler, *Reforming the Poor*, pp. 44, 55–57.

60. See, for example, George S. Hoshino, "Will the Services Provisions of the 1962 Public Welfare Amendments Reduce Costs?" *Social Casework* 44 (1963): 439–40, 442–43.

61. Hoshino, "Money and Morality," p. 20; Elizabeth Wickenden, "A Perspective on Social Services: An Essay Review," *SSR* 50 (1976): 577.

62. Mildred Rein, "Social Services as a Work Strategy," *SSR* 49 (1975): 517–18; Alfred J. Kahn, "Public Social Services: The Next Phase—Policy and Delivery Strategies," *Public Welfare* 30 (1) (1972): 16.

63. James R. Dumpson, "Public Welfare and Implementation of the 1967 Social Security Amendments," *Child Welfare* (1968): 386–87, 389.

64. For expressions of these sentiments, see ibid., p. 382; Wickenden, "A Perspective on Social Services," p. 579.

65. Patterson, *America's Struggle Against Poverty*, pp. 175–76; Rein, "Social Services as a Work Strategy," p. 518.

66. Rein, "Social Services as a Work Strategy," pp. 515, 518–21.

67. Bradley R. Schiller, "Welfare: Reforming Our Expectations," *Public Interest* 62 (Winter 1981): 55–65; Katz, *Undeserving Poor*, pp. 225–28, 231–32; Andrew Hacker, "Getting Rough on the Poor," *New York Review of Books* 35 (13 October 1988): 12–17. For a recent statement that voices strong support for workfare, see Michael Novack et al., *The New Consensus on Family and Welfare: A Community of Self-Reliance* (Washington, DC: American Enterprise Institute, 1987), esp. pp. 74, 82, 84, 85–86, 102, 111–12, 114. Hacker's essay offers a careful critique of this approach to welfare reform.

68. Neil Gilbert, *Capitalism and the Welfare State: Dilemmas of Social Benevolence* (New Haven: Yale University Press, 1983), pp. 176–77; Kahn, "Service Delivery at the Neighborhood Level," p. 38.

69. Dorothy C. Miller, "Children's Services and Title XX from a National Perspective," *Child Welfare* 57 (1978): 135.

70. Winford Oliphant, "Observations on Administration of Social Services in

the States," *Child Welfare* 53 (1974): 283; Mark D. Jacobs, "The End of Liberalism in the Administration of Social Services," *Administration and Society* 18 (1986): 15–16.

71. Wickenden, "A Perspective on Social Services," pp. 583–85.

72. Martha N. Ozawa, "Issues in Welfare Reform," *SSR* 52 (1978): 53.

73. On resistance by the states to Reagan administration budget policies, see Frances Fox Piven and Richard A. Cloward, "Popular Power and the Welfare State," in Michael K. Brown, ed., *Remaking the Welfare State: Retrenchment and Social Policy in America and Europe* (Philadelphia: Temple University Press, 1988), p. 76.

74. Moynihan, "Crises in Welfare," p. 29; Edward D. Berkowitz, "Social Welfare and the American State," in Donald T. Critchlow and Ellis W. Hawley, eds., *Federal Social Policy: The Historical Dimension* (University Park, PA: Pennsylvania State University Press, 1988), p. 192; Paul Adams and Gary Freeman, "On the Political Character of Social Service Work," *SSR* 53 (1979): 568–69; Katz, *Undeserving Poor*, pp. 117–20.

75. Patterson, *America's Struggle Against Poverty*, pp. 192–98.

76. George Hoshino, "Social Services: The Problem of Accountability," *SSR* 47 (1973): 376–78, 380. Social workers resented the way evaluation studies were conducted. For a defensive statement, see Kahn, "Service Delivery at the Neighborhood Level," pp. 31–32.

77. Patterson, *America's Struggle Against Poverty*, pp. 122, 161.

78. For evidence of this mode of thought, see ibid., pp. 187, 191; Ozawa, "Issues in Welfare Reform," pp. 42–47.

79. Patterson, *America's Struggle Against Poverty*, p. 185.

80. On the poverty research, see Katz, *Undeserving Poor*, p. 120; Nathan Glazer, "Reforming the American Welfare Family: 1969–1981," *Tocqueville Review* 6 (1984): 149–68.

81. Katz, *Undeserving Poor*, pp. 120, 122–23.

82. Burton Gummar, "A Power-Politics Approach to Social Welfare Organizations," *SSR* 52 (1978): 358–59; Oliphant, "Observations on Administration of Social Services in the States," p. 282; Withorn, *Circle Game*, pp. 3, 97–99.

Chapter Nine
The Tenacity of the Therapeutic

1. See, for example, Richard Korn, "The Private Citizen, the Social Expert, and the Social Problem: An Excursion Through an Unacknowledged Utopia," in Bernard Rosenberg, Israel Gerver, and F. William Howton, eds., *Mass Society in Crisis: Social Problems and Social Pathology* (New York: Macmillan, 1964), pp. 576–93; Willard Gaylin et al., *Doing Good: The Limits of Benevolence* (New York: Pantheon, 1978). The broad skepticism about rehabilitation is also noted by Allen. See Francis A. Allen, *The Decline of the Rehabilitative Ideal: Penal Policy and Social Purpose* (New Haven: Yale University Press, 1981), pp. 24–25.

2. For an insightful review of the studies on "street-level" personnel, see Clarence N. Stone, "Whither the Welfare State? Professionalization, Bureaucracy, and the Market Alternative," *Ethics* 93 (1983): 588–95.

3. Among the first proponents were Gordon Hamilton, Samuel Mencher, and George Hoshino. See Samuel Mencher, "Perspectives on Recent Welfare Legislation, Fore and Aft," *Social Work* 8 (July 1963): 63; George S. Hoshino, "Will the Services Provisions of the 1962 Public Welfare Amendments Reduce Costs?" *Social Casework* 44 (1963): 443; Alfred J. Kahn, "Social Services in Relation to Income Security: Introductory Notes," *SSR* 39 (1965): 381. Eveline Burns seemed to endorse this position, though her statement is less clear. See Burns, "What's Wrong with Public Welfare?" *SSR* 36 (1962): 115–16.

4. Kahn, "Social Services in Relation to Income Security," pp. 381–82; Herman Levin, "The Logic of Merging Public Services for Family and Child Welfare: Historical Support," *Child Welfare* 47 (1968): 468–69; Winifred Bell, "Too Few Services to Separate," *Social Work* 18 (2)(1973): 69–70.

5. Davis McEntire and Joanne Haworth, "The Two Functions of Public Welfare: Income Maintenance and Social Services," *Social Work* 12 (January 1967): 28; Alan Keith-Lucas, "A Critique of the Principle of Client Self-Determination," *Social Casework* 8 (July 1963): 69–71; George Hoshino, "Money and Morality: Income Security and Personal Social Services," *Social Work* 16 (April 1971): 23–24.

6. McEntire and Haworth, "The Two Functions of Public Welfare," 27–28; Burns, "What's Wrong with Public Welfare?" pp. 114–16.

7. Karl Birnbaum, "A Court Psychiatrist's View of Juvenile Delinquents," *Annals* 261 (January 1949): 57–58; Alfred J. Kahn, *A Court for Children: A Study of the New York City Children's Court* (New York: Columbia University Press, 1953), pp. 129–30.

8. H. Warren Dunham, "The Juvenile Court: Contradictory Orientations in Processing Offenders," *Law and Contemporary Problems* 23 (1958): 523; Paul W. Tappan, "Judicial and Administrative Approaches to Children with Problems," in Margaret Keeny Rosenheim, ed., *Justice for the Child: The Juvenile Court in Transition* (Free Press, 1962), p. 152. But this view was not universally accepted among social personnel. See Kenneth L. M. Pray, "The Place of Social Case Work in the Treatment of Delinquency," *SSR* 19 (1945): 235–44; Gerald A. Tracey, "A Social Worker's Perspective on Social Work in Probation," *Crime and Delinquency* 7 (1961): 131–36.

9. Harris B. Peck, "Resistance in Delinquency," *Social Work in the Current Scene* [NCSW, *Proceedings*, Selected Papers] 77 (1950): 379–81; Elliot Studt, "The Client's Image of the Juvenile Court," in Rosenheim, ed., *Justice for the Child*, pp. 209–10.

10. The notion that the label itself inflicts harm and produces the very behavior it purports to signify has become a commonplace among sociologists and social workers. See, for example, Alfred J. Kahn, "Social Work and the Control of Delinquency: Theory and Strategy," *Social Work* 10 (April 1965): 12.

11. Sol Rubin, "Protecting the Child in the Juvenile Court," *JCL* 43 (1952): 427–28; Lewis Yablonsky, "The Role of Law and Social Science in the Juvenile Court," *JCL* 53 (1962): 433.

12. On the overuse of status offender categories for girls and the fears about "escalation," see Randell G. Shelden, John A. Horvath, and Sharon Tracy, "Do Status Offenders Get Worse? Some Clarifications on the Question of Escalation,"

Crime and Delinquency 35 (1989): 215; Meda Chesney-Lind, "Girls' Crime and Woman's Place: Toward a Feminist Model of Female Delinquency," *Crime and Delinquency* 35 (1989): 18.

13. David Gilman, "How to Retain Jurisdiction over Status Offenses: Change without Reform in Florida," *Crime and Delinquency* 22 (1976): 48–49.

14. For discussions of diversion, see the various essays in Robert M. Carter and Malcolm W. Klein, eds., *Back on the Street: The Diversion of Juvenile Offenders* (Englewood Cliffs, NJ: Prentice-Hall, 1976); Margaret K. Rosenheim, ed., *Pursuing Justice for the Child* (Chicago: University of Chicago Press, 1976).

15. Deinstitutionalization in mental health was propelled by several developments during the late 1950s and early 1960s. Medical technology played a part, as the invention of psychotropic drugs made possible the regulation of acting-out behavior without the need for confinement. Just as important were a number of studies of institutions that suggested how damaging the carceral setting was to inmates. Far from restoring the ill to a normal status, institutional life made patients even less fit for social intercourse than they had been before commitment. Legal advocates, reflecting upon this literature, began to challenge the validity of involuntary placements in institutions that did no good for patients yet deprived them of liberty. Unless their "right to treatment" was honored, it was contended, they ought to be released. Ellen L. Bassuk and Samuel Gerson, "Deinstitutionalization and Mental Health Services," *Scientific American* 238 (February 1978): 46–47; Andrew Scull, "Deinstitutionalization and the Rights of the Deviant," *Journal of Social Issues* 37 (3) (1981): 7; Donna E. Renn, "The Right to Treatment and the Juvenile," *Crime and Delinquency* 19 (1973): 477–84.

An alternative approach, community mental health, captured the fancy of mental health professionals, lawyers, and social workers. Patients would be placed in a less restrictive environment, even treated on an out-patient basis instead of facing confinement, all in their own community. Beyond assuring better care, and so proper respect for the right to treatment, this arrangement would permit them to enjoy living arrangements that roughly approximated those found in ordinary society. (Advocates termed this "normalization," but since the word better describes the entire mission of the human services I choose not to follow their usage.) National policymakers in the Kennedy Administration took notice, leading in 1963 to legislation to establish a comprehensive network of community mental health centers. Federal funds would be made available to build and operate small local facilities, especially in impoverished neighborhoods where mental illness seemed to have reached epidemic proportions. Scull, "Deinstitutionalization and the Rights of the Deviant," pp. 7–8; Martha M. Dare and Karen Guberman Kennedy, "Two Decades of Turmoil: Child Welfare Services, 1960–1980," *Child Welfare* 60 (1981): 372–73; Bassuk and Gerson, "Deinstitutionalization and Mental Health Services," p. 48.

16. Ira Glasser, "Prisoners of Benevolence: Power versus Liberty in the Welfare State," in Gaylin et al., *Doing Good*, pp. 114–15; Michael H. Langley and H. B. Drone, "Juvenile Justice: Reneging on a Sociolegal Obligation," ssr 47 (1973): 564–65.

17. "New Structure in Washington," ssr 41 (1967): 428. Even this reorganization came to seem an inadequate expression of the principle of separation. In

1977 income maintenance was placed under the Social Security Administration and all service programs were grouped together in the Office of Human Development. Neil Gilbert, "The Transformation of Social Services," *SSR* 51 (1977): 631–32.

18. For contemporary discussions of the effects of this reorganization, see Gilbert G. Dulaney and Kenneth J. Badel, "Crisis in the Counties," *Public Welfare* 30 (Fall 1972): 32–36; Winford Oliphant, "Observations on the Administration of Social Services in the States," *Child Welfare* 53 (1974): 281–82.

19. Jan L. Hagen, "Income Maintenance Workers: Technicians or Service Providers," *SSR* 61 (1987): 262. In the late 1970s some states evidently moved to reunify the administration of services and assistance to take advantage of federal reimbursement rules. See Bill B. Benton, Jr., "Separation Revisited," *Public Welfare* 38 (Spring 1980): 18.

20. Florence W. Kaslow, "How Relevant is Family Counseling in Public Welfare Settings?" *Public Welfare* 30 (Fall 1972): 19.

21. Hrasura Rubenstein and Mary H. Bloch, "Helping Clients Who Are Poor: Worker and Client Perceptions of Problems, Activities, and Outcomes," *SSR* 52 (1978): 77–83; Hagen, "Income Maintenance Workers," p. 268. In part this may be due to the physical arrangements that have accompanied separation, which often result in services being housed apart from income maintenance. Recipients under this arrangement must extend themselves, inquiring about services and then expending time and effort to secure them at another office. This discourages those under the heaviest burdens from learning about services or actively seeking help. Joel F. Handler and Ellen Jane Hollingsworth, "The Administration of Social Services and the Structure of Dependency," *SSR* 43 (1969): 417–18; Thomas P. McDonald and Irving Piliavin, "Impact of Separation on Community Social Service Utilization," *SSR* 55 (1981): 632–34.

22. Handler and Hollingsworth, "Administration of Social Services and the Structure of Dependency," p. 417; George Hoshino, "Social Services: The Problem of Accountability," *SSR* 47 (1973): 379; Dulaney and Badel, "Crisis in the Counties," p. 34; Ann Withorn, *The Circle Game: Services for the Poor in Massachusetts, 1966–78* (Amherst: University of Massachusetts Press, 1982), p. 50. Certain problem cases—those which involve abuse, neglect, or adoption—were exempt from separation, and services remained mandatory. McDonald and Piliavin, "Impact of Separation on Community Social Service Utilization," p. 630.

23. Irving Piliavin and Alan E. Gross, "The Effects of Separation of Services and Income Maintenance on AFDC Recipients," *SSR* 51 (1977): 403; "Stone, Whither the Welfare State?" p. 590. For a compelling account of how the experience of dealing with an assistance agency has changed since the separation policy has gone into effect, see Susan Sheehan, *A Welfare Mother* (New York: New American Library, 1977). The same criticism has been made of child welfare agencies in which tasks have been divided. See Jerome H. Zimmerman, "Negotiating the System," *Public Welfare* 45 (2) (1987): 23–24.

24. Michael Sosin, "Emergency Assistance and Special Needs Programs in the AFDC System," *SSR* 56 (1982): 197; Evelyn Brodkin and Michael Lipsky, "Quality Control in AFDC as an Administrative Strategy," *SSR* 57 (1983): 2, 4, 7–9.

25. Richard Weatherly et al., "Accountability of Social Service Workers at the

Front Line," ssr 54 (1980): 568–69; Brodkin and Lipsky, "Quality Control in AFDC as an Administrative Strategy," pp. 3, 6, 10, 12, 23–24; Withorn, *Circle Game*, p. 61. Some social workers have responded to these developments with a plea to reprofessionalize the eligibility determination function, on the grounds that this would be better for clients while lowering the error rate still more. Norman L. Wyers, "Income Maintenance and Social Work: A Broken Tie," *Social Work* 28 (1983): 261–68. Evidently Massachusetts has attempted to follow such an approach, redefining the job of its eligibility technicians to include service coordination. Jolie Bain Pillsbury, "Reform at the State Level," *Public Welfare* 47 (2) (1989): 10–11.

26. Thomas Blomberg, "Diversion and Accelerated Social Control," *jcl* 68 (1977): 274; Dare and Kennedy, "Two Decades of Turmoil," p. 375; Irving A. Spergel, "Community-based Delinquency Prevention Programs: An Overview," ssr 47 (1973): 19.

27. Langley and Drone, "Juvenile Justice," p. 568; Spergel, "Community-based Delinquency Prevention Programs," pp. 27–28; Blomberg, "Diversion and Accelerated Social Control," pp. 276, 278, 280–81.

28. Blomberg, "Diversion and Accelerated Social Control," p. 276; Gilman, "How to Retain Jurisdiction over Status Offenses," p. 51.

29. Tappan, "Judicial and Administrative Approaches to Children with Problems," p. 145; Angel Castillo, "Juvenile Offenders in Court: The Debate Over Treatment," *New York Times*, 24 July 1981, p. B4; Peter S. Prescott, *The Child Savers: Juvenile Justice Observed* (New York: Alfred A. Knopf, 1981), pp. 29–30, 219–20; Chesney-Lind, "Girls' Crime and Woman's Place," p. 18. Public pressure can also make itself felt more directly: in many communities the juvenile court judge has held his post either through election or periodic popular reaffirmation. He therefore has had to remain sensitive to public sentiments about delinquency and to complaints in the local press that his institution can do nothing to stem the tide. Paul W. Alexander, "Constitutional Rights in the Juvenile Court," in Rosenheim, ed., *Justice for the Child*, p. 86.

30. Prescott, *Child Savers*, pp. 120, 238–40; Paul Lerman, "Child Welfare, the Private Sector, and Community-Based Corrections," *Crime and Delinquency* 30 (1984): 28.

31. Gilman, "How to Retain Jurisdiction over Status Offenses," pp. 49–51.

32. Blomberg, "Diversion and Accelerated Social Control," pp. 275–76; Lerman, "Child Welfare, the Private Sector, and Community-Based Corrections," pp. 22, 33; Castillo, "Juvenile Offenders in Court," p. B4.

33. Chesney-Lind, "Girls' Crime and Woman's Place," pp. 7, 9, 11, 18, 20–21, 24.

34. Dare and Kennedy, "Two Decades of Turmoil," p. 375; Paul Lerman, "Trends and Issues in the Deinstitutionalization of Youths in Trouble," *Crime and Delinquency* 26 (1980): 292–93.

35. Lerman, "Trends and Issues in the Deinstitutionalization of Youths in Trouble," pp. 282–89; Paul Lerman, "Deinstitutionalization and Welfare Policies," *Annals* 479 (May 1985): 134, 140, 143–45, 148; Lerman, "Child Welfare, the Private Sector, and Community-Based Corrections," pp. 7, 9–12, 22–23. See also Dare and Kennedy, "Two Decades of Turmoil," pp. 376, 379–80.

36. Scull, "Deinstitutionalization and the Rights of the Deviant," p. 16; Lerman, "Child Welfare, the Private Sector, and Community-Based Corrections," p. 29.

37. Lerman, "Trends and Issues in the Deinstitutionalization of Youths in Trouble," p. 289; Lerman, "Deinstitutionalization and Welfare Policies," p. 148.

38. Martha Derthick, *Uncontrollable Spending for Social Service Grants* (Washington, DC: 1975). See also Elizabeth Wickenden, "A Perspective on Social Services: An Essay Review," *SSR* 50 (1976): 570–71, 578.

39. Gilbert, "Transformation of Social Services," p. 626; Mildred Rein, "Social Services as a Work Strategy," *SSR* 49 (1975): 518–19.

40. Gilbert, "Transformation of Social Services," pp. 617–28; Neil Gilbert, *Capitalism and the Welfare State: Dilemmas of Social Benevolence* (New Haven: Yale University Press, 1983), pp. 51–54; Sanford F. Schram, "Politics, Professionalism, and the Changing Federalism," *SSR* 55 (1981): 87–88.

41. For a particularly clear statement of this position, see Alfred J. Kahn, "Service Delivery at the Neighborhood Level: Experience, Theory, and Fads," *SSR* 50 (1976): 23–24, 47. See also Kahn, "Child Welfare: Trends and Directions," *Child Welfare* 41 (December 1962): 459, 467, 474–75; Kahn, "Social Services in Relation to Income Security," p. 387; Kahn, "Public Social Services: The Next Phase—Policy and Delivery Strategies," *Public Welfare* 30 (1) (1972): 18–19. Other social personnel adopted the same view. See Harold L. Wilensky and Charles N. Lebeaux, *Industrial Society and Social Welfare* (New York: Free Press, 1958, 1965), pp. 138–40; Winifred Bell, "Services for People: An Appraisal," *Social Work* 15 (July 1970): 8–9.

42. The connection to the social living standard was explicitly drawn early in the postwar era in Donald S. Howard, "The Social Services and the Maintenance of Optimum Standards of Living," *NCSW, Proceedings* 74 (1947): 114–21.

43. Kahn, "Public Social Services," pp. 19–20; Mencher, "Perspectives on Recent Welfare Legislation," p. 64.

44. Gilbert, *Capitalism and the Welfare State*, pp. 59–60, 66; Allen, *Decline of the Rehabilitative Ideal*, pp. 25–28.

45. Gilbert, "Transformation of Social Services," p. 631; Gilbert, *Capitalism and the Welfare State*, pp. 55, 57–58.

46. Gilbert, *Capitalism and the Welfare State*, pp. 61–63; Gilbert, "Transformation of Social Services," p. 638.

47. The 1967 amendments authorized the purchase of services from private providers; under the 1974 Title XX amendments, private funds could be used to meet the federal requirement for state matching funds. Through these changes, private agencies were made eligible for direct receipt of federal funds, a reversal of a policy first established by Harry Hopkins during the New Deal. Wickenden, "Perspective on Social Services," p. 579; Gilbert, "Transformation of Social Services," pp. 632–33; Ralph M. Kramer and Bart Grossman, "Contracting for Social Services: Process Management and Resource Dependencies," *SSR* 61 (1987): 33.

48. Rein, "Social Services as a Work Strategy," pp. 527–31.

49. Hoshino, "Social Services," pp. 373–74; Gilbert, "Transformation of Social Services," p. 625.

50. Barbara Gottschalk and Peter Gottschalk, "The Reagan Retrenchment in Historical Context," in Michael K. Brown, ed., *Remaking the Welfare State: Retrenchment and Social Policy in America and Europe* (Philadelphia: Temple University Press, 1988), pp. 63, 71.

51. Michael K. Brown, "Remaking the Welfare State: A Comparative Perspective," in Brown, ed., *Remaking the Welfare State*, pp. 15–16; Frances Fox Piven and Richard A. Cloward, "Popular Power and the Welfare State," in Brown, ed., *Remaking the Welfare State*, pp. 76, 90–92; Steven Rathgeb Smith and Deborah A. Stone, "The Unexpected Consequences of Privatization," in Brown, ed., *Remaking the Welfare State*, pp. 239–40; Sidney L. Gardner, "Building New Constituencies," *Public Welfare* 42 (1) (1984): 40.

52. Michael Lipsky, "Bureaucratic Disentitlement in Social Welfare Programs," *SSR* 58 (1984): 6, 8, 11; Michael B. Katz, *In the Shadow of the Poorhouse: A Social History of Welfare in America* (New York: Basic Books, 1986), p. 287.

53. Mildred Rein, "Work in Welfare: Past Failures and Future Strategies," *SSR* 56 (1982): 223; Katz, *In the Shadow of the Poorhouse*, 286; Sheldon S. Wolin, "Democracy and the Welfare State: The Political and Theoretical Connections between Staatsrason and Wohlfahrtsstaatsrason," *Political Theory* 15 (1987): 477–80.

54. For comments along these lines, see Gilbert, *Capitalism and the Welfare State*, pp. 72–73, 139, 156. For an example of a broad appeal for services that fails to set priorities, see Withorn, *Circle Game*, p. 143.

55. Theodore J. Stein, "The Child Abuse Prevention and Treatment Act," *SSR* 58 (1984): 302–8; Schram, "Politics, Professionalism, and the Changing Federalism," pp. 85–86; Michael S. Wald, "Family Preservation: Are We Moving Too Fast?" *Public Welfare* 46 (3) (1988): 34, 36.

56. For example, see Suzanne Daley, "A Strained Welfare Unit, Another Child Dead," *New York Times*, 19 January 1989, p. A1.

57. The dimensions of the phenomenon are explored in Ken Auletta, *The Underclass* (New York: Vintage, 1983), chap. 2.

58. Michael Novak et al., *The New Consensus on Family and Welfare: A Community of Self-Reliance* (Washington, DC: American Enterprise Institute, 1987), pp. xiii–xiv, 13, 74; James Q. Wilson, "The Rediscovery of Character: Private Virtue and Public Policy," *Public Interest* 81 (Fall 1985): 3–4.

59. Katz, for example, suggests the term "underclass" be abandoned because it leads to a focus on a narrow subset of the poor. Michael B. Katz, *The Undeserving Poor: From the War on Poverty to the War on Welfare* (New York: Pantheon, 1989), p. 234. On the reluctance of liberals to discuss the underclass, see William Julius Wilson, "Cycles of Deprivation and the Underclass Debate," *SSR* 59 (1985): 539–59.

60. For a vivid example, see Lisbeth B. Schorr (with Daniel Schorr), *Within Our Reach: Breaking the Cycle of Disadvantage* (New York: Doubleday, 1988).

61. Tappan, "Judicial and Administrative Approaches to Children with Problems," p. 155; Oliphant, "Observations on the Administration of Social Services in the States," p. 285; Spergel, "Community-based Delinquency Prevention Programs," pp. 19–21, 26.

62. John B. Turner, "In Response to Change: Social Work at the Crossroad," *Social Work* 13 (July 1968): 12–13; Alvin L. Schorr, "The Tasks for Voluntarism in the Next Decade," *Child Welfare* 49 (1970): 433; Shirley M. Buttrick, "On Choice and Services," *ssr* 44 (1970): 430–31; Archie Hanlan, "Casework beyond Bureaucracy," *Social Casework* 52 (1971): 199.

63. Smith and Stone, "Unexpected Consequences of Privatization," pp. 243–45; Kramer and Grossman, "Contracting for Social Services," pp. 35, 38, 41–42, 44–48; Steven Rathgeb Smith, "Changing Governance in the Welfare State: Government Contracting with Nonprofit Service Organizations," Working Paper #28, Center for the Study of Philanthropy and Voluntarism, Duke University, December 1989, pp. 16–17.

64. Michael Lipsky and Steven Rathgeb Smith, "Nonprofit Organizations, Government, and the Welfare State," *Political Science Quarterly* 104 (1989–1990): 625, 631–32, 640, 644–45.

65. Ibid., pp. 631–32, 635–36, 639–40, 647–48; Smith, "Changing Governance in the Welfare State," pp. 19–20, 21, 23–24; 27–28.

66. Lipsky and Smith, "Nonprofit Organizations, Government, and the Welfare State," p. 638.

67. On the split within the helping professions brought on by the conflicts of the 1960s, see Max Siporin, "Practice Theory and Vested Interests," *ssr* 52 (1978): 421–22; Burton Gummar, "On Helping and Helplessness: The Structure of Discretion in the American Welfare System," *ssr* 53 (1979): 214–15; John H. Ehrenreich, *The Altruistic Imagination: A History of Social Work and Social Policy in the United States* (Ithaca, NY: Cornell University Press, 1985), pp. 197–203. For a contemporary statement of the radical position, see John B. Turner, "In Response to Change: Social Work at the Crossroad," *Social Work* 13 (July 1968): 7–9.

68. George L. Kelling, "Poverty: Problems, Programs, and Proposals," *Child Welfare* 50 (1971): 21.

69. Daniel P. Moynihan, "The Crises in Welfare," *Public Interest* 10 (Winter 1968): 19–20.

70. Martin Rein and Sheldon H. White, "Knowledge for Practice," *ssr* 55 (1981): 26.

71. Francis A. Allen, "The Borderland of the Criminal Law: Problems of 'Socializing' Criminal Justice," *ssr* 32 (1958): 113, 115; Eileen L. Younghusband, "The Dilemma of the Juvenile Court," *ssr* 33 (1959): 11, 18, 20; Dunham, "Juvenile Court," pp. 516, 522, 526; Tappan, "Judicial and Administrative Approaches to Children with Problems," pp. 148–49; Moynihan, "Crises in Welfare," p. 23; Maude M. Craig and Philip W. Furst, "What Happens After Treatment? A Study of Potentially Delinquent Boys," *ssr* 39 (1965): 170–71; "Has Social Work Failed?" *ssr* 46 (1972): 427, 429; Korn, "Private Citizen, the Social Expert, and the Social Problem," p. 582.

72. Dunham, "Juvenile Court," p. 521; Younghusband, "Dilemma of the Juvenile Court," p. 11; Langley and Drone, "Juvenile Justice," p. 566; Gummar, "On Helping and Helplessness," pp. 222–23.

73. Allen, "The Borderland of the Criminal Law," p. 114; Robert G. Caldwell, "Juvenile Court: Its Development and Some Major Problems," *jcl* 51

(1961): 509; Rein and White, "Knowledge for Practice," p. 15; Malcolm Bush and Andrew C. Gordon, "Client Choice and Bureaucratic Accountability: Possibilities for Responsiveness in a Social Welfare Bureaucracy," *Journal of Social Issues* 34 (4) (1978): 25, 29–31.

74. Marvin Silverman, "Children's Rights and Social Work," *SSR* 51 (1977): 171–72; Bush and Gordon, "Client Choice and Bureaucratic Accountability," pp. 27–29, 31, 38–41.

75. For an anguished expression, see Harry Specht, "The Deprofessionalization of Social Work," *Social Work* 17 (2) (1972): 3–15.

76. Ehrenreich, *Altruistic Imagination*, p. 206; Kathy E. Ferguson, *The Feminist Case Against Bureaucracy* (Philadelphia: Temple University Press, 1984), pp. 136–37.

77. Kahn, "Public Social Services," pp. 20–21; Kahn, "Service Delivery at the Neighborhood Level," pp. 23, 33–34; Aleanor Merrifield, "Implications of the Poverty Program: The Caseworker's View," *SSR* 39 (1965): 295–97; Helen Harris Perlman, "Can Casework Work?" *SSR* 42 (1968): 435–47.

78. Kahn, "Service Delivery at the Neighborhood Level," pp. 46, 52–53.

79. Alfred Kadushin, "Myths and Dilemmas in Child Welfare," *Child Welfare* 56 (1977): 142–45.

80. Gilbert, *Capitalism and the Welfare State*, pp. 23–24, 26; Yeheskel Hasenfeld, "The Administration of Human Services," *Annals* 479 (May 1985): 74.

81. Linda Cherrey Reeser and Irwin Epstein, "Social Workers' Attitudes toward Poverty and Social Action: 1968–1984," *SSR* 61 (1987): 621.

82. William M. Epstein, "Science and Social Work," *SSR* 60 (1986): 145–60; Rein and White, "Knowledge for Practice," pp. 35, 37–38; Robert Morris and Delwin Anderson, "Personal Care Services: An Identity for Social Work," *SSR* 49 (1975): 157–74.

83. See, for example, Schorr, *Within Our Reach*.

84. Epstein, "Science and Social Work," pp. 148–50, 152–55.

85. Martin Bloom, "Challenges to the Helping Professions and the Response of Scientific Practice," *SSR* 52 (1978): 584–87, 590–93; Patricia Hanrahan and William J. Reid, "Choosing Effective Interventions," *SSR* 58 (1984): 244–45.

86. For the general argument about dividing sovereign power, see Theodore J. Lowi, *The End of Liberalism: The Second Republic of the United States*, 2d ed. (New York: Norton, 1979). The increased use of private confinement is discussed in Lerman, "Trends and Issues in the Deinstitutionalization of Youths in Trouble," pp. 282–85; Lerman "Child Welfare, the Private Sector, and Community-based Corrections," p. 29.

87. On the problem of accountability under service contracting, see Kramer and Grossman, "Contracting for Social Services," pp. 39–42; Smith, "Changing Governance in the Welfare State," pp. 20–21.

88. Stein, "Child Abuse Prevention and Treatment Act," p. 309; Douglas J. Besharov, "Right versus Rights: The Dilemma of Child Protection," *Public Welfare* 43 (2) (1985): 19–27; Douglas J. Besharov, "Contending with Overblown Expectations," *Public Welfare* 45 (1) (1987): 7–11. For a more general discussion of the problem of "at risk" classifications, see Gilbert, *Capitalism and the Welfare State*, pp. 151–52.

89. Blomberg, "Diversion and Accelerated Social Control," pp. 279–81.
90. Chesney-Lind, "Girls' Crime and Woman's Place," pp. 24–26.

Conclusion
Captive to the Past

1. New Yorkers were stunned by the death of six-year-old Lisa Steinberg in 1987 at the hands of her lawyer father. In the immediate aftermath of the event, much of the editorial comment in the local newspapers reflected upon the failure of neighbors and the child's teachers to report earlier evidence of abuse to child welfare officials. Yet the city's child welfare department has failed repeatedly to protect the children who have been called to its notice.

2. On the influence of the physical sciences, see Richard Korn, "The Private Citizen, the Social Expert, and the Social Problem," in Bernard Rosenberg, Israel Gerver, and F. William Howton, eds., *Mass Society in Crisis: Social Problems and Social Pathology* (New York: Macmillan, 1964), pp. 581–82.

3. I hasten to add that child abuse is less frequently reported where income is adequate, a condition that neighborhood government alone can do little to promote. To reduce dangerous behavior, we need not only grassroots involvement but also increased material supports.

4. Richard C. Cabot, "Treatment in Social Case Work and the Need of Criteria and of Tests of Its Success or Failure," Presidential Address, NCSW, *Proceedings* 58 (1938): 3–4.

5. Some interesting suggestions may be found in Douglas J. Besharov, "Right versus Rights: The Dilemma of Child Protection," *Public Welfare* 43 (2) (1985): 21–25. On the difficulty of making a rights strategy work, see Jack Tweedie, "The Dilemma of Clients' Rights in Social Programs," *Law and Society Review* 23 (1989): 175–208.

6. Linda Gordon, *Heroes of Their Own Lives: The Politics and History of Family Violence* (New York: Penguin Books, 1988), chap. 9.

Index